Re-make/Re-model

D0872706

Re-make/Re-model

Becoming Roxy Music

MICHAEL BRACEWELL

DA CAPO PRESS

A MEMBER OF THE PERSEUS BOOKS GROUP

Cataloging-in-Publication data for this book is available from
the Library of Congress.

First Da Capo Press edition 2008
Reprinted by arrangement with Faber and Faber Limited
ISBN: 978-0-306-81400-6

Published by Da Capo Press
A Member of the Perseus Books Group
www.dacapopress.com

Da Capo Press books are available at special discounts for bulk purchases
in the U.S. by corporations, institutions, and other organizations. For more
information, please contact the Special Markets Department at the Perseus
Books Group, 2300 Chestnut Street, Suite 200, Philadelphia, PA 19103,
or call (800) 255-1514, or e-mail special.markets@perseusbooks.com.

10 9 8 7 6 5 4 3 2 1

For
Jon Savage
Peter York
Maxwell Sterling
Linder

is trying to 'retain the freshness and imme̶
art music "... with an outrageous mixture o̶
electronic.' Robin Denselow on a new phenomen̶

̶ST PIECE of news I have
̶onths from the British rock
̶ Bryan Ferry has just had
̶out. If that seems more
̶e weak, then perhaps I
̶ain : Ferry is lead singer
̶with Roxy Music, the most
̶ British band to have
̶the seventies. In the four
̶t they have been playing
̶y have enlivened that mori-
̶ution, the Top Ten, with
̶lain," the best single I can
̶ince the Who's " I can see
̶ They have also released
̶ht (and very different)
̶ their stage performances
̶led surprising openers for
̶ Alice Cooper and David
̶ey were about to tour
̶ an attempt to consolidate
̶ss, but now—at the most
̶ of their career—they are
̶on, and will be for some

̶ Ferry languishes in the
̶nic, with £10,000 worth of
̶s cancelled, it is worth
̶what we are missing. Roxy
̶opularised by their image :
̶r case of the glitter and
̶ndrome. They come on—
̶is reference to Sha Na Na
̶are—in gold lamé trousers,
̶rd skin, and Brylcreem.
̶fifties science fiction movies
̶e Day The Earth Stood
̶s Ferry. And why ? " We
̶ on to stage without some
̶esentation, it makes it more
̶e don't associate sincerity
̶th drabness in appearance."

̶thesiser controller, Brian
̶ge St John Le Baptiste de
̶o (who prefers, for obvious
̶ be known as Eno) takes
̶ further : " Hearing is con-
̶ what one sees. Presenta-
̶egral to how we think the
̶ear the music."

̶ut there is a strong danger
̶se of the image Roxy will
̶d for climbing on the camp-
̶vagon, when what they are
̶o is far more adventurous.
̶ is to solve one of rock's
̶roblems : how to retain the
̶nd immediacy of the fifties

and part electronic. The result ought
to be a terrible mess, but it works :
Danny and the Juniors meet Cornelius

" Phil Spector
girl groups lik
material sound

cy of the fifties rock 'n' roll while still prog
tyles: part revivalist, part forties nostalgi
in rock music

xy Music : Bryan Ferry (top left) and Eno (below centre)

realised you didn't have
to play anything to be
music ") who shocked h
the electronic avant-gard
ing fascinated by rock 'n'
synthesiser not as a n
ment, to reproduce the
fake French horns, or a
to make strange noises,
the sound from other
Such experiments are
travelling rock band. The
has to travel from the in
is to be modified (pian
saxophone) to a mixer
of the hall, then back to
back to the mixer, and
amplifiers—a journey of
Special equipment is b
cope.

Eno is also trying to
concept of " systems " in
means " each musician p
part over and over agai
different parts overlap i
phase relation at any g
gives the appearance o
piece of music progressin
really very simple. The
not in the music, but in t
of the listener, whose e
more and more detail." O
use a systems section a
" Bob Medley."

Roxy have more unconv
about recording. While m
delighted to use over
16-track studios, Ferry ge
old US Bonds records v
as if they were recorded
chip shop." The idea
" raw and exciting and
not to become too clinica
up the nice bits but le
hidden." Their single is a
how all that should sou
But not the album. It's
polished.

This may all sound a cu
mic approach to the hit
doesn't work out that way
compare the enthusiasm
ginia Plain " with that of
single. " For me, what
is an incredibly joyous
Ferry. " It is the first ti
been able to think that
or communication, involv

l the New York
rystals," but his
like frantic Vel-
ntage Hollywood

to the movies ("Two HB" is about
Bogart).
He refuses to print them on the
record sleeve because "there is

'Rosemary had the detached false-and-exalted feeling of being on a set and guessed that everyone else present had that feeling too.'

F. Scott Fitzgerald, *Tender is the Night*, 1934

contents

cast

Bryan Ferry
Marcus Price
Tim Head
Stephen Buckley
Nick de Ville
Marco Livingstone
Richard Hamilton
Rita Donagh
Mark Lancaster
Jeremy Catto
Viv Kemp
Roger Cook
Andy Mackay
Polly Eltes
Brian Eno
Roy Ascott
Carol McNicoll
Anne Bean
Adrienne Hunter

Antony Price
Juliet Mann
Keith Wainwright
Duggie Fields
Wendy Dagworthy
Jim O'Connor
Pamla Motown
Janet Street-Porter
Judith Watt
Paul Thompson
Eric Boman
Peter Schlesinger
Peter York
Duncan Fallowell
Phil Manzanera
David Enthoven
Tim Clark
Richard Williams

illustrations

Text Illustrations

Plates

acknowledgements

My thanks are due firstly to all of the people who so kindly agreed to be interviewed for this book, whose story this is, and whose names are listed on its opening pages. My thanks to them is doubled, in many cases, for the further generosity they have shown in sharing not only their insights and recollections, but photographs and documents from their personal archives.

In addition, I am especially grateful to Philip Gwyn Jones, who was vital in the origination of this project; to Antony Harwood and James Macdonald Lockhart at Antony Harwood Ltd; and to Lee Brackstone, Darren Wall, Lucie Ewin and Stephen Page at Faber & Faber for all of their tremendous enthusiasm and support.

For their assistance with aspects of my research I would like to thank: at Newcastle University Fine Art Department, Professor Frances Spalding; and at the Newcastle University Fine Art Library, Angela Horn. At the University of Reading Special Collections Service, and for his invaluable knowledge, Mike Bott. At Opal, Jane Geerts and (during the early days of the mission) Catherine Dempsey. At Studio One, Juliet Mann, Christelle Villanueva and Isaac Ferry. At Warholstars (www.warholstars.org), for his gracious permission to quote from transcripts of his fascinating two-part interview with Mark Lancaster, Gary Comenas.

To the following, for the interest and support that they have shown to this project, heartfelt thanks: Philip Hoare, Michael Collins, Andrew Renton, Murray Chalmers, Ian Massey, Jennifer Higgie, Dan Fox, Polly Staple, Rick Poynor, Hari at Hari & Friends, Annette Bond, John

Hampson, Phil Johnson, Joe Kerr, Marc Camille Chaimowicz, John Robb, Austin Collings, Peter Saville, Jeremy Deller, Teresa Gleadowe, Neil Tennant, Julian Evans, Richard Wentworth, Robin Robertson, Jonathan Coe, Morrissey, Alan Cristea, George Shaw, Matthew Higgs, Gilbert & George, Andrea Rose, Andy Hastings, Jeremy Millar, Howard Devoto, Rhett Davies, Richard Boon, Judy Nylon, Paul Bayley, Richard Riley, Brian Dillon, James Roberts, Marcus Field, Lynne Tillmann, Bertie Marshall, Christina Birrer, my father George Bracewell and my sister Rosamund Bracewell.

note on the text

All of the interviews in this book were conducted by the author, and are quoted in the present volume for the first time. Any quoted material from other sources is credited in the main body of the text.

Re-make/Re-model

introduction

The subject of this book is a particular constellation of determinedly creative individuals, some of whom, between the first half of the 1960s and the opening years of the 1970s, would become friends, and nearly all of whom – across the same period – would at least become acquainted. How this cast assembled, their interests, activities and relationship to one another, is also the story of one of their most spectacular manifestations.

In 1953, the artist Richard Hamilton was appointed to the post of 'teacher of basic design', at what was then known, confusingly, as the King Edward VII School of Art, within King's College, University of Durham at Newcastle upon Tyne. His arrival would mark the beginning of an era, inaugurating a chain of events and a gathering of participants that would include, almost twenty years and many fortuitous encounters later, the creation by Bryan Ferry – a former student of Fine Art at Newcastle, between 1964 and 1968 – of the group Roxy Music.

Roxy Music would be one of the most original and successful British groups to emerge in the early 1970s, citing an eclectic range of influences from modern music, popular culture and fine art. From their earliest public recognition, the group would also stand for an assertion of exclusivity – a conjuring of *la vie deluxe*, inculcated by a bravura use of style. Achieving fame within the pop mainstream almost immediately, Roxy Music became, as Bryan Ferry would observe in 1975, 'above all . . . a state of mind'.

The line connecting Richard Hamilton's appointment to Newcastle (he would leave the university in 1966, acclaimed as an artist, intellectual and founding guru of Pop art) and Ferry's realisation of his own pop vision, is drawn between a complex but distinct configuration of points. What emerges from its tracery are various semi-casual *cenacles*, comprising networks of art-student friendships forged across the span of the 1960s. The tenets of these friendships spliced artistic enquiry with bedsit bohemianism, and a devotion to the shrines of pop music and personal style. One consequence of such a lifestyle – however buoyed up by more traditional undergraduate pursuits – would be an inclination to balance the creative possibilities opened up by an education in fine art against the conscious honing of a pose: the sharp inheritance of pop cool meeting the wily strategies of Duchampian aesthetics.

The cast of this account, therefore, comprises a set who chose to inhabit the point where fine art and the avant-garde met the vivacity of pop and fashion as an almost elemental force within modern society and culture, and who were eager to work with the potential of both. Dissolving the boundaries between 'high' and 'low' art forms, how might ideas within the visual arts, cinema, electronics, fashion, the musical avant-garde, science, performance art or philosophy be fused with the intense, erotic energy – the capacity for myth making – of pop? And how might one dress, and socialise, with the same attention to personal style that a Hollywood set designer of the 1930s would devote to the detailing of a big musical number?

In one crucial sense, Roxy Music would be a modern triumph of the applied arts, and on the journey to its realisation, Smokey Robinson and Marcel Duchamp (for example) or the Velvet Underground, John Cage and Gene Kelly, could and would acquire equal importance – all, in their different ways, forcefully and glamorously modern.

As a meticulously considered and presented montage of cultural forms, Bryan Ferry's concept of Roxy Music would be in every sense a work of Pop art. But how to describe such exploratory rearrangements of creative intention, and their consequences? Before beginning, mark the solemn words of 'Nigel Norris' – a fictitious freelance writer for *Rolling Stone*, setting out his stall in Howard Schuman's television drama of 1976, *Rock Follies*, episode three, 'The Road': *Norris:* 'I think one should apply the same critical standards to rock music as to any other art form.'

Such an idea (met on screen by the exclamation, 'You did say you write about music, didn't you? That sounded more like the *Times Literary Supplement!*') would be central to the conception of Roxy Music.

With the release of their debut album in June 1972, titled simply *Roxy Music*, Ferry presented his *carte de visite* to the world. The record was arch, thrilling, elegant, unique, clever and richly romantic. Like a manifesto written in the language of heavily stylised, nuanced and atmospheric pop and rock music (the songs made use of both genres, in their broadest sense, and at times simultaneously), the album was made all the more alluring by its presentation.

The principal musicians, cosmetically beautified, looked sinister, louche, imperial, remote, maniacal and leeringly self-preening. By contrast, the auburn-haired beauty queen whose image lay across the record's ice-blue gatefold sleeve appeared beseeching, yielding, yearning – at once seductive and seduced. She seemed to have been ravished – or to be achingly desirous of being ravished – by the very music that her glamour was being asked to represent.

Roxy Music, as such, proposed a masterclass in charisma. To those responsive to its infectious charms, the album suggested a hitherto hidden and instantly desirable demi-monde – a place of declamatory style and sophistication, part cabaret, part carnival, simultaneously futuristic and archaic, but swaggeringly self-assured in its balancing of contradictions. The greater formula of this effect, nearly twenty-five years later, was summarised by the artist and ideologue Brian Eno (credited on *Roxy Music* as 'Eno: Synthesiser & Tapes'); in correspondence to the author he wrote: 'I thought, and still think, that pop music isn't primarily about making music in any traditional sense of the word. It's about creating new, imaginary worlds and inviting people to try them out.'

And herein lies the greater theme of this present volume; for it is the prehistory and founding constitution of the 'new, imaginary world' summoned up by *Roxy Music* with which this book is most concerned; with the processes that comprised its moment of becoming, and the participants involved in and witnessing its creation.

Once established as a major pop act (in effect, by the late summer of 1972), Roxy Music – as a 'state of mind', in Ferry's words – would come to represent the portal through which one might glimpse, or even reach, the empyreal world brought to mind by their intense romanticism: a place where the bewitching half light of the Parisian violet hour, or the shocking elegance of Jay Gatsby's 'gorgeous pink rag of a suit', might be brought to life in a song.

That Bryan Ferry was the author of Roxy Music – as an idea, and as a specific musical and imagistic concept – all the principal musicians agree. (Although it is more than likely, interestingly, that between them they all had differing ideas of what, exactly, they were trying to achieve.) Likewise, Ferry himself is equally clear that on the journey to realising his vision, he encountered or sought out a succession of individuals who made vital contributions to the overall creative process, and without whom the project would never have proceeded.

These collaborating artists in turn possessed their own relationship to one another, and to a further network of friends, observers and acquaintances. Nearly all would recognise that exuberant *vie deluxe* – a pop, fashion and fine art society, fixated on glamour, newness, wit, stylistic and creative virtuosity – that *Roxy Music* so invitingly proposed, and would perhaps consider themselves to be amongst its initial inhabitants.

Making their operational headquarters, as the 1960s gave way to the 1970s, amidst the red-brick mansion blocks, black-railinged squares, stucco-fronted houses and broad grey streets around Chelsea, Kensington, Notting Hill and Olympia – with orbital settlements in Battersea, Camberwell and New Cross – a further characteristic of this young, artistic milieu would be their consciously heightened engagement with the concept of modern style: in the acquisition of 'cool', as the term then used between these contemporaries to acknowledge the perfected signature of stylistic self-assurance. Individually and collectively, many of the figures within this book became semi-seriously concerned with the dimensions of their own exclusivity; and as connoisseurs of an intoxicating sense of pose – in one sense aloof, separatist – played games with not only the reinvention of themselves, but the entire notion of class.

In this, these artist bohemians of the late 1960s would emerge in the earliest years of the 1970s as both their own art movement and their own high society – fulfilling to the letter the edict of Charles Beaudelaire, a century before, that:

> Dandyism appears above all in periods of transition, when democracy is not yet all-powerful, and aristocracy is only just beginning to totter and fall. In the disorder of these times, certain men who are socially, politically and financially ill at ease, but are all rich in native

energy, may conceive the idea of establishing *a new kind of aristocra-cy*, all the more difficult to shatter as it will be based on the most precious, the most enduring faculties, and on the divine gifts that work and money are unable to bestow. Dandyism is the last spark of heroism amid decadence . . .

Achieving swift fame as the house band, therefore, of 'a new kind of aris-tocracy', revered and emulated for their dramatic energy no less than their poise, Roxy Music's founding stance – part studied hauteur, part rock and roll panache – would make articulate their constitution of balanced but opposing qualities: of the suave flippancy of popist fashion and the inten-sity of dedicated musicianship; of intellectual sophistication and the sheer exuberance of pop and rock music; of nostalgia and the avant-garde; of heterosexual eroticism and ambiguous sexual identity; of artifice and authenticity; of fast and slow; of warm sensuality and a cold, machine-like perfection.

It is this last fusion of opposites, of sleek mechanisation and sensuous romanticism (of sexual glamour and technology), which most links the founding temper of Roxy Music to the genealogy of Pop art, as pio-neered by Richard Hamilton; and which will prove to be the common denominator of their vehement modernity. For while it is equally impor-tant to recognise the punishingly hard work and uncomplicated ambition demanded by such a fast-track career in pop and rock music, the newness and originality of Roxy Music was the consequence in one vital sense of this collision or dialogue (or both) between an array of seemingly opposed ideas.

Speaking with the author in 1997, Andrew Mackay (credited on *Roxy Music* with 'Oboe & Saxophone'), described the group as follows: 'If Roxy Music had been like cooking, it would be the dish in Marinetti's *Futurist Cookbook* called, I think, "Car Crash": " . . . an hemisphere of puréed dates and an hemisphere of puréed anchovies, which are then stuck together in a ball and served in a pool of raspberry juice . . ." I mean, it's virtually inedible – but it can be done.'

The circumstances under which such a recipe might even be con-ceived are thus the concern of the following pages, as are those eager and able to prepare, and willing to consume, such a dish.

part 1

newcastle 1953–1968

one

Bryan Ferry, born 26 September 1945 to Frederick, a mine worker and former farmhand, and Mary Ann, a factory worker, in Washington, County Durham. He has an older sister, Ann, and a younger, Enid. Bryan attends the Glebe Infants School in Washington, and in September 1957 goes to Washington Grammar School.

First, a temple in the Greek style. The sense is one of abandonment. On a cold, steep hill of wind-toughened grass, eighteen sandstone pillars (Doric, broad to the verge of squat), blackened with age, weather and soot, support the entablatures and twin pediments – there is no roof – of a mid-Victorian copy, half sized, of the Theseum of Athens.

Approached on foot, its immensity drawing nearer, the heroic ideal of the place falls away. Grandeur gives way to mere enormity, statement to silence, substance to emptiness. Sometimes known as the Penshaw Monument, this solid memorial to John George Lambton MP, first earl of Durham, landowner and mine owner, was designed, like stage scenery, to be appreciated from a distance.

Dominating the summit of Penshaw Hill near Houghton le Spring, slightly to the south and west of Newcastle upon Tyne, the foreboding pillars of Lambton's memorial are visible and impressive for miles around – visible from west Durham and north Tyneside, and from as far south as the Stang Forest in Teesdale. The gravitas of classical architecture, its language of straight lines, makes eloquent its superiority; the pillars and pediments add the tone of their imperial style, like the chime of a sombre bell.

Incongruous within the sparse surrounding countryside, aloof, remote, the Penshaw Monument surveys from one side what once were mines. Stand within it and study the view: you will see a flat landscape stretching away towards the North Sea; to the west, there are the hills of Durham; and further north, towards the River Tyne, the suburbs of Washington – once a village, now a small town.

And so the imperial looks down on the post-industrial; and in the late 1940s and early 1950s, looking back up, was Bryan Ferry, then a boy. Absorbing the rhetoric of this chilly *hommage* to classical architecture (designed by the brothers Green of Newcastle, and built in 1844), a child of England's austerity years looked up to the Empire style, entranced.

Ferry to play:

Bryan Ferry: 'When my parents were first married they lived in a farmhouse; and there was a hill nearby called Penshaw Hill. On top of the hill was a local landmark – a Greek monument built for the first earl of Durham. This was where my father was brought up; and his family had farmed on the sides of the hill. Years later, when I showed this place to Antony Price, he said, "Now I know why you're so interested in visual things: it's because of that monument."

'And it seemed to me like a symbol – representing art, and another life, away from the coalfields and the hard north-eastern environment; it seemed to represent something from another civilisation, that was much finer . . .'

We first glimpse Ferry as a child; somewhat reserved, of promising imagination, conscious of a finer world, but taking his place in the raw and shabby landscape of the Peace: the grid of local streets between farmland and coalmines; fog on the allotments, a few shops and cinemas – the Washington Carlton, Regal and Ritz. It is a region which despite its proximity to Newcastle and the sea can seem desolate and remote; a landscape that would enter industrial decline even as Bryan was growing up, to be unkindly described in the 1960s as 'the Rust Belt', stilled beneath an immensity of sky.

At the beginning of the 1950s, some rows of new properties were built in Washington, one of which the Ferrys would subsequently occupy (on Gainsborough Avenue: a broad road of low, semi-detached houses, some gabled, ascending a gentle hill, suburban, almost, in aspect, with grass verges on the street corners). Ferry was aware of both inhabiting and being a product of a space between opposing qualities: between the industrial and the pastoral; community and isolation; the modern and the traditional. And aware moreover of being the son of parents who embodied these differences: a shy, retiring father (although a good boxer, on occasion), who loved animals and the countryside, and a vivacious, strikingly attractive mother, more urban, who had worked in a factory and enjoyed conversation and company.

At the infants' school, Ferry showed some evidence of having imaginative gifts – an access to his inner world. He was drawn by temperament to the arts – writing and drawing; he enjoyed football. Aged eleven, he went to the local grammar school. His boyhood and early adolescence would then unfold to be dominated by a particular interest in jazz music, cinema, and, after some initial hesitation, early rock and roll releases in their original American form, rather than British beat boom interpretations.

In his early love of film and popular music, Ferry was specifically drawn to the transformative magic commanded by glamour, and to the agency of glamour in personal style. He would also recognise the talismanic energy, itself a vital aspect of glamour, of musical instruments themselves.★

Ferry was discerning, by way of his favourite things, the ways in which glamour comprised a rare concentration of character and activity: fluid, exuberant, deft, indelible within the memory once seen, addictive, joyous – above all conveyed with no apparent effort. The coolly aristocratic qualities of the Greek style, transposed to the iconography of modern mass age. Meanwhile, if we could look into the depths of Bryan Ferry's eyes – when he was, say, fourteen years old – what might they have seen?

Bryan Ferry: 'My childhood took place in Washington, which at the time was a small pit village in County Durham. It stands about five miles from Sunderland, and five miles from Newcastle, and a few miles from

---

★ A generational characteristic, perhaps, of the times; the actor Malcolm McDowell, as a young man in Liverpool in the late 1950s and early 1960s, once told me of looking down into the windows of a music shop from the top deck of a bus en route to Lime Street Station, and seeing twin rows of shining, new electric guitars; 'they gave you *hope*, somehow'.

Durham as well – so it's in the triangle between those three cities. It was a typical pit village, in as much as there was a small pocket of quite heavy industry surrounded by very rich farmland; and then there'd be another village which had its own pit, and maybe a factory – and then more farm-land. So it was quite strange, with the combination of being close to the countryside yet in this very tough working environment as well.

'My parents were from both places in a sense. My father was born on a farm about two miles away from where my mother lived, and he used to come and see her on one of his carthorses – they courted every night for about ten years. I remember her saying she was embarrassed, when he came along on this farm horse; he was wearing a bowler hat and spats – something from another age, really. Whereas I guess she was more used to motorbikes, and she worked in a factory.

'She had had a very hard life, my mother – they both had. But I got the impression that my dad had enjoyed being in a country environment. Even though they were only two miles from each other, they had had completely different childhoods. Both were from very big families – they both had seven or eight brothers and sisters; and both were very poor in their own way.

'My dad's stories were about chopping the ice in the mornings so they could wash in a big wooden tub outside the cottage; and of getting up at five o'clock to milk the cows before going to school. He didn't really like school, and was always running away – chased by the teachers. All sorts of stories . . . They created their own entertainment; they played football with a ball made out of a pig's bladder . . .

'In the 1930s, when the great depression came, the farm that my father worked on went broke – there was no money. Not that they'd ever had any, but they couldn't exist really. So he went and worked in Washington, in the town – just a mile or so from where he was born, but down the pit, looking after the horses. That was all he really knew – looking after the ponies that lived underground. So for him it was quite hard. Someone who loved the outdoors to be working underground. I always felt very sorry for him. He did that until he retired – until the pit closed down. All through my childhood he was there . . .

'And so it was a very strange, Thomas Hardy-type existence that my father had had; while she, my mother, was from the town. I guess they were attracted by their opposites. My mother was very vivacious, and full of life – very sociable; she liked to talk and to meet people. Whereas he was very quiet, very thoughtful, and didn't really care about what was going on in the world much. He just smoked his pipe – and he liked racing pigeons. He kept hens, and had a vegetable garden; he used to win prizes for his vegetables; and he used to win prizes for his ploughing – with a team of horses. That was his thing; he was a ploughman really ...'

With regard to his early education and formative influences, Ferry would be constantly studying and absorbing the world as he found it, as well as filtering those impressions through both his own imaginative world and the worlds of music and cinema. What emerges is the picture of a boy entirely focused on the processes of perception and a kind of analytical refinement – coupled with the fondness of his generation for the burgeoning new delights of popular culture.

Bryan Ferry: 'I think the first person who found that I had any talent was Miss Swaddle. That was before, even, I went to grammar school. She took a real shine to me. She was the teacher in my final year at infants' school, and I wrote a couple of essays which astounded her, I think. I remember her taking me to one side – it was quite hard for her to concentrate on anybody, because there were fifty people in her class. I think that I was top of the class. She said, "Where did you get this from?" – and it was just a story, but quite tragic, or heartfelt; I think it was quite moving. And so she thought that I had real talent as a writer. I didn't really feel that again until sixth form, at some point, studying art and thinking: I can be an artist myself. I had a depth of feeling; it was a case of where to channel it ...

'When I was a boy, I had a paper round, and so I used to read *Melody Maker* before I put it through someone's letterbox. I dragged my uncle Bryan off to see the Chris Barber Band at Newcastle City Hall; and then, when I got a little braver, I started to go into town on the bus to see concerts on my own. I would be dressed in a white trench coat – at the age of twelve. I would probably have seen the adverts for Strand cigarettes; I was very interested in *style*.

'My sisters and I would sit in the cinema and watch any old rubbish. I started going to the pictures early on – even when I was at junior school. My dad had an allotment where he grew his vegetables, and that was right next door to the cinema – the Carlton. It was a local fleapit really; but it was my Cinema Paradiso from a very early age, because my mother used to make tea for the projectionist – cakes and scones and sandwiches. So he got these free teas, and we got free tickets. There were wooden benches that you sat on . . . I saw *Gone With the Wind* there and all sorts.

'Of course, when you got old enough to have a girlfriend, or to go on a date, the only thing you did was take her to the pictures – that was your date. But that was in the High Street of Washington, where there were two cinemas – which were bigger, and had proper velveteen seats rather than benches. One was called the Regal, and the other the Ritz. None of them are there now. I liked science fiction films . . .

'When I went to university I would go to the cinema club, which is where I became aware of cinema classics and film-as-art – all that kind of thing. Up until then it was film-as-entertainment. That was all you did – you didn't have television. We got one in 1955 when Newcastle were in the Cup, but so did everyone in Newcastle. We were very poor, you see – so I think it's fair to say that Roxy Music, from my point of view, would be the reverse of this background.'

And of his early interest in music:

Bryan Ferry: 'It's always sad when I go back to Newcastle and see that certain places don't exist any more. But it's great that one shop – which was very important for me also – is still there, in a wonderful old arcade, with extravagant tiled floors, rather like the Bond Street arcades. It's a shop called Windows, which is a family music shop and the only place you really go to buy records. The windows are full of clarinets, saxophones, electric guitars – a proper music shop, which sold everything. But just to see a trumpet in the window – a real instrument, to look at it and study it!

'I started being a jazz fan at the age of ten or eleven; and I bought my first records at Windows. You'd go in, and they had about six booths where you could listen to records. You'd go to the counter and ask for a particular release, and could you hear it please . . . Then off you'd go to booth number four or whatever, which would be a little cubicle lined inside with pin-board. You didn't have headphones, there was just a little speaker, and you'd stand there listening to your record. You'd listen to it right to the end before you bought it . . .

'Those first records were all 78 rpms – I've still got them. I bought the 78 by the Tony Kinsey Quintet, whom I must have heard on the radio.* But then there was one, a classic record actually, by Humphrey Lyttelton, called "Bad Penny Blues" (1956), which was produced by that person who went mad and killed himself – Joe Meek. He mainly produced pop records, but I subsequently discovered, years later, that he produced "Bad Penny Blues" – and it did have a *weird* sound, all of its own. Strange.'

'Bad Penny Blues' is a record of exemplary stylishness – as slick as it is unusual, its atmosphere memorable. Heard fifty years after its initial release, its vitality as fresh as ever, like many iconic records, it has a quality which jars, an oddness almost, within the context of its times.

As recorded in 1956 at IBC for Parlophone Records by Lyttelton (ex Eton College and Camberwell Art School), and sound engineered by Joe Meek, the structure of 'Bad Penny Blues' is carried on a chassis of big, rolling piano chords; dipping in and out of emphasis, paced by drums and bass, the rhythm allows Lyttelton's trumpet to slink about with teasing panache, sliding in mood from playful to sinister to suggestive; there are sudden dead drops into briefly re-emphasised piano playing, accelerations of tone and tempo as the bass and drums maintain their unwavering candour. In a little over three minutes, the style has touched the swirling hems of skiffle, boogie-woogie, trad jazz, ragtime – at times, almost, rockabilly – yet retained its own singularity. Hence, a UK hit for Lyttelton in July 1956; hence, for Ferry, an early study in the physics of musical style. (The piano introduction to 'Bad Penny Blues' would be reprised in 1968 by the Beatles, on the introduction to 'Lady Madonna'.)

By chance or insight, Ferry's recognition and liking for the 'weird sound' on 'Bad Penny Blues' also touches upon the qualities of creative incongruity that will later enhance the early output of Roxy Music. From an early age, Ferry assembled a palette of influences, which would then

---

* Kinsey was a founder member, in the early 1950s, of the Dankworth Seven. With his own group he would later hold an eight-year residency at the Flamingo Club in Soho, London – a jazz venue that would achieve even greater fame by the mid-1960s through the leading Mod acts who played there, and its consequent importance on the map of Mod London.

be worked with in much the same way that a painter works with colour. His selected shades all tend to be distinguished by their intensity; but the phosphorescent presence of Joe Meek – a self-tormented homosexual and future drug addict, who would take his own life in 1967 – provided a touch of formative and telling strangeness to Ferry's colour chart of tonal moods and styles. Meek's best known creations – John Leyton's 'Johnny Remember Me', 'Wild Wind', 'Son This is She' and 'Lonely City', all produced between 1961 and 1962, and recorded in Meek's tiny flat in the Holloway Road, north London – have an air of racing, eerie melodrama; 'Telstar', meanwhile, the transatlantic chart-topper recorded with the Tornados in 1962, sounds like a Pop art hymn to the glamour of the space age. All of these qualities – the Meekian other-worldliness – will find their way, as hues or nuance, into the creation of Roxy Music.

One of Roxy Music's first and most important supporters, the critic Richard Williams, working as a features writer on the staff of *Melody Maker* in the early 1970s, would make a point of identifying the subtle but undeniable touch of Joe Meek's influence on the second track of the first Roxy Music album, the sensually titled 'Ladytron'. In his review of *Roxy Music* published on 24 June 1972, Williams wrote: 'Best of all is "Ladytron": it begins as a little lovesong, with flickering castanets, but soon shifts into a "Johnny Remember Me" groove, all echoing hoofbeats.' A week later, in a short interview for *Melody Maker* with Bryan Ferry, Williams noted again, 'the Joe Meek-style production touches on "Ladytron"'.★

Meek's pop futurism was descriptive of the enthusiastic awe with which space exploration and rocketry were regarded in the late 1950s and early 1960s – occupying an enchanted place in the popular imagination where the eerie fables of science fiction combined with a specifically modern kind of glamour. It is an eloquent coincidence, therefore, that in the same year that 'Bad Penny Blues' became the first jazz record to chart in the UK Top Twenty, thus catching the attention of the ten-year-old

★ As a somewhat Gothic aside, some Meek enthusiasts like to suggest that the subsequent failure of the actual AT&T satellite Telstar – due apparently to radiation damage from a nuclear test – was more than coincidentally related to Joe Meek's quickening decline into troubled, occultist, drug-addicted collapse (and in this he resembles somewhat Jack Parsons, the Faust-like, pioneer rocket scientist, California based, who became increasingly entrapped within the black arts).

Bryan Ferry, the exhibition 'This is Tomorrow' opened at the Whitechapel Art Gallery, London – itself an address, in part, to the effects of technology and mass media upon the present and the future.

The exhibition (of some thirty-six artists and architects, divided into twelve three-person teams) would, of course, feature a spectacular contribution from Ferry's future tutor at Newcastle University, Richard Hamilton, who worked in a group with the architect John Voelcker and the artist and critical theorist John McHale (who would subsequently move to America to become a futurologist). A dramatic visual aspect of the Hamilton team's contribution was the image of Robby the Robot, from that year's film *The Forbidden Planet*, carrying off in its mechanical arms a swooning, mini-dressed blonde starlet – an early example, in this context, of Pop art's fusion of eroticism and machinery, romanticism and mass media. Thus the heady aura of the space age – its reality appearing in many ways as exotic as its fantasy – could be seen as a significant factor within both the popular imagination and the cultural climate of Britain in the mid-1950s.

Ferry's earliest, barely adolescent interest in music, however, was most heavily inclined towards black American jazz and folk blues.*

Bryan Ferry: 'My greatest treasure was an EP that I bought, which was the first record that wasn't a single and wasn't a 78. I remember thinking it looked rather flimsy and small, but it cost more than a usual record. It was four tracks – the Charlie Parker Quintet with Miles Davis doing four songs. And I listened to that again and again and again, and learned every note of it – memorised all of the solos.

---

* Speaking with the author, Ferry summarised his principal musical influences and inspirations as follows: 'It's very difficult really – like what are your favourite colours. I'd have to say Charlie Parker, because he was the one I got really very passionate about, and I thought was very exciting. They'd probably all be American. There would have to be a blues artist, so I'd probably say Lead Belly. Then it starts getting difficult. Maybe Otis Redding, because he represented a whole school of music that I liked – Stax, Memphis, R&B, which I thought was very melodic and very soulful. I don't really listen to those records as such, but I do like to hear them when they come on. So that's three. Maybe Billie Holiday, that's four. And if there's going to be a white band I wouldn't really choose the Beatles or the Stones, although they were both really good. I'd probably say the Velvet Underground, because they represented a kind of art interest that I had. So that might be your five.'

'The first person I actually heard on the radio was Lead Belly. That's the first memory I have of hearing something. There was the skiffle boom, so that sort of music – early folk blues from America – started getting on to the radio. Lonnie Donegan was a big star, doing "Rock Island Line" [in April 1956] which was actually a Lead Belly song. So I remember hearing a few Lead Belly things on the radio and thinking "What's that?" – it caught my imagination . . .'

For Ferry, the music of Lead Belly (aka Huddie Ledbetter, 1888–1949) would remain a career long enthusiasm. Songs such as 'Goodnight Irene' and 'Midnight Special' have been described as 'so central to [American] popular consciousness, that most Americans are unaware of where they came from'; and there is an entrancing, profoundly elemental quality to recordings of Lead Belly, which seems to be drawn from some deep crease in the psyche. The songs recorded in New York during the 1940s by Moses Asch and Frederic Ramsey Junior for the Folkways label (founded as much as an ethnographic resource, to document songs, sounds, spoken word and music from around the world) have an edge and an intensity which makes them sound simultaneously ancient and modern. The more they are heard (the famous 'Shout On', for example, or 'Governor Pat Neff') the more their seeming simplicity, verve and temper begin to take hold, at once infectiously melodic and touched with strangeness.

Photographs of Lead Belly from the same period show a handsome, white-haired black man, impeccably turned out in a sharply pressed double-breasted suit, white shirt, silk tie and highly polished shoes. One can see how for Ferry, in addition to the emotional and musical vigour of the music, there would be an attraction to Lead Belly that was derived from his almost mystical presence as an archetype – a founding figure in modern popular music, a black dandy, a precursor to Bob Dylan. Above all, a very 'cool' figure – of which there were rather few, it could be added, amongst the undeniably cheerful ranks of the British beat boom stars of the middle to late 1950s.

Bryan Ferry: 'You'd quite often get the same song coming out twice. An American record would be quickly covered by an English artist. I remember "Singing the Blues" was recorded by Guy Mitchell in America [also in 1956], and then Tommy Steele did the English version. So whenever there was a good song from America, there'd be a cover version fighting it up the charts. Usually the American ones were more interesting in a way, or had more of a sexual potency about them. It wasn't really until the Beatles that you started to feel the English had something – up until then they had always seemed a bit inferior – quite a lot inferior. The Shadows were interesting; some of their records had a uniqueness about them; and I thought the first Cliff Richard record, "Move It" [1958], was very good – had a really good sound . . .'

All of this, within sight of the Lambton memorial, imperious on the summit of Penshaw Hill.

two

Once at Washington Grammar School, Ferry is a talented, diligent, if at times – by his own account – somewhat lazy student. He is inclined towards the arts, and in the sixth form will play Malvolio in the school production of *Twelfth Night*. He manages nine decent O levels before entering the sixth form on the Arts side. More important, he discovers between the ages of eleven and sixteen, in the following order: rock and roll, team cycling and tailoring, and makes early studies of certain styles. But first, Ferry recommences his recollections with a memory from the early spring of 1957 – of 'Bill Haley's Rock and Roll Show', Teddy boys, and 'Jazz at the Philharmonic'.

Bryan Ferry: 'I didn't think I had any gift for music – it didn't even occur to me. It just grew, this interest, and shifted from one thing to another as you discovered different kinds of music. You would develop certain musical snobberies and dislikes for some music which you didn't think was *cool*. Then you'd overcome those and maybe get into that music. I remember my sister was very much into Little Richard, Fats Domino and Elvis – all the early rock people. At first I was a bit resistant to that – and then I got the hang of it and started liking it. I must have got over it very quickly actually, because in 1957, when I was still eleven, I won tickets to the front row of the Bill Haley tour – which was the first rock and roll tour of Britain.

'It was the first time that that music had come to Europe, and it made the front pages of all the newspapers: "Teddy boys wreck cinema" – that sort of thing – and there were people dancing in the aisles . . . It was a whole new youth culture that nobody had ever seen before, and there I was on the front row when it came to the north-east – to the Sunderland Empire.

'I think I must have taken my sister, Ann, or she took me. I had won a competition on Radio Luxembourg, where you had to place, in order, Bill Haley's favourite six songs. I remember "See You Later Alligator", I thought, was the best – and it was; that's all I can remember. But it was fantastic – really exciting – and so I started going to concerts after that, mainly jazz.

'Bill Haley seemed loud, raucous – very dangerous. Even though now, when you see photographs of the Bill Haley band in their tartan jackets, and Haley with his kiss curl, they look like old men – in the way that those deep southern American people did, with their redneck hairstyles and short back-and-sides. But the sax player played upside down, that sort of thing. It was really electric guitar that did it – that was the thing, that was the birth of the electric guitar. It was something to see.★

'I missed a lot of great things, but I did see the Platters, whom I thought were wonderful, and the Modern Jazz Quartet; various big bands – Count Basie. There were these tours called "Jazz at the Philarmonic" that used to come round Europe – Dizzie Gillespie, Ella Fitzgerald, those sort of people. And they would be part of the packages of jazz stars who would tour – I thought it was magical, really I did. They were all grown-up things, and I was there as a young teenager, often on my own. I must have cut quite a curious figure, wearing my trench coat. But my parents let me go – a half-hour bus ride to town and back ...'

As with his identification of Joe Meek and early black American folk blues, Bryan Ferry's vivid recollections of Bill Haley and His Comets add a further colour to his palette of influences and inspirations. The music of Bill Haley was a potent new fusion of existing styles – hillbilly swing, white country and western and black rhythm and blues. The signature of this new sound was first read in Haley's release from 1953, 'Crazy, Man, Crazy', which was the founding example of commercially successful white rock and roll, hitting the US charts that year.

Haley and his Comets were then catapulted into unlikely international superstardom, subsequent to the choice of MGM to use Haley's 'Rock Around the Clock' in a Glenn Ford film about rebellious high school students, *The Blackboard Jungle*. Although the record had initially sunk without

★ Andy Mackay would also witness the arrival of Bill Haley at Victoria Station, London. Sixteen years later, with Roxy Music, he would play his own saxophone upside down – a piece of musical theatre caught on German television – *Musik Land* – in early 1973.

a bubble, by the time the film was released in 1955 (the same year that Mary Quant opened her first 'Bazaar' boutique in the Kings Road, London), Haley had enjoyed no fewer than three US Top Twenty singles, thus making him a huge star and prompting the international release of *The Blackboard Jungle*, and almost immediately afterwards, the (reasonably excruciating) rock and roll musical *Rock Around the Clock*. So began the importation to Europe of the so-called rock and roll revolution, to arrive a little under eighteen months later right before the very eyes of Bryan Ferry at the Sunderland Empire.

The 'Rock and Roll Show', as witnessed by Bryan and his sister, would have added a memorable theatrical dimension to the already intoxicating musical excitement of this new phenomenon. While many young people were somewhat dismayed to discover that the impious buddha of teen rebellion, Haley himself, was a decidedly portly married gentleman in early middle age (thus encouraging, once seen, the imminent cult of the young, beautiful and single Elvis) there was a circus-like showmanship to the live performance of the music, with the auxiliary drama being added by the fashion amongst not just Teddy boys, but teenagers in general, to contribute their jiving war dance, seat slashing and general ballyhoo – the likes of which (as confirmed to the press the same year by the chief constable of Manchester), 'had never been seen before in our streets'. *

It is difficult to imagine, now, the unheard-of impact that early rock and roll would have had on not just the United Kingdom, but particularly on the industrial northern cities of England which were still, in many places, in the rain-swollen ruins of their war damage – in appearance looking closer to the nineteenth century than the twentieth. Photographs taken of the mayhem caused in British theatres and cinemas by both the new rock and roll films and the 'Rock and Roll Show' of 1957 itself, however, are as interesting for the drab, class-bound appearance of the overly excited audiences and fuming management (the latter all brass-framed spectacles and dusty dinner suits, the former oppressed by their belted raincoats, thick woollen socks and mufflers) as they are for the scenes of astonishing devastation that they depict.

* In Liverpool, at the same period, it was reported that 'a thousand jitterbugging teenagers were pursued by the Fire Brigade and the Police' through the city centre, to be 'hosed down'. A riot of carnivalesque high spirits, which presumably the teenagers enjoyed immensely.

Here and there in such pictures, one catches a glimpse of some boy's greasy hair which has been carefully and defiantly shaped into an approximation of a quiff; and somehow these abbreviated attempts at sartorial rebellion, often worn with sullen, damply shapeless, sturdily unglamorous clothes, have more resonance, as signs of the kicking and spitting newness of the scarcely born pop age, than the extravagant splendour of fully assembled and ready-to-knife-you Teddy boys.

Much has now been written and documented about this pivotal phase in British cultural history, which occurred towards the end of the 1950s: the massive increase in teenage spending power, the consequently rapid rise of youth as a new, financially and therefore culturally powerful social group; and the rallying cries of the various kinds of music which would start to bring together all the strands we now recognise as comprising the beginnings of pop and rock musical culture – new sexuality, new technologies, new confrontationalism, new informalities, new media, new stimulants, new fashions, new music. (Mass production, mass media, acceleration and sex thus being the four founding conditions of this new pop age, and becoming to the Pop art of the period what nature was to the Lakeland poets.)

The colour and clamour of early white American rock and roll, its energy and electric vibrancy, the band's stage clothes often reminiscent of music hall and vaudeville (pushing the notion of style to the very brink of absurdity), will all reappear in their mutated, concentrated form in Ferry's early pop vision. Similarly, the idea of music being performed as a total event – its sensory power compressed to capacity; the image, sound and demeanour of the musicians achieving an eruptive, above all startling, display of bravura effect.

For all of his artistic inclinations, however, Ferry was far from being a frail or retiring adolescent. Rather, he was equally interested in physicality (hence football) – and also physicality as might take its place as a further element of the periodic table of personal and creative style which he was assembling for himself. Ferry was thus concerned throughout his late childhood and early teenage years with the identification of those activities, individuals or ideas which might best assist with his reinvention of himself as more open to elevated, energised experience. He was researching glamour, intuitively.

The forcefulness of a certain vigour, intensifying the signature of one's identity, was a vital observation in Ferry's earliest study of style – a study conducted from beyond his considerable (and enduring) shyness. Quentin Crisp's pronouncement in *How to Have a Life-Style* (first published in March 1975) retrospectively summarises the stance: 'Style is the way in which a man can, by taking thought, add to his stature. It is the only way. Style is never natural; its nature is that it must be acquired. The finishing touches of style are best self-taught but the basic exercises that lead to style can be learned from others. If a tutor of any subject does not also teach style, he must at least teach the need for it.'

Ferry's initial extracurricular tutors in style – before attending university – would therefore include musicians and Teddy boys, also racing cyclists, and the old guard of salesmen at the gentlemen's outfitters, Jacksons, in Newcastle. Racing cyclists, first.

Bryan Ferry: 'When I was about fourteen, one of the things I got into was cycling – racing cycling. I was very much into that as a *style* thing – it was quite important for me. It was a very cool sport; it had a uniform. You wore these brightly coloured cycling shirts, and you read the *Tour de France* cycling magazine. I became quite obsessed by it for a couple of years – from about thirteen to sixteen. With the money which I'd earn by working in the tailor's shop [Jacksons of Newcastle] or by delivering newspapers [for Anderson's shop in Washington], which I did before I went to school in the morning, and when I came home in the evening. It was a very big newspaper round and it gave me thirty shillings a week, which was a fortune – I could buy records and cycle parts.

'I joined the cycling club, which was called Houghton le Spring Clarion, and I went there for time-trial races. I wasn't particularly good, but I had beautiful bikes that I built. That was a great style moment for me. Because I thought it was a very beautiful thing, that kind of cycle sport . . .'

In a further side-step to the activities that Richard Hamilton had been pursuing in Newcastle during the middle years of the 1950s, there is a coincidental but insightful similarity between Ferry's fervent enthusiasm for cycling and the introductory note co-written by Lawrence Gowing (who was then director – until 1958 – of Newcastle University's Fine Art department) and Hamilton himself, to accompany Hamilton's didactic exhibition, 'Man, Machine and Motion' – held at the University's Hatton Gallery in 1955.

The exhibition (as described by Hamilton in his *Collected Words*), was 'a survey of appliances invented by men to overcome the limits imposed on them by the physical attributes provided by nature', and it took the form of 'approximately 200 photographs and photographic copies of drawings' which were mounted in Formica sheets and fixed within thirty open frames. As such, this was intended to be as much an exhibition about exhibition design, as it was about the subject of its exhibits.

In describing the exchange by modern man of horse and rider for machine and rider, Gowing and Hamilton (although Hamilton subsequently attributed the final authorship of the exhibition catalogue's introduction to Gowing alone), describe a dramatic shift of intensely romantic experience, which might also serve well to define the temperament of Bryan Ferry, and the allure for him of the 'very beautiful thing', the sport of cycling. Gowing wrote: 'The relationship is now different, and more profound. The new rider has not merely exchanged the potentialities of one creature for those of another. He has realised an aspiration which lies deeper than thought, the longing for a power with no natural limits; he finds himself in real life the super-human inhabitant of his dearest fantasy.'

As a 'new rider' at Houghton le Spring Clarion, Ferry clearly took delight in the whole mythology of team cycling. The somewhat continental chic of the cycling jerseys, the masculine elegance of the bikes themselves, their construction and maintenance; the Gallic sophistication of *Tour de France* magazine. What was on offer, in addition to the sensory and physical thrill of the sport, was the whole kit of a further romantic role – and one to which Ferry had responded with obsessive dedication.

Bryan Ferry: 'I sold all my bikes when my mother asked me to give it up, because I was spending all my time on it. I was always very obsessive you see, and I could think of nothing else but that. This was just before I sat my O level exams, I guess.'

The cycling club, however, would later provide a pivotal figure in Ferry's early musical career – the first of what Ferry himself describes as vital, chance encounters, without which his life would have been very different.

On an interpretive level, there is a dialogue between the sentiments of

Gowing's pronouncement, 'in real life the super-human inhabitant of his dearest fantasy', and Ferry's formative, already entrenched romanticism – a determination to transcend, and to do so with exceptional, impeccably executed panache. There is an echo of that same ambition, too, in a comment made by Brian Eno to the author in 1997, regarding the earliest stage costumes worn by Roxy Music – that they 'were quite deliberate takes on the space nobility of the 1950s – the Masters of the Galactic Parliament and so on.'

On a more terrestrial level, Ferry was discovering the social strata of subcultural Washington and Newcastle, as those layers existed on the cusp between the 1950s and 1960s. Washington, much smaller, could deliver small-town aggression, with its home-grown gangs of Teddy boys. Their presence appealed to Ferry's connoisseur's taste for a certain vulgarity – the aesthete's penchant for the enlivening, contrary energy of the loud, brash, colourful and outrageous.

A short film, *Gala Day*, made in July 1962 by John Irvin, funded by the British Film Institute's Experimental Film Unit, gives a good portrait of working-class youth in the industrial north-east at the beginning of the 1960s. As the Durham and district miners gather one July morning for their day of celebrations, we see the simultaneous, tornado-like arrival of vast gangs of teenagers – still, at this time, a reasonably recent sociological invention. Arms linked in long lines, some wearing fringed novelty cowboy hats, with here and there a knot of local rockers, they thread and swirl their way through the older generations – most of whom look on with a mixture of bewilderment or disgust.

Amidst the ceremonial trades union banners, an end-of-day service in Durham cathedral, the open air speeches from political worthies (including the young Anthony Wedgwood Benn), the new youth appear freshly, wantonly liberated from the old formalities of a workers' holiday.

Teddy boys would be important to Ferry, and had emerged in the UK during the middle years of the 1950s, the first of the major pop teen tribes, swiftly becoming demonised (not without cause) within the popular imagination as knife-wielding, bigoted folk devils, high on sex, rock and roll, vandalism, intimidation, and anything else that happened to be to hand. Their title came in part from an abbreviation of 'Edwardian', referring to their chosen style of clothing – the velvet-collared, long-sleeved, thigh-length jacket, the high-collared shirt, bootlace tie and narrow, tapering trousers. It was above all a mutant style, calling in to play not simply the aristocratic British fashions of the early years of the twentieth century, but also the black American 'zoot suit', white, southern American dandyism, and – as Philip Hoare has described in his essay 'I Love a Man in Uniform: Twentieth-Century Military and the Dandy Esprit de Corps' (2004) – a working-class appropriation of the covert, fetishistic customising of military uniforms by homosexual officers within fashionable London regiments, known as 'New Edwardians':

> Now, in the mid-twentieth century, through Soho pubs and the less frequented byways of Hyde Park, a stylistic baton was passed from the New Edwardians of Pall Mall and Belgravia, back to the East End and South London, where the fashion was street-abbreviated and mediated as the Teddy boys, an urban battalion armed with switchknives instead of sabres, and with razor blades hidden in those black velvet collars.

Ferry would always be interested in the potential of uniforms as stylistic statements. In addition to his admiration for the ceremonial swagger of the Teddy boys, and the jerseys worn by the cycling teams, he will later describe how his collaboration with the fashion designer Antony Price – himself interested in the sartorial relationship between uniforms, fetishism, and the erotic, romantic glamour of classic formal styles for men and women – would suggest both the white tuxedo (made famous by Eric Boman's iconic *l'heure bleu* portrait of Ferry on the cover of *Another Time Another Place* in 1974) as a kind of *uber*-uniform, and of course the Weimar and fifties GI militarism of some of Ferry's stage clothes from the middle years of the 1970s. For Ferry, the relationship between the uniform as a style, and the classic dandyism of formal correctness, is of certainty intimate.

But in one sense, Ferry's earlier liking for the 'vulgar' style of the Teddy boys served to frame and sharpen the decorum and poise of his other aesthetic enthusiasms, adding the vital grit which gave a keen edge (a semblance of volatility, perhaps) to what otherwise might have been merely a rather precious assimilation of good taste. In addition to which, more prosaically, such vulgarity could be slick and joyous in the same way that melodrama could prompt a luxuriance of melancholy.

The Teddy boys would find their place on Bryan Ferry's formative palette of influences and inspirations – above all, in their dedication to a certain outrageous style, through which they both defined themselves and made a forceful statement about their sense of identity and personal attitude. Like the racing cyclists (and, as we shall see, the grandly mannered older assistants at the traditional tailors' shop Jacksons) the Teddy boys contributed to Ferry's youthful study of 'auto-faction' – to be self recreated as a virtually mythological version of yourself. Or, to quote Quentin Crisp once more, 'to know who you are – and be it like mad'.

Bryan Ferry: 'The town [Washington] was kind of dangerous – it always seemed quite physical, with gangs of Teddy boys, and rival gangs fighting each other – rather like *West Side Story*. It was Teddy boys against other Teddy boys; people were very territorial, and if you came from one part of town you would automatically have to fight someone from the other part of town. I was apart from that, being a grammar-school boy; but as a grammar-school boy, in your bottle-green blazer and green-and-yellow-striped tie, you had to keep an eye out for the Teddy boys at a certain bus station, just outside the ice-cream parlour where they used to play billiards.

'I actually became quite friendly with the local gang, who were quite a bit older than me, so I think that made me more acceptable. I learned to play snooker quite early on, and I used to spend a lot of time playing with these wonderful Teddy boys, wearing their long Edwardian coats – real dandies, really into their clothes, even though, of course, they weren't effeminate in any way; they were very, very hard. And very proud of their suits. I suppose that I was no threat to them, being quite a bit younger. When I used to go and play there in the snooker place I must have been about five years younger than the people I was playing with; so I was a bit of a junior.

'One night, all in that same period, maybe when I was sixteen, I went to see Puccini's *La Bohème* at Newcastle Theatre Royal. I was completely captivated by it. I remember coming out crying – I was in tears because it was so beautiful. Strange, isn't it? I obviously felt music very deeply . . .'

three

Newcastle in 1961, and its trinity of gentlemen's up-market clothing shops: Jacksons the Tailors – traditional, City Stylish – flashy, and Marcus Price – very American, modern and cool; Bryan Ferry takes a Saturday job at Jacksons and studies tailors' pattern books from the 1920s and 1930s, and the notion of style as the agency of social mobility.

At the beginning of the 1960s, Newcastle city centre retained both the grandeur and the parochialism which had distinguished the provincial cities of northern England – their wealth, and hence their architecture, civic institutions and topography, linked almost entirely to their industrial and mercantile heritage. But if the docks, shipyards and quayside were heavily industrial, tough, and even dangerous after dark, then other quarters of the city centre, and the inner residential districts favoured by the university students, just slightly to the north towards Jesmond Dene park, were historic and bourgeois in appearance.

In many ways, it was a city that at this period was both time-locked in the inter-war years of the 1920s and 1930s, and entering the mass consumption and mass production boom of the late 1950s and 1960s. The truism 'austerity Britain' does much to describe the lingering, drab quality of much of British life during the 1950s, but it tends also to deny the equally important emergence of the new consumerism, with its innovations in product design, bigger, brighter shop windows, evolving advertising and signage. At the time when Bryan Ferry was first exploring Newcastle, he would have been aware of both the sombre gravitas of the city's older institutions, and the promise of newness which was beginning to emerge through the more popular cultures of music and fashion.

To walk through Newcastle at this time – as photographs from the period describe – would be to wander through a typically bustling, in places architecturally imposing, northern British city – the vastness of its Victorian buildings still relatively free of the regeneration and rebuilding schemes that would soon come to dominate British towns and cities later in the 1960s. Newcastle was a city, moreover, with a certain kind of glamour, deriving in part from its dependence on the docks and shipyards, and in part from the grandeur of its heritage. Indeed, 'cool' and 'stylish' are two terms which Ferry, Richard Hamilton and the Mod outfitter Marcus Price all use in defining the city at this time.

Thus there was a sense of both immense, industrial strength, and of warren-like streets, alleys and arcades. And within these, of both elegance and seediness, mercantile propriety and something approaching a youth-cultural underworld. By the time that Ferry would enter the department of fine art at Newcastle University in the early autumn of 1964, the city's relation to modernity would have accelerated, and its art student cliques be proudly conscious of their particular, somewhat Americanised stylishness. But Newcastle's provincialism would render its tastes and fashions markedly different from those of London, as well as amplify and draw attention to the styles of the local followers of fashion.

In terms of its geography, one might imagine the city centre itself as being marked by Grey's Monument – an elegant pillar commemorating the statesman and tea lover Earl Grey (built in 1893, with the head of the statue, having survived the Luftwaffe, being hit by a bolt of lightning in 1941) – which stands at the junction of Grainger Street and Grey Street; the latter being a stately curved street of early nineteenth century, imperious looking buildings (including the Theatre Royal) and described by John Betjeman as 'one of the finest in western Europe'. The city centre had been largely rebuilt from the 1830s, led by a partnership of Richard Grainger (developer), John Clayton (town clerk) and John Dobson (architect). Newcastle's finest buildings and streets – Grey Street, Grainger Market and the Theatre Royal – date from this period.

Taking the university buildings along King's Walk and Haymarket as the 'top' of the town centre (north of them, heading towards the open space of the Town Moor) one can think of the city's principal streets as leading down towards the quayside of the River Tyne. The main streets were Newgate Street, Clayton Street (in both of which there were branches of Jacksons), Percy Street (home of the Marcus Price menswear shop and proto-boutique, also, later, of the equally celebrated Club A-Go-Go) and Northumberland Street – the last being the site of the white stucco magnificence of Fenwick's department store (founded in 1882), in whose restaurant (since the turn of the twentieth century) dinner-suited dance bands had played *thé dansant* tunes from a small podium, flanked by potted palms. The Fenwicks themselves (an heir of whom, Mark Fenwick, would become Roxy Music's manager) were one of Newcastle's oldest leading families.

In sartorial terms, this period between the mid-1950s and the rise of Beatlemania in 1963 saw a fusion of American 'college' styles and the more continental, early Mod clothing. Add to this the cigar-and-mahogany masculinity of the old fashioned, traditional British styles to be bought off-the-peg or bespoke at Jacksons, and you have the basis for Bryan Ferry's early education in menswear. Never a practising Mod, but sympathetic to its credo of ultimate stylishness, Ferry was absorbed, rather, by the transformative qualities of fashion and style: how image becomes an agency of social mobility.

Bryan Ferry: 'When I worked in Newcastle – at sixteen years old I suppose – a lot of great Teddy boys used to come into Jacksons, where I worked on Saturdays. And I used to advise them on suits. My main job was to write down measurements as the tailor measured them and called them out; he had special books to take down all the measurements, and you had to do all kinds of specific things with them: ask them how many buttons they wanted and what sort of lapels. Sometimes they were just dead straight suits, and other times these fancy things which the Teddy boys would invent: wanting to have velvet piping, or a certain number of buttonholes. It was quite interesting.

'They [Jacksons] had all these wonderful old books of styles, so I'd spend ages when the place wasn't busy just looking through these illustrations of gents with pencil moustaches and bowlers in Bond Street. Wonderful books which you could show to the customers . . . And there were some marvellous characters who worked in the shop. I enjoyed that very much, and that's when I became interested in sartorial things.

'There was an old boy who worked downstairs in the "deluxe" department, where toffs would come for suits. Some of the suits were very expensive, and others were quite cheap; most of the time the suits would be about ten quid, which was quite good considering that they were made to measure.

'This marvellous old boy was the type who had been in tailoring all his life, and had assumed a certain kind of poshness which I thought was rather good. As you can sometimes find in some of these old department store people, or guys who work in Savile Row – they seem to "construct themselves" from the people they have met over the years. The manager was a fabulous piece of work; he had a wonderful moustache and haircut – it's amazing how these people invent themselves, and give themselves incredible airs and graces, but I think it's good fun.

'At the time I thought, God, these guys are really something, really smart, really posh; but looking back I suppose they were poor little salesmen in a tailor's shop in Newcastle. But really immaculate they were, dandies – always with the handkerchief – they dressed very well. The Teddy boys and these tailors had a very different look, but the fact that they took such great pains, both in their different ways, made them similar.

'But for me, I quite like the anonymity of dressing almost like Philip Marlowe or something. I was always fascinated by men's clothes, although they didn't determine my life. Having worked in a tailor's shop for two or three years when I was a teenager, I think it had some impact on my taste in what to wear and my knowledge of what to wear. Because I suddenly knew about three-button, single-breasted suits with side vents, or which buttons you were supposed to fasten, and which you weren't, and all the rest of it. Apart from that, there was the interest I had in different musicians from different times – I always liked the cool ones. Like Miles Davis and Charlie Parker – the Modern Jazz Quartet, or Chet Baker. They all had a sense of being quite chic. So I felt that I wasn't doing anything particularly new, but taking bits from here and there which I liked, and assembling my own doctrine.'

As Ferry approached his mid-adolescence, in the opening years of the 1960s, his interests and enthusiasms would begin to correspond in part to those cited by the founding, purist devotees of the Mod movement – the rise and peak of which can be dated, loosely, from 1960 to 1965. Ferry's early liking of Charlie Parker and the Modern Jazz Quartet; his subsequent love of soul music, Tamla Motown, Stax releases and R&B; his increasing fascination with esoteric personal style (in particular the Gallic chic of the cycling club). Similarly, as he entered the sixth form, his maturing inclination towards arts subjects: the romantic ideal of the bohemian intellectual, whose creative philosophy is style and vice versa. All of these tastes and attitudes have been claimed as central to the earliest, pre-commercialised credo of Mod. It was at around this time that Ferry would pin poems by T. S. Eliot, then being in serialised in a newspaper, to his bedroom wall.

In essence, Ferry's relationship to Mod (and, later, that of his immediate circle at Newcastle University) could be summed up as the enshrinement of pose: of cool deportment in all things – the endless subdivision of one's activities into an index of correct mannerisms (almost, but not quite, a form of performance art); and, accordingly, the refinement of one's taste to increasingly specific garments, styles and accessories – worn to omnipotent codes of design, cut, manufacturer, fabric and, perhaps most important, manner of dress.

As Mod was in many ways a direct reaction by lower-middle-class and working-class youths of the early 1960s against what they perceived as the drab, creepy, quotidian dullness of prevailing fashions and attitudes (still mired in Mod's worst nightmare – the past), the movement was thus dedicated to a new ideal, summarised by notions of clean, sharp 'modernist' lines, acceleration, consumerism, black jazz derived 'cool' and sleek continental and American styling.

Likewise, contemporary French and Italian cinema and fine arts, the vibrant aura of young British film stars such as Tom Courtenay and Albert Finney ('just popped out of the Garrick for a smoke') – the smart, confrontational, working-class anti-heroes they had played seeming related to Mod in their youth and disaffection, as much as the slick modernity represented by Hollywood's depictions of the fast-paced, intoxicating exhilaration of Madison Avenue, were all contributing ingredients to the perfecting of Mod cool.

All of these qualities are cited in the copious literature on early Mod, and have been set down by those for whom the movement shaped their every waking minute. Jonathon Green, in his oral history of the 1960s, *Days in the Life: Voices From the English Underground 1961–1971* (1988), quotes the words of Steve Sparks, that, 'Mod before it was commercialised was essentially an extension of the beatniks. It was to do with modern jazz and to do with Sartre. It was to do with existentialism.' A fellow intervie-wee in Green's survey, David May, cites the writings of Genet and Camus, as much as amphetamines, shopping, dancing and getting one's hair cut at the women's hairdressers, as being intrinsic to the purist Mod lifestyle.

In its founding form, Mod was a genuine conflation of the cultural and the subcultural – above all the desire to declare a separatist devotion to newness. Richard Barnes, more succinctly, states in his account *Mods!* (1979) that, 'It was from their Modern Jazz tastes that they named them-selves. They called themselves Modernists.'; also, that 'The Mod way of life consisted of total devotion to looking and being "cool".'

David May's reminiscences for Jonathon Green touch upon two other qualities of Mod as a catalyst of personal and social development. Firstly, how Mod was one of the principal factors to urge young people in the provinces to move to London (mythic example: Billy's cool girlfriend, Liz – 'she's crazy, man' – actually does get on the train south at the end of the film *Billy Liar* [1963]); secondly, May touches upon the relationship between Mod and sexuality – 'There was always a large gay element in it.'

Roxy Music would also employ sexual ambiguity ('to look beautiful, but in ways that men had not thought of looking beautiful before', as Brian Eno would later observe), while at the same time creating its own sense of maleness and its own romanticised heterosexual eroticism. As Ferry would happen to have several close homosexual or bisexual male friends, he would also recognise in their acuity, wit, and sense of style, an outlook and ambition which was similar in some respects to his own – to the singular creation of identity through style; pursued with such intent as to seem simultaneously effortless and a triumph of artifice. 'There was an unstated camp streak running through all this masculine preening . . .' Green comments in his further study of British counterculture in the 1960s *All Dressed Up* (1998), adding, 'Hardcore Mod was above all an incestuously, narcissistically male environment.'

But Mods were also, for the most part, the sons and daughters of the working classes or newly suburbanised lower middle classes. The elevated ideals ascribed to early Mod should thus be understood within the usual, rather more spotty and leery concept of adolescence – as photographs of

Mod crowds of the early 1960s reveal. But this also makes their 'revolt into style' all the more extraordinary, for being in many ways an amalgam of received ideas – a translation of various subcultural fantasies into a new expression of modernity.

Coinciding with the wider availability of further education for working-class children, enabled by the Butler Education Act of 1944, this would make Mod especially linked to the art college environment – indeed, art students and Mod were entwined from the very beginning of the movement. Hence, also, Mods being amongst the first junior employees of the new, younger creative industries – advertising, media, design, television and fashion.

Studying the alternately exasperated and sensationalist newspaper coverage of early Mods,* one is immediately struck by the collision between the movement's dedicated sense of exclusivity and its context – the shabby streets and clubs which typified the lower-middle and working-class teenage haunts of the period.

Against such a backdrop, what stand out are the sudden vivacity and significance of the new, youth-created and youth-oriented trends in retail design. At the beginning of the 1960s, clothes shops aimed towards the younger, fashion-conscious, typically Mod customer began to assume their own importance as both venues and, vitally, as embassies of new attitudes.

The term 'boutique' (first appearing in October 1957 in *The Times* newspaper, to describe departments within big stores where both couture and wholesale garments were available) would define this new trend; but away from central London and Carnaby Street, in a big provincial city such as Newcastle upon Tyne, the latest cool fashions – made almost more audacious and striking in their provincial context – were sold only by a very small, select number of local retailers, the most celebrated – the 'coolest' – being Marcus Price, on Percy Street.

Throughout the 1960s, the importance within provincial British cities of such lone, independent, meticulously sourced and stocked shops – be they clothes shops, bookshops, record shops or early health food stores –

---

* 'Inside the Mind of a Mod', for instance, written by Marjorie Proops for Saturday 23 May 1964's *Daily Mirror*, concluding: 'They'll get as bored with it all in the end as I am with them already.'

would be of paramount importance. Away from the social, cultural and commercial vastness of London, in cities where attitudes and fashions took far longer to change (or failed to change at all), the availability of what is now termed 'otherness' – alternatives to the local orthodoxy – would become vital life blood to the inhabitants of those places who cared to look beyond the known and acceptable, to that which was new, different or emblematic of change.

Thus the exclusivity and poise of Mod held an appeal for Ferry, its rigorous commitment to personal style, and much of the music, but here his affiliation to the cause as a specific movement reaches its limits. As with so many of the subcultural and cultural phenomena he was discovering during this period, Mod would find its place alongside a whole array of other interests. No single flag held his allegiance; Ferry was curating the accumulation of his influences.

Bryan Ferry: 'Jacksons was one of the principal outfitters in Newcastle at that time. I guess there were three or four – but it was one of the best of the High Street tailors. There were also two other very different clothes shops in Newcastle, which I used to go to. One was more trashy, but I really liked it; it was called City Stylish, and there you could buy incredibly pointed Italian shoes, and also Teddy boy wedge-soled shoes. All the more outlandish clothes came from City Stylish: pencil ties, really good Teddy boy clothes and extreme Italian suits – tiny thin lapels, lots of buttons down the front and very narrow trousers. Pin-stripes – very good; wild clothes . . . I really liked that shop; I used to go and look in the window every night when I was in Newcastle . . . Windows into a doorway . . .

'I couldn't really afford things from the other, which was called Marcus Price – a shop for top-end Mod clothes. There you would have American shirts – it was like a very early boutique. The man who owned it, Marcus Price, was a great jazz aficionado and he was part of the jazz scene – a very cool scene. But Newcastle was a very cool town in some ways – a leading Mod town. And the very expensive Mod clothes came from Marcus.'

four

Marcus Price – a very cool, top-end Mod shop in Newcastle; its owner and its history, from 1953 to the mid-1960s.

Marcus Price: 'I was going to say that Newcastle was a "cloth cap" kind of city – back in 1952, 1953. But it was starting to leave that image behind, as I remember from the clothes that we sold. We used to sell flat caps, for instance – this would have been when I was eighteen or nineteen, and just going into the trade; and I remember my father taking the guy who sold them outside, on to the street, and saying: "This is why we're not buying any caps from you: just count the number of fellers on the street in caps." And there were hardly any. It was a significant change in dress. And we were selling *modern* clothing . . .

'My father had started the business through other shops. After I did my year at university, I went into the army to do National Service. I was in Germany for a while, and when I came back I went into the business at the shop in Percy Street – Number 31. While I was in the army, my father had acquired the shop and shopfitted it. It was lino-floored; and the counters were from other shops that he'd had – they weren't brand new, that's for sure. The fixtures were maybe ten years old, so there was a quaint look about it – the lino had a checked pattern . . .'

As Marcus Price proceeds to describe the interior and stock of his shop, one begins to see a near-perfect example of how the cool, commercial styling of the late 1950s and early 1960s corresponded to the modern urban folk art which was so central to Pop art, as well as to the heightened sartorial tastes of the Pop-art generation. There are also distinct touches of the kind of imagery which would become associated with Roxy Music's 'imaginary world'. Price's name spelt out in red neon, for example, and the shop's logo – of a dinner-suited, man-about-town in the style of Maurice Chevalier or Fred Astaire. The slick modernity of the back-shop lino in the pale blue and yellow of the Swedish flag; also the labelling of garments 'Continental Styled' or 'US Styled', and the importation of US styles and popular culture by way of the army.

In one sense, we can see how Marcus Price's shop, and the passion for jazz of its owner, are like a secular version of the themes of Pop art, as well as becoming a finishing school for art student style. All the pop influences and inspirations are there – modern music, US film styles, American popular media, the latest fabrics and synthetics – the culture of a new, streamlined, sexy, technological, mass consumerist world. In describing the fashions stocked, and the garments which became particularly popular, Price also sets down an index of styles and of stylishness – the sartorial expression of pop age modernity.

Marcus Price: 'When we opened up the back shop, which I had designed, we got pale-blue lino with yellow stripes and a slightly more modern fabric for fitting-room curtains. That was the younger person sort of pushing his way in! The curious thing was that the colour of the lino was from the Swedish flag, because I'd been to Sweden for a quick trip. It looked terrific! It wasn't the most modern shop in the world – we were definitely in the provinces; but the clothing we kept was up to the minute.

'It was a big shop – about sixty feet in depth, so you went back a long way. There was a lot of window to dress, and I did the window dressing. Again, one tried to be as modern in that as you could – influenced by Cecil Gee in London, because they were a terrific company in the fifties, absolutely marvellous. You always wanted to beat Cecil Gee.

'It's quite curious how you start out looking at the most modern thing you could find, which was Cecil Gee; and then there was another shop, Davis, in Shaftesbury Avenue, that was a very American kind of shop, and also Williams in Tottenham Court Road. Those three shops were very, very influential in our thinking. And so we went after the same merchandising that they were getting. Sometimes, that was a bit ahead of the provincial town style – but it did work, it worked very well indeed . . .

'To describe the shop, starting with the window: it was black glass on the outside, and had Marcus Price – with Marcus above the Price in red neon. Down the side was this guy in claw hammers [a dinner suit], cape and black bow tie, which my father had had on his letterheads. That's where the design came from, and he had it etched in the glass – which of course Mark [Lancaster – Newcastle University Fine Art graduate, British artist, friend and 'superstar' of Andy Warhol, pivotal style guru to Bryan Ferry and his contemporaries] saw as some wonderful iconic thing!

'In the windows in those days we used to take a shirt, and put a stiff bit of hardboard in it and then pin it so that it was incredibly tight. Then we put a tie around the collar, and cufflinks in the cuffs – we sold huge, American-style cufflinks. We had two labels for own label stuff. One was 'US Styled' and the other was 'Continental Styled' – just to cover everything. I remember we bought five hundred ice hockey type pullovers; they had a slash neck and stripes. Mainly black, with red, white and yellow stripes down the arm. We had a marvellous time with that.

'So you had the window; and you had fifty or sixty shirts all in lines, with ties and cufflinks; then in the next window you had jackets and trousers. You only did one jacket in those days, and it was a black and white Donegal tweed – made of rayon! And black rayon trousers with a sheen on them and quite a turn-up.

'With the fashions of 1952, '53 and '54, you were only eight years after the war, and there had been nothing happening. But then the American influence came in through the army. I remember my father came back from Germany after the war and the first magazines we had in the house were *Esquire* and *Life*. He had been in the international area, meeting other soldiers in Germany, and those things had influenced him.

'I was collecting jazz from 1945 onwards, I guess, and Dizzy Gillespie was the modern jazz trumpeter of the time. Then there was a marvellous article in *Esquire* on Dizzy Gillespie. So that was how information was filtering through to the family, and that was how you built up your sense of modernity. I was aware of the meaning of "cool" through "cool" jazz. They say of Miles Davis's pianist Bill Evans, that he was "cool", as was Miles himself. It was a phrase used around all of those areas; and people were cool. So it's a term from music which transfers to people.'

The American men's magazines of the period – their pin-ups, as much as their totemistic style – were important to British art students in terms of the aspirational, glamorous world which they described. During the time when Bryan Ferry was doing his Saturday job in Newcastle, in the autumn of 1962, an article would appear in *Esquire* about the author James T. Farrell, under the title 'Another Time, Another Place' – the title of Ferry's second solo album, released in 1974.

Marcus Price: 'Going back to the shop. You went in, and there were trays of wonderful socks – which were mainly black, but hooped in brilliant colours: electric yellows, heliotrope – things like that. Ties were "Slim Jim". It was pretty smart, because if you look back Teddy boys were wearing ties with their long jackets. We didn't do so much of the Teddy boy thing – that was done by Jacksons the Tailors made-to-measure, in the main. But we would supply the shirts and the narrow ties. I can't tell you the number of shirts we sold! They were all cutaway collar, under the brand name Jaytex – and we sold thousands of them, seriously. So the collar was straight across, and then with the slim tie. That was back in the 1950s.

'Once you were in the trend you just kept it as sharp, smart and up-to-the-minute as you can get away with. And there were certain things that you couldn't get away with in those days; things that you had seen down in London, and which just didn't apply here until a year or two later, but that was okay . . .

'The jean thing went from 1959, 1960 – when it was English jeans – to Levi's, which were very difficult to get hold of. The first we got were the unshrunk ones. Seamen used to want them – they'd put them over the side, and after a few miles at a few knots they'd softened up considerably! We also did Wrangler jeans as well. The Levi shirts with press-studs were massive; they had diamonds and clubs in mother-of-pearl. Richard Hamilton showed me the originals from the States – real Wrangler cowboy shirts with big cuffs, and studs. Then we did them in cord and in cowhide.

'"A sophisticated, top-end Mod shop" is absolutely right to describe what we were doing. Because I think we moved on in the sixties. By the time of the Beatles and Mods, there were the three-button jackets in the Madison Avenue advertising style from the States. If you look at American films from the late 1950s and early 1960s – Doris Day films and things like that – you'll see executives wearing three-button jackets with the top button done up. In the sixties we had a fifteen quid suit; we also did a twenty-five quid suit which was Italian imported, lined trousers to the knee – which I couldn't get makers to make for me here, even when I offered them more money, mainly because they hadn't got the facilities. But that suit – three buttons, a sheen on it, incredibly smart. Twenty-five quid being quite a lot of money in the sixties – fifteen was the average.

'We started doing Ben Sherman shirts in the 1960s. They were very special, because Ben had been to the States and had got the answer to the button-down. It wasn't simply a question of putting a button on a shirt and fastening it at the collar; it was a very special twirl which got you a nice rounded area. They did it so perfectly, with a button at the back – like the old American song, 'Does your collar button at the back?' – a kind of Brooks Brothers thing. And a hanging loop on the seam. They were in the Oxford cloth, which was a big American influence, and as cool as hell. It was one of those things – we sold thousands and thousands of them. They were de rigueur – everyone wanted to have one. We even did frocks in them – a long shirt. I think we dressed the staff in them from time to time.

'The high-collar shirts were "giraffe collars" – you couldn't get them high enough, with a tab, so the tie came through and held the collar in tight. And then a pin through – which was also big.

'So all of that was your modern menswear of that era, near enough.'

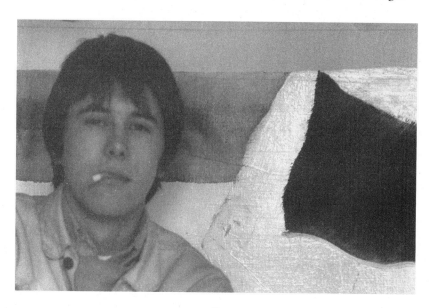

five

1962–1964. Bryan Ferry in the sixth form of Washington Grammar School; his academic choices; his discovery of jazz clubs and his first group, the Banshees.

When, in 1961, Ferry had entered the sixth form at Washington Grammar School, he was most drawn to those subjects which assist the romantic ideal. But in terms of his aspirations, his choice between acting and painting, art school and perhaps studying English at Oxford University, appears to sit somehow within the broader matrix of his outlook: these subjects as career choices were immediately transposed by him into the received idea of the romanticised lifestyles pertaining to each.

Equally important, this was also the first period during which Ferry would begin to experience the tension between his practical relationship to fine art and music. His involvement in his mid to late teens with the local rock and roll covers group the Banshees would thus be most extraordinary in its sudden conversion of a relatively shy, reflective youth, into the occupant of the exposed and perilous position behind a microphone in front of a band.

Bryan Ferry: 'Academically, I seemed to go in phases, of when I liked the idea of studying or didn't. Generally I did all right. I became quite lazy I think; I had to be pushed to study, because I'd find other things to distract me. I was drawn to the arts subjects, and when I was just about to go into A levels, in the sixth form, I became interested in art itself. Literature, too – I liked reading and I liked poetry. I liked history. So those were the three subjects that I chose to do in the sixth form. History was something

44

I really enjoyed. I just didn't particularly like writing essays, or the hard work.

'History of art I was very interested in, and that's what I wanted to be at first – an art historian. And then, I didn't have any natural facility for drawing, but I started to get better. I wasn't brilliant, but I had a very good teacher, and I became interested then in the idea of becoming an artist myself. So that's what I decided I wanted to do.

'My English teacher, however, was also very good. He used to walk around in a black gown, and he'd been to Oxford, and he was different from my rather louche art teacher who used to take me to the pub. We'd go drinking and so on. But the English teacher really wanted me to study English. He put me in a play at the school, *Twelfth Night*, where I played Malvolio. It was the first time that I'd been on stage, and I got rave reviews – I was quite good at it, I think.

'And so the English teacher said that I must go to Oxford and study English and become an actor. I would never have studied hard enough to do that, I think; and the art thing had got hold of me by then, and I decided that I really wanted to be a painter. I suppose that I liked the *idea* of being a painter: I liked the lifestyle, I liked the Bohemian ideal of the Left Bank of Paris – lots of wine, lots of models to paint; beards, pipes . . . It was this whole Bohemian vision that I had for myself. I had almost styled a vision of what I wanted to be, and I was drawn to that image of living.'

At this same time, a friend and patron of Richard Hamilton called William Copley – a collector and surrealist – was actually living out the 'Bohemian ideal' in Paris. Speaking with Paul Cummings, shortly before his death, Copley would observe with ironical fatalism: 'What I do think, and it's a terrible thing to say, is that in New York the atmosphere forces you to feel you have to make it. And Paris, I think, traditionally was the place you went to when you didn't want to make it. People went to Paris to paint, to get away from their rich families – you know, and live in cafes and paint and be beatniks . . .' In his more *Billy Liar* moments of fantasy, the young Bryan Ferry might well have been drawn to the fantasy of escaping a rich family in order to become a beatnik painter in Paris.

It was also at around this time that Bryan Ferry first identified his interest in the ways that music or art could animate a pose – the fantasy lifestyles of the romantic imagination, as embodied through particularly suave, intense forms of creative activity. This was an equation which became increasingly important to the cast of people involved with not just the creation of Roxy Music, but the rise of a whole art school forged cult of the 'poseur' – a simultaneously profound and ironic code of deportment, halfway between performance art and 'dressing up'.

Back at the New Orleans Jazz Club (on Melbourne Street in central Newcastle), Ferry especially liked the way in which the club and its denizens had a filmic, other-worldly air. At the same time, there was a robust muscularity to this reasonably tough, smoke-filled Newcastle jazz club – certainly not peopled with the socialites, dandies and exquisites one imagines creating the cocktail hour chatter at the opening of *Roxy Music*, but filled none the less with a particularly heady atmosphere, working on Ferry's imagination to refine a dash of heightened romance. From a musical point of view, these early visits to Newcastle clubs provided Ferry with his lasting admiration for the kind of solid, bravura musicianship that typified the Stax, Motown and R&B music so sacred to Mod.

Bryan Ferry: 'On Saturday nights – this is when I was in the sixth form – I used to go to a jazz club in Newcastle called the New Orleans Jazz Club which had really a great atmosphere. To me it was just like being in a movie set: people smoking and drinking, and then this band playing who were really good. A very good trumpet player. They were doing be-bop sort of stuff, and they were called the Mighty Joe Young Jazz Men. John Walters was the trumpet player – he had been an art student at the university where I was dreaming of going at that point. He later became John Peel's producer – he's now dead, poor thing, but he was a great character, a really funny man and a great be-bop trumpeter. He was the producer when I was with Roxy Music on the John Peel show in the early 1970s – in '72, before even our first record came out.

'Then there was a tenor player who was very, very good called Nigel Stanger who later played on one of my records ['Taxi', 1993]. I wish that I had played with him more – he was a fantastic player. He played with Herbie Goins [Herbie Goins and the Night-Timers – whose early recordings would also feature the Mahavishnu Orchestra founder and guitarist John McLaughlin] and people like that, at the Flamingo Club in

London. And Eric Burden from the Animals would get up to sing, and he was outstanding. I thought that he was very good, singing in the Jimmy Rushing-type style of blues shouter. So Newcastle was quite a home for the blues, I think. It was very rich and varied, my early years growing up there, before I went to university . . .'

Bryan Ferry's very first involvement with singing in a group is described with the under-stated but prophetic explanation: 'I thought this might be a way of making some money.' But as the singer with the (very young) group the Banshees, Ferry was clearly doing more than simply messing around in a teen band. Not least because the group did comparatively well – playing working men's clubs around the Newcastle area, as well as, impressively, at the famous Club A-Go-Go, a little further up Percy Street from Marcus Price's shop.

There is a particularly vivid detail within Ferry's description of his audition for the Banshees, as it was held in a women's hairdressers in a neighbouring village to Washington called Shiney Row: the image of a traditional rock and roll group, with their equipment set up within a frame of what Ferry describes as 'weird-looking, space age hair dryers', has the visual resonance and comedy of a Pop art montage.

Bryan Ferry: 'When I was just about to leave school, I bumped into this guy, Bruce, who had been in my cycling world. He said, "I've got a group – I play drums in a band. We're looking for a singer – can you sing?" And I said, "Er – yeah."

'Usually I worked every holiday – I was quite hard working! I'd work in the local steel factory – Washington Steelworks – doing odd jobs and labouring. Or on a building site, depending on what was going at the time. At Christmas time I worked on the post, delivering parcels and letters. There was always something going on to earn money.

'So Bruce asked me to come along for an audition, which was held in his dad's hairdressing salon in Shiney Row, another village about three or four miles away. And there in this hair salon, with all these hair dryers around the room – weird looking space age hairdryers – was this band set up. I had never sung in my life before, except at home, singing along with my records. So I thought this might be a way of making some money.

'I got the job, anyway, and became their singer. And for someone who was as shy as me, I was quite amazed that I could do it. His dad was the manager, and he had a whole diary full of bookings for that summer period. So suddenly, instead of working in the factory for maybe ten pounds a week, I was getting that per night. Incredible.

'They were called the Banshees, and they did all these Chuck Berry songs like "Sweet Little Sixteen" and "Johnny B. Goode" – the sort of things that people did then. And some pop things as well. They were very good, in that very basic way of two guitars, bass, drums and me. We played working men's clubs and that sort of thing. I blush to think – because I was painfully shy. I'd just try to imitate records, whichever song it was. I'd try to sing like Chuck Berry or whoever. But we played really good places as well. We even played Club A-Go-Go which was the big venue in Newcastle. While I was in that band I met Jane Mackay – Jane McNulty then – who a few years later I introduced to Andy (Mackay) and they married. She's dead now, sadly – she was a local girl.'

The A-Go-Go would become a frequent meeting place for Ferry and his art student friends; it would also be a venue which he would play with his second and third bands, while he was still at the university: the City Blues and the Gas Board. Along with the Quay Club (somewhat rougher and more sinister, down on the Quayside) and the New Orleans Jazz Club, the A-Go-Go (not without its own frisson of risk) was Newcastle's leading venue for modern pop and rock music. Lunchtime dances – rather like early versions of those described by Tom Wolfe in his essay on the psychedelicising of London Mod, 'The Noonday Underground' in 1968 – were held at the Majestic Ballroom, and also in the Oxford Galleries Ballrooms. These catered more for the young Newcastle workforce of office boys and shop assistants, looking to let off some steam in their lunch hour.

Bryan Ferry: 'The Club A-Go-Go was great. That was near the bus station. You'd go up these stairs, past all these bus drivers and bus conductors who had a tearoom or an office there, and the club was at the top. It was in two sections: there was what they called "Young Set" and then there was the "Old Set" or "Jazz Set". So you had to set up in one part of it for the first set, and then you had to move all your equipment through to the other side – there were two rooms, in other words, and the second was more sophisticated. The first was bigger, maybe.

'Later, I saw all sorts of people there: Cream, the Spencer Davis Group, Wilson Pickett, Captain Beefheart – I was DJ at the club the night Beefheart played there. I remember helping my friend David Sweetman to paint the mural in the club: a New York skyline in fluorescent paint, so at night it appeared lit up – rather like David Letterman has behind him.

'There was this marvellous Jewish man called Mia Thomas, who was the boss of the A-Go-Go. He was like a Sidney Greenstreet figure – this big, big man in a double-breasted suit. He was a great character – really scary. And some quite hard men used to go there – like gangsters: dressed in mohair suits, with beautiful girls – the best-looking girls in Newcastle: quite tarty. It was really exciting – it felt really "It" to go there. Beautiful girls . . .'

Marcus Price: 'There's an odd link there, because Mike Jeffries, who actually owned the A-Go-Go, had done social studies [now sociology] at university. He then had an older man who fronted it, who was from a retail background – Mia Thomas; he had a deadpan manner, and used to pop in to the shop for ties. Initially Mike had had a coffee house, and then he translated that into a club – the A-Go-Go. He was up-to-the-minute you see.

'The A-Go-Go became a bit like the Cavern, in Liverpool. Women's styles at the club varied – some of it was flash Newcastle, but a lot of the time it was just sweaters and jeans. Slightly better dressed in the older "Lounge" section. The hair was that Cathy McGowan kind of thing. Black pullovers, Ben Sherman shirt dresses. Little Levi jackets . . .

'They put on a lot of American stuff – John Lee Hooker, Muddy Waters, Sonny Boy Williamson – mainly blues. Then we had the local stuff – the Animals, of course. Also, Long John Baldry, Rod Stewart when he was just starting off, Julie Driscoll, Eric Clapton. The Junco Partners were the resident group . . .

'Newcastle, then, was a lively, lively place – a lot of fighting, a lot of blood in the streets. We once got broken into three times over one weekend. It was a rough area of town. But Percy Street was nice during the day: a seafood counter, a pipe shop, a wool shop; and then this home of modernity in black glass, which was very unusual. When we first opened, the shop next door was a skin yard – skins piled high . . .'

So a picture of Newcastle's Mod scene in the early 1960s begins to emerge, with Ferry already singing covers of rock and roll standards in a suitably lively band, as well as exploring the city's sartorial subculture – from archaic pattern books to 'top-end' Mod styling. There is also something keen-edged about the fact that both Marcus Price and Mike Jeffries – Newcastle's modern outfitter and modern club owner, respectively – have some background within academic humanities and social studies.

Such informal dialogue between mass culture and cultural theory is in line with the fact that Richard Hamilton, then in residence at the university's Fine Art department, would find himself testing – albeit informally – the socio-cultural observations of the artists and academic theorists at the Institute of Contemporary Art, London (the 'Independent Group'), against the fervid realities of Newcastle's front-line of popular culture. There is even a touch of the Independent Group's anthropology of mass and pop cultural Americana in Hamilton showing genuine western denim shirts to Marcus Price.

In joining the Banshees, Ferry had made a vital act of affirmation: that rather than being content to remain in the audience, one of hundreds of locally cool, modish youths, he would prefer to be in the spotlight, elevated.

Bryan Ferry: 'The group did really well, but when it came to September it was time to leave them and start university. If I hadn't bumped into Bruce, this drummer, I would never have done anything in music, I'm sure of it. So if I hadn't been in the cycling club and met him then . . . It's funny how things can lead one to another in a strange way. So it's best not to question why you do certain things. It was a chance meeting.

'I can't remember what we wore. We didn't have any stage suits or anything like that. There are no photographs from that period. Isn't that strange? You might have one ten by eight photograph of the group which you'd send out maybe, and get them to pin up "Appearing next week" – that kind of thing. I don't think we even had one of those; the band was thrown together so quickly . . .'

six

In the late summer of 1964, Bryan Ferry takes leave of the Banshees and enters the Fine Art department of what by now is known (since 1963) as the University of Newcastle. It is a highly dynamic period in the history of the department, with Richard Hamilton on the teaching staff, and studio demonstrators including the former students, now artists, Mark Lancaster and Rita Donagh. At Newcastle University, between 1964 and 1968, Ferry will also pursue his musical ambitions and become friends with fellow art students Stephen Buckley, Tim Head and Nicholas de Ville, as well as with Hamilton, Donagh, and Lancaster. Ferry and Stephen Buckley will also become close friends with Jeremy Catto, an historian – who along with Mark Lancaster and Richard Hamilton would become a vital personage in the aesthetic education of Bryan Ferry.

The importance of Bryan Ferry's education and social experiences as a member of the Fine Art department of Newcastle University, in relation to his subsequent career and artistic ideals as a musician and singer, cannot be overestimated. On an academic level, Ferry and his immediate circle of acquaintances might be said to comprise a generation for whom pop had replaced nature as the principal, elemental subject matter of fine art. Linked to this, the presences of Richard Hamilton and Mark Lancaster would provide Ferry with two very different kinds of mentor – a common denominator of their influence being a fascination with modernity, the potentiality of art-making and all that was vibrantly thrilling about the accelerating technological world of popular culture.

As for many young people of his generation, tertiary education within the arts would free Ferry from the immediate prospect of the drudgery of working-class labour, and introduce him to a liberating form of mildly bourgeois bohemianism — a new experience of life, 'beyond the coalfields' of the industrial north-east.

Professor Janey Ironside — mother of Virginia Ironside, agony aunt, and the first Professor of Fashion at the Royal College of Art — would later describe a post-Second World War generational shift in class values and arts education, which, as well as applying specifically to young fashion designers in the 1960s, might be seen as true of many 'working-class' art students — whether of the fine arts, design, or fashion — in the late 1950s and early 1960s. Certainly, it would be true of Bryan Ferry.

Ironside writes:

> Class has always influenced fashion in Britain and the working class influence has been strong. They have a wider outlook, are inventive and are not hidebound by convention. Indeed, one of the best results of the social revolution in Britain since the Second World War has been the release of many young designers to the world. By a system of local and government grants, young people are enabled to go to art schools and colleges and have freedom to experiment. Before the war, most of the people who are now well-known designers would probably have been maids in other people's houses, miners, or working in shops, and would never have had a chance to show what they could do. But now they have this chance.

Entering Newcastle's Fine Art department in 1964, Ferry was only just in time to benefit from the charismatically influential presence of Hamilton, who would leave in 1966 to pursue his own increasingly successful career as an artist. Throughout the early 1960s, the development of British and American Pop art was delivering a formidable canon of new art-making — its energy, poise and glamour overthrowing, for the more progressive minority of the young art students of the period, the lingering mystical quietude of neo-Romantic British art, or the enshrined dominance of European painting and sculpture. (This move towards pop was a process of detachment and reaction summed up in the poetically adversarial title of Alex Seago's account of the development of the Pop art sensibility at the Royal College of Art, London, in the late 1950s and early 1960s — *Burning the Box of Beautiful Things*.)

Bryan Ferry: ' . . . of course when I did eventually go to the university, I discovered that it was very non-U to be interested in the School of Paris. Because suddenly it was the New World of New York, and Warhol, Jasper Johns, Rauschenberg – these were the people who were the heroes at university, and of course Richard Hamilton, who was the famous teacher there. I quickly became enamoured of the whole American dream.'

The university itself and the department of Fine Art have been described in some detail by the cultural critic and art historian John A. Walker, who was a student at Newcastle between 1956 and 1961. His autobiographical essay *Learning to Paint: A British Art Student and Art School 1956–61* gives a lucid and engaging account of both university life at that time and the prevailing artistic trends and fashions within the department. Walker's description of the departmental buildings – somewhat old-fashioned collegiate – paints a picture of the surroundings in which Ferry and his contemporaries would be studying a few years later into the 1960s:

> The department itself was housed in two buildings making up one corner of the quadrangle around which several departments of [King's College] clustered. One building was a red-brick, neo-Tudor structure; the other neo-classical. The neo-Tudor building stretched above a double archway that gave access to the quadrangle . . . Entrance to the department was via the neo-classical building, just through the archways. It had an imposing entrance hall, with a marble floor, dominated by a large plaster cast of a classical sculpture . . .
>
> Off the entrance hall were administration offices, a lecture theatre, a library and a shop selling artists' tools and materials [all still in place]. Also off the entrance hall was the Hatton Gallery, a large room named in 1925 after the memory of Richard G. Hatton, the first Professor of Fine Art in the University.

It was in the Hatton Gallery that Richard Hamilton would create three important exhibitions during the 1950s: 'Man, Machine and Motion' (1955), 'An Exhibit' (1957) and 'Exhibit 2' (1959).

Walker, describing the university during the closing years of the 1950s, recalls how, in 1958, 'CND marchers with traditional jazz bands' would assemble in front of the Students' Union before leaving on protest marches. For many of Ferry's generation, Tamla Motown, Stax and Mod style, as opposed to politics and trad jazz, would become the prevailing ide-oloies. Rounding off the departmental geography, Walker describes how, 'The two upper floors and attics of the building were devoted to painting studios . . . ; there was a life-drawing room; stained glass and printed tex-tile studios; a humid conservatory for the study of plant life, and a studio for the purpose of still life painting.' Hamilton would be fascinated with morphology, introduced by the artist, surrealist and photographer of East End life, and contemporary of Hamilton's at the Slade, Nigel Henderson, to D'Arcy Wentworth Thompson's classic book on the subject, *On Growth and Form*.

The picture therefore is of a traditional, provincial red-brick universi-ty, firmly rooted in academic respectability and seriousness (the ideals of which were reflected in the imposing institutional architecture and plas-ter casts of classical sculptures) but at the same time full of lively enquiry and in places refreshingly unstuffy. Walker's memoiristic essay has been published with some photographs from the period: the female art stu-dents looking chic, beatnick, *gamin*esque (white raincoat, bat's-wing eye-liner), and the boys (a generation older than Ferry) more kitchen sink bedsit – closer to the 'Angry Young Men' than to Mod. Alongside the stu-dent digs around Jesmond Dene park, and the fashionable venues in the town, the university as Walker describes it is an almost perfect articulation of 'town and gown' – barely sloughing off the damp post-war tweediness which had dominated student life through much of the 1950s.

During Ferry's time at Newcastle University, his principal friends and acquaintances would include Mark Lancaster (at Newcastle from 1961–5), Stephen Buckley (1962–7), Tim Head (1965–9), Nicholas de Ville (1965–9), credited on *Roxy Music* as 'Art – Nicholas de Ville', and Rita Donagh – who studied at Newcastle between 1956 and 1962, and would then teach there as a student demonstrator (a semi-tutorial role, often taken up by star pupils of the immediately previous generation) between 1962 and 1964.

The teaching staff, also, were extremely impressive. In addition to Hamilton and Donagh, Director of Fine Art from 1959 (successor to Professor Lawrence Gowing) was Kenneth Rowntree – a painter from the older generation whose studies of British life and landscape in the 1940s and 1950s were filled with twilit stillness and a sense of reverie. In

1950 he made a series of 'Projected designs' of covers for *Vogue* magazine, and in 1954 accepted a commission to paint a mural for the first-class dining room of the P&O liner *Iberia*.

The 'master of painting' in the department until 1961 had been the abstract artist – and consultant architectural designer of Peterlee, a new town in County Durham – Victor Pasmore, who collaborated with Hamilton on several exhibition and publication projects at Newcastle, including 'An Exhibit' at the Hatton Gallery in 1957. Hamilton would also design the catalogue for Pasmore's exhibition at the Hatton in 1960. In 1961 Pasmore was taken up by the prestigious Marlborough Fine Art gallery in London, and thus released from teaching. By remarkable coincidence, one of the former students turned studio demonstrators (between 1959 and 1961), the lively and demonstrative Roy Ascott – later proponent of 'telematics' (computer networked creativity) – would subsequently teach Brian Eno on his foundation course at Ipswich Civic College in the mid 1960s.

As recounted by John A. Walker (and alluded to by Rita Donagh), during the late 1950s Pasmore and Hamilton between them came almost to represent the schism, tension and dialogue between abstraction and figuration – with early Pop art being regarded by the supporters of abstraction as somewhat reactionary, owing to its adoption of personal, anecdotal and vernacular imagery. Despite this rift between differing schools of thought, however, John Milner, Professor of Art History at the University of Newcastle, writing in his biography of Kenneth Rowntree in 2002, would state that: 'Hamilton and Pasmore both approached visual creativity as an investigation.'

The model for the first year 'Basic Course' was derived in part from

Bauhaus teaching, one aspect of which involved the notion, as Hamilton would write in his article, 'First Year Studies at Newcastle', published in 1960 in the *Times Educational Supplement*, 'that artists should join with craftsmen in the design of goods for mass production'; another of which being 'the emphasis on technical training and research into problems of form which are required to be solved without recourse to artistic considerations'.

A later assessment of Hamilton's teaching methods would state:

> The constant factor [in all of the work of Pasmore, Hamilton and Hudson] . . . was a resolution of opposites – in its simplest and most obvious form a combination of intellectual and intuitive faculties within entirely fresh approaches to creativity. Their experimentation as a whole is seen as having been concerned with minutest technicalities of grammar, and yet as having pursued implications of even the smallest creative act upon the realms of three-dimensional construction, of 'architecture', and of the real world presented in popular culture and in performance art. Their images were not conceived as isolated from the real world: such images, to paraphrase Klee's famous dictum, were to make the world real.

Several stages along the cultural food-chain from the rigorous academic intentions behind Hamilton's thinking for the Newcastle Basic Course, the idea of a dialogue between art and mass culture , and of a resolution of opposites, would evolve to permeate the cult of style surrounding Roxy Music.★

A kind of postmodernism lite, such aesthetic strategies will be seen to contribute to the ways in which both Ferry's creation of Roxy Music,

---

★ Peter York, in his essay 'Them' (1976), would subsequently evolve the idea of extended creativity to define, New Journalistically, a whole subgroup of social anthropology: 'Thems are the word made flesh,' he would write in *Harpers & Queen*. 'Thems put the idea into their living; they wear their rooms, eat their art.' York would also identify that this exclusivity-minded trend, occurring amongst a certain type of person during the 1970s, for a highly art-infused lifestyle, was the consequence of what he termed, 'the art school bulge and the assimilation of camp'. He then cites the way in which these same aesthetes are directed by a certain understanding of Pop art, namely, 'Pop Art taught them how to look at things in a cock-eyed way, i.e. in the way that somebody else had already looked at them . . . This led to a widespread use of pastiche.'

and the creative outlooks of many of his principal collaborators, will have become by the beginning of the 1970s heavily steeped in quotation, collage and a stylistic exaggeration based largely on iconographical fantasies of the past and the future.

Ferry's circle at Newcastle would be distinguished in the mid-1960s – at something more of an undergraduate level – by their fusion of fine artistic enquiry, a keen interest in music, and a dedicated stylistic cool. Owing to Hamilton's presence within the Fine Art department, his close contact with the legendary French artist and ideologue Marcel Duchamp, and his consequent intimacy with leading members of the New York avant-garde (including both Andy Warhol and the surrealist and patron William Copley), there would also be forged a connection between Newcastle and the white-hot core of American Pop art that could rival that enjoyed within the London art world.

During Bryan Ferry's time at Newcastle, Hamilton would also undertake his famous reconstruction of Marcel Duchamp's so-called *Large Glass – The Bride Stripped Bare By Her Bachelors, Even* (1915–23). Mark Lancaster, close friend of Ferry and at that point studio demonstrator at Newcastle, would take several of the photographs of the process of this reconstruction, which then appeared in the illustrated record published to accompany the showing of the finished work at the university's Hatton Gallery, in April 1966.

seven

Richard Hamilton – modern art guru: his early career and influence; *On Growth and Form*, the Independent Group, and a brief flash-forward to June 1975.

'I have, on occasions, tried to put into words that peculiar mixture of reverence and cynicism that 'Pop' culture induces in me and that I try to paint. I suppose that a balancing of these reactions is what I used to call non-Aristotelian or, alternatively, cool.'

Richard Hamilton, *Romanticism*, 1972

While it would be perilous indeed to claim Richard Hamilton and Bryan Ferry to be in any sense generational reflections of one another, there was nonetheless a powerful constellation of ideas in Hamilton's art and teaching that would leave an imprint on aspects of Bryan Ferry's creation of Roxy Music.

These would include: a connoisseur's appreciation of the rhetoric, signage and allure of popular culture; a particular interest in the conflation of warm, erotically romantic, often feminised imagery, and a colder, mechanistic, meticulously designed artistic representation; the concept and practice of drawing on a wide range of artistic potentialities and solutions, rather than remaining within one narrow approach; the blurring of 'high' and 'low', 'intellectual' and 'mass cultural', 'popular' and 'esoteric' forms and ideas; an exploration of recreating and replicating existing works by either other artists or oneself; the perfecting of a work's surface – preferring the pristine and the polished (the machine fresh, so to speak) to the ragged edges demanded by self-conscious authenticity; and lastly the idea of being both artist and art director within the realisation of a work – perhaps the heaviest creative burden and challenge to undertake.

One of the best assessments of Richard Hamilton's artistic and cultural importance was written in 1991 by the distinguished critic, the late David Sylvester:

> Defining Hamilton as the founder or father or grandfather of British Pop diminishes him inasmuch as it focuses on a secondary element in his work. His preoccupation with mass culture is only an aspect of his consuming obsession with the modern – modern living, modern technology, modern equipment, modern communications, modern materials, modern processes, modern attitudes. He has a passionate involvement in the modern for the sake of its newness.

Hamilton, therefore, was regarded by his disciples as the artist representative of modern cool – the bringer of tomorrow today – at the dawn of a decade during which youth, modernity, pop culture and technology would comprise a leading socio-cultural fixation. As an undergraduate, Ferry would come to know Richard Hamilton and Rita Donagh socially – it was a time of many parties; more directly, as a first-year student, Ferry would have attended Hamilton's Basic Course – with its emphasis on ridding the fresher students of their pre-conceived ideas about art-making, and teaching them the value, in Hamilton's words, of 'developing modes of thinking which will induce a self-critical attitude in the student'.

Beyond this, Ferry and his contemporaries were unanimous in regarding Hamilton as an inspirational presence above all, whose ideas – as though atomised into the academic environment – permeated both the departmental studios and the prevailing regard for what 'being an artist' might actually mean. In this they were the direct beneficiaries of the pioneering research into mass culture and technology, and the relation of those subjects to fine art, that Hamilton had undertaken throughout the 1950s – that most misunderstood of axial modern ages, a vexed, tentative, cuspate period between the trauma and ruination of the Second World War and a future which looked to space and the atom for both its salvation and its shadow.

Richard Hamilton: 'I was teaching at Newcastle from 1953 to 1966. It was the impression I got when I taught these eighteen-year-olds at the university, that when they came in they'd all been stuffed with the art education provided by people at secondary schools; and that it really was pretty irrelevant – so you'd better clear the board first. It did seem a necessity at the time.

'All sorts of people applied to study art. We [the staff] all used to be available at interview times, and it was extraordinary to find, for instance, that there was this girl from some village in Wales who said that she had never seen a painting – had never, ever seen a painting in her life! How you can come to an art school, never having seen a painting, seemed so extraordinary that we thought she had to be admitted – so that she might at least have an opportunity later.

'And so it ranged from that, to people who were very sophisticated, and who might come there simply because they'd heard of Victor Pasmore and wanted to study with him – and a few even knew my name ...'

Hamilton is being modest as regards his own reputation as an artist concerned with what might be termed the cultural physics of the modern mass age – from the vivacity of early rock and roll to the lunar stillness of a society cocooned in technology and media. By the time that Ferry became one of the first year students to attend the Basic Course at Newcastle, Hamilton – then on the verge of being recognised as a major artist in his own right, his own painting having been barely acknowledged within the department until this point – had already established, and become known for, his investigations into the relationship between art, design, media and popular culture.

His background, as a former teacher at the Central School of Arts and Crafts in London, was one in which the boundaries between art and product design had been encouraged to be traversed, and this, in addition to his keen interest in the latest developments in popular culture, established him as a figure completely up to speed with the fastest, sharpest, concepts of the modern.

Richard Hamilton: 'I was teaching at Central School of Arts and Crafts in London. The only person of any power who was teaching in the London art schools was William Johnstone, who was a Scottish painter – very dour, but very good and knowledgeable, and he employed lots of people because there were mainly part time teachers.

'It's strange that in a school of arts and crafts – which is what the Central School was at that time: furniture, jewellery, industrial design, and a very small art department – Johnstone was getting people into the different departments who were operating at a different level. He got Eduardo Paolozzi, for instance, to work in the textiles department – Eduardo was probably the first of the people he employed. I think he had an idea that this could be a kind of Bauhaus, and at the Bauhaus they had these artists who were a spanner-in-the-works in a way, but they could contribute something useful. And then Bill Turnbull went to teach in the furniture department – there were a lot of unexpected people; even Victor Pasmore was teaching in the industrial design department ...'

By the early 1950s, Hamilton had contributed to a notion and practice of modern art education which was both rigidly practical and steeped in an attitude to art which was entirely in step with the latest technical, social and cultural developments. Also, the idea of rearranging the norms of method and process will have its echo in the concept of colliding seemingly opposed ideas in order to create an utterly new effect.

Between 1952 and 1955, Hamilton had been one of the principal members of the Independent Group – a small gathering of artists and theorists, whose meetings were held under the auspices of the Institute of Contemporary Arts in London (then based at Dover Street, just opposite the Ritz Hotel on Piccadilly) but whose opinions were by no means in line or sympathy with the beliefs of the ICA's president Herbert Read. As described by Independent Group member, artist and futurologist John McHale, it was a 'small, cohesive, quarrelsome, abrasive group', and included the critics Lawrence Alloway, Peter Reyner Banham and Toni del Renzio, and the artists Nigel Henderson, Eduardo Paolozzi, William Turnbull and Richard Hamilton.

The group's discussions centred on art theory and the analysis of popular culture and mass culture – as art historian Martin Harrison summarises, 'Many Independent Group members had a common interest in Hollywood cinema, American comics and science fiction, and if Lawrence Alloway was most active in analysis of these popular art forms then Banham was the most solidly demotic in his support for American product styling and technology.'★

The key issues under discussion within the Independent Group were the relationship between 'high' and 'low' art, the developing roles of advertising and mass media (hence the group's espousal of Marshall McLuhan's early study of advertising and media, *The Mechanical Bride: The Folklore of Industrial Man* [first US publication, 1951]), the potential dialogues between art, science and technology, and the philosophical examination of the purpose of 'design'.

Almost inaugurating the study of these concerns was the exhibition 'Growth and Form', curated at the ICA by Hamilton in 1951 and described by Martin Harrison as '. . . a prototype multimedia or environmental art event that included film loop projections and the stroboscopic lighting of water droplets'. (Thus described, the exhibition sounds almost like a precursor to Andy Warhol's 'Exploding Plastic Inevitable' 'happenings' with the Velvet Underground, staged in New York a decade and a half later, and witnessed first hand by Mark Lancaster and Rita Donagh. Installation photographs of the exhibition, however, show a design system and a selection of images which appear simultaneously scientific and austere – dramatic and enigmatic, educational and unknowable.)

The Independent Group were thus concerned with how a conflation of modern phenomena – from art, science, industry and media – might be refined philosophically to assist with a renewed understanding of the art-making process. For Hamilton, the consideration of 'pop' imagery

★ In a quick fast-forward to the evening of 18 June 1975, Professor Peter Reyner Banham can be seen in an epoch-defining photograph taken of a group at a table in the roof-garden of Biba's (the former Derry & Tom's department store in Kensing-ton High Street), the occasion being the launch party for Bevis Hillier's book *Austerity/Binge: The Decorative Arts of the 40s and 50s*. Against the London summer evening sky we see Janet Street-Porter, Bevis Hillier himself (later renowned for his great biography of Sir John Betjeman) and – dressed in singlet, satin boxing shorts and boxing gloves – 'Little' Nell Campbell, star of *The Rocky Horror Show* (playing Columbia), and later nightclub impresario (of 'Nell's') in 1980s New York. Hillier's elegant shawl-collared tuxedo and satin bow tie sit at odds with Banham's dark suit and professorial beard.

There is an ironical neatness to the cultural historical circuitry which will somehow bring this group together in the Biba roof-garden, to celebrate a nostalgia for a past style, as part of an evolving analysis of pop forms and ideas which might almost be said to have begun with the enquiries of the Independent Group – the commencement of which had in turn been contemporary to the period surveyed by Hillier's book.

and sources, as they related to his own art-making processes, would also be held within an intellectual framework that was underpinned by his equally rigorous study of the art and ideas of Marcel Duchamp. (It was Nigel Henderson, again, who had first introduced Richard Hamilton to Duchamp's 'Green Box', which Hamilton would subsequently translate and, famously, typographically interpret.)

As McLuhan's *Mechanical Bride* would read like the first cultural manual of the pop age – a means of responding to the new bombardments of advertising rhetoric, rather than being merely passive consumers – so the interests of the Independent Group, sifting through the cultural and philosophical extrapolations of the new popular culture, would eventually persuade Richard Hamilton in his view (given in the *Fathers of Pop* Arts Council TV documentary transmitted in 1979) that, 'we were able to say everything we can think of is right and can be used'.

Richard Hamilton: 'I've always been unhappy at the idea of being labelled as a Pop artist; but I can see that I tried to create something for myself – a way of looking at the contemporary world. I don't know whether I have ever mentioned that I had seen the work of Frank Stella, and read his writings. And I couldn't see why he would want to produce work that he described as "non allusive" – an art detached from all possibility of having allusions to anything else: it is the work, and nothing else. That seemed to me to be sad in a way – rather like pulling out the plug. My ambition was to be multi-allusive! I wanted to relate to everything that was going on in the world.'

By the late 1950s and early 1960s, Hamilton's art and writings would be investigating – on a sociological level, apart from their profound enquiries into artistic technique – what might be termed the erotics of consumer culture, from pin-ups to film stars to product design. And this investigation would be founded upon a methodology and perception which owed much to a fusion of art and technology – a Marshall McLuhanite melding of 'warm' and 'cool' media.

Richard Hamilton: 'I do tend to analyse and think of making art as problem solving; but I caught it largely from Marcel Duchamp I think, when reading the notes of Duchamp. He thought a great deal; he didn't do that much, but he did a hell of a lot of thinking; and he wrote enough clues into his notes to be able to tell you that what he did was very deliberate and considered.

'In a way, I felt that what I'd been doing before the mid-1950s was floundering, and going through a whole gamut of styles. It was all a kind of parody. When I look at drawings which I did at the Royal Academy Schools when I was sixteen, I can think, well, that's got a tinge of Picasso, and the next day a bit of Cézanne, and the next Ingres. It was all about style. And I could do it all but I wasn't really thinking much. I was developing technical capabilities which were quite useful later, but by 1951, doing the "Growth and Form" exhibition, I was beginning to think "What's it all about, Alfie?" And trying to rationalise it with texts – with words.

'When I went to Newcastle, it was because of Hugh Casson – whom I knew very vaguely. I'd done exhibitions in London – "Growth and Form" was the first in 1951, which architects knew about at least. And so Hugh Casson, who was very much involved with the Festival of Britain, would have known that this was the ICA's contribution to that and had probably been along to see it. He was very charming, a nice man, and he wrote to me and said that they needed somebody in Newcastle who might take a job as lecturer in design.

'Hugh Casson thought of me as a designer of some interest, I suppose. The reason that there was a job at all was because Lawrence Gowing had arrived at this university, taken the job as professor, and thought, "This isn't an art school, it's more like a craft school," and begun to see what he could get rid of. And he got rid of the chap who was teaching design, and replaced him with me. I suppose that I was sufficiently associated with design, having come through the auspices of Hugh Casson, to be acceptable. So I was lecturer in design which meant I didn't really have much of a job, so I had to make a job for myself.'

Hamilton's acknowledgement of going through an apprenticeship phase of making work which was largely in the style of earlier great artists – as 'parody', to use his own term – is echoed in Bryan Ferry's earlier statement that when singing with the Banshees he was primarily copying the vocal style of whatever number the group were covering. Likewise, speaking about his own work as an art student, Ferry speaks of becoming caught in an imitative phase – of making works in the style of great or iconic modern artists. Both Hamilton and Ferry would of course transcend the imitative phase in their own work – Ferry by deciding on music as his medium, and Hamilton largely through his encounters with the work of Marcel Duchamp, whose notes (known as the *Green Box*) for his *Large Glass* painting *The Bride Stripped Bare By Her Bachelors, Even* he would be reading closely towards the end of the 1950s.

Bryan Ferry: 'My work as an art student varied every year . . . It changed. When I was at school, just about to go to university, I remember doing a whole series of Francis Bacons – like screaming heads and so on. I love those pictures.

'Much later, I met Francis Bacon at a party, and he said that he wanted to do my portrait; so we started this correspondence, but sadly we were never in the same place at the same time, plus I sometimes get preoccupied with things in my own work that preclude me from doing things like that – it's a sadness, really. It would have been great to have a portrait done by him, I guess. He seemed a really amusing character – very sharp. I enjoyed talking to him when I met him.

'But when I was a student, in addition to my Francis Bacon phase I did a whole series of stained canvases in the manner of Morris Louis, whom

I also liked. And, of course, there was a Richard Hamilton period.'

Richard Hamilton: 'When I was at the Royal Academy Schools, as a student, I realised that I was doing pastiches of everyone. I don't think I'd done anything before *Hommage à Chrysler Corp.* (1956). I had done the *Ulysses* illustrations, but I don't rate those as having invented an image. Those were just trying to illustrate what went on in Joyce's mind.

'But with *Hommage*, I felt that I was doing something that was really necessary.

'I had to break through this barrier of what was mine and what was an image I recognised as belonging to somebody else. When I look at it now, there's a hell of a lot of Duchamp in it. It really comes directly out of my encounter with Duchamp and the *Large Glass* – so it's not that original!

'The next, *Hers Is A Lush Situation* (1958), was more original; but *Hommage à Chrysler Corp.* was a big departure for me – unlike anything I'd done before, and unlike anything that I'd seen before, which was more important. Although there is this Duchampian mythology in there somewhere. And that's when I was actually immersed in the notes [the *Green Box*] – 1957.'

On a daily basis, Ferry and his contemporaries would be particularly aware of absorbing the inspiration and influence of Hamilton's ideas – rather as though Hamilton were creating a particular artistic and intellectual ambience in which the students developed. But this was also a time when the social side of the art department was almost as important: parties, dances, trips to the neighbouring seaside towns for picnics and cricket on the beach. Hamilton would subsequently recall Ferry's social presence, 'I remember him often going to parties, because I was a great partygoer. I think in some ways I initiated the party spirit in Newcastle. So I remember him always being at the parties, and being terribly good looking . . .'

eight

'Man, Machine and Motion'; Rita Donagh; 'This is Tomorrow'; lunchtime rock and roll dances at the Majestic Ballroom; Polaroids and performance lectures: 'Glorious Technicolor, Breathtaking Cinemascope and Stereophonic Sound'; Hamilton and the technology of mass culture.

Hamilton's approach to art would extend the notion of the artist by recreating the role as one which might also include being a designer, typographer, printer, photographer, technician, writer, theorist, teacher – the 'total artist' in this respect. Thus, his early exhibitions, concerned with exhibition design itself, as much as their subject matter – morphology, mechanical extensions of the human body – could in one sense be seen as works of art in their own right, although they were unlikely to be regarded as such at the time. But this idea of an expanded, inclusionist creativity, in which the media that art might be made in proliferates across the range of seemingly industrial, artisan or commercial technologies, is central to Hamilton and his influence. As is seen from the following recollection, Hamilton was responsible for re-routing much of the university's 'service' departments – printing and photography – to new uses within the Fine Art department. Oddly, until then, the divide between fine art and technological services had been so vast that the two had seldom, if ever, become acquainted. In his forging links with the 'service' departments of the university, Hamilton further endorsed that quality of modernity which David Sylvester would later see as defining his identity as an artist.

Richard Hamilton: 'In 1955 I made the exhibition "Man, Machine and Motion", primarily because I thought: this university happens to have an art gallery; we don't have a collection, just an art gallery. It was only a short-term exhibition space called the Hatton Gallery, but having got that under my wing, it became a kind of responsibility.

'So if, for instance, they needed an exhibition of Tiepolo drawings, which the art historians wanted to do, then I would be the one who sorted it all out in the gallery: hanging the exhibition, and making a catalogue – because there was also a print department as a service organisation. There was a photography department, too – mainly because of the needs of the medical school and the dentistry department – photographing mouths and operations. But the man who ran it was wonderful, in that he saw a service department as something that should be available to the whole university. We became good friends, and he was always very interested in new possibilities, such as: the printing machine was really an Addressograph company offset litho printer, printing only an A4 sheet or something. But it could cope with more, and we were soon printing these really rather good catalogues after a while – with spiral binding – for exhibitions at the Hatton Gallery.'

'Man, Machine and Motion', with its Kraftwerkian 'Mensch Maschine' interpolation of the machine becoming one with human beings, reveals Hamilton's fascination with the taut, almost erotic relationship between product design and human physicality – sensuality, even – which would in many ways be the foundation of his ultra-modernity as an artist. Installation photographs – in modern colour, naturally – show the fine, complex, geometric design of the exhibition: the panels displaying the photographs are arranged in groups relating to different forms of manned mechanistic transport – aquatic, terrestrial, aerial and interplanetary. Images of diving suits, midget submarines and underwater robots, biplanes and spacemen (the latter images actually roofing one of the other sections – precursing the 'moon ceiling' which would be seen the following year in Hamilton's iconic photomontage: *Just What Is It That Makes Today's Homes So Different, So Appealing?*) acquire a certain inscrutability and enigma, for all the world like some ethnographic museum display from the twenty-third century.

Richard Hamilton: '1956 was a critical moment; because as a result of discussing things for three, four years at the ICA – coming backwards and forwards from Newcastle, and engaging in these discussions with my peers – I learned a great deal. And we thought about all sorts of things, and put them into words. Which I felt to be a necessary thing.

'At the ICA, one of my collaborators came back from the States with a lot of material including Elvis Presley records, which nobody had heard, and "Rock Around the Clock" – the very beginnings of the big rock and roll movement. So he came back with these, and *Mad* magazines and lots of interesting things that I suppose would be regarded as ephemeral material. And these were discussed and played at the "This is Tomorrow" meetings; it was like a social analysis of what was going on. And I found myself getting very interested in particular people: all of those early rock and roll groups and the Detroit stuff – the 45s.

'Rita [Donagh] also did something rather extraordinary when I was there in Newcastle, a little later. I didn't know her very well in those days, but she said that she was going to the local ballroom in the evening, and that she often went at lunchtime to the same place. So I went with some other people – Mark Lancaster amongst them, I'm sure. But Rita used to go, by herself, or with another girl student, and watch these office girls dancing with each other to rock and roll music at lunchtimes. And then we all started to go – with the students from the art school. And I think we gained a lot of experience from seeing the thing from the level of where the action was, rather than the Institute of Contemporary Art's discussion of it ...'

Rita Donagh: 'It was at a place called the Majestic and it was a ballroom – a very fine ballroom. Peter Moore took us. He was a student who was a local boy, whose father was a piano player in Newcastle, and he discovered it. It was the place where American rock and roll was first heard in Newcastle. They were all wonderful dancers, the office girls; they would make long lines and do these incredible moves. I started at Newcastle in 1956, and then it was all about discovering these different things. By the early 1960s, the city had become quite famous for music ...'

Hamilton would also recommend to the students that they attend certain rock and roll concerts – those by Little Eva, for example; Rita Donagh suggests that coming up from London, in touch with the latest music and magazines, Hamilton had a profound influence on broader issues of taste beyond the teaching of art.

Historian Martin Harrison also recounts Hamilton's description, itself a statement on cultural status, of John McHale's importation of early pop Americana into the UK: '. . . the package contained,' Hamilton recounts, 'the first Elvis Presley records to land on these shores . . . protectively interleaved with copies of *Mad* magazine so that no one knew what was ballast and what was cargo.'

Within the earlier generations to benefit from Hamilton's teaching – when he was simply teaching Design prior to being invited to co-teach the Basic Course with Victor Pasmore – Rita Donagh was a brilliantly gifted student. Arriving at King's College, Newcastle, in 1956, she would later teach within that same department from 1962 to 1964. Her work as an artist being centred around profound aesthetic enquiry (specifically the capacity for representation within art), the mapping of social identity and politics, Donagh would then teach in the department of Fine Art at Reading University, between 1964 and 1972, through which she became acquainted with Andrew Mackay and his circle of friends.

Rita Donagh – like Richard Hamilton, and, as we will see, Mark Lancaster – is a pivotal figure in the network of friends and acquaintances who will form the broader milieu out of which Roxy Music emerges in the early 1970s. Most important, she is a principal figure in the relationship between the Fine Art departments at Newcastle and Reading universities – the only two universities in England, outside London, where one could study fine art as an honours degree at that time.

As a teacher, Donagh's interest in the relationship between contemporary music, performance and art (pursued during her time as a tutor at Reading University), would be of particular importance to Andrew Mackay's generation of art students, as would her encouragement to work within the broadest definitions of art, and her constant awareness of gender roles within society. At the same time, when in partnership with Richard Hamilton, the couple would be acknowledged as the ultimate arbiters of modern cool. The seriousness of Donagh's subsequent concerns as an artist – in particular her examination of what are known as the 'Troubles' in Northern Ireland – sits in sharp relief to the enthusiasm with which she would be recognised by her students as a teacher, intellectual and iconic figure.

Rita Donagh: 'While I was still at the convent [Our Lady of Mercy Grammar School, Wolverhampton] I got permission to go to life drawing evening classes in Bilston, which is a town between Walsall and Wolverhampton. I thought that this was what artists did – they drew from life. The teacher there had been at the Slade when Stanley Spencer was a student; and I got this idea that I wanted to study art. I began to feel that I was studying art, rather than 'doing pictures' at the convent school.

'So I asked her about becoming an art student. I really wanted to go to Wolverhampton, because I knew they had a good art school, but I discovered that I wasn't eligible because I lived outside the borough. So I would have had to go to Walsall. And then the teacher at Bilston began to talk to me about the Slade, so I said to my art teacher at school, "There's a place called the Slade. Maybe I could apply to go there?" And she replied, "To get into the Slade, you've got to be either very rich or a genius." So she rather dampened that.

'I left school after O levels, and felt so insecure that I went back to do A levels. And when I got back I discovered that there were universities where you could study art. One was the Slade, which was out, the other was Reading and the third was Newcastle. I had interviews at both Newcastle and Reading. At Reading I did an exam, and they were very nice; but they wouldn't take me because I was too young. I think I was only sixteen, and you had to be eighteen to matriculate.

'I went for the same exam at Newcastle, where Lawrence Gowing was then professor; I went into the interview and he said, "Of course you can't come into the first year because you're not eighteen. But we have a scheme where we can take students for a year before they matriculate, called 'occasional student'." So I went to Newcastle and did that, and didn't become a first-year student until 1957. My birthday was in April, so by the time I got to Newcastle I was seventeen.

'When I went to Newcastle, all these boys came who had just done their National Service, so they seemed very old to me. They were probably twenty, twenty-one, but when you're seventeen a twenty-one-year-old seems very old. John Walker was a contemporary of mine, as was Adrian Henri, the poet [born 1932, graduated in Fine Art in 1955]; Mark

[Lancaster] came later. I didn't meet Mark until 1961, when I'd already been there for four or five years. Mark and I are more or less the same age, but he'd gone to work in his father's mill . . .'

Ferry, de Ville, Buckley, Head and Lancaster all confirm Rita Donagh's observation that Newcastle's Fine Art department at this time was a place of extraordinary creative dynamism – the sense that one was plugged right into the circuitry of the latest ideas in art and culture, and that an intellectual system held sway which shaped one's approach to art-making – and, it would later transpire, a certain nuance of one's social discourse: a propensity for light, self-deprecating irony, set alongside a keen sense of artistic enquiry, and a natural sympathy towards the avant-garde.

Rita Donagh: 'The experience of going to Newcastle was a bit like the experience of going to hear Beckett at the Birmingham Rep when you'd never heard of Beckett. The powerful influence, initially, was Victor Pasmore, because Richard wasn't teaching the Basic Course at that point. When I first went to Newcastle, Richard taught something called "Design", which was associated with textile design. I think it was because Lawrence Gowing, and the people teaching painting, were very much Euston Road school [a factual, largely anti-romantic form of naturalistic painting from life], and thus thought of Richard's work as "design". He was doing all those paintings, but they thought that it was some kind of design work. But Victor Pasmore had just started and he was very dynamic, very messianic, and preached modernism! And the impact was stunning. Even the older painters at the school were doing abstract expressionism and action painting – that was very much the thing amongst the bright, older students; but Victor was something different. He talked about abstraction in a way which was . . . It was almost as though he'd been converted, and wanted to convert all of us.

'So I very quickly gravitated from Euston Road – which was working from life, which I'd been doing anyway at Bilston – into thinking about form, and eventually abstraction. Victor taught the first year, and so this was the first time I encountered Paul Klee – an incredible thing to hit the *Pedagogical Sketchbook!* (1925; English edition, trans. Sybil Moholy-Nagy, New York, 1953).

'Richard came in one day every fortnight to teach design, and that was very interesting because it was all based on growth and form – organic form, movement. The two combined were extraordinary. It was Victor who invited Richard to join him to make a Basic Course; and they then made it much more clear. But when I was there, we did Victor's work, which was modernism and abstraction, and Richard's work which was a design course coming out of D'Arcy Wentworth Thompson [*On Growth and Form*]. And then we would have painting from life, and sculpture and fabric design – that's how it worked. Later it all became integrated into a Basic Course, that I taught on briefly, and Mark did too. So it was an exciting time – things were being formed; it was just all beginning to come together.'

Vitally, Donagh also identifies the fundamental importance of the confluence of seemingly opposing influences – in this case, Pasmore's abstraction and Hamilton's enquiries into pop. This idea of colliding opposites – soul music and manipulated electronic sound, for example, or chanson and free-jazz inspired rock – will also be intrinsic to the musical and imagistic creativity within Roxy Music. (Hence, Andrew Mackay's astute comparison of the group to the melding of opposed ingredients in a Futurist recipe.)

As Donagh recalls, during the period when Hamilton was beginning to make some of his most important early paintings – *Hommage à Chrysler Corp.* (1957), *\$he* (1958–61) *Pin-up* (1961) and *AAH!* (1962) – he would scarcely have been acknowledged by his employers and colleagues at Newcastle as an artist. Rather, he was seen as a tutor in design who undertook work of his own which had little direct bearing on his role within the department. It would not be until the middle of the 1960s, subsequent to his second solo exhibition in 1964 at the prestigious Hanover Gallery, London, and an article he wrote and art directed for *Living Arts* magazine, that he would begin to attract serious attention from the art world.

Richard Hamilton: 'By 1956, when the suggestion was made that we do an exhibition, ['This is Tomorrow'] I had to begin to think about what is important, what have we been thinking about, and how does it relate to anything one might produce? Also that this was not a work of art that I was making, but a kind of didactic presentation, wrapping up the ideas that we've all been concerned with over the years – people like Lawrence

Alloway and Reyner Banham and all the rest of it. I think that anything I did then would have been acceptable to at least fifty per cent of those people. Because it wasn't art, it was what one might think of now as a factual assemblage . . .

'Having been engaged in that experience, I was left out on a bit of a limb until I got this letter from Peter Smithson [Peter Smithson and his wife, Alison, were an architectural team, pursuing radically modern ideas] saying, "Suppose we follow this up, what should we do?" And I thought, you can do your architecture, and anybody else can do their criticism; but this output that we might develop within our own fields, should be related to the thinking that's gone on in the important events of the last five or six years – which included, Smithson's *House of the Future*; and I listed that among them – or the exhibition that they'd done "Parallel of Life and Art", which I don't think would have existed without *Growth and Form*.'*

'The House of the Future' had been made by the Smithsons for the *Daily Mail* Ideal Home Exhibition in March 1956 (just before the 'Fun House' exhibit made by Hamilton, McHale and John Voelcker for 'This is Tomorrow'). The 'House of the Future' – a predicted dream home of 1981, minus the heartache – was furnished in fibreglass, plastic and tubular steel, the effect being a kind of sci-fi minimalism – heightened, during the exhibition, by the presence of some futuristic female inhabitants, in appearance part Flash Gordonette and part elfin.

Richard Hamilton: ' "Growth and Form" came first. It goes back beyond – I don't say that it starts there. There's a long line going back to 1851 of exhibition design, so it's not something that starts in 1951! I was inspired by seeing a lot of historical models and admiring them – it's a form, and it's an interesting form.

* In September 1953, at the Institute of Contemporary Arts, London, Eduardo Paolozzi, Nigel Henderson and Alison and Peter Smithson had held their exhibition 'Parallel of Life and Art'. Martin Harrison again: 'The images in "Parallel of Life and Art" were deliberately un-pretty, raw and grainy. A conscious democratisation of visual information juxtaposed works by Klee, Dubuffet and Alberto Burri with non-art material such as huge, commercially produced blow-ups of micro-photographs, fossils or news photographs. Reyner Banham located the origins of New Brutalism in this display, but the non-hierarchical disposition of the objects was central to the concept of "image" – of an image, that is, as the conveyor of meaning irrespective of its status as high or low art.'

'I don't know, in fact, where the title "This is Tomorrow" comes from, because it was decided at a meeting that I wasn't able to attend. I would have argued against it – and I did argue against it, in a sense, in the little statement that I made. I say: "Nobody can say what tomorrow's going to be like – let's concentrate on today." And this was the premise on which I based the whole of my contribution to the exhibition although, actually, it looks a little more far-out than any of the other contributions to the exhibition.'

The Hamilton, McHale and Voelcker 'Fun House' contribution to 'This is Tomorrow' (assisted at 'every level', Hamilton later wrote, by his first wife, Terry) was visually dramatic and powerfully eloquent of a modern sociology. Nearly billboard-sized in scale, an ecstatic Marilyn Monroe, from the film *The Seven Year Itch* (1955), plunging her hands into the billowing folds of her skirt, cased one side of a structure through which the viewer could walk, experiencing multimedia representations of a set of themes which Hamilton later recounts in his *Collected Words* of 1982: 'Imagery – Journalism, Cinema, Advertising, Television, Styling, Sex Symbolism, Randomisation, Audience ˙participation, Photographic image, Multiple Image, Mechanical conversion of imagery, Diagram, Coding and Technical drawing.' And, 'Perception – Colour, Tactile, Light, Sound, Perspective Inversion, Psychological shock, Memory, and Visual Illusion.'

Read back with the hindsight of fifty years, these qualities might also be listed as fundamental components – machine parts – of the ultimate pop or rock group as a mass-media project. At the time, however, 'Fun House' was made as a carefully considered statement about the potential creative relationship between artist and architect, as well as the sociological diagnosis which the multimedia structure undertook. Vitally, this proto-pop structure – part booth, part museum of the modern quotidian, part, perhaps, shrine – established an aesthetic formula between machine culture and eroticised female glamour. This would describe one half, so to speak, of Hamilton's infectious understanding of the pop age, which would then be further enhanced – rendered intellectually operational – by his work on Duchamp's *Large Glass*. All of which, in the manner of disciples and gurus, would be absorbed by Bryan Ferry and his contemporaries within Newcastle's Fine Art department.

Most famously, in January 1957, in a letter to the husband and wife architectural team Peter and Alison Smithson, Hamilton had penned what is usually taken to be the founding definition of Pop art: 'Pop art is: Popular (designed for a mass audience), Transient (short term solution), Expendable (easily forgotten), Low cost, Mass produced, Young (aimed at youth), Witty, Sexy, Gimmicky, Glamorous, Big Business.'

It is important to remember, however, that at the time when Hamilton wrote this list, there was no such movement or school as Pop art. Rather, there was the small gathering of artists, critics and thinkers who were increasingly interested – from many differing points of view – sociological, technological, aesthetic, semiotic and futurological – in the workings and challenges of (particularly American) popular culture.

Marco Livingstone [art historian, curator]: 'Trying to find a definition of pop was something that they'd been discussing at the Independent Group, as a general subject of interest; but the way Hamilton was using the term pop in that letter was not defining an artistic movement or style; he was talking more about what they called the Pop art/fine art continuum, which they saw as a whole area of culture from the "popular" end to the "high culture" end. And this was really talking about the popular end of it – and more what became the subject matter and source material of Pop art rather than as a definition of Pop art.'

Hamilton's reasoning led to his identifying a breadth of artistic possibility which Nicholas de Ville, as a fellow student at Newcastle under Hamilton during the early and middle years of the 1960s, and close friend of Bryan Ferry, would see as having a direct relevance to Ferry's later concept of a modern musical group. Extended a little further, one can see how Hamilton's analysis of the relationship between pop culture and fine art would resonate through that swathe of subcultural activity in the late 1960s and early to middle 1970s that was championing a total aesthetic lifestyle of self-recreation – of actually 'living the idea', as Peter York would later put the cause.

Richard Hamilton: 'I probably sat down and wrote it ['Pop art is . . .'] in less than an hour. I did it because I wanted to inform the people I was sending it to: what is the thing that we call pop? And then what is fine art? I was able to make a list of what I thought – like "glamorous", "big business", "expendable"; and then go through it and think: in what way are these characteristics of Pop art – and I was talking about popular art [as Pop art in the art historical sense had not yet been labelled as such] – distinguishable from fine art?

'So I looked at this list, and thought, "big business?" Well, there was lots of art in the past which had been big business: Rubens – that was big business. And glamorous: Boucher was glamorous, for instance. So I was able to go through the whole of this list and say that each quality has always been a possible characteristic of certain individuals who have been thought of as fine artists, who fit the bill. But when I came to the word "expendable" I thought, no – nobody in the fine art world has ever thought of themselves as being expendable. And then I was wrong. I've learned later that my list was definitive, there were no exclusions. [Hamilton would later consider Andy Warhol to be the artist who accepted expendability as a characteristic of his art.]

'And that's what I think I found rather inspiring: you can do anything and it's fine art. There are no limits. You can justify all these characteristics if you want, but why bother? Because anything that you're going to do is going to come within the boundaries of possibility.'

Like other pioneers of mass-age culture, such as Marshall McLuhan or Roland Barthes, by the mid-1960s Hamilton had defined a critical acuity and an artistic language which not only anticipated the flamboyance of postmodernism, but had already assigned such thinking to its place in a white, chilled museum of contemporary thought and culture: the coming to terms with the supremacy and immediacy of surface; the conversion of the artist into an ambiguous brand; the identification of glamour as perhaps the most determined form of peace-time social energy; the usefulness of transgressive or absurd imagery, its potency increased by the meticulous punning on materials and contexts; the adaptation of technology to aesthetic purpose; the role of selective vision in a culture of information anxiety and visual stress; the seductions of colour and the erotics of form.

Above all, Hamilton conjured with the refined capacities of replication and montage – sustaining a creative chemistry which fused the cold sheen of freshly minted machine parts with sumptuous painterly aesthetics. And the dynamism of Hamilton's art appears to be the maintained and controlled collision between the sensual and the mass-produced – between the respective cultural force-fields of art and artifice.

For his students, one of the ultimate consequences of Hamilton's teaching and ideas was a sense of grand liberation – an authorisation to explore the broadest possible concept of what being an artist might be. Ferry, too, would be very much caught by this idea.

Nick de Ville: 'My memory is that when we were in Newcastle we were very interested in the idea of personae – that things didn't have to be an authentic reflection of your personality, and you could adopt a persona. To my way of thinking, this was a moment of self-conscious realisation: that being a rock star, or being an artist, was a pose which could be manipulated – rather than it being an authentic reflection of an inner person.

'All these ideas are very familiar today, but there was a version of these ideas around, particularly in Newcastle, where there was something about Hamilton, and a chimeric quality to his work at this period. Everything he did bore very little relation to the thing which he'd done before; his style subsequently settled down into a much more conventional sense of an oeuvre, but at that point I think a lot of people really admired the fact that he'd do a scaled-up badge [*Epiphany*, 1964], then *My Marilyn* [1964–5], and so on. The way these works panned out as a group was really extraordinary to us, because we were used to somebody having a fixed style, which they did in a very particular way from painting to painting, and the idea of someone making a huge button, then a painting, then a photograph – it just seemed to be an entirely new way of being an artist, which didn't rely on that notion of visual consistency, but seemed to depend on something else – some kind of intellectual continuity, rather than a purely visual one.

'I felt that Bryan had picked up on this really strong idea; in Roxy Music you could have personae, rather than a group of hippies doing this hippy thing that they were stuck with. So there was this idea that you could be something, then something else, then something else.'

Hamilton had already prophesied the ambient nature of the total pop environment in the 'Fun House' installation of 1956 – a work which briefed the viewer with his view of the post-1946 consumer age as a kind of unyielding bombardment of slick, gaudy, eroticised signifiers – at once seductive and disruptive. His subsequent mixed-media work would seem the product of a near future age, and described the tension between the social appetite for the compensatory pleasures of modern living (the hunger for glamour, celebrity, and the sheer aesthetic gorgeousness of a refined, product-led culture) and, vitally, the ways in which those desires were duped by the same obsessions.

Thus Hamilton would both celebrate the fetishised surface of mass-age culture, while being busily at work within its contradictions – creating an epic narrative of modern experience, the principal theme of which, perhaps, was the relation of technology to desire. Photography, and the idea of the art-directed photograph, would become intrinsic to this concern. Hamilton – fluent in the imagery of advertising, fashion and glamour photography – was above all concerned with the relationship between image and design, in both medium and message.

Richard Hamilton: 'The first Polaroid camera I ever encountered was through the head of the photography department at Newcastle; because he knew Edward Land, who was the inventor of the Polaroid camera. He sent him a wonderful pigskin case with all the cameras and accessories and lenses, and I had access to all of this three or four years before the public had heard of Polaroid.'

Hamilton's immediate, enthusiastic uptake of the latest technologies would inform both his thinking and, during his time at Newcastle, an almost performative aspect to his lectures – the then impressively futuristic event of him taking a Polaroid picture of his audience (those taken at Newcastle, Cambridge University, the Institute of Contemporary Arts, and the Royal College of Art show an almost entirely male and rather defensively self-conscious contingent). But Hamilton's use of Polaroid technology anticipated that of Warhol's fascination with the medium, and would become an important strand of his art-making, notably the 'Polaroid Portraits' series (in four volumes to date, published between 1972 and 2001), in which other artists would be invited to take a Polaroid portrait of Hamilton – an act which can become one of self-portraiture for the guest photographer. Hence, for example, Bryan Ferry's Polaroid portrait of Hamilton, taken in August 1985 is composed and lit in a sumptuous, painterly manner – like that of a Rembrandt portrait (as Ferry would later explain. Richard Hamilton, on the other hand, felt more that Ferry was photographing him in the same manner that he would himself be photographed for one of his album sleeves).

The most famous of Hamilton's lectures was written in 1959 and entitled 'Glorious Technicolor, Breathtaking Cinemascope and Stereophonic Sound'. The snappy, pop title of Hamilton's lecture is drawn from the promotional rhetoric of Hollywood feature films, and is a slogan used by Cole Porter in one of his songs for the Fred Astaire and Cyd Charisse musical of 1957, *Silk Stockings*.

As a lecture, 'Glorious Technicolor, Breathtaking Cinemascope and Stereophonic Sound' was anything but a foray through the cultural studies of Hollywood camp. Rather, it was a highly detailed account (as its subtitle stated) of 'technical developments in the entertainment industries in the Fifties' – how the technology of cinema actually worked, right down to its optical systems and aspect ratios. In this, the lecture examined in near forensic technical detail how the bewitching power of cinema was designed and developed.

Read now, the lecture can be seen as equally important – in terms of Hamilton's interests as an artist – in its accounts of the achievements, responsibilities and rivalries between the big Hollywood studios – their brand names and corporate logos (MGM, Paramount, 20th Century Fox) perhaps the ultimate signifiers of mass cultural romanticism. The lecture thus expanded upon his interest in the relationship between design, mechanics, technology, and the vast, near elemental forces of modern glamour.

Rita Donagh: 'Richard gave two lectures when I was there, and I'm not sure whether the Duchamp one was first. He did one lecture on the *Large Glass* and then "Glorious Technicolor, Breathtaking Cinemascope and Stereophonic Sound". It was the Duchamp lecture that impressed me most, and that was because the "Glorious Technicolor" was wonderful in terms of presentation – there were three screens and stereophonic sound – but it was very technical, and I couldn't follow it; I didn't know enough about cinematography or photography. It was wonderful visually, but it was very seriously about optics and cameras. But the Duchamp lecture was extraordinary in a different way. That was art history; and the thing I remember from that was how he managed to get across the mechanomorphic aspect of the painting.

'Which again, I suppose, as we were already reading Klee and Kandinsky – it fitted in: a gap that was missing in the other things we had done. Because Richard, of course, wasn't teaching any of that. This was a lecture which he just did. Sometimes he did lectures because he just wanted to do them – he was interested in lecturing as a form, doing a presentation – "the Hamilton lecture" – which was always a great experience.'

Richard Hamilton: 'Rita was a student at about that time, and it came as a surprise to me when she later told me that she and the other students used to go to my lectures. I only gave about one a year, but I used to do a sort of set piece – "Glorious Technicolor, Breathtaking Cinemascope and Stereophonic Sound"; and she said "I don't think any of us knew a word of what you were saying – we didn't understand it at all. But when we went away, we realised that maybe it would make sense. And after a lapse of time it began to make sense. But it was only in retrospect." You couldn't make a programme of it and say, "This is what you've got to learn." You just did it, and it gave them this strange, almost theatrical experience. It even happened that towards the end of my stay there [at Newcastle University], and afterwards, students would perform lectures – as though to say, "This is rather interesting, I'll do one of these." I didn't see much of it, but I'm told that it occurred . . .'

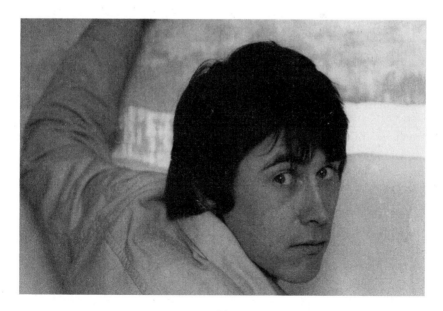

nine

Mark Lancaster – 'the coolest of the cool'. His first trips to London; arrival at Newcastle
University in 1961; the Majestic; rock and pop heroes; acceptance by the art department
'in crowd'; 'Maxwell House'; travels with Philip Trevelyan; photographing the Town Moor
fair, summer 1962.

The pale colours of the photograph show a sunny day in June 1962. The
scene is the paved quadrangle outside the Percy Building at the
University of Newcastle. In the furthest corner, half in shadow, a deeply
recessed door is crested with an imposing coat of arms; to their right, the
bare expanse of the exterior wall is topped with a line of oblong windows, beneath which a further three coats of arms are set in concrete
relief. The plain, somewhat stern building is an example of twentieth-
century institutional British architecture at its most respectable – not so
much grand as oversized.

Crossing from brilliant sunshine to shade, two men in flannels and
sports jackets are passing one another in the midday hurry, one with his
briefcase under his arm. A woman wearing a cap-sleeved blouse and blue
tartan skirt is walking the other way towards a shallow flight of concrete
steps. To the right is the concrete kerb of a flowerbed, within which are
crowded, around a staked spiral of silvery, ornamental ivy, a blaze of
brightly coloured summer blooms.

Brisk and orderly, the quotidian scene thus amplifies the visual equivalent of a sudden, undampened major chord. For facing us square on
across the flowerbeds, unattended, from its position leaning against the
Percy Building, is a portrait format, hoarding-sized picture of a jar of

Maxwell House instant coffee. The red of the label lets out its cheerful shout in a bright yellow flash of declamatory jitterbugging capitals: 'COFFEE-POT FRESH'.

This being 1962, in the sober precincts of a British provincial university, during the examinations season of a summer term, the panel (a work of Pop art) appears so incongruous, and so culturally adrift, as to be freed of any projected meanings. It is solely itself, visually exuberant, inscrutable – as blank or as meaningful as you like. And in the middle ground of the photograph, standing black-jacketed, his expression too distant to read, but set, serious, is the work's creator, Mark Lancaster, then a second-year student. The photograph itself was taken, that fine summer's day, by Lancaster's friend and tutor, Richard Hamilton.

Mark Lancaster takes his place within this story, by the accounts of his contemporaries, as a legendary figure who embodied the apparently effortless, all important 'cool' that was in many ways a shared ambition of his friends and acquaintances. Only Richard Hamilton and Rita Donagh would be regarded as his equal in this most elusive

and potent of personal qualities. As such, Lancaster might be read as part James Dean, part Tom Courtenay, part Jay Gatsby, part Oscar Wilde – a compelling character, a youthful pioneer, and above all arbiter elegantiae of his circle. Within the aesthetic education of Bryan Ferry, and occurring at a time during which, as Nick de Ville recounts, the notion of playing with 'personae' was very much in the air, Lancaster assumes an additional importance – a role model within a cast of role models: a masterclass in the correct use of style.

Bryan Ferry: 'Mark Lancaster was the coolest of the cool, after Richard. He was slightly older than the rest of us, and having his final show not long after I arrived at the University – really beautiful pictures . . .'

Tim Head: 'Mark Lancaster was the pivotal figure. There was this thing about "cool" going around then, and Mark epitomised the coolest of the cool. Whatever Mark said and did he was super cool – and nobody could quite match that. You've probably heard about Marcus Price's shop in Newcastle – he had all the latest American shirts, and all the cool styles. Well, Richard [Hamilton] and Mark would go down and get first choice of these shirts – and then the rest of us would get what was left. Then, at the weekend, Richard would have his cool American shirt with amazing western patterns on it.'

Viv Kemp (artist, close friend of Andy Mackay, subsequently married to Tim Head): 'Mark Lancaster was the King of Cool. He'd been up in Newcastle, and everybody was in love with him – like Rita, and Richard and . . . everybody. He just had this charisma; he was just so cool and so ahead of his time. Later he bought a flat in Belsize Park Gardens. I remember being in his place, and I used to smoke Kent cigarettes – and Mark just looked at me and said, "You must be the only person left on this earth who smokes Kent." And I just withered – I completely withered! So much for being an individual – I just knew I could never smoke Kent again.

'Mark later worked for Warhol. He'd been a student at Newcastle, and then he became a student assistant – which was like the coolest appointment. I'm absolutely sure that Mark would have been a big influence on Bryan . . .'

Marcus Price: 'I seem to remember Mark Lancaster coming back from the States in '64, and he had a seersucker jacket – blue or yellow and white stripes – and that was cool! Mark's personal style, and what he was interested in – were all cool. I think he pushed the boundaries before other people; he was terribly influenced by Richard, obviously, but also by America – as everybody was in those days.'

A second photograph, taken in 1964, shows Lancaster standing outside Marcus Price's shop on Percy Street. Dressed in a single-breasted black leather jacket (the first leather jacket, in fact, to be worn in the Fine Art department), shirt and tie, he is leaning against the lustrous black glass panels of the famous sign which ran down the left hand side of the shop, depicting at its top the jazz age boulevardier in top hat, tails and red satin-lined cape. Lancaster's expression is unsmiling, a little stern almost, yet somehow utterly assured.

During the early and middle years of the 1960s, Lancaster would live with fellow art student Stephen Buckley (who studied at Newcastle, including an extra scholarship year, between 1962 and 1967) in Eslington Terrace, near Jesmond Dene park in Newcastle. On Lancaster's departure to London in 1966, Bryan Ferry would then share the flat with Buckley. Their neighbours would include fellow students Nicholas de Ville and Tim Head.

Slightly older than most of the students in his academic year, Lancaster was a provincial child of the immediately post-Second World War period. As such he joined that generation of art students who had grown up during the quietude and ruination of the 'Austerity Years', and whose tertiary education coincided with the accelerating new culture of the youth-fixated, mass media, mass age. This was a generation for whom America – and New York in particular – would be the promised land of modernity. (One might imagine the contrast, for example, to the eyes of a restless eighteen-year-old from the north of England, between the bright, breezy New York of *Pillow Talk* or *Breakfast at Tiffany's*, and the soot-blackened brick, melancholy war memorials and terrace ends of their own home towns.) Lancaster himself would be a pioneer in this regard, first visiting Manhattan in the summer of 1964, and subsequently returning there to work with both Andy Warhol and Jasper Johns. He would also pursue his own career as a successful artist, and eventually settle in America just under a decade later, in the early 1970s.

Marco Livingstone: 'Mark Lancaster, whom Hamilton clearly regarded as his star pupil, and who got a First at Newcastle, was a kind of systemic painter in the 1960s, using grid formats – a much more cerebral painter than Stephen Buckley was at that time, who was playing with the materials and using a very rough and ready aesthetic – deliberately crude. Lancaster's work was more elegant and considered, and compared to Buckley's rather lacking in emotion because of that. Lancaster went to the States very early on, and with an introduction from Hamilton went to Warhol's studio – sweeping floors, stretching canvases and so on. So it was quite exciting for his student contemporaries to think that someone had actually met Warhol and worked for him.'

In his own work as an artist (of which, more later), his sense of personal style, relationship to music and fashion, acuity as a photographer, but above all, his awareness of the holistic relationship in which all of these qualities might reside, Lancaster can be seen as a supremely 'pop' figure. He takes his place as an artist-settler of the modern world, for whom the Yellow Taxicabs of mid-town Manhattan, no less than the McGraw-Hill building on West 42nd Street, no less than the lunchtime dances at the Majestic Ballroom, no less than the folk art of the fairground stalls at Newcastle's Town Moor fair, no less than Motown, *Breakfast at Tiffany's* and the photography of Alfred Stieglitz (the subject of his student dissertation) would cohere into both his subject matter (although his own art would change significantly between the early and late 1960s) and the sophisticated patterning of his lifestyle.

Lancaster's career as an undergraduate at Newcastle runs parallel to his personal development as an equerry of modern glamour. Around him and finding him, one can see the exhilarating cyclone of the pop experience, and of the honing of a social sense. Dancing to Bobby Vee, the Marvelettes, the Shirelles or the Crystals, becoming aware of the aesthetic potential of commercial imagery and the finer points of American styling, in his early years at Newcastle Lancaster became friends with both Hamilton and Hamilton's first wife, Terry, as well as with Rita Donagh.

As for Hamilton and Donagh, the lunchtime hops at the Majestic

Ballroom were vividly recalled, central features of Lancaster's life in Newcastle at the turn of the 1960s.

Mark Lancaster: 'One day last week we were having clam chowder in a waterside cafe called George's, unchanged since the seventies I would think, in a little place near here called Galilee, where the fishing boats still go out, and the ferry goes to Block Island.

'I noticed that the music playing was first of all, "Walk Right Back" by the Everlys, followed by "Twisting the Night Away" by Sam Cooke, then "Can't Get Used to Losing You" by Andy Williams. And I thought, it's exactly like the Majestic. That sequence of three songs doesn't quite make sense chronologically, although at the Majestic they played favourites like Dion and Bobby Vee, and, I'm sure "Walk Right Back" for over a year or more after they came out. Also lots of Brenda Lee, Adam Faith and Billy Fury. The Andy Williams hit was in '63, by which time they would have been playing the Beatles' first records too. I'd forgotten how good "Can't Get Used to Losing You" is, and of course it's by Pomus and Schuman, one of the great songwriting teams, up there with Lieber and Stoller.

'I was once refused entry to the Majestic for wearing Levi's, and had a big fight with the manager about it. But it was great, especially in the immediately pre-Beatles era, the twist era and after. There was nothing better to dance to than "The Wanderer" and "Take Good Care of My Baby" – and they would play them almost every time. They had three lunchtime sessions a week, for a shilling I think, and by far the majority there were not students, but boys and girls from the offices and shops ...'

These were the same office boys and working girls (Wolfe's 'Noonday Underground') whom Hamilton has noted as revealing more about the physics of popular culture than the discussions of the Independent Group at the Institute of Contemporary Arts. Popular culture and pop music, for Lancaster and his generation of astute and receptive student contemporaries, might almost be seen to have existed simultaneously in three different forms: vernacular, intellectual and elemental. The first was as sheer exuberance and nervous excitement – a sensory, social experience; the second, as channelled through the ideas of Richard Hamilton, re-routed these stimuli to an intellectual form of art. The final, 'elemental' quality is more fanciful in concept but no less apparent in fact: that of pop as a kind of living, socio-cultural energy, comparable perhaps to both a force of nature and a machine-generated essence of pure glamour, itself defined as 'enchantment'.

As for Ferry, the discrepancy between Lancaster's family background (from deeply respectable, hard-working, Yorkshire 'middle-middle to lower-middle classes' – in his own words) and the life opened up by studying art at university, was considerable. Indeed, this very discrepancy – a shared experience for many art students of the time – served to amplify massively the sense of personal freedom and intellectual curiosity which was suddenly allowed. Thus, for these young men and women, the emotional acoustics of their lives had been radically heightened. Lancaster's early adulthood also reveals the allure of London, a four-hour train ride and a world away from the big northern cities of the time. In a sense, the template of Lancaster's mature interests – art, society, the city – would be summarised in these early excursions to the capital.

Mark Lancaster: 'I left school (Bootham, a York Quaker school) in 1955, having "decided" to go into the family textile business (as every male for four generations had). I was unenthusiastic, but had no strong sense of what else to do, and no encouragement to do anything else. My brother was doing National Service and so I took his place, as it were, at the mill and took textile technology courses at Huddersfield Technical College. These also kept me from conscription into the army.

'I would say now that I became depressed over the following four years, and planned – in a kind of fantasy – an escape. I dreamed of running away to London and working at Foyle's, or Better Books, or even Harrods – things like that. But what I did in fact was go to London for as many weekends as I could and see things. My best friend from school, Richard Morphet, was already there. [Morphet was a writer, art historian, curator, subsequently Keeper of Modern Collection, Tate Gallery, until 1998.]

'In 1959, when I was twenty-one, my grandmother, whom I loved, died. She had been a good pianist – playing Schumann and Chopin even in her eighties. When I was a kid, about ten years old, I fell in love with that wonderful song from *Pal Joey* – "Bewitched, Bothered and Bewildered". We didn't have a gramophone, and so I bought the sheet music and asked to play it – which she did on her Bechstein grand in the style of Chopin. I started painting that same year, 1959, out of doors on the moors, and self-portraits and so on . . . I also started taking evening classes at Huddersfield School of Art – which was in the same place as the textile department.

'In Sheffield I saw an exhibition called "The Developing Process", which was an Arts Council touring show about the Basic Course which had been introduced by Victor Pasmore and Richard Hamilton at Newcastle University, and by Harry Thubron and others at Leeds. After I failed to get an interview at the Slade, which disappointed but did not surprise me, I immediately applied to Newcastle. I couldn't stomach the idea of studying in Leeds – it was too close to home, and I was desperate to leave home.

'I remember going on the train for the interview, reading *Mr Norris Changes Trains*, and one of the questions they asked was, "What was I reading on the train?" That was my best answer I guess . . . I was petrified, almost paralysed. Victor Pasmore and Richard Hamilton were there, and Kenneth Rowntree the professor, and a few others. Richard asked me about one of my paintings based on the mill interior, which had a certain mechanical quality. Victor Pasmore asked me which painters I liked and I could only think of Cézanne. So when I was accepted I was ecstatic of course.

'I took the advice of somebody there and decided to live in a hall of residence. Newcastle was an exciting place to me, visually first – arriving by train over the high-level bridge and seeing the Tyne Bridge and the low-level bridge and all the activity.

'I became pretty conscious of my being five years older than almost all the others, and also that I was in a state of enormous excitement. I spent a lot of time exploring the city and taking photographs. The hall of residence was deadly dull and pretentious – formal dinners with table service – and I made a small number of friends in other fields. After staying up talking most of the night a couple of times, I actually had sex with a guy down the hall – a languages student who came from a background not unlike mine.

'There was a film society which met one night a week and showed French classics and Bergman, Antonioni, and so on; I realised after the first show that all the "cool" people from the art department were there, including Richard, and I think that is where I first met Rita Donagh. At some point towards the end of that first term I was starting to help Richard with some of the graphic design he was doing for the Hatton Gallery catalogues, and he taught me how to use Letraset. He invited me to the Christmas end-of-term party in his studio there, and that was the night I felt I had "arrived". That was the first time I talked to Rita, I think.

'In Newcastle in 1961, as well as the new Twist, there was a terrific following for Piaf's "Milord", which was still quite new then. The Fine Art department had a small group of Francophiles led by Eric Dobson, who chewed garlic and read Huysmans's *A rebours* – a fabulous book. David Sweetman [later a distinguished critic, poet, dramatist, restaurateur and film-maker] was also one of the trendsetters in the Fine Art department. He brought the first Dylan album in before anybody else knew of him, and earlier had been the first to find out about the Beatles, and had their first single before anybody else.'

The impact from 1962 onwards of the Beatles (for whom Hamilton, of course, would seven years later design perhaps their most strikingly modern record sleeve and packaging – the so-called *White Album*) would mark in one sense the end of the 'beat boom' era in British pop music – and with it the faint embarrassment and lack of interest (shared, generationally, by Ferry, Mackay and Eno) with which much UK pop music was regarded in comparison with its US counterparts.

Rita Donagh: 'At Newcastle there was an art history lecture once a week, maybe more, but always at five o'clock. The lecture theatre was a rectangular room with banks of seats, and you entered a door on the side where the lecturer was speaking. So you came in at a lower level, walked across the stage and went up the front. If you were late you were very conspicuous – the lecturer had to stop and so on. We were gathered there – it must have been in the first year – and in came David Sweetman. He had great charisma too – that theatrical quality which some people have. And he opened the door and he had this record in his hands. And he held it aloft and said, "I've just bought this incredible record! You've all got to listen to it." And this was 1962, and the record was "Love Me Do". It was the first time that any of us had heard of the Beatles . . .'

Lancaster's keen interest in Hamilton's ideas can be seen in both his 'Maxwell House' piece – made during the summer term of his second year – and in his friendship with the artist and his first wife. As students from the time point out, Hamilton was not so much 'teaching' his ideas on Pop art, as allowing them to be represented through his presence within the department. As such, Pop art itself had a quality at this time that was not so much 'underground' as restricted to a few exclusive initiates within a pioneering cult of modern studies. The whole pop ethos – the opening up of what it might mean to be an artist in the modern world – was thus a very heady pursuit.

Marco Livingstone: 'Certainly in terms of looking for encouragement and inspiration, the whole Pop art generation in the UK – the slightly younger ones, who were at the Royal College from '59 onwards: Peter Phillips, Allen Jones et al. – wanted to escape from what they felt was the dreariness, the drabness of life in England during the 1950s, in which they'd been brought up. And also to escape from the art that they'd been confronted with, which they thought was polite and rather tame – the St Ives painters, the 'Kitchen Sink' painters. But they started making their work without an awareness that there were Americans doing similar things. Once they became aware of Warhol, Lichtenstein, Oldenburg and so forth, that was a great encouragement to them. It sounds so unbelievable now, but in Britain the first colour Sunday supplement magazine didn't come out until 1963, and so those sorts of images just weren't available here.'

Hamilton's pop thinking – as further described by such key texts as his 'For the Finest Art try – POP' (1961) and 'An exposition of $he' (1962) – was coming from a position of pronounced technological enquiry and diagnostic sociological vision. Rather than making an art about quotidian pop subjects which was primarily or solely concerned with youthful exuberance, Hamilton's ideas were underpinned by a richly creative, intellectual refinement – a literary quality, perhaps, which steered a course between glamour, romanticism, aesthetics, irony, technology, critique and cultural studies. Hence the tutor's delight in Lancaster's simultaneously declamatory and inscrutable 'Maxwell House' construction.

Mark Lancaster: 'One of the last projects in the foundation year of 1961–2 was about imagery. We were asked to explore any kind of imagery and make something of it. Somebody in the class found a place where they distributed large posters in sections for billboards, and I went with this girl and we brought back a ton of stuff, in pieces I guess about two by six feet each. Everybody went crazy cutting and collaging them, but I found a big panel which on one or two pieces had a five-foot-high Maxwell House jar, which I pasted on to an old painting I covered with white paint. (This was May 1962 and as far as I know I was unaware of Warhol.) I had previously taken the Coca-Cola can (then a new thing) as a still-life object, and made paintings under Richard's influence from Coke ads, but this Maxwell House piece was the most "radical"; and one sunny day, Richard, who loved it, said let's take it around the campus and photograph it in various settings.'

Coincidentally, it would be as a consequence of this project on 'imagery' on the Basic Course that Hamilton would later find, amidst the discarded materials on the studio floor at the Fine Art department, the publicity still from Douglas Sirk's 1949 film noir thriller *Shockproof*, starring Patricia Knight, on which he would base three collaged studies and two paintings – including the famous *Interior II* of 1964. The 'assembling' process of these works, and the placing of the image of Patricia Knight in modern-looking interiors, thus creating the extraordinary impression of a *mise en scène* that appears both realistic and artificial, figurative and deconstructed, glossily modern and rooted in the Hollywood film styles of the 1940s, would echo in a commercial form through the meticulous mixed media construction of the cover image for Roxy Music's second album, *For Your Pleasure*, released in 1973.

Between 1961 and 1963, Lancaster's work within the Fine Art department showed extraordinary sophistication and promise. Working with such 'pop' subjects as Philip Morris cigarette advertisements, the Everly Brothers singing duo, the actor Paul Newman and the television character *Dr Kildare*, Lancaster made pieces across a range of media – the Philip Morris painting was made on an old veneer tabletop, for example, while his paintings of the Everly Brothers were 'sleeved' in plastic sheeting like long-playing records.

A further source of interest and inspiration lay in the 'folk art' of the signage to be found at the famous Town Moor fair which came to Newcastle in the summer. As photographed by Lancaster in the summer

of 1962, the booths and rides of the fair, the confectionery and tea stands, present their own vivid world of appealingly skewed imagistic hyperbole: Superman and a vast 'OK' in powder pink on a sherbety orange background (which Lancaster would later make a painting based upon); panels inscribed with barely literate enticements ('Don't be a squar- enjoy yourself') outside the hall of mirrors; the vast trucks with 'Northern

Amusements' emblazoned along their sides; two bright-eyed schoolboys leaning suggestively towards glistening candy bars; a painting of a wasp-waisted showgirl – 'Alive Alive' – propped up to advertise 'Beauty and the Beast'.

It is a world contemporary to the miner's festivities in the BFI short film *Gala Day*, filled with that somewhat seaside cheerfulness which is never too distant from melancholy but equally intimate with a slick variant of glamour – the grease in the hair of a speedway operator, and so forth. Lancaster's photographs of the fair are in some ways a rehearsal, in their emotional resonance, for his later photographs of New York (made two years later, in the summer of 1964). Both series of images identify romance and melancholy within well-worn thoroughfares of public space; the monolithic grandeur of Manhattan appears no less begrimed, exhausted but intensely vibrant, than the coarse adornments of the fun-fair; each is a common place landscape shot through with exotica: textbook examples of the pop form in its raw state, simultaneously intimate and distant, deafening and mute.

Socially, Lancaster was also expanding his horizons. Like Ferry, he would be drawn towards the company of people whom he regarded as fundamentally smart; unlike Ferry, he was less possessed of profound shyness. In his first year, Lancaster made friends with Philip Trevelyan, with whom he would go on excursions to both junkyards and the homes of literary and artistic aristocracy. Theirs might almost be seen as a version of the undergraduate friendship between Charles Ryder and Sebastian Flyte, in Evelyn Waugh's novel *Brideshead Revisited*, but up-dated to the pop era of the early 1960s.

Mark Lancaster: 'Philip arrived at the same time as I did in 1961 and we rode around on his motorbike and sidecar to cafes for lunch and to scrapheaps of which he particularly was fond. He later became a movie-maker. His father was Julian Trevelyan [artist and printmaker, introduced to surrealism at Trinity College, Cambridge by a fellow student, the future documentary film-maker Humphrey Jennings]; and his mother, whom I visited with him at Newhaven, was Ursula Mommens, the potter.

'Philip and I visited Leonard Woolf's house at Rodmell, that same weekend, in 1962. Leonard had said on the phone that he was going up to London but the house would be left open. He also told her that he had just had a letter from an American who had written a play and wanted to know if it was all right to call it "Who's Afraid of Virginia Woolf?" I told Edward Albee this story twenty years or so later. We went to Monks House and wandered all over, looking at the pictures and painted furniture by Duncan Grant and Vanessa Bell.

'At Newcastle we also visited Philip's great aunt, Lady Trevelyan, widow of Charles Trevelyan, Liberal MP, I think, at the incredible Wallington Hall in Northumbria, where she still lived, with its wonderful gardens and William Bell Scott murals . . .

'But also at this time there other things going on, outside the university: films that meant a lot included *Psycho*, *Saturday Night and Sunday Morning*, *A Taste of Honey* and *Billy Liar* and *We are the Lambeth Boys* [a documentary about the Alford House youth club in Kennington, South London] – also movies by Truffaut, Antonioni, Resnais and Godard. And in the late 1950s and early 1960s there was the play *Five Finger Exercise*, involving homosexuality and a boy's relationship with his family. I took my parents to see it in Leeds (I had already seen it in London) and told them that it was about a family like us. Afterwards my mother said, "It's not a bit like us – your father doesn't even play golf."

Lancaster's early years at the Fine Art department were clearly enjoyable and filled with influences and inspiration. More remarkable, however, was the locally originated network of connections being made between the new iconoclasts of the art world; as participated within by Lancaster, and as revealed in the assurance of his student work, an axis between New York and Newcastle was being established by Richard Hamilton – the principal coordinates upon which would include Warhol and Duchamp.

As established within that era at Newcastle University when Hamilton was teaching, Lancaster's career as an art student thus began to gather momentum on a larger stage: for a provincial student of that time, he would be the beneficiary of an astonishing breadth of experience – rather as though he were the student hero of a nineteenth-century *Bildungsroman*, but finding his way through the charismatic society of modern artists, as opposed to the drawing rooms of Parisian high society. (The drawing rooms of Parisian high society would come later, in fact.) Lancaster's valued presence within this world is perhaps summarised by his appearance in a collage (made in 1966) by the brilliant and enigmatic American Pop artist Ray Johnson (who, in 1985, would take his own life, seemingly as a final art work) wearing a T-shirt with his name printed across it.

Mark Lancaster: 'Richard Hamilton in fact commuted to Newcastle every week from London, where he lived with his family. In summer of 1962 his wife, Terry, told me she had seen David Hockney at a party, and he had on a T-shirt with DAVID printed on it. She asked him about it and he told her he had made it at the Royal College of Art, where he was a student, using old wooden letter blocks. She asked him if he would make one for her friend Mark, and he said he would, if she supplied him with a T-shirt with the position of Mark's nipples marked on it, so that he could print the name between them. I sent a new white T-shirt to Terry, via Richard, and eventually it got back to me ...'

Tragically, Terry Hamilton was killed in a car accident in the autumn of 1962. A photograph of her by Lancaster shows a pale, dark-haired young woman, seated in a low-slung modernist chair, and dressed in black T-shirt, a dark, high-collared tweed jacket, black ski-pants and black, laced, suede shoes. Wearing thick-framed dark glasses of the sort more associated with Italian film stars of the period, she is holding up an LP as though it is a manifesto. As a portrait it doubles as a study of total 'cool'.

Mark Lancaster: 'The photo of Terry sitting in the Fine Art Department – I love it so much, partly because we had just been talking about the Bach Unaccompanied Cello Suites, and that is the album she is holding up. Mostly we talked about Roy Orbison, the Marvelettes and the Shirelles ...'

ten

Newcastle–New York 1963–1964. An encounter with the young David Hockney at the Royal College of Art; Hamilton's *Self Portrait* for *Living Arts 2*, 1963; Hamilton's trip to Pasadena, California, for the first Duchamp retrospective; Lancaster's first trip to New York City in the summer of 1964; meeting Andy Warhol and Henry Geldzahler; introduction and work at the Silver Factory; starring in *Kiss*; work on student dissertation on Alfred Stieglitz; a coda – Florine Stettheimer's *Cathedrals of Broadway* (1929).

During the early years of the 1960s, Richard Hamilton had yet to be fully accepted by the power-brokers of the art world. While frustrating, doubtless, there was also the sense in which such outsiderdom might ultimately serve to strengthen the singularity and verve with which Hamilton's identity as an artist would eventually be acclaimed. Entering the world of fine art by way of design, technology and popular culture, Hamilton appears as intensely and uniquely modern – directly connected to the new world of electronics, sign systems and mass media, rather than being immured within a more salonistic, aloof appraisal of modern themes.

Marco Livingstone: 'I think one of the reasons that it took a while for Hamilton to be properly recognised as an artist, was that his work was very complex from the beginning, and there were many things going on in each work – which took a little time to unravel, and for people to understand, which I suppose some people also resisted because they thought it was a little too clever and a little too intellectual. During the years that he was teaching, he hardly showed his work at all; so when pop

97

happened, he wasn't visible in the art world. He was known to his students, and to a few other artists, but his first solo show for many years wasn't until 1964. So he missed that whole period when everything was happening for everybody else. Kitaj had shown in 1963, Hockney had shown, Peter Blake had had various shows. So even people younger than him had been presenting their work as Pop artists before Hamilton did.'

But even by the early 1960s, Hamilton's presence as a pop ideologue, whose approbation as a taste-maker was no less influential than his visual and written statements on pop, would be having a profound effect with the Royal College – even though he was unattached to the painting school, and as a consequence unacknowledged there as an artist. But to the younger generation, Hamilton was a guru. This would lead to his identification of the young David Hockney as a new artist of tremendous promise – who in his turn, by the end of the 1960s, would have become a central figure in the Ladbroke Grove, Notting Hill milieu of artists, designers and creative industry workers (including fashion designer Antony Price) with whom the young Bryan Ferry would socialise at the end of the decade.

Rita Donagh: 'The Royal College seemed to come at everything from a different angle. The Pop art at the Royal College [Hockney, Kitaj, Phillips, Boshier, Boty, Jones] was not the kind of work Richard did – it was much more influenced by American pop.'

Richard Hamilton: 'If somebody was doing an exhibition of Pop art – as it was called – they would invite me. But for no other reason than that they could see some association there with what I was doing, but I was really a little outside it because I was older than the others.

'My first encounter with David Hockney was when I was invited to the Royal College to do a crit. I was working at the Royal College, but in Hugh Casson's department [Interior Design]- he had asked me to go and teach one day a week, so I was able to mix my commuting to Newcastle with a day in the Royal College. And I was there for a few years. Then I had an invitation one day from the Painting School – "Would you come and give us a crit?" – where you put up all the pictures, and somebody comes around and talks about them.

'The interesting thing was, it was the students who invited me – not the teaching staff. In fact, they were rather irritated I think by the request. Roger DeGrey I knew quite well because he taught at Newcastle when I was first there. But same as in Newcastle, I didn't have anything to do with painting at the Royal College – I wasn't seen to be a good influence on painters. So I went in – it was the first time I'd ever done anything like this – and I found it very difficult. I'd talked about students' work in Newcastle, of course, but there I knew them. But here you walk in and you're a complete stranger – not only to the people, but to the work. You have to concentrate very hard to see what's going on, and it all has to be done in the space of minutes – maybe ten minutes to take a look around and then start talking about them.

'I had to give a prize at the end – twenty-five shillings or something. And so I happened to choose a picture of David Hockney's. He always says that was the first moment of recognition that he had; and when I came out with Roger DeGrey – we sort of trooped out in procession from the room – Roger said to me, "I'm sorry you picked David Hockney, because he's a very difficult student. He hasn't done any written work, he hasn't produced a thesis, and he's not complying with the examination procedure. We don't know what we're going to do . . ."

'It turned out that David got the Gold Medal in 1963; and he says that my intervention and twenty-five shillings had changed the whole thing! He got the Gold Medal – the best student of the year! And he collected this on the podium wearing a gold lamé jacket. It was in the press; there was a colour photograph of him in one of the colour supplements getting his diploma.'

In his autobiographical volume *My Early Years* (1976), Hockney confirms that Hamilton's influence and support were responsible for radically altering the department's view of his work: '. . . from that moment on the staff of the College never said a word about my work being awful'; and adds, 'Richard was quite a boost for students; we felt, oh, it is right what I'm doing; it is an interesting thing and I should do it. Then the press began their interest . . .'

It was fitting, therefore, to Hamilton's particular ideas about pop, that his eventual 'arrival' as an artist of major importance would come in part by way of a work which took the form of a magazine cover, entitled *Self-Portrait* and published by *Living Arts 2* in 1963, accompanied by

Hamilton's pop/beat/ad-man text *Urbane Image*. As an image (conceived and assembled by Hamilton, and photographed by Robert Freeman — who would also work on the photography and design of three albums by The Beatles), *Self-Portrait* can be read as a crucial — to say nothing of prophetic — statement regarding not just the construction and positioning of modern visual culture, but the role of the artist. In this single work, Hamilton conflates the notion of artist, art director, stylist, technician, producer/director and auteur. *Self-Portrait* therefore takes its place on the Pop-art/fine-art continuum as relating to fashion shoots or advertisements or film stills, as well as to a 'fine' artistic work.

This is what you get: on a bubblegum pink background paper, a cream, open-topped '63 Ford Thunderbird with scarlet upholstery is parked between a Mercury space capsule and an open white refrigerator, filled with groceries. Positioned between the back of the car and the shadow of the open refrigerator are a typewriter, a toaster, a vacuum cleaner, a portable 'Wondergram' record player, a Gene Vincent album and a white telephone. (Hamilton would later tell me that of the early rock and roll singers, 'Gene Vincent was my favourite – "Be-Bop-A-Lula" ') Sitting on the car's bonnet, poised as if to throw deep-field, is a man dressed in full American football kit; lying across the car's boot, clad only in black underwear, is a young female model.

But of equal importance to the image itself is its meticulous list of photo credits – unheard of, heretical, even, within a fine arts context. The list begins 'Producer – Richard Hamilton', and continues (as though in a flash forward to the extravagant accreditations in fashion magazines) to include the names of the photographer, the stylist, the female model, the suppliers of the American car, ditto the Mercury capsule (Shepperton Film Studio), the display foods, the refrigerator, the lingerie, the background paper, the football uniform, and so on – right down to the site managers (Taylor Woodrow Construction Ltd).

The combination of the image and the list of photo credits, as conceived and produced by an artist such as Hamilton, acquires a double impact. On the one hand, the *Self-Portrait* image itself is a honed depiction of modern, American (and therefore doubly modern) consumerist desires – sex, cars and rockets against a rock and roll background of domestic technologies. On the other, the accompanying list of credits bestows both a sense of elevated aesthetic status – an investiture of exclusivity and importance – on all the individual components of the finished image, and a sense of commerciality and commodified glamour, rather than fine art.

Thus the space capsule and the lingerie model, the Ford Thunderbird and the set of display foods, are simultaneously granted parity with one another as deserving of precise and conscientious accreditation – a gesture at once somewhat camp and winningly self assured. The industrial– commercial ring to such notation resembles that of film credits; at the same time, it is as though one is being shown the infrastructure of a total art work. Thus, the fine-art/Pop-art continuum is effectively blurred, cultural status is rendered ambiguous, the lecture in American socio-futurology is delivered, but from a potentially ironic position of one remove. Add to this the context of the published image (an art magazine) and the whole thing takes on a glorious, declamatory insouciance, maintaining a balance between candour and ambiguity, entertainment and manifesto.

Such a bravura manipulation of image, irony and intentionality, similarly supercharged on the high-octane erotics of pure pop glamour, will be revisited by Bryan Ferry's 'cover concept' for the cover image and accompanying photo and styling credits of *Roxy Music*, in 1972 – and indeed across the whole series of Roxy Music's hyper-eroticised yet meticulously poised cover art.

Hamilton's pioneering deconstruction and reassembling of modern American pop imagery is described by the artist in his accompanying *Urbane Image* text:

In real close; what's in the finder? With a long-focus lens opened up to f2, depth of field is reduced to a few millimetres when you're not too far from the subject. Definition swings in and out along a lip length. A world of fantasy with unique erotic overtones. Intimacy, trespass yet, on a purely visual plane. Sensuality beyond the simple act of penetration – a dizzy drop into swoonlike coloured fuzz, clicked, detached and still, for appreciative analysis. Scale drifts that echo Van Vogt's pendulum swing of time; fulcrums of visual fixity that Penn engages with the twist of a knurled knob.

Hamilton also includes – in a further gesture of commentary – a 'Glossary' to assist with the reading of his text. For the quoted paragraph, the entries include, with suave eclecticism, 'f2', 'Depth of field', 'Van Vogt' ('A master of the science fiction genre') and 'Penn (Irving)'. There is then a visual glossary, depicting names and terms from 'Harley Earl' to 'Bug-eyed-monster' to 'Playmate' to 'Michelangelo's God'. Despite their evident humour and knowingness, neither *Urbane Image* nor *Self-Portrait* nor their glossaries are exercises in mere ironical pageantry. Rather, they comprise the totality of a pop image, its rhetoric, semiotics and temper, as well as – primarily – providing an audit by title of Hamilton's own recent paintings up to this point. In short, it's a total production.

Richard Hamilton: 'Ted Powers – he was the only big collector in England at the time and a marvellous man; he bought Lichtenstein, and Oldenburg – he said to me, after I'd done this magazine piece, "I'd like to buy something of yours." And I said, "Why, after all these years, are you interested in my stuff?" And he said, "Well, I saw that article you wrote for *Living Arts* and I thought it was very interesting." "What about it made you change your mind?" And he said, "Before I read that, I didn't know you were serious."

'It was as though I was playing with this idea – that pop was a sort of game. *Urbane Image* is the only piece of writing that I've ever done that satisfied me. I managed to achieve in that text something that was the equivalent of the paintings. I've never been able to reach that standard again.'

Hamilton, therefore, as a commentator on the workings of mass media, image and advertisement, would find himself recognised as an artist by way of his mediation of image and identity – an elegantly effective calling into service of pop's own systems.

As *Self-Portrait* and *Urbane Image* were being published in *Living Arts 2*, the first major retrospective of the work of Marcel Duchamp was being shown at the Pasadena Museum in California. Arguably Hamilton's greatest influence, and an artist whose iconic presence would be an inspiration to succeeding generations of progressive thinking art students, Duchamp was none the less a surprisingly obscure figure in the early 1960s. Hamilton would be one of his greatest interpreters and artistic colleagues, having made his 'typographic translation' of Duchamp's notes (known as the *Green Box*) for his *Large Glass* in 1960, and then making his reconstruction of the actual work – *The Bride Stripped Bare By Her Bachelors, Even* – at Newcastle between 1965 and 1966, the processes of which would be photographed by Mark Lancaster.

Hamilton travelled to Pasadena to see the Duchamp exhibition in October 1963 (his first trip to America), and he and Duchamp were subsequently photographed together at the Museum of Modern Art, New York. Through Duchamp, Hamilton would become friends with some of the leading artists in America at the time, including Warhol, Oldenburg and Jim Dine. According to Hamilton, his growing acquaintance with Duchamp led to his being treated as 'an insider' by the American artists, and thus he 'knew enough people to provide an entrée to that world for Mark'. In addition to which, Lancaster was of course welcomed and accepted on his own merits.

Hamilton would later describe his first trip to America as being that of both 'a missionary and an explorer'. And, to some extent, the same could be said of Mark Lancaster's experience the following year. Certainly, Lancaster departed for the US with an explorer's zeal; similarly, on his return to Newcastle he would be searching for ways in which to translate his experiences into the language of his art, including, his 'New York lecture' (more resembling an audio-visual installation, in today's terms) which he gave in the autumn of 1964, and which would be a significant event in Bryan Ferry's first term in the Fine Art department.

There is a coincidental neatness in the fact that Hamilton's first major work on returning from America was titled *Epiphany* – an oversized copy of a cheap badge (or button) which he had bought in Los Angeles, and which blazed the funkily cryptic phrase 'Slip It To Me' in blue sans-serif letters against a vivid orange background. The phrase seems to suggest the desire for answers and initiation – couched in the cool suggestiveness of US hipster speak of the pop era. That Lancaster – ostensibly in New York to research his student dissertation on the work of photographer Alfred Stieglitz – would almost immediately be accepted by the white-hot core of the Warhol circle, during perhaps one of Warhol's most intense surges of artistic consolidation, would immediately place the Newcastle University art student in the realm of living, volatile, seductive myth.

But just the experience of America, for Lancaster, was steeped in heady glamour – another total production. His first impressions – airliners, television, baseball, pay-phones, fast food – thus read like a directory of pure pop phenomena.

Mark Lancaster: 'When I went to New York in 1964 I was doing research for my BA thesis on Alfred Stieglitz and the 291 Gallery – which, with Richard's support, I had got the art history department to accept (I don't think they had a clue what it was about). And so I actually got a grant of about £100 towards my trip from the Local Authority. It was arranged via BUNAC: the British Universities North America Club, which was a very enterprising outfit that organised charter flights. Mine was via Aer Lingus from Manchester to New York and cost, I think, £60 for the round trip. But basically I had been saving for this trip for ever.

'The TV in New York was black and white; there were about eight channels (which seemed a lot) and a couple were on all night. I saw my first colour TV in a shop window in August 1964 – it was a baseball game, and people were crowded round. The telephones were all rotary, and the Factory's only phone was a pay-phone on the wall (painted silver). Calls were 5 cents or 10 cents. A slice of pizza was 15 cents. The subway was 15 cents. Somebody once wrote that there was a correlation between the price of the subway token and a slice of pizza in NY which held up pretty well until at least 1980.

'At Horn and Hardart (the Automat) the coffee was either 10 or 15 cents, baked beans were 25 cents, sandwiches 50 to 75 cents and hot plates 4 quarters. At Tad's on 42nd Street where I had my first NY meal on July 4th, the steak and baked potato was $1.19 which came to something like $1.28 with tax. The Seagram building was then just a few years old and had the Four Seasons [restaurant] at the south side and the Brasserie at the north side in the basement. This was open twenty-four hours, and sometimes I would go there late with Andy and Henry Geldzahler [then Assistant Curator for Twentieth Century American Art at the Metropolitan Museum]. This was where Andy once insisted he had to talk to Henry, and Henry and I met him there about midnight and Andy said, "Say something."'

'Art galleries were mostly closed for the summer in those years, but the Green Gallery was open and tended for the summer by Samuel Adams Green (coincidentally named) who later ran the Pennsylvania Institute of Contemporary Art – site of Warhol's first museum show in 1965. He was a friend of Greta Garbo. I don't think my hair was especially long at that time, but long enough to be asked more than once on the street "Are you a Beatle?" The English accent opened doors in New York then as it has continued to do.'

The 'entree' provided to Lancaster by Hamilton would prove exceptionally rewarding. Lancaster immediately responded to the scene at Warhol's first 'Silver' Factory, and the circle there were equally prepared to welcome the young Englishman as temperamentally and artistically simpatico to the extraordinary social environment which Warhol was creating around himself, and which was becoming the template and subject matter of much of his art. That Lancaster would appear in two of Warhol's movies that summer *Batman Dracula* and *Kiss* (with Gerard Melanga) is some indication of the speed with which he responded to the Factory scene. At the same time, his principal reason for visiting America – to research his dissertation on Alfred Stieglitz – would lead to a friendship with Henry Geldzahler, himself brilliantly connected in American fine arts circles.

It was all some distance from dancing to the Shirelles at the Club A-Go-

Go in Percy Street – but at the same time, in effect, this initial New York sojourn was the intensified continuance of a particularly romantic sensibility. In part as a process of self-realisation, Lancaster was exploring the very source of American pop's iconography and glamour, even as pop itself was being routed by Warhol through the gay, outsider, drug-friendly, sex-obsessed, intensely urban demi-monde of the Factory entourage. In this respect, Hamilton had enabled Lancaster to connect with a scene that was then being driven by its first, heroic, youthful momentum – energised by a permissiveness and volatility which would be brought to a violent end four years later, with the attempt on Warhol's life by Valerie Solanas. (An earlier shooting had taken place at the Factory in the late spring of 1964, when a 'mole person' casual visitor called Dorothy Podber, accompanied by her dog, Carmen Miranda, fired four shots into a stack of *Marilyn* canvases – which promptly became 'shot *Marilyns*' and highly collectable.)

By the time that Lancaster arrived in the summer, the Factory was in its first full flowering as a drug-fuelled, rock and roll filled, silver-coated den of underground activity – out of which Warhol was creating his first great art. As Victor Bockris described the Factory at the time of the party held by Warhol following the opening of his 'Brillo Boxes' show at the Stable Gallery, on 21 April 1964: 'Rock music played at top volume as the lights bouncing off the silver created a hall of mirrors effect. The reception was the first time the New York social and art worlds were at the Factory and it was a huge success. The look of the Factory, with Andy's paintings on the walls and Brillo boxes stacked up on the floor, was striking. "It was like a crash," recalled Billy Linich. "It was really a smash."'

Mark Lancaster: 'Richard Hamilton was not at all well known as an artist at that time [1964], but had gone to Pasadena the previous year – his first trip to the US – to see the Duchamp exhibition which Walter Hopps had organised. Marcel Duchamp and his wife (Teeny Duchamp) were there, and Andy must have been having a show in LA [his second at the Ferus Gallery, in fact] – at any rate they met at a party.

'Richard told me when he came back, that if I went to New York I should call him [Warhol]. I only knew Warhol then from a couple of reproductions in magazines, and I think a photograph of him in *Life* or something, with some paintings in a Bonwit Teller window. He was still thought of as less "important" by the critics than, say, Lichtenstein.

Warhol wasn't included in a big Painting 1954 to 64 show that was at the Tate in Summer of '64, even though Jim Dine, for example, was . . .'★

Warhol, having already courted controversy earlier in the year with his contribution to the New York State Pavilion at the World's Fair – *The Thirteen Most Wanted Men* (mostly Mafiosi – which Warhol painted over with silver paint after the work was pronounced by the governor to be 'offensive to Italian Americans') – would go on to make some of his important early work in 1964, including the film *Empire*. This would also be the year when Baby Jane Holzer (profiled in *New York* magazine by Tom Wolfe as 'The Girl of the Year') became a central star of the Warhol coterie, and – crucial to Warhol's dealings with the world – the year when he bought his first tape recorder. In short, 1964 would see the beginnings of the consolidation of the mythic Warhol.

Mark Lancaster: 'I had little sense of Andy in any particular way. I was nervous about calling him, but I had at that point been in New York for three days without speaking to anybody. He was so friendly when he called me back, and invited me right away to come by the Factory; but it was walking into that incredible place when I immediately thought, "Well, this is it; this is absolutely the most exciting place I have ever been and there is something extraordinary going on here."

'Even though Jane Holzer was sitting there, I sensed "gay" immediately. There was never any sexual pressure from Andy, who just wasn't like that in those days, though soon he would ask about my sex life. "Does he have a problem?" was almost his first question about anyone. I think I sensed right away that Andy was a more interesting artist than the other "pop" artists – with the exception of Jasper Johns, whose work I knew a bit about by then. At the MoMA I had made the connection that Johns's *Target* was a kind of precedent for the *Marilyn*.

'The Factory was extremely "modern" and up to date for me – and Andy was utterly cool in a way I had never experienced. Working for Andy never involved getting paid, but if you were still around at the end

★ It is ironic to note that not only was Warhol excluded from the Tate's 54–64 painting show, so – amazingly – was Richard Hamilton. Marco Livingstone says: 'There was a show at the Tate in 1964 called "Painting of a Decade 1954–1964" which had at least thirty artists in it; and Hamilton was left out – which seems incredible now, as Hamilton is one of the great artists of that period.'

of the day he would take the group down to the Village and we would have hamburgers and stuff at one of the cafes like the Figaro and he would always pick up the check.

'The *Kiss* film with Gerry [Gerard Melanga] was made in August 1964 at 231 East 47th Street. I think we were standing in front of the couch, and Andy suggested we do it and we did it. Nobody else was there. I think he [Andy] knew that Gerry didn't like me and that I was wary of him. So his wanting us to kiss could be interpreted in several ways. I found Gerry attractive in his somewhat swaggering "macho" way, but I figured he was basically straight – but we did kiss, heavily, for the three minutes of the film, and I enjoyed it. I never discussed it with him, it was like "work".'

The research for his dissertation on Stieglitz would also provide Lancaster with a further series of fascinating introductions, which would ultimately lead to his close relationship with Jasper Johns. But Lancaster's experience of New York in 1964 was far from being merely 'social'; his work at Warhol's Factory, assisting with basic tasks around the studio, as well as observing Warhol's working methods, would have a significant influence on his own work when he returned to Newcastle in the autumn. But there is also a profoundly Warholian conflation of art, work and society at the heart of Lancaster's first trip to New York – an immersion in a total lifestyle, which was itself a reflection of both the vibrancy of the city itself, and the possibilities being opened up by art.

Mark Lancaster: 'When I told Andy that the official reason I was in New York was to write my degree thesis on Alfred Stieglitz and the gallery he ran called 291; and that I had been reading old copies of Stieglitz's magazine *Camera Work*, in the library of MoMA, and the ancient Edward Steichen had looked over my shoulder at them but didn't say anything, Andy's reply, almost verbatim, was: "Oh, you must meet my best friend Henry Geldzahler. He is at the Met. [Metropolitan Museum of Art] where they have all those Stieglitz things, in the basement, and he will show you the paintings by Florine Stettheimer. She's my favourite artist – she is sooo great."

'And so I did, and saw a lot of wonderful things. Demuth's *Figure Five in Gold* was on view, but most of the works of that period were in storage. The huge Stettheimer *Cathedral* paintings with their wonderful magical narrative and amazing frames – *Cathedral of Wall Street* and *Cathedral of Broadway* which can now be seen in the galleries – were then banished to storage, along with wonderful Arthur Doves, John Marins and Georgia O'Keeffes. I love those artists.

'Henry took me under his wing, and took me with him when he visited artists. He was close to Frank Stella and his then wife Barbara Rose, who became friends; and he took me to Roy Lichtenstein's studio, where he was making beautiful simple sunset and sunrise paintings that summer; also to Jim Rosenquist's, who was making a picture (which I love), of a cut-off detail of an ad for a contest, with the letters cut off by the edge of the picture so it didn't make sense. We visited Ellsworth Kelly in his studio in the Hotel des Artistes, where he was making a huge red, black and blue painting.

'Henry was going to visit Iran with Frank Stella in August that year, and lent me his apartment on West 81st Street while he was away. He asked me if there was anybody else I wanted to meet and I immediately said "Jasper Johns" because I loved his work – what I had seen. The first painting of his that I saw was *False Start,* which was shown in the US Embassy gallery in Grosvenor Square, London, probably in 1961 or '62. (Those were the days, again, when the State Department sponsored art shows.) Henry said that it might be difficult, but he contrived a meeting, and later took me to a reading by John Ashberry in Jasper's apartment. He lived then in a penthouse on Riverside Drive at 106th Street with marvellous views to New Jersey and Palisades Park.

'When Andy knew I had met Jasper he said, "Ohhh, Jasper's sooo Famous," which was true compared with him. "We'll never see you any more." I told him that was silly. But Jasper was very glamorous, always, to Andy, who had bought a drawing of his around 1960. Jasper was very good looking too, but quite private. We became close friends.'

Lancaster returned to Newcastle for his final year as an undergraduate art student at the end of the summer. One can imagine the wealth of impressions and experience that he must have been aware of bringing back from New York, and which would have a profound effect on the subsequent course of his life and art. A closing word, however, concerning Lancaster's exposure to the work of Florine Stettheimer – Andy's 'favourite' artist.

Born in 1871, Stettheimer would become best known for a series of four large paintings called the *Cathedrals*, which she made between 1929 and her death in 1944. All are dense with opulent colour, richly detailed – literary in their imagistic commentary on a city and an epoch. The first, *Cathedrals of Broadway* (1929) seems to bring the vertiginous, glamorous world of F. Scott Fitzgerald's jazz age Manhattan to life on canvas; the painting is a dizzying, vivid depiction of a city of fabulous, monolithic entertainments – of stage musicals and talkies, nightclubs, neon, limousines, liveried commissionaires, bell-hops, fountains, elegant, flapperish ladies and dinner-suited gentlemen (the American ancestors of the top-hatted boulevardier at Marcus Price's shop) preparing to enjoy the city's show.

Made during the Depression, *Cathedral of Broadway* – in all its glitter and carnival – doubles as an almost ironic reflection on the ways in which, at the same time, impoverished and struggling Americans were turning to the great spectacles of cinema and musicals to distract them from the bleak realities of life. (In a further quirk of art historical neatness, it would be Marcel Duchamp who organised the first retrospective of Stettheimer's work, in 1946.)

And as one studies the painting, drawn into its compelling montage of illuminated signs, a cinema screen (the Mayor of New York on the newsreel, about to pitch the first ball of the season), banners, grand lobbies and velvet ropes, there is an entirely coincidental frisson in the fact that on the left of the painting is the name 'MARK' and on the right, aglow, the endlessly evocative but ultimately meaningless word 'ROXY'.

eleven

Mark Lancaster's return to Newcastle in the autumn of 1964; the importance of style for fellow undergraduate Stephen Buckley; a glance back to the Picabia retrospective, curated by Richard Hamilton at the Hatton Gallery in April 1964; Bryan Ferry joins Fine Art department; Ferry's impressions of Hamilton teaching the Basic Course; Mark Lancaster's New York lecture; Lancaster's 'Ho Jo' paintings.

Lancaster returned from New York to Newcastle just as Bryan Ferry was beginning his first year in the Fine Art department. Ferry's immediate circle of fellow undergraduates and graduate students over the next four years – Stephen Buckley, Tim Head, Nick de Ville, and through Stephen, Mark Lancaster – would share an educational and social experience which was bordered on the one hand by their desire to be artists in the most modern sense, and on the other by a certain student bohemianism, in which Mod styles and pop music played a vital role.

The year before Ferry's arrival, in 1963, Stephen Buckley had made a painting entitled *Middle Class Interior with Ballroom* – later described by the artist: 'The upper section is a schematic rendering of the Majestic Ballroom, Newcastle upon Tyne, which offered popular lunchtime rock and roll sessions. The lower section has elements of domestic interiors taken from colour supplements.' Of this painting, Marco Livingstone writes in his monograph on Buckley, *Many Angles* (1985), that 'his [Buckley's] concern with "taste and style and how environments reflected taste and style" was rooted in the pop aesthetic and in themes which Hamilton, in particular, had dealt with.' Also that, 'In retrospect Buckley thinks that one of the missions of his work has been to redefine taste.'

Middle Class Interior with Ballroom could be read as an allegory of the undergraduate's sense of newfound freedom – the exchange of the parental home (often with all of its restrictions and formality) for a swallow dive into the welcoming waters of youthful subculture, music and fashion. As an early example of Buckley's art, *Middle Class Interior* points up his interest in colliding opposing ideas, in quotation, and in a certain application of irony. Livingstone again: 'It is as though even the most basic forms employed by Buckley are offered within inverted commas, so that they are not true abstractions but pictures of abstractions, and in that sense not abstract at all.' (One might imagine, nine years later, a similar strategy being applied to the creation of a new kind of rock music – a fusion of quoted styles, in which even the act of quotation is stylised.)

Buckley had arrived at Newcastle in 1962, from Leicester, where he had been taught art in the sixth form by William Varley, himself from Tyneside. In common with his generation, a substantial attraction of university education for Buckley was the chance to leave home. In addition to which, particularly to the art students arriving at Newcastle in the early 1960s, the presence of Hamilton was a major draw.

Marco Livingstone also notes how Buckley would have come under the influence of three other major figures of the pop era, who were coming to Newcastle as visiting lecturers: Joe Tilson, Richard Smith and Eduardo Paolozzi. Livingstone points out that Tilson, in particular – during the autumn term of 1963 – was making, 'in full view of the students, some of his earliest pop objects'.

For Buckley, the processes of Pop art would be maintained by a commitment to the pop lifestyle – a pursuit in which he joined with Mark Lancaster, with whom he would share a flat not far from the university, in Eslington Terrace, for nearly four years. In keeping with the pop lifestyle in Newcastle at this time, Marcus Price (where Buckley had a Saturday job), the Majestic Ballroom and the Club A-Go-Go were central fixtures. And again, as with Lancaster's leather jacket and paintings of the Everly Brothers or Dr Kildare, Buckley's student career demonstrates that particular fusion of art and pop as a targeted exercise in style – the mercurial nature of which both their art would subsequently explore.

Stephen Buckley: 'Of course, Pop art went part and parcel with music – and the fact that along with Mark Lancaster I had a great collection of records. I used to go along most Wednesday lunchtimes to the Majestic Ballroom for the lunchtime twisting sessions. It was Motown that we were mostly interested in – the Shirelles, the first Phil Spector achievements, the tail-end of rock and roll. I saw Gene Vincent fall off the stage at the Majestic Ballroom, but that was an evening performance.

'The premises of the A-Go-Go must have been a warehouse of some sort, originally. There were two very large dance areas, coming up from a central staircase, and there was a vicarious danger about it, as well. I suppose I went there three or four times a week; and it had a late night licence. But curiously enough it was the dancing that was the thing, rather than drinking. One wasn't getting drunk, one was dancing. So I saw the Stones and the Who – we slightly knew Pete Townshend because of Richard Morphet, who had been a schoolfriend of Mark Lancaster: his younger brother, Chris Morphet, was a film cameraman and had known Townshend from way back.

'And then the Quay Club opened during my last two years in Newcastle – I was in Newcastle for five years because I got a scholarship, which was when Bryan Ferry and I started living together. There were four or five clubs open by that time, but the thing about the Quay Club was that it has an Eastern European atmosphere to it – or rather, like one's fantasy of Berlin in the 1930s. It was a different group of people – there were visibly criminals about. The Quay Club was much more about having a drink.

'At Marcus Price, I remember, Ben Sherman shirts at 49s. 11d and poplin ones at 52s. 6d. The things we mostly sold were Ben Sherman shirts – during the great period of Ben Sherman, before he sold the company; button-downs in Oxford cloth – imitations of Brooks Brothers standard things, but very, very sharp. Then we sold Levi's, which nobody else had at that time, and we also sold these incredible split-hide Levi jackets. And these wonderful cowboy shirts which we all had, with a triple cuff, a yolk, with pearl pop-on buttons – the material was called Dan River Wash and Wear, so they were drip-dry, which of course was very attractive to a student. They were very narrow cut so you had to breathe in a little bit, but they were wonderful – wonderful . . .

'It was Newcastle's equivalent to Carnaby Street. Also these wonderful jackets that were made by a firm in Leeds: grey tweed, three button, Ivy League style but with raised, rolled, double-stitched seams. I worked at the shop on Saturdays, during term time, and most of the week during the holidays – £1 a day. I also got discount. I don't know that working there gave one status; but it did mean that I got to know a great many people in "town" rather than "gown" – and right across the spectrum of the conurbation. Because you see, Newcastle itself was quite tiny around the university area, and it was wonderful to meet all these kids who came in from Gateshead, and across the river, all the way up Tyneside, to visit Marcus's shop.'

Influences and enthusiasms would therefore be in place, through Hamilton, Lancaster and Buckley, to exert an influence over Ferry when he arrived at the Fine Art department: Pop art, Duchamp, Warhol, Motown, Mod, America, and a profound enquiry into the nature of style. Earlier in 1964, Richard Hamilton had also curated, with Ron Hunt, the first ever retrospective of work by Francis Picabia (1879–1953) – an artist whose friendship with Duchamp (co-founding American Dada with him in 1913) and artistic restlessness across many different ideas, forms and styles were enough in themselves to place him in the forefront of Hamilton's intellectual ancestry, and endorsed by his interest in what have been described as 'functionless machines' and 'mechanistic fantasies'.

For Ferry's generation within what he will later call the 'in crowd' at the Fine Art department, Hamilton's interests and research thus combined Dada, surrealism and pop into a particularly heady brew – the volatility of these ideas being contained and earthed by Hamilton's belief in the fundamental importance of creative problem-solving within art. The Picabia exhibition would have a significant influence on the work of Stephen Buckley, and also – via Picabia's involvement with Stieglitz – a direct relevance to the interests of Mark Lancaster. A substantial portion of the works in the show at Newcastle were lent by the collector Ted Powers – who had shown a keen interest in Hamilton's own work subsequent to his text and layout in *Living Arts 2*; many of the remainder were lent by Picabia's widow, Gabrielle Buffet-Picabia.

Mark Lancaster: 'I was involved very much with the Picabia show, and helped Richard with the catalogue. It was a revelation to learn of somebody like that for the first time and of course it tied in with my Stieglitz thesis – he showed Picabia at 291 and published things, including *The*

Blind Man which had the Duchamp urinal in it, photographed by Stieglitz. And of course the show introduced Stephen to a lifetime's interest and influence of Picabia. I took some catalogues to New York and remember giving one to Jasper Johns, who owned a Picabia drawing.'

Stephen Buckley: 'A significant event was the first Picabia show, most of which belonged to Ted Powers – a rather crucial collector of that period. He made his money out of television. The Picabia show was important because Richard got me on to cleaning frames and helping with the hang, so these were the first famous paintings that I had actually touched.'

Marco Livingstone also quotes from an interview given by Buckley in 1972, on the occasion of an exhibition of his work in London at the Kasmin Gallery, that Buckley particularly admired Picabia's 'mobility of style' – going on to endorse an attitude which he likens to changing one's ideas as often as one's shirts. This idea of working across a range of styles and forms seems key to the prevailing ethos amongst some of the Hamilton faction at Newcastle in the early 1960s.

One also gets the impression of a tremendously exciting and engaging array of new ideas and new inspirations being available within the Fine Art department to those who cared to explore them. In addition to the Picabia retrospective and Hamilton's own work and teaching, there was the transfer of Kurt Schwitters's *Merz* wall from Ambleside in the Lake District to a permanent home in the university's Hatton Gallery; and then, the great reconstruction of the Duchamp *Large Glass*.

It is important to note that both these curatorial, installation and reconstruction projects, as undertaken by Hamilton, and his teaching methods, were in one vital sense complete fusions of technical and artistic problem solving; seen in relation to Hamilton's own work and thinking, they extend his interest in design and construction – in the mechanical and technical aspects of the 'service' departments of the creative process. At the same time, they are aesthetically and conceptually profound.

Bryan Ferry: 'Richard was in charge of the foundation year, so when you first went to Newcastle you were all put together into this large group and he would give you certain projects to do. You then got on with it, and he would give you a critique of it all at the end of the week. It was stimulating, and quite challenging; sometimes you wouldn't know what he was talking about – it could be quite intellectual and difficult to follow.

'But in the sense that he led by example, it was also very inspiring. Because you were always aware that he was doing his own stuff, off in his studio somewhere. And as the months went by in that first year, you got the sense of his importance as a leading artist. The school was polarised into the "in crowd" and the hip, who followed Richard and that modernist approach to art – which was both the Duchampian tradition of conceptualised art and Warhol – and a few who preferred the more European, older school of thinking.

'I think that there is a wide scope, or a breadth of vision, in Hamilton's work which I found inspirational. It's not just one picture that he's painting – in the way that with some artists you get the impression that they do a particular kind of picture very well, and then perfect that one picture throughout their career. Mark Rothko would immediately spring to mind as an example of that, and while Rothko aficionados will probably howl with dismay, to the outsider you'd say that there's basically one sort of picture that he does. With Richard, I think he's much more diverse, and you get the sense of an intelligence leaping around. Some people found the work soulless I suppose, but I didn't. My favourite pictures of Hamilton's are the ones I find very lush and sensual – celebrating their subject matter in a good way.

'For me, it was great to be somebody who wanted to be an artist, who was avidly exploring the world of art – which you do as an art student, studying different periods and styles of art – and suddenly coming across someone like Richard, who seemed so incredibly modern at the time. It was great to find pictures where the inspiration was the shape of a modern motorcar or Marilyn Monroe; it was very exciting, and seemed very fresh and of the time that we lived in.

'And yet, there was a sense of great skill there too; so it was somebody who could obviously draw, and who was taking pains over something – which means that you take it more seriously in a sense. Whereas some of the more slap-dash of the Pop art movement may not have impressed you so much in that way. I always felt that about Jasper Johns as well – that there was a great skill there, taking incredible pains, which is something I quite like.

'The famous collage that Richard did [*Just What Is It That Makes Today's*

Homes So Different, So Appealing (1956)] was very exciting to me, and I suppose that when I try to analyse my own work, certainly some of the early songs were very collage like – where I'd actually throw different styles of music into the same song, or try to . . .'

During Ferry's first term at the university, Mark Lancaster would present his 'New York' lecture – an event which on the one hand picked up on Richard Hamilton's idea of the 'performance lecture', and on the other seems to rehearse the emotional dynamics of much later exercises in audio-visual installation.

Comprising the screening of a selection of slides to a musical soundtrack played on a record player, Lancaster's lecture created a vivid, intensely felt portrait of New York City. The slides were of photographs which Lancaster had taken (some from the fire escape of Andy Warhol's Factory) of New York taxicabs, the modern movement curves of the McGraw-Hill building, and the dizzying tessellation of hoardings and signs around Times Square. He also showed slides of photographs taken at the Factory, and of Jasper Johns working in his studio.

In retrospect, one might think of this lecture as a summary of all that was considered, at the time, to be so culturally important and thrillingly glamorous about America and Manhattan in particular. It was also, clearly, a paean to New York from Mark Lancaster – almost an announcement of his betrothal to the city – and as such would have maybe contributed to the glamour and superlative 'cool'

with which he was perceived by so many of his contemporaries. To be sitting in late autumnal Newcastle upon Tyne, the afternoon chilly and damp, seeing images of sun-baked Manhattan – and this at a time when undergraduates very rarely travelled in such a manner to America – would have appeared breathlessly romantic. In addition to which, for Lancaster, the presentation was also in part an artistic homage to the spirit that he had witnessed and participated within at Warhol's Factory.

Mark Lancaster: 'The lecture was Richard Hamilton's idea. I don't remember it being particularly well received. I was so nervous, and though I loved that I had managed to put it together and pulled it off, I had a sense of anticlimax, thinking that about half of the students had no interest in it or what I was trying to get across.

'I showed slides of the city and then showed the Factory photographs, with Lesley Gore singing "You Don't Own Me" and Dionne Warwick "A House is Not a Home"; then I showed Jasper Johns working in his studio. At the end there was a sequence of multicoloured taxicabs seen on 47th Street, taken from the Factory fire escape, and accompanied by the *Breakfast at Tiffany's* music "Moon River". [by Johnny Mercer and Henry Mancini, 1962]. It seems to be the taxicabs that remain most in people's mind – they have always mentioned that. The taxis are all yellow now, but then they were often red and yellow, green and yellow, and for the 1964 World's Fair, blue and orange. There are so many taxis in *Breakfast at Tiffany's*, and my slides made me think of it.'

Bryan Ferry: 'Mark's lecture was very beautiful: "Moon River", and yellow taxicabs . . .'

Stephen Buckley: 'In those days one didn't just go to America – one couldn't afford it. And Mark came back to Newcastle having met so many people, and there we were in our little student flat in Newcastle with a Warhol on the mantelpiece and a Jasper Johns . . . I think that that little group of us knew more about what was going on in New York than in London.'

Mark Lancaster: 'What Stephen said is of course completely true – New York was unknown to most of us then, except from movies. One of the reasons I used "Moon River" was because the film of Capote's *Breakfast at Tiffany's* was such a "love letter" to New York – as in their ways had been, for me, *How to Marry a Millionaire*, *The Seven Year Itch* and *The Apartment*, as well as the more sinister New York movies of the 1950s.

'I am not sure how I decided to have music accompany the slides – partly because I didn't know quite what to say. But also partly because of the way the music had been so vital to my experience: those particular songs as well as the whole thing at the Factory, where "People" by Barbra Streisand was also played a lot, as well as the Supremes, the Dixie Cups ("Chapel of Love"), and some 'Music of Majorca' thing I can't now identify. People would change the record, but Andy never would, he would always simply repeat the same record if he happened to pass by when the record had ended. So I guess back at Newcastle I wanted to evoke that – I just had a little record player there by the projector control; and I changed the records shakily as I remember, because the whole thing made me very nervous . . .'

Lancaster's trip to New York had a significant effect on his work as an artist. In a short essay intriguingly titled, 'Mark Lancaster, Andy Warhol and Bryan Ferry' (1998), John A. Walker quotes from an article on Lancaster's 'Paintings, 1965–67' by Richard Morphet, published in *Art and Artists* in June, 1967: 'Lancaster's first paintings when he returned from the States in 1964 centred round the imagery of the Howard Johnson company – whose urban restaurants and highway Motor Lodges are immediately recognisable by their vivid house style . . .'

This series of paintings would be Lancaster's principal excursion into pop – his work otherwise being concerned with process, grids and systems.★

Mark Lancaster: 'I returned for my final year after New York and had a small studio in what had been a shop on Barras Bridge [a road very near to the University]. I started my "Howard Johnson" paintings there (though I had made two small ones in New York) and I made about five large paintings on the various Ho-Jo themes, the map of the locations, the roof and tower.

★ This would be extended further in the later 1960s, in paintings such as *Zapruder* (1967) in which a grid of rectangles becomes a visual transposition of the famous footage shot in 1963 of the Kennedy assassination by Abraham Zapruder. The conversion of vivid, empathetically charged 'human interest' media into a form of abstraction would also be seen in the work of Rita Donagh during the mid 1960s – notably her semi-sculptural work *Contour* (1967–68), based on a photograph from *Life* magazine, published in 1964, of young gay men taunting police surveillance on 42nd Street, New York.

'The most interesting was probably a 10-foot-square painting based on a Howard Johnson napkin, almost all white and off-white, with an undulating ribbon-like border punctuated by the little roof and tower image, in those two great colours they used, turquoise and orange. It was shown at the 1965 "Young Contemporaries" in London, an annual show for students from around the country, where the people who ran the Rowan Gallery saw it and eventually offered me a show in November 1965.'

Marco Livingstone has pointed out that, 'By and large, the work produced by Hamilton's students bore a tangential relationship to pop.' That Bryan Ferry would eventually use pop music – and even pop stardom itself – as a medium for creating art was at this point unknowable; but during his time at Newcastle University, certainly, he would feel the equal pull of music and art, as creative media and as lifestyles, and would find himself initially torn between them in his search for romantic self-expression.

twelve

Newcastle University: 1964–1966. Bryan Ferry's first acquaintance with Mark Lancaster and Stephen Buckley; arrival of Tim Head and Nicholas de Ville. Attitudes to art, style, taste, exclusivity and America; 'Virginia Plain' – the painting and the song; for Bryan Ferry, 'music is a strong drug'.

By the autumn of 1964, Mark Lancaster had experienced at least fragments of the dizzyingly glamorous escapades that Ferry's cascading lyric for the first single released by Roxy Music, 'Virginia Plain', would describe nearly eight years later.

Unlike most British art students of the early 1960s, Lancaster really had made the acquaintance of 'Baby Jane' (Holzer), and discovered how New York's art world 'opens up exclusive doors – oh wow!'

In this, while 'Virginia Plain' would read like an inculcation of American pop imagery, doubling as a prayer for success, it also set out a mythic territory that Mark Lancaster had gone some way to exploring in actuality. Speaking later about 'Virginia Plain', Bryan Ferry remarked: 'The American Dream, that's what the single was all about: dreaming of going to New York and living in an attic and painting. The whole Warhol set-up was fantastically attractive then . . .'

During his first year at Newcastle University, when Ferry made an initial acquaintance with Mark Lancaster and Stephen Buckley, they were of course his senior and as such more established within the department. (It would not be until 1966 that he would share a flat with Buckley.) Ferry's striking looks and shyness were combined within Lancaster's first impressions:

Mark Lancaster: 'Being so busy with the huge spurt of energy and new ideas after New York, and working on my thesis on Stieglitz as well, I didn't hang out in the lobby of the art department as much as in previous years, though I spent a good deal of time in the library. I remember noticing Bryan and hearing his voice before I knew him. I could tell from his accent that he was a "local" – and I noticed his striking hair, which I don't think was very long then, but well-groomed – maybe he even used Brylcreem . . . He was very dapper, and shy. I don't remember when we first spoke, but he might have asked me about New York.'

Stephen Buckley: 'I suspect that he came up to me, because I would have been older. But once I met Bryan, we were pretty much doing things together a lot of the time. I then shared a flat with him in Eslington Terrace during my sixth year. I had actually taken the flat over from Mark Lancaster, and Mark and I had lived there for about three years. Then Mark left, and I stayed on for another year with a scholarship.'

With the subsequent arrival at the Fine Art department of Tim Head and Nicholas de Ville in the autumn of 1965, a small coterie of soon-to-be friends and acquaintances – Ferry, Buckley, Lancaster, de Ville, and Head – would be based around various of the student flats in the three-storey, late-Victorian houses on Eslington Terrace, in lower Jesmond, not far from the university. Set back from the road behind low-walled front gardens, Eslington Terrace had a somewhat dignified air. Many of the houses retained their pilastered, heavy, fanlit front doors, and some their double-storey bay-fronted windows. As rented accommodation in the mid-1960s, the terrace was rich in an atmosphere of somewhat mysterious, faded gentility, which – colonised in the later 1960s by the pungent tracery of hippy domesticity – would become such a prominent feature of student 'digs' in the inner suburbs of the provincial cities.

Bryan Ferry: 'When I was living in Newcastle, Tim lived in the flat below me and Nick lived almost next door – in Eslington Terrace, which was the coolest street, a beautiful street near the railway track, just behind the girls' grammar school.

'Tim was very cool, too – he would go to work for Claes Oldenburg in New York, and he was the first person who played me the Velvet

Underground when I was at college. He was always ahead of the game a bit – a year younger than me.'

Tim Head: 'There was a group of us, a little coterie, who were tuned in to American pop – and I knew a little about what was going on in Europe as well. But then, importantly, there were also those who were not that interested. Our group would have been smallish. Later we shared the house on Eslingon Terrace for at least a year and a half; it very conveniently backed on to a girls' school. We used to entertain the girls at lunch – Bryan would get them pissed, and then they'd go back to school for the afternoon.

'We used to go to this wonderful club, the A-Go-Go, which was very near the university in the Haymarket. That's where all the R&B and bands would play – I saw Hendrix play there; in fact, he came back to a student party with us. Bryan did some DJ'ing there later. And that was our social life; there were other places, but they were a bit smarter. There was the fantastic Mayfair Ballroom – I remember Chuck Berry on stage there; and City Hall had Ike and Tina Turner, and the Rolling Stones . . .

'It was a friendly city – I mean, it was heavy – there were bouncers on the door, and what would later be seen in all that *Get Carter* gangster stuff; but Newcastle people are friendly. It was quite bleak, and cold in the winter, but it was a great student town. The National Film Theatre opened up there when I was a student – so you could spend your day in the cinema. *8 ½* and the Antonioni stuff, *Alphaville* – all those films that leave a big impression you. But Club A-Go-Go was where we used to go – they specialised in R&B – Geno Washington, the Who – even though we were also listening to the progressive stuff as well.

'Then there was the Quay Club, which got burned down, and nobody knew who by. The Club A-Go-Go had these steep steps going up to it, and I remember a guy getting pulled out by the bouncers – as I was going back into the club this poor guy was being hurled down the stairs and thrown into the street. The Mayfair Ballroom was fantastic; a massive thing with a big revolving stage . . . Newcastle would have been a good place on a tour: big audiences, its own music scene – the Animals and so on.'

Academically, the 'little coterie' would respond in their different ways, as students, to the influence of Hamilton's teaching on his Basic Course. But if the extended thinking of this teaching would be that art-making could comprise a virtually limitless spectrum of possibilities, then the basis of these artistic freedoms was rooted in a strict, problem-solving approach, rather than a riot of experimentalism and free expression. Indeed, the problem-solving exercises set by Hamilton on the Basic Course actively discouraged any 'artistic' enjoyment of image making.

In his article, 'About Art Teaching, Basically', written for *Motif 8* in the winter of 1961, Hamilton had noted the gap between the training of tex-tiles, furnishings and industrial designers, and the education of fine artists, suggesting: 'In art school training, at least, it seems to be imperative to bridge the gap between the disciplines of the life room and the rigours of basic design.'

Richard Hamilton: 'When I was a lecturer in design, Lawrence Gowing didn't like me talking to painting students. Then, when Victor Pasmore came along, he rather liked the idea that I could feed into his empire. I'd been doing one session a week. Then I did more or less what I'd been doing at Central School – the growth and form idea. It was really getting across my principles that you have to wipe the slate clean in a way that I had had my slate cleaned at various times in my life.'

Rita Donagh: 'Richard was the only person who would talk to us about Paul Klee for instance – about artists who were also thinkers. And that all became a part of the Basic Course.'

Richard Hamilton: 'But I was very careful not to present the idea that I could teach them how to paint – teach them a style. I've always thought I was teaching them how to think about art.'

Rita Donagh: 'Also, Richard worked in the school, so if you had to see him about anything you could also see his paintings. And these were the great paintings – *Hommage à Chrysler Corp.* and so on. And so you can imagine, as a student, seeing these works . . .'

Richard Hamilton: 'But I would never be encouraged to ask my students to talk about it. That was just something I did in my spare time.'

Rita Donagh: 'Yes, but you didn't explain what you were doing, or what these strange pictures were all about. Your teaching was very much about thought processes.'

Ferry and his immediate circle of friends in the Fine Art department were also all under the spell of modern America. With the exception of Ferry himself, all would eventually follow Mark Lancaster's lead and visit New York during their undergraduate or postgraduate careers. The creative atmosphere around Hamilton being directly linked to the sense of intimacy with America and the New York art scene, there was an awareness amongst Ferry's generation that they were studying at a time and in a place that were particularly magnetised to pioneering the latest developments in art and ideas.

Tim Head: 'Hamilton opened your eyes to a more outward-looking view of things, in terms of art. Certainly, I don't know what we'd have been doing in Newcastle if Richard wasn't there; it was almost like he gave us a licence to do what we did, in a way. And although we were all quite different, I think that Richard was responsible for making you feel that you were part of something important that was happening at the time. And I think this sustained us – the feeling that we were a part of something . . .'

A common denominator of the artistic thinking proposed by Hamilton would be the active pursuit of diversity as a creative virtue. This, coupled with the development of analytical discernment, would urge a sensibility in which the analytical and communication skills of an intellectual technician were merged with the visual awareness of a professional aesthete.

Marco Livingstone: 'One of the defining characteristics of Hamilton's work is to escape the straitjacket of a single style, and to find the correct form for any idea. This perhaps had more effect on some of the people whom he taught than on others. Buckley has a very unified, coherent style; whereas Tim Head's mentality is maybe more like Hamilton's – where he'll move from a photographic installation, to a drawing, to a painting; he'll print the paintings, he'll paint them by hand – he'll do whatever's necessary that seems logically in tune with the concept.

'So there is a certain, what might appear to be eclecticism in Hamilton's work, which is really to do with that desire to escape a signature style; he got this from [his reading of] James Joyce, he says, more than from

Duchamp – that idea of constantly speaking in different voices.

'It could also be said that there's certainly something in the early Roxy Music material, the references to other people's music – a little bit of the Beach Boys or French chanson or whatever – that was very self-conscious and very clever in a way that Hamilton's work can be. And which was rather new to pop music.'

There is a tangible connection between aspects of the art education which Ferry et al. were receiving, and their espousal of an in crowd lifestyle. Summarised, the students were experiencing an opening-up of cultural identities, in addition to pursuing their different ideas with regard to actual art-making. There was also (of course) a considerable vein of light-heartedness running through their student lifestyles in which wine, women and song played an integral role. At the same time, their awareness of witnessing, by way of Hamilton and his encouragements to absorb new ideas, a confluence of cultural stimuli – including Hollywood films, pop music, new technologies, art history, design, pop imagery – would pro-pose a vastly exciting range of possibilities.

Nicholas de Ville: 'The scene at Newcastle in the mid-sixties was quite complex. Richard Hamilton was an incredibly important influence; but I don't think that either Bryan or I were doing what you'd call Pop art. Richard had a studio assistant teaching the first year called Mark Lancaster, who shared a flat with Stephen Buckley. Mark by this time was into a kind of pretty cool, colourfield painting, post-abstract expression-ist; Stephen Buckley was painting in a post-Jasper Johns abstraction. Bryan himself was painting in a way which was abstract, although there were fig-urative elements in them.

'I think there was an attitude coming from Richard Hamilton which had various strands to it. There was the fact that he was very interested in, and supported a revival of interest in, the Hollywood films of the 1930s and 1940s – which at that time, the early 1960s, were quite an undiscov-ered continent of cinema. That was about the time people were starting to take John Ford and Billy Wilder seriously as auteurs.

'Hamilton also brought quite a few people to Newcastle, like Hockney, Joe Tilson, Richard Smith, Ron Kitaj and Eduardo Paolozzi. So that was an introduction to the art world, which had a glamour attached to it. Also, Hamilton's relationship with Duchamp and his recreation of the *Large Glass*, and that becoming the centrepiece of Duchamp's first retrospective at the Tate, later in the decade – all of that . . . So to say that Newcastle was a provincial centre, that was pretty extraordinary, really; because it was very well connected internationally, and it was very ambitious and cutting edge, for that time, in its ideas about contemporary art. There were quite a lot of bright students there, so the milieu was quite exciting. And there were a lot of different things going on in the department simultaneously.'

As a student, de Ville became particularly aware of the ways in which Hamilton's teaching, in addition to the generational enshrinement of America, and set against the lingering ethos of the 'less modern' faction within the department, created a particularly charged and unique creative atmosphere. (A significant aspect of this energised sensibility derived from the sense of 'burning the box of beautiful things' – of rejecting the ideas of the 'old school' in favour of pop, Duchamp and the American avant-garde.) His own student work reflected the conflation of sometimes opposed sensibilities. His identification of 'new hybrids' seeming possible within artistic practice is particularly prescient.

Nicholas de Ville: 'It was a strange amalgam of ideas coming through Hamilton from Duchamp; and an interest in semiotics – the idea of a painting being a series of signs, and an interest in what might constitute a meaningful sign. Also of things coming from New York – very cool ideas about contemporary art: colourfield painters like Noland and Olitski, and the beginnings of people like Judd and Morris coming to prominence. All of this was being gleaned by a lot of eager art students through the pages of *Artforum* and *Art International*.

'Now, thinking about it, these were pretty irreconcilable influences; but at that time, what you had on one side was a very traditional notion of art education – and a lot of the teachers in the art school were pretty traditional, teaching from a veneration for Picasso and Matisse, and strands of British Academy life drawing, which was still seen as being important, if not compulsory.

'On the other, that all seemed to us to be very embedded in a pre-war notion of art education. You have to remember that the 1960s was a time of considerable ferment; it was really to do with counter culture, and people getting fed up with certain things that were part of the social settlement that politicians envisaged as a consequence of the war – which had held, pretty much, during the fifties and was disintegrating during the 1960s. Full employment was becoming a thing of the past, and the trade unions were kicking over the traces. So there was this sense of ferment, that things were possible, and who knows what hybrids might have seemed a good idea.'

Moving to London in the late 1960s and working as a studio assistant for Richard Hamilton (his tasks including sanding down Hamilton's *Guggenheim Reliefs* [1970]), de Ville would maintain his friendship with Bryan Ferry and become a major contributor to the art direction of the sleeves for *Roxy Music, For Your Pleasure* (1973), *These Foolish Things* (1973) and *Another Time Another Place* (1974). He would subsequently work on the art direction of many of the later Roxy Music albums, as well as becoming a successful artist in his own right and a senior academic.

But de Ville's work for Roxy Music could be seen as a bravura example of the capacity to transpose artistic ideas across the 'fine-art/popular-art' continuum, and to think both conceptually and in the technical, 'problem-solving' terms demanded by design – an approach demonstrated, for instance, in the assembling of a meticulously honed image in praise of stylishness (as in the case of *For Your Pleasure* or *Another Time Another Place*) in which the heavy amplification of romantic detail would play a pronounced part. He would be heavily involved in the presentation of model Kari Ann as an early seventies reclamation of Rita Hayworth on the cover of *Roxy Music*, and likewise Amanda Lear, with panther, on the cover of *For Your Pleasure*.

In the mid-1960s, however, Ferry and his contemporaries would share the sense that the ultimate distillation of Hamilton's teachings might be said to include the understanding of that elusive and ceaselessly seductive quality, 'cool'. The quality that Nick de Ville defines within Hamilton's thinking as 'intellectual continuity' could be granted an extension that connected the making of art to the making of an artistic lifestyle – an outlook which seemed in part a pop/Duchampian reclamation of aesthetic movement poise, and in part an assertion (simultaneously profound, camp and semi-ironic) of glamour. To treat one's life and creativity, perhaps, as 'a total production'.

Tim Head: 'It was a certain kind of lifestyle, perhaps – that included music, and the way you live, and what you're interested in. A sense of stardom is maybe a part of it. I go back to Mark Lancaster as a model: that everything you do is cool – how you drink your tea, what kind of cigarettes you smoke; all that kind of stuff. With Mark it was taking Richard's notion of being as interested in the design of the furniture as in the paintings, and applying it to the whole conduct of lifestyle. And I think that rubbed off on Bryan. Because with Mark – everything he said was Cowardian, almost.'

Central to this sensibility was a certain connoisseurship as regards the understanding and appreciation of the broadest range of visual imagery; equally vital was an avoidance of academic earnestness, or mere intellectual neatness. Tim Head, who would also go on to a highly successful career as a visual artist, having worked as a student for both Niki de Saint Phalle in Amsterdam and Claes Oldenburg in New York, had arrived at Newcastle University at the same time as de Ville. His experience of the department in the mid-1960s re-emphasises the importance of Hamilton and the American influence, and the idea of transposing fine artistic ideas across a whole rage of possible media and activities. Head would become particularly interested (as would Rita Donagh) in the work of the American 'land' artists.

Tim Head: 'I was looking for an art school to go to, and suddenly I realised that Richard Hamilton was teaching at Newcastle; I was living in Yorkshire – I grew up there – and so it seemed to be the right place. That was all I knew about it: that Richard had started this Basic Course there. I started in 1965. Bryan was a year above me.

'The professor was Kenneth Rowntree – he was a big Francophile; he used to play boules on the bit of lawn in front of the department. His paintings all had Gitanes packets collaged into them. And we of course all thought this was a load of crap – we looked to America for exciting Pop art. And not only had Richard looked at all that material in the 1950s, way before the Americans, he was obviously the link to all that.

'The department was perhaps very much divided between the people who responded to Richard, and his new way of thinking about art – that it could include all of these other things from other worlds: pop culture, design – and the more conventional people, who presumably had been there in Newcastle teaching for a long time. Richard had instigated this way of breaking down how you might think about art – not just fine art, but visual images. His idea was that from that you could do anything; you wouldn't necessarily be a fine artist. You could go off and design cars – or even be a pop star . . .'

In an interview with Tony Godfrey for *Artlog* magazine, in November, 1978, Stephen Buckley would also offer several aphoristic statements concerning, taste, style and art-making. The Wildean tone of these pronouncements is nuanced by the corresponding seriousness of Buckley's influences, and the artists whom he admired – Richard Smith★ (for whom he would work as an assistant on leaving Newcastle), Picabia, or Rauschenberg.

Buckley, too, connects a somewhat dandyfied 'aesthetic movement' approach to the artistic life, to a profound reflection upon the capacity of fine art to involve the viewer's emotions – not least when the artist follows the Duchampian route of embracing diversity and rejecting set patterns. His suggestions seem also to connect to the work and performances made in the 1970s by artists as diverse in background as Bruce McLean (with his 'Nice Style' pose band), 'The Moodies' performance group, Andrew Logan or Carol McNicoll (the latter being an artist and ceramicist, who would make some of Brian Eno's most extravagant stage costumes in the early 1970s).

'What I regret is that Art is no longer recognised as entertainment, nor as something that is socially enjoyable . . .' Buckley states in *Artlog*, adding, 'I intend to do some woodcuts soon. I'm also hoping to do a teaset and have it editioned, but you'll be able to make tea in it – it

---

★ Richard Smith, who had worked in America between 1963 and 1968, possessed a studio on Bath Street, near Old Street in East London, which would become well known to several of the Roxy Music milieu towards the end of the 1960s. It was a mythic place, having been the location for the famous party scene – featuring Pauline Boty, Peter Blake, and David Hockney – at the end of Ken Russell's documentary film for BBC *Monitor*, *Pop Goes the Easel*. The lease had been won in a poker game off the film director John Schlesinger, and after Smith it would be occupied by Mark Lancaster, as well as offering temporary space to Bryan Ferry.

wouldn't be an arty one.' There is a *fin de siècle* ring, also, to his observation: 'I think both style and taste are axes which everything revolves around. They are alike but they are not the same thing . . . but they are interdependent. Everyone has got taste and they can't escape it. There is no such thing as good taste and bad taste: there is only your own taste and someone else's taste.'

Ferry's own work during the first year would include making his painting, *Virginia Plain* – the title being a reference to the type of tobacco used in many American and British cigarettes, as well as a pun upon a girl's name. Ferry's personal iconography had already included his barely adolescent admiration for the mystique of romantic solitude conjured up by the advertising for 'Strand' cigarettes ('You're never alone with a Strand' ran the slogan); *Virginia Plain* continues the equation between cigarettes and a cinematic concept of romance. As a first year exercise *Virginia Plain* was faintly Hamiltonesque in its use of popular imagery, and not without a touch of surrealist fantasy.

Bryan Ferry: 'It was a watercolour or a painting on paper. It was just like a surreal drawing of a giant cigarette packet, with a pin-up girl on it, as a monument on this huge Daliesque plain. I liked that phrase "Virginia Plain", which was what they always put on cigarette packets. So it later became the title of the first single I put out with Roxy Music – with a slightly imponderable lyric, which I also rather like because it's just a torrent of images, really, and free association of images. There's a reference to Baby Jane Holzer in there, who was part of the Warhol Factory set, of course; and even my lawyer's mentioned – Robert Lee. I believe I was his first client. He was a young lawyer, and we met when I was rehearsing with Roxy Music . . .'

An unused and unpublished lyric by Ferry, also titled 'Virginia Plain' and dating from the same approximate period of composition in the very early 1970s, appears closer to the imagery and temper of the student painting made six or seven years earlier. In this alternative lyric the tone is reflective and romantically melancholy – an authorial voice within which Ferry would create classic pop lyrics, and which stands in contrast to his more declamatory, witty style – as though Cole Porter had tutored with Edith Sitwell. In this version, we find Ferry ruminative:

Serene she stands
– a monument
on this horizon
only the sun breaks
behind her running
along stiff boards
stained and shining
Brilliant.
Her box can lure
When primaries
come first
on the hard
pack begging
at each breath
to consume.
In clothes she walks
the middle way –
but very little
to detect. (confound)
Never taking off
To soar aloft
– only choking
on the ground.
She'll never make
Havana sound
or smell or taste
the same,
she's on her own
so fair and sweet
that pure
Virginia Plain.

Given how seriously he took his studies as an art student, Ferry would be drawn, slowly but surely, with even greater force towards his interest in music. The two groups with which he would sing while still a student, the **City Blues** and the **Gas Board** (of which more shortly) would acquire enough local success, however modest, for his friends and acquaintances – with mixed reactions – to be aware that his musical ambitions were more than simply casual.

More important, Ferry's long-standing love of music also began to entwine with his developing sense of how he might operate as an artist – and this would lead him, by the time of his creation of **Roxy Music**, into wholly new territory.

Bryan Ferry: 'None of my pictures were any good, really. I hadn't really found myself as an artist, but I enjoyed doing things. I was kind of fiddling around with music while I was still there, so I wasn't as devoted a student as I could have been or should have been. Maybe my heart wasn't totally in it, although when I first went there it was. Music is a very strong drug, and it became more and more clear to me that that's what I wanted to do – although it wasn't until after I graduated that I really knew.'

thirteen

1965–1966: Re-making and re-modelling; Richard Hamilton's reconstruction of Marcel Duchamp's *The Bride Stripped Bare By Her Bachelors, Even*; mannequins, machines and sexuality; the CPLY connection; Bryan Ferry and the pop song as ready-made; an encounter with Monsieur et Madame Duchamp in Carnaby Street, London, in the summer of 1966.

Marcel Duchamp's *The Bride Stripped Bare By Her Bachelors, Even*, also known as the *Large Glass*, is generally considered to be a pivotal but perplexing work of art. Its reputation, like that of its creator, is steeped in glamorous inscrutability, and unchaperoned excursions into its possible meaning, despite the suave reassurances of initiates into Duchamp studies, are largely deemed perilous.

As an object, *The Bride Stripped Bare By Her Bachelors, Even* is a painting in two halves on two separate sheets of plate glass, one above the other, with a total size of 274 x 170 cms. The work was declared 'definitively unfinished' by Duchamp in 1923. In 1926 it was displayed in Brooklyn (its first public appearance) and on being returned from the exhibition was accidentally smashed. In the mid-1930s, Duchamp reassembled the pieces, and the work – in its reconstituted, shattered form – was finally put on permanent display at the Philadelphia Museum of Art in 1954.

Duchamp's greatest interpreter – and, as far Duchampian ideologies allow, his direct artistic successor – would be Richard Hamilton. In 1960, with the encouragement and assistance of the artist, Hamilton had made his 'typographic translation' of Duchamp's hand-written notes for *The Bride Stripped Bare By Her Bachelors, Even*, which are also known as the

Green Box. As Rick Poyner describes in his essay 'Typotranslation' (2000) this process:

> was an undertaking of deep significance for both men. For Hamilton, the forensic insight he gained into the thinking of one of the twentieth century's most enigmatic artists was to have a decisive impact on his paintings of the period, such as *Hommage à Chrysler Corp.*. And for Duchamp? Hamilton heard later that the artist who embraced 'the beauty of indifference' carried the slim *Green Book* with everywhere. He didn't read it or even look at it, but placed it by his bedside, like a Gideon Bible found in a hotel room.

Thus forearmed with unique insight into Duchamp's thinking and working methods, Hamilton would be engaged during his final year at Newcastle University on a meticulous reconstruction of the *Large Glass*. Destined to be the centrepiece of the first major Duchamp retrospective – 'The almost complete ,works of Marcel Duchamp' – held at the Tate Gallery, London, in June 1966, this phenomenal task of recreation would be a major event within the Fine Art department at Newcastle between 1965 and 1966. Of Bryan Ferry's generation and milieu of students, Mark Lancaster and Stephen Buckley would assist Hamilton with aspects of the work – Lancaster photographing the process of recreation, and Buckley polishing the (now bullet-proof) glass on which Hamilton made the replica. Wafts of the Duchampian legend, and an interested awareness of the artist's working methods, would subsequently inform Ferry's discussion of his own creativity within the medium of pop music.

The recreation of the *Large Glass* – which Hamilton titled, with elegant wit, *The Bride Stripped Bare By Her Bachelors Even, Again* – served to extend Hamilton's profound interest in the relationship between design, technology and fine art. To recreate the work presented above all a formidable technical challenge, in addition to the exhaustive processes of decipherment required to retread, from the notes within the *Green Box*, (and at times with the artist's assistance), Duchamp's mental and creative processes.

The process of re-making the *Large Glass* was funded 'with the enthusiastic support', as Hamilton later reported, of Duchamp's close friend, the onetime art dealer, subsequently collector, surrealist painter and maker of pop assemblages William Copley, who painted under the name 'CPLY'. Born in New York in 1919, Copley had been adopted by Colonel Ira C. Copley, a congressman and newspaper publisher. Assured a lifetime of financial independence, he attended Andover and Yale, and served in the army between 1942 and 1946 before developing a passion for surrealism – spending much of the 1950s and early 1960s in Paris.

Copley would also establish a charitable institution for the support of the arts (subsequently re-christened the Cassandra Foundation at Duchamp's suggestion), the documents of which, relating to the period 1954–1967, include a substantial correspondence with Hamilton and reference to the funding of his re-making of the *Large Glass*. (Copley died at Key West, Florida, in 1996. Both he and his son, the artist Billy Copley, would be on the fringes of the Warhol milieu – Billy Copley also being an acquaintance of Mark Lancaster, attending with his then girlfriend Susan Johnson Warhol's birthday party at Montauk in August, 1977.)

On one level, the *Large Glass* might be interpreted as the description of a machine of semi-ironical complexity – a device within a surrealist comedy – the purpose of which is to disclose, with prodigious fetishism, a sexual encounter between nine male archetypes (the 'bachelors') and a mechanised feminine, 'the bride'. For Hamilton, however, the work was foremost a technical manifestation of an intellectual exercise – the enabling work of conceptualism, and an act of profound, artistic revelation. He finally started work on the replica of the *Large Glass* in June 1965.

Richard Hamilton: 'That last year I was in Newcastle, from 1965 to 1966, I hardly saw any students, except socially, because I was working on the *Large Glass* in my studio; and I didn't move out of the studio – I just had to work like mad all the time.

'I could read drawings – that was the important thing. When I was building my house in Highgate I was making models, and I had worked during the war in a drawing office. I was a draughtsman, so I knew about plans and elevations; and I knew a little about perspective, which most draughtsmen would not be expected to know.

'So when I encountered Duchamp, I knew enough to understand what he was doing. To see these drawings in the *Green Box* – which were done on little scraps of paper – and to realise that all the dimensions were there: he'd put everything in; and you could reconstruct the whole thing without seeing, knowing, or having any idea what the original was like! You weren't following a picture of it; you would be using just the dimensions that were available, and following the perspective.

'Sometimes I got into difficulties. On one occasion there was a dimension along the horizon, and I thought – I don't understand what this dimension means and there it is marked on the horizon. And so I had to ask him [Duchamp]. It was marked "D2"; he said, "Oh, I didn't have the room on the piece of paper to put the real dimension, so I put half of it on and called it 'D2'." He had got a specific distance, and a specific mark, but you had to double it to get the vanishing point. It was all very precise.

'And of course it is quite revolutionary. You have to remember that the whole idea of the *Large Glass* was fully formulated – apart from a few elements which were added ten years later – in 1912. Conceived, and written about and detailed. But I don't think of it as being modern in the sense of a 1950s pop idea. It's very scholarly, the approach to it; and it's also terribly personal. It's almost more like a scientist doing something – working out problems.

'But the thing that strikes me all the time, and I never get bored with any of it, is the wonderful invention which goes on in it at every level. A little marginal image in a note that goes over twelve pages of the text; and then he talks about this picture which he might make. And there's this very easy little sketch, and at the top it says "MAR", and at the side of the bottom part it says "CEL". The whole of this imagery of the *Large Glass* is being developed out of his name! He starts with nothing – nothing that's got anything to do with anything else that's ever happened. And then he developed this "marie" and "celebature" – and then it all comes, miraculously. Building little bricks one on top of another until you get this vast edifice and mythology. It's unbelievable. You can't imagine that that early on, in a 1912 note, he would have put this detail, and that nobody had noticed – until I did.'

One summary of the arcane and erotic romanticism that the *Large Glass* seems to describe has been given by Calvin Tomkins – art critic for the *New Yorker* magazine during the 1960s, and a friend of Duchamp. Here he outlines an allegory at work within the epic imaginary scope of the *Large*

Glass, the echoes of which one could identify right across modern romantic iconography, from the writings of F. Scott Fitzgerald, to the Hollywood film drama *Gilda*, to the songs of Johnnie Ray – and indeed the 'cover girls' on Roxy Music's album sleeves.

'Again and again in Duchamp's notes, there is the joyous sense of a mind that has broken free of all restraints', writes Tomkins,

> – a mind at play in a game of its own devising, whose resolution is infinitely delayed. The bride, who is queen of the game (as powerful and as mobile as the queen in the game of chess, to which Duchamp gave so much of his imaginative energy), will never achieve her ardently desired orgasm. Her 'blossoming,' Duchamp tells us, is merely the last state of this nude bride before the orgasm which may (might) bring about her fall. She is like Keats's maiden on the Grecian urn, forever in passage between desire and fulfilment, and it is precisely this state of erotic passage that Duchamp has chosen as the subject of his greatest work. Sexual fulfilment, with its overtones of disappointment, loss, and 'fall' from grace, was never an option. The bride, the bachelors, and by implication the onlooker as well are suspended in a state of permanent desire.

As such, the *Large Glass* becomes above all a statement of romanticism, and of the classically romantic need to maintain a state of ecstatic frustration above all – yearning always for the moment of infinite possibilities, prior to consummation placing limits on the dream. Thus the work describes both the moment of becoming, and the deeper sense of being 'definitively unfinished'.

Within predominantly male fables of acute romanticism, such frustrated longing, when routed through surrealist tastes, has fixated on the notion of a mechanised, artificial female that exists in a condition of permanent cosmetic perfection. Brought into the age of mass culture and pop, such mannequins become newly eroticised versions of the figures Keats studied on the Grecian urn. Painstakingly constructed, mass produced and mass mediated, the 'ideal' females of cinema, pin-up, or even showroom dummies, could thus be reposited as the modern, romantic-erotic muse.

Hamilton himself had written about the commodified and stylised constructions of erotic femininity, as described by advertising for domestic fridges and pin-ups, in his essay, 'An exposition of $he' published in *Architectural Design* in October 1962. This essay provided background information to Hamilton's painting, *$he* (1958–61) and extended a warm, if tongue-in-cheek, welcome to the new school of idealised females that had arisen in commercial visual culture beyond fine art. As such, it was in one sense an essay in praise of artifice.

In a stunning example of aesthetic paradox, Hamilton likens what he calls the 'curiously ingenuous' quality of his (in fact vibrantly intellectual) paintings to Marilyn Monroe, later asserting: 'But I would like to think of my purpose as a search for what is epic in everyday objects and everyday attitudes' – referring back, perhaps, to his remark earlier in the essay that, 'The relationship of woman and appliance is a fundamental theme of our culture; as obsessive and archetypal as the western movie gun duel.'

But as Duchamp suggests, such heightened romanticism is not without its comic possibilities. In 1946, Hans Richter's film *Dreams That Money Can Buy* would include (alongside a sequence created by Duchamp based on his *Nude Descending a Staircase* of 1912, with music by John Cage) an alternately eerie and camp musical number, created by the artist Fernand Léger and 'performed' by showroom mannequins, titled 'The Girl With the Pre-Fabricated Heart'.

Sung in a quavering soprano by Libby Holman, the song is a rolling ballad describing a female mannequin's determination to evade her male showroom dummy of a suitor. The film concludes with the dipping and rising of a female mannequin, dressed as a runaway bride, eternally (stationary) bicycling through an artificial dusk – away from the constraints of love, marriage or consummation (as represented by her morning-suited bachelor grooms), her manufactured perfection unsullied.

In all of this quasi-comic peculiarity, one feels, there is a psychological allegory of intense romanticism – its need for romantic-erotic perfection so acute, that human interference would only disturb the flawless balance and surface of the poise. Hence, in the lyric of 'The Girl With the Pre-Fabricated Heart', we hear: 'A goddess today, if she is "Grade A", is constructed upon the assembly line.' Similarly, 'You float in my new pool, deluxe and delightful.' Ferry will write of a vinyl companion, in his song,

'In Every Dream Home a Heartache'; while the cover conceived by Bryan Ferry and Antony Price for Roxy Music's darkling, 'sort of disco record' (as Ferry described the release) *Manifesto*, in 1979, would divert from the alluring, sensual, all-too-human femmes fatales of the previous covers to present instead a Studio 54 style party of posed mannequins.

Allegorical speculations were not, however, Richard Hamilton's main concern during his work on the *Large Glass*. Rather, his interest lay in understanding the relationship between Duchamp's creative processes and artistic ideas – the ramifications of which he knew were nothing less than revolutionary, and had prompted him to pronounce (in his essay on Duchamp's Pasadena Retrospective, written for *Art International* in January 1964): 'He [Duchamp] simply changed the terms by which painting had lived for centuries. In changing the rules, in re-inventing art as though it had never existed, he re-opened the possibility of working. The new rules were these: Art is conceptual – that is to say it has nothing to do with visual stimuli external to the artist's mind. It was to be as absolutely conceptual as much of the art of the past had been retinal ...'

It would be this rule breaking and iconoclasm which would establish Duchamp as a cultural hero for a new generation of progressive-thinking art students. His name would become linked to a wider sense of rebellion and questioning of authority, and as such his impact on modern art-making would be rivalled only by Picasso and Warhol. Hamilton would later write in his catalogue essay for the Tate Gallery Duchamp retrospective of 1966: 'In his purpose of "changing the definition of art" Duchamp had no power to exclude, he could only widen the language, only make us more aware that art is all pervading.'

In this one can also see how the 'new hybrids' of art suggested by Nick de Ville, inspired by Hamilton's belief that 'there are no limits' to the capacity of art, have if not their basis in Duchampian thinking then a place within its immediate influence. For culturally enquiring students to be in such close proximity to ideas as forceful as these was as exciting as it was inspirational. The tang of revolution hung around such heresies – the sincerity of the revolt underlined by Duchamp's insistence that he was not to be imitated, save in further acts of iconoclasm. 'No living artist,' Hamilton wrote, 'commands a higher regard among the younger generation than Marcel Duchamp.'

1 The Marcus Price shop, Percy Street, Newcastle-upon-Tyne – 'a top end Mod shop' in the early 1960s

2 Marcus Price – shop interior with twin emblems of Mod modern style: Pan American poster and action painting

3 Richard Hamilton in installation of *Man, Machine and Motion*, Hatton Gallery, University of Newcastle, 1955

4 Installation shot, 'This Is Tomorrow', Whitechapel Art Gallery, 1956
5 *Self-portrait* cover for *Living Arts 2*, 1963 by Richard Hamilton (photograph by Robert Freeman) A total production of Pop imagery

6 Mark Lancaster – 'the coolest of the cool' – outside Marcus Price, Newcastle, early 1960s. 'The first black leather jacket in the Fine Art department'

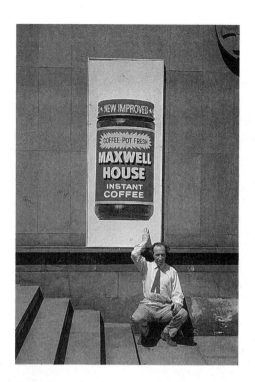

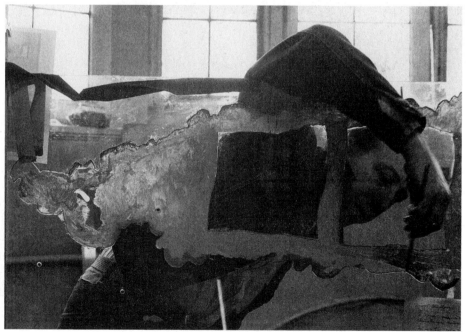

7 Richard Hamilton with Mark Lancaster's 'Maxwell House' – Summer term, University of Newcastle, 1962. Exemplary work from the 'Found Imagery' project set for students

8 Richard Hamilton at work on his reconstruction of *The Bride Stripped Bare By Her Bachelors, Even* by Marcel Duchamp, Newcastle, 1965

9 Bryan Ferry in Fine Art Department, University of Newcastle, mid 1960s. 'I remember him being terribly good looking'

10 Editions of Bryan – studio passport photographs of Bryan Ferry as art student, mid 1960s

11 (from top, left to right) a) Bryan Ferry and Stephen Buckley on their Italian holiday with Jeremy Catto, August, 1966; b) Jeremy Catto, August, 1966 – 'an interest in style . . .'; c) & d) Bryan Ferry playing croquet in the garden of Susie Cussins's house, Newcastle, summer, 1967; e) Susie Cussins – the only named person to whom *Roxy Music* would be dedicated. She would later marry an advisor to President Reagan; f) Bryan Ferry, summer, 1967, at the Cussins' residence, Newcastle

The mention of Duchamp's appeal to a younger generation would have particular relevance to the young Bryan Ferry, who became sufficiently interested in Marcel Duchamp to make substantial reference to the artist during interviews, nine years later, when Roxy Music were touring America. That Ferry quite clearly regarded his work as a musician to be entwined with his awareness of, and training in, the visual arts, is matched by the immediacy with which he cites Duchamp alongside his musical heroes. At the same time, such pan-cultural pronouncements were regarded with suspicion and incredulity by some music fans and most journalists.

Jonathan Takiff, however, the pop correspondent for the *Philadelphia Daily News*, would interview Bryan Ferry for the issue dated 24 May 1975, under the retina-enlarging headline, 'A CROSS BETWEEN MARCEL DUCHAMP AND SMOKEY ROBINSON?', continuing: 'A diffident, detached, though not unfriendly character, this twenty eight year old, Newcastle, England native obviously relishes his role as a "rock elitist". A former artist, he cites Marcel Duchamp and Smokey Robinson as equal musical influences.* 'Why Duchamp? Because he never established any particular style, just flitted around from one thing to the other,' says Bryan. 'That's why our music was full-born – sensual, physical, and also fairly intelligent, I think. And that's why people accepted it so quickly. The whole British music scene was very stale, desperately craving something new.'

For Hamilton, the recreation of the *Large Glass* would be forensic and almost archaeological, presenting him with a job that would include calling upon the skills which he had learned as a student at the Royal Academy schools – most notably highly detailed draughtsmanship. It is typical of Hamilton's modesty that he refers only to the technical challenges of re-making the *Large Glass*, when his engagement with the piece as an artist, in relation to the methods and ideas within his own work, is also of crucial importance. For Hamilton, the manoeuvrings of

---

* The San Francisco edition of *Rolling Stone*, three months later, would also acknowledge the breadth of Ferry's conceptualism – a faint snag of wariness on the edge of their pronouncement: 'The difference between Ferry's "Sympathy for the Devil"' (wrote Dave Marsh, referring to a track on Ferry's album of 'ready-mades', *These Foolish Things*) 'and Rod Stewart's "Street Fighting Man", is the difference between the approach of a pop intellectual and that of a Rolling Stones fan.'

Duchamp's creative consciousness, to work without interference from external influences, artistically unfettered, would be of particular interest – mirrored in his belief in 'wiping the slate clean' as the beginning of an art education.

Richard Hamilton: 'It is astonishing, when you really get into the notes, to find how inventive and how personal they are – also the determination to wipe everything that has ever happened before out, so nothing would influence him. And I think that stayed with Duchamp all his life. That privacy was important to him. Not because he was a private man; not because he was jealously guarding something; but because he refused to allow the possibility of being influenced by anybody or anything.

'I didn't instil in my students any urge to learn about perspective – that would all have been considered a very old-fashioned kind of thing! They were interested in Duchamp, but more in a vague, mythical sense.'

For the students in Ferry's circle, Hamilton's work on the *Large Glass* was recognised as an important event. In Stephen Buckley's words, 'One observed it, and watched it, and saw how it was done, and one was privileged to be involved.' In retrospect, one might think of the recreation as both a practical summation of Hamilton's teachings and a lesson in the workings of influence and discipleship.

Tim Head: 'I saw the recreation of the *Large Glass* happening. And *The Bride Stripped Bare By Her Bachelors, Even* is a mythic work. It divides people: those who think that it's the Anti-Christ of art, and those who think it's the Saviour. The department had a copy of Richard's rendition of the *Green Box*, which was fantastic for me: the idea that this work had all this background of imagery and symbolism and connections was very exciting.

'Richard was obviously one of those people who felt that Duchamp needed to be better known in this country. True to his philosophy, Richard didn't see himself simply as an artist but as a typographer and a lot of other things. And I suppose that his idea of resuscitating this work was a labour of love, but it fitted into his philosophy of extended art works.'

One of Mark Lancaster's photographs of Hamilton working on the *Large Glass* shows the artist holding up a pane to study it. In his signature denim rodeo shirt with pearl buttons, and belted blue jeans, Hamilton looks every inch the artist hero, at once reflective and intense. The pane he is examining is a study for the *Oculist Witnesses* ('Peeping Toms', as Hamilton called them) of the *Large Glass* – their likenesses resembling machine parts of a device from the distant future.

There is a cosmology to the *Large Glass*, just as there is a mythic presence to Duchamp, which allows both to slip without effort into a broader iconography. In one sense, the *Large Glass* seems to exist as a diagrammatic representation of glamour, romance and sexuality – as a silent comedy, a cavernous mystery, a folly, a romance, a manifesto, an absurd pornographic fable. Ultimately, as Hamilton suggests, its possible 'meaning' is of less significance than its multi-layered articulation of a conceptualist way of thinking about art-making, the language of which is deeply personal to Duchamp.

Bryan Ferry's subsequent references to Duchamp contributed a further finesse to his pop vision – an awareness of artistic process, and the resonance of myth. Combine Duchamp's name with that of Smokey Robinson, and you present a cocktail of inspirations and influences which is as colourful as it is intoxicating.

Bryan Ferry: 'Later, I used the title "The Bride Stripped Bare" for a record of my own. It was just a conceit really, where I thought that it was such a wonderful title – a very curious title, in many ways – and especially for the mass public; that maybe it would lead them into learning about something more interesting.

'I like the idea of Duchamp taking something like a bicycle wheel and just placing it in a different context and putting his signature on it, really. And I guess I was thinking that when I took a song that was by somebody else, and did my own version of it: that I was adding my stamp to it, my signature. Like a ready-made – a song as a ready-made.'

There is a reflective quality to Duchamp's iconoclasm, which becomes a mirror of intentionality – his disciples and interpreters tend to find their own attitudes and interests reflected in the flawless surface of his conceptualism. Thus, for Ferry, Duchamp's identifies the power of selection and signature – a form of elevated connoisseurship. Thirty years later, by contrast, Brian Eno would make a somewhat more direct intervention into

Duchampian conceptualism by releasing a pipette of his own urine into Duchamp's 'ready-made' urinal, *Fountain* (1917), when it was on display at the Museum of Modern Art in New York. Eno's art school anarchism and creative questioning of cultural status and artistic systems might be discerned in this act – which, in its slapstick insolence, is also entirely in keeping with Duchamp's demand for art to be above all 'hilarious'.

Mark Lancaster's recollections of his two meetings with Marcel Duchamp in London in 1966, then have a pop panache of their own – flippant, deadpan, astute, cool . . .

Mark Lancaster: 'I met Marcel Duchamp at Richard Hamilton's house in London, when he came for his exhibition at the Tate Gallery in 1966. He asked me, "Etes vous artiste?" and when I said yes, or "Oui," he said, "Moi aussi." I met him and his wife, Teeny, in Carnaby Street, a few days later, where I had just bought a bright yellow suit. They admired it, but I didn't have the nerve to ask him to sign it . . .'

fourteen

Photographs of Bryan Ferry taken during his time at university show a noticeably good-looking young man. An abbreviated quotation from F. Scott Fitzgerald's posthumously published, unfinished novel, *The Last Tycoon* (1941), will serve to both describe his romantic appeal and provide an uncannily prophetic portrait of the future star:

> His dark eyes took me in, and I wondered what they would look like if he fell in love. They were kind, aloof, and, though they often reasoned with you gently, somewhat superior. It was no fault of theirs if they saw so much. He darted in and out of the role of 'one of the boys' with dexterity – but on the whole I should say he wasn't one of them. But he knew how to shut up, how to draw into the background, how to listen . . . He was born sleepless, with no talent for rest or the desire for it.

As good looks tend also to be an agent of social mobility, so Ferry would gradually become more involved in undergraduate life in Newcastle – slowly bringing to consciousness his attempt to combine his interests and ideas as an artist, with the possibilities and lifestyle offered up by music.

Casually, at this point, he occupied a divided ambition, being both a (reasonably) conscientious art student and, through his singing with two student groups, the City Blues and the Gas Board, a determined apprentice soul singer. As such he remained both an acolyte of the Bohemian ideal (maintaining his long-standing fantasy of life as an artist in a New York loft or a Left Bank garret), as well as an eager denizen of jazz and soul clubs.

The inherent conservatism of both pop music and fine art, however, as mutually sympathetic but rigidly separate, insular, and self-regarding professional worlds, would discourage a young art student such as Ferry from imagining that there might be a ready way to creatively combine the language and intentions of both. And yet Ferry's interests, artistically, were drawn from a source which admitted no particular distinctions of aesthetic or cultural status. As evidenced by his admiration for Hamilton's vision as an artist and choice of above all modern subject matter ('the shape of a car, or Marilyn Monroe') Ferry was immersed in a pop world where 'cool' could be conveyed across a range of media – from how you dressed, to the art you liked, the car you drove, the cigarettes you smoked, the company you kept, or being a singer in a soul group.

But it would not be fair or accurate to think of the student Bryan Ferry as an other-worldly pop aesthete, dedicated solely to the refinement of an artistic masterplan. As important were the traditional pleasures of independent undergraduate life ('It was a time of many parties,' as Richard Hamilton remarks); and in particular the sweaty, dynamic, muscular world of working as a young musician in demanding north-eastern clubs. Music, that 'very strong drug', as Ferry describes it, was exerting its addictive influence.

With both the City Blues and the Gas Board, the idea was to play forceful soul and R&B music – arguably Ferry's first musical loves. Andrew Mackay would later observe to the author that Ferry's first solo record, *These Foolish Things* (1973), subsequent to the success of the early Roxy Music material, would be a selection of his favourite soul songs, their temper refracted through Ferry's Englishness.

The City Blues began life as the earthily titled the City Blues Jug Blowers and were a four-piece group which included, on piano, a fellow resident of Ferry's hall of residence at Newcastle during his first year, one

Phil Chugg. At local north-eastern venues such as the Blue Note in Sunderland and the Manhole Club in Wallsend, the group played blues standards including Fats Domino's 'Blueberry Hill', and 'Crawling Up a Hill' and 'St James Infirmary' as recorded by John Mayall's Bluesbreakers. They also (as recounted by Chugg) played a cover of 'The Doctor's Cure' – a somewhat risqué number that the pianist had heard Alex Harvey perform at the Disc A Go Go in Bournemouth. (Glaswegian Alex Harvey, finding fame as the frontman of The Sensational Alex Harvey Band would later, briefly, be represented by Bryan Ferry's future friend and collaborator Dr Simon Puxley.)

The City Blues considered themselves 'too cool' to go in for the usual student photographs that might be taken around the university campus. And there must have been some substance to their sense of self-worth: Mia Thomas, manager of the Club A-Go-Go, was sufficiently impressed by them to consider backing them to record a demo. As chance would have it, Thomas's money was subsequently committed on another act, and the group missed their chance.

If the City Blues were to some extent a continuation of Ferry's experience of singing with the Banshees, then the Gas Board, with whom he sang between late 1965 and 1967, were a far more serious proposition in every respect, and would achieve considerable local success. The group would also include both Graham Simpson (later credited on *Roxy Music* as: 'Graham Simpson – Bass') and John Porter, who would play bass guitar as a 'guest artiste' on the second Roxy Music album, *For Your Pleasure*.

Performing regularly at the Club A-Go-Go, the Gas Board was an up-market seven-piece R&B group, with members also including Ian Watts, Mike Figgis (the future film director) and John Laws. This time, a publicity photograph was issued, in which Ferry wore a sharp needlepoint jacket and button-down shirt: 'Representation', the publicity shot announced, was by 'Dix Enterprises – 31 Byron Close, Ouston, Chester-Le-Street, County Durham'. A telephone number on the Birtley exchange followed. Thus established, the Gas Board became a firm favourite on the Newcastle scene.

Marcus Price: 'Everyone in Newcastle used to converge on the A-Go-Go on a Thursday night, when very often the Gas Board were playing. This was around 1965 to 1967. The Gas Board were very popular, and had quite a big following. They were always thought of as being quite arty – you were always aware of that with them. Bryan was very tall, very good look-ing and usually wore dark clothing . . .'

Bryan Ferry: 'When I got to university, I quickly looked around to see if there was anybody else [who might make music]; and in my hall of resi-dence [Henderson Hall], where I lived in my first year, there were a cou-ple of guys who were putting together a band, and I became the singer. That was the City Blues. By the following year I had found some people from other parts of the university who were better players, and that became the Gas Board.

'It was kind of weird; because there I was in what was supposedly the cool place to be studying art, but coincidentally I had discovered this other thing, which I guess was both a way of making money and a form of self-expression – although at this point, remember, I hadn't written anything. So it wasn't particularly deep – it was a bit lighter because you didn't feel that it was anything, really, you had invented or created your-self. But it was good fun.

'The City Blues band was "more of the same" – a bit more ethnic R&B than I'd been doing in the Banshees. But when it changed into the Gas Board we started doing some really good stuff. We discovered all the Stax people; and the guitar player was very good and could do Freddie King instrumentals. He had a fantastic collection of R&B records from America. It would be great to have a set list from that period to see what exactly we were doing. I do remember we did that song "Hey! Baby", which was more of a pop thing by Bruce Channel; and Bobby Bland – we did a few of those, because we had a horn section, and so it was quite sophisticated in that sense. We were guitar, bass, drums, tenor, alto, trum-pet and me – by which time I was playing a bit of harmonica as well. One or two people said that I "had a distinctive voice" – but that was as much as I got, I think. But I enjoyed playing with them, and by then we weren't playing working men's clubs, we were playing cooler sorts of places – music clubs and so on.

'When I knew Graham Simpson he was really bright. He read English when he was at university with me, and we lived in the same house when we were in the Gas Board. He used to drive the van; I booked the gigs and arranged the rehearsals, but he did everything else. He had a fantastic collection of Blue Note albums which were his pride and joy; he was very meticulous about anybody touching them. And he had some great girl-friends – he was maybe two years older than me. He was a bit of a char-acter. I liked Graham, and Roxy Music would never have happened without him. Just the fact that he spent all that time with me when I was writing the first songs – just plugging away on his bass, encouraging me. Being somebody to play something to, and with . . .'*

But the seriousness with which many of Ferry's friends and acquaintances took his pursuit of a singing career was tempered by the fact that most of them assumed he would put his studies as a painter first. And, ultimately, it would be the awareness that he was falling behind with his studies that would lead Ferry to leave the Gas Board, and return, initially, to his hard-held intention of becoming a full-time visual artist. By 1967, however, Ferry would have realised that what he actually wanted to do (and what then became his all-consuming, full-time artistic ambition) was find a way of combining fine art with pop music to create a new form – a new medium, almost – of meticulously honed, montaged and amplified pop stylishness.

In the meantime, as the rigours and demands of gigging with the Gas Board began to take their toll on Ferry's work as a student, it was a peri-od of change within the department of Fine Art. Mark Lancaster, in addi-tion to deepening his relationship with America, and with New York in particular, would move to London in 1966. Similarly, Richard Hamilton, had decided to leave his teaching post at Newcastle (by his own account, he had only meant to stay a few years, and ended up staying thirteen), and return to his own work in London.

The latter half of the 1960s would see Hamilton making some of his best known works, most notably his *Swingeing London '67* series (based on a newspaper image depicting the arrest of Mick Jagger and Hamilton's friend and now art dealer, Robert Fraser) and one of his masterpieces, *I'm Dreaming of a White Christmas* (1967), based on a Panavision 70mm nega-tive frame from Paramount's 1942 film *Holiday Inn*, starring Bing Crosby. In 1968, Hamilton would also be approached by Paul McCartney, via

---

* The 'listening' collaborator would become an increasingly important factor in Ferry's creative chemistry – a role within which, as discussed later, Dr Simon Puxley would become virtually indispensable.

Robert Fraser, to create the design and packaging for what became known as the *White Album* (due to Hamilton's design) by the Beatles. Arguably, Hamilton's design for the *White Album* is rivalled only by Warhol's portraits of Elvis Presley, Marilyn Monroe, Elizabeth Taylor and Jackie Kennedy as one of the great statements in art about modern global celebrity. Certainly, the design might be read as a 'last word' in the broader cultural etymology of Pop art.

In his career-long fusion of art, design and mass media, with a specific interest in the object/multiple, Hamilton's work with the Beatles enabled him to undertake a print job of virtually unlimited editioning. And the power of the Beatles was such that, as he later wrote, 'they could override the usual commercial niggling'.

Richard Hamilton: 'Robert Fraser threw the best parties of any of the galleries. And if there was an Oldenburg opening or a Jim Dine opening all the major musicians would be there. So when the Beatles asked me to do the *White Album*, it was because Robert Fraser had put me up for it. But I was a bit reluctant really. I knew what album covers were like, and I couldn't see myself doing something within that genre. Which I suppose is the reason I had apprehensions about it.

'When I got to this meeting that had been arranged in the Beatles' office in Savile Row, I was sitting waiting in an outer office watching beautiful girls in mini skirts taking dogs out for a walk and things like that. The whole thing was so artificial and silly – and I was getting bored stiff, thinking what am I doing here? Then I was allowed into the presence of Paul, and by that time I was bad-tempered. So when he said that they wanted me to do the cover of this album they were working on, I said "Why don't you do it yourself?" That was my first reaction.

'Then Paul said, "Come on, haven't you got any ideas?" and I said, "Well my best idea is to leave a white cover" – and it went on from there. So I hadn't gone in with the intention of doing a white album cover. It was just provoked by this irritation I had at seeing all this nonsense going on.

'As it developed, I realised that I couldn't leave it white and I'd better do this inside poster. Paul was very good and went along with everything I said. I had thought that it was going to be too difficult, really – that they'd have trouble selling it to EMI. But they were so powerful that they could do it – no arguments.

'And so Paul would come up every afternoon and see what was going on. The recording of the album was done, but they were mixing it. He'd come to mine at about half past two, or three, and stay until about five, then go off to Abbey Road – we were quite near. He was always interested in what was going on, and I don't think that I could have really had any success with what I thought I might do, without his help.

'I said that I'd need material [for the collage that became the poster insert that came with the double album], and asked Paul if he could get photographs of himself, George, Ringo and John, and just give me the ones which haven't been used. And to my surprise, they each sent up a tea chest filled with stuff – so a lot of the time was spent with sifting through this, and coming up with strange photographs . . . There was everything. I have a photograph still, in the studio, which is of Paul – a passport photograph, but he's got glasses and a black moustache like Groucho Marx.

'When we were doing the record [the *White Album*] we had to put numbers on them; and I said "I'll have Number One"; and Paul said "Not on your nelly – we'll have the first four!" So I made mine . . . Zero! To get some idea of how many digits would be required, I asked Paul first of all. He said "Well, over a million"; and so I said "Do you mean, over ten million?" And he said "eight million" – he wouldn't go further than that! But maybe they did run out of numbers . . .'*

As Hamilton returned to London in 1966, so Mark Lancaster – having already had a successful exhibition in November 1965, at the prestigious Rowan Gallery in Belgravia, of sixteen acrylic on canvas paintings – would also settle in the capital, then commuting four days a week to teach at the Bath Academy of Art, where Michael Craig-Martin was also teaching. His exhibition at the Rowan had reflected his burgeoning passion for modern, popist Americana (as well as including, with fetching incongruity, a painting based upon the striped pattern of his parents' lawn in Yorkshire). This aside, the paintings took subjects including the department store Bonwit Teller, Lesley Gore, Third Avenue, Bloomingdales, Baby Jane Holzer, the architect Raymond Hood, baggage reclaim, Sears Roebuck and Marlene Dietrich.

---

* One wonders what the result would have been had Richard Hamilton 'produced' the first release by Roxy Music, in the same way that Andy Warhol had lent his influence, artwork and charisma to the production of *The Velvet Underground & Nico*.

Lancaster's abiding attraction to America took him back to New York in the summer of 1966, where once again he was at the white-hot centre of Andy Warhol's increasingly heady and volatile milieu. This would lead, in September that year, to Lancaster's witnessing of the filming of *Chelsea Girls*, and to experiencing first hand the volatility and emotional fragility of Andy's 'superstars'.

Mark Lancaster: 'I hung out at the Factory a few days, and one day arrived as they were setting up a scene. I think the filming of *The Chelsea Girls* was mostly completed. This was early September. A set had been built to look like a small room, and in it was a kind of throne/bed for Ondine. I don't remember how many people were there, but Andy was at the camera and he asked me to hold the microphone, just out of camera range at the side of the "set". The film started rolling. Does he shoot himself up with speed on camera? I don't remember. This girl, a kind of idiotic creature, I had already decided, starts this "confession" dialogue with "Pope" Ondine, who after a few minutes calls her a "phoney". I think the second time he says this, Ondine gets visibly angry, screams at her, throws a glass of Coke at her, then lunges towards her and starts hitting her.

'By this time I felt sure that this was not "acting" as it were. I was quite scared, and saw that other people were backing away. I put the mike down on something and backed away myself, noticing then that Andy had also done so, leaving the camera running. I think the girl ended up running out screaming.

'Oddly enough, a friend of mine from England, Roger Cook [artist and academic, expert on Warhol, who taught at Reading University where he would also know Rita Donagh], was on his first trip to New York, and I had invited him to the Factory that day to meet Andy. He was on a bus coming uptown from the village and that girl was on the bus, and he had thought her odd, from her appearance if nothing else, and he had followed her into the Factory and arrived right as the filming started. His original account was that after this scene I was totally nonchalant and introduced him to Andy. I told him I was actually terrified, and I was "acting cool".'

Roger Cook: 'I had come over to the US on a Stuyvesant scholarship, which I had won through the Whitechapel New Generation exhibition. Rita [Donagh] was in New York at the same time. So I phoned Mark — who invited me over to the Factory; and although I was twenty-six at the time I was probably far more naive than a postgraduate student would be now. I'd bought this rather smart suit from Jaeger — it was the time of Beatle suits worn with thin ties — and this was what I was wearing.

'So Mark told me to get on the bus to East 47th Street. The first thing I noticed when I got on the bus was this woman sitting opposite, whom I now recognise was dressed as a hippy — but at that period such a thing barely existed. She was wearing an oriental skirt — an odd figure. But when I reached my stop, she got off at the same time, and lo and behold walked up the same street. I had been told to shout up to the window, where somebody would throw down the keys; I had also been told that the lift was a big industrial sort, and I should be careful not to be noisy because they would be filming.

'Anyway, before I could shout up, this woman had shouted up, and got the keys. She let herself in and went up the stairs, while I took the lift. When I got to the top I tried to open the door as quietly as I could, and then squeezed in to what I now know is the most mythical space. There seemed to be people lounging around, and leaning against pillars; and they all seemed to be completely stoned, and most probably were.

'Pope Ondine was on the couch, starting this extraordinary part of the film where he's asking "Anyone wanna confess? Anyone wanna confess?" At which point this woman who had been on the bus, ran onto the set and started this dialogue with Pope Ondine. It was all obscenities, and it remains in the finished film. And then all of a sudden, Ondine says to her, "You're nothing but a phoney", and throws a glass of water over her. He then started to hit her, really violently, around the face.

'It was so bad that I was on the verge of running on to the set to stop it; but before I could she had run off — with Warhol following her with a camera. Mark was recording the sound, and he just sort of emerged from behind the set and said, "Oh hi, Roger — come and meet Andy." By which time I was shaking like a leaf. I think I said that I didn't want to meet Andy, I just wanted to get the hell out of there. What had happened was just horrible. And Mark said, "Oh, this kind of thing happens every day around here, don't worry about it . . ." So then I went and met Warhol —

all I remember of which was that his skin was grey and his hand was like a wet dishcloth.

'A few nights later we went to the premiere of the film, and then to see the Velvet Underground at the Dom – where we also met Rita. I think she was staying with the Copleys . . .'

As Cook recalls, this same late summer, he and Lancaster saw the Velvet Underground perform as part of Warhol's 'Exploding Plastic Inevitable' multi-media show. The group – at that time, like hippies, barely known, and largely dismissed by those who did know about them – would become perhaps the only musical reference point to be shared by all the founding members of Roxy Music. The group's collision of 'pop' songs and avant-garde improvisation, artistic sophistication and 'street' style, intellect and physicality would be qualities included amongst Roxy Music's formative influences.

Mark Lancaster: 'I think it was a few days after the Ondine scene that Andy invited us to go to the first night of the "Exploding Plastic Inevitable" at the Dom on St Mark's Place. The Velvets and Nico had performed there earlier in the year, but I had been under the impression that this was the first performance. It was a kind of reunion, I guess. This was before any of their records were out, so it was a totally new experience. I remember approaching the place, I think it had been one of those Polish ballrooms they had on the Lower East Side, in the dark, and seeing Jonathan Miller on the street. I had met him once in London, and I told him about what we were going to see, but he said he was late for something and couldn't go. I guess I had a ticket or invitation or something, but it was very crowded and I spotted Andy upstairs in the balcony and went up. That may have been the first time I met Paul Morrissey.

'There were slide projectors and movie projectors and spotlights and as soon as the Velvets and Nico came out on the stage below, everything happened at once. The sound, the lights, the movie against the back wall, the slides of stars and cut-out shapes, the strobe lights, the coloured beams of light. The sound was overwhelming and stunningly raw, but Nico's droning voice on "I'll Be Your Mirror" was also clear and mesmerising. My memory tells me that was the first song, but I really don't know.

There was a seemingly endless version of "Heroin" and there was "All Tomorrow's Parties" and more and more.

'Andy looked ecstatic, in the glow of lights in the balcony. It was like this was his new world. I think they showed whatever reels of film were around, and I'm pretty sure some of it was from the yet to be finished *The Chelsea Girls*. Gerry was in leather pants, dancing with Mary Woronov, and he had a whip and also two huge flashlights which he danced with, beaming them into the audience. The old mirror ball from the Factory was hanging in the middle, and the strobe lights flickered and it was a kind of excess I had never experienced before. And I loved it. It was kind of crummy at the same time, with things being improvised, feedback. I seem to remember somebody was projecting some slides Andy didn't like, but overall it was amazing. This was before the big light shows went around with rock groups, but it was the almost non-musical sound of the early Velvets that was shockingly raw. It was so close to "noise" and yet it was hypnotic, and it was, of course, years before their influence turned out to be huge.'

In his notebook for 1966, Lancaster wrote down his immediate impressions of the EPI, as a list of remembered details:

Andy Warhol's Plastic Inevitable
Balloon Farm
The Velvet Underground and Nico
Upstairs at the Dom – mirrored and marbled ballroom
Two slide projectors (Carousels) striped, dotted, check, coloured filters,
on time changers every 3 seconds – on end and ceiling
movies from 3 points – on balcony. Reflections of projections.
2 electric bubble making machines
3 stroboscopic lamps
2 long electric torces danced by Gerard
Nico's child.
Mary Woronov stands there after covering G with gold paint,
& he does it all so well so badly, like an Italian epic movie.

Lancaster's reference to Warhol seeming to have created through the EPI and the Velvet Underground a 'new' world that he was now inhabiting, chimes directly with Brian Eno's comment about the capacity and effect of pop music to make new, imaginary worlds, and invite people to try them out.

Rita Donagh also attended this show, later recalling the same impression that Mark Lancaster observed of Warhol directing and watching the events from the balcony: 'Andy stood alone on a balcony high up directing the performance. This strange figure seemed to me, with my Roman Catholic upbringing, to be the prince of darkness. This was a side of life that I had not been instructed in at the convent.'

Roger Cook: 'I remember vividly Warhol up on the balcony at the Dom. And what is incredible now is quite how crude it all was, technically: just projectors aimed at the stage that Warhol orchestrated. It seemed to me that everyone was on drugs. I remember Nico and her child on stage, and the whip dance. I suspect it was all far more innocent than it seemed at the time. I thought that all these people were about to go over a cliff – which in fact a lot of them did. But the music was danceable. At the time, one simply didn't know who they were.'

Warhol would be an important figure in some of Donagh's 'Figure Compositions' series – notably appearing in her *Shadow* (painted in 1964–65, before Donagh actually saw the EPI in New York) and in Holbeinesque, elongated form in her aptly titled *42nd Street* (1965–6) and *Underworld* (1966). Donagh's representations of Warhol within her art seem to capture the glamour and enigma which swiftly became a part of his legend – he takes his place within her work as both static and fluid, his image transposed in such a way that he seems both factual and auric.

This was a time that would also mark a significant change within the Fine Art department at Newcastle. The departure of Richard Hamilton, and the fact that Rita Donagh (having been a studio demonstrator at Newcastle between 1962 and 1964) was now teaching at Reading University, meant that by the time Mark Lancaster made his move to London towards the end of 1966, a generational shift had occurred within the department.

The fates of those students who had been directly within Hamilton's coterie were now in the hands of the remaining members of the faculty – some of whom were less disposed to recognise or reward the lines of enquiry which were being explored. But help was at hand in the shape of

Northumbrian born and Newcastle educated abstract artist Ian Stephenson (1934–2000), who would subsequently be based at Chelsea School of Art. Immediate to Hamilton's departure, it was Stephenson – himself exploring ideas in the late 1960s such as 'throwing' paint on to a canvas placed flat on blocks on the floor – who would represent the more modern faction within the department.

Tim Head: 'Ian Stephenson, really, protected a group of us. I nearly got failed, at one point; and there was a slight antagonism towards people who had been part of Richard's "group". Ian was somebody we could talk to. I don't think his sensibility was ours; but he took an interest in what we did, and supported us. Obviously, when it came to the marking, we all got 2:1s or whatever it was. Otherwise, we'd probably all have got failed.'

But the 'group' would survive, maintaining their interest in the latest developments in American art in particular. Between 1966 and his own graduation in 1968, Ferry's divided ambition, attracted to both music and fine art, would steer its course between the two until his last eighteen months at university. Life as a student was proving interesting and liberating, with recognition as a good-looking young singer being matched by the sociable pop bohemianism of life as an art student.

It was also in 1966 that Bryan Ferry and Stephen Buckley made the acquaintance of an historian and aesthete called Jeremy Catto, who would become a lifelong friend of Ferry and a formative influence on his aesthetic and social education. Brought up in Newcastle and educated at Balliol College, Oxford, Catto was then teaching at Durham University, and would later teach History at Oxford, specialising in the social and religious history of fourteenth- and fifteenth-century England.

A connoisseur and scholar, with an interest in aesthetic style that included on the one hand the boutiques of the King's Road (buying clothes from Granny Takes A Trip, as well as from Carnaby Street), and on the other the imagism of Ezra Pound's *Cantos*, Catto represented an elevated, academically assured sophistication and sense of taste – the attributes, in one sense, of an 'upper', socially confident class, at ease in both their leisure and their intellectual outlook. As the brilliant agent of a particular glamour Catto helped make real the finer world of art and culture that had been signified to the young Bryan Ferry by the classicism of the Penshaw Monument, back in Washington.

Jeremy Catto: 'In June 1966, I had been to a party in Newcastle with some students from Newcastle University. At that time, I was lecturing in the University of Durham, and I knew Newcastle well, anyway. I didn't meet Stephen and Bryan at the party, but I was having a drink in a low bar in the big market, the Royal Court, and they came in. Stephen, who was always the more forward of the two, said to me, "Weren't we at the same party the previous night?" and I said, "Yes, we were" – and indeed we had been. So we got drinking, and then we decided we'd go off to a nightclub in South Shields – which, typical of the north-east in those days, turned out to be shut. And so we came back again.

'After that I came to see them. They lived in Eslington Terrace in those days. So we decided to go off and have a little Mediterranean holiday, because I had to go on a research trip to see some manuscripts. I drove, because neither of them could – although Bryan did learn at that point, a little. We ended up somewhere south of Naples. It was very good. We had quite a lot of friends as it turned out in Newcastle, and we have remained friends ever since. Bryan must have been about twenty . . .'

Photographs taken during the first years of their friendship, and in partic-ular of the holiday in southern Italy which Buckley and Ferry took with Catto in August 1966, show a supremely cool trio of travellers: Ferry in pink button-down shirt and slick aviator-style dark glasses; Buckley in pristine white T-shirt and brown fedora; Catto, his hair Hockney blond, wearing jet-black Ray-Ban sunglasses. And Catto clearly found the com-pany of Ferry and Buckley equally stimulating – taking specific interest in Buckley's ideas on the artistic relationships between style and taste.

Jeremy Catto: 'I liked these guys very much, but I didn't know anything about modern art. I learned about modern art from speaking with Stephen. I had two or three lunches with Mark Lancaster in London. He was extremely nice. I could see he was a very brilliant man, and they revered him enormously. He was a little bit older than them.

'But I do think our trip to Italy had quite an effect on Bryan. I think it was the first time he had been there, and he was affected by both the obvious historic beauties of Florence, where we stayed for a day or two, and by Assisi. And of course Italy in the 1960s was very much a land of style. Italian youth dressed well in those days; now they wear reach-me-down American grunge of the worst kind. In those days, I think both Stephen and Bryan were affected by the people they saw. Crossing into Italy is a different world – it feels like a different world.'

Catto also identified the shifts in taste and cultural fashion which would occur between the closing years of the 1960s and the first half of the 1970s. As the underground ideology of drugs, radicalism and revolution had dominated much of the British subculture throughout the latter half of the 1960s, so the early 1970s would see their replacement, in certain more urbane quarters, with a modish nostalgia for elegance – an attitude that Roxy Music would make so eloquent and of which they would be hailed as the chief exponents.

Jeremy Catto: 'I think that Bryan and I were both in search of style, of various kinds – a desire to be at the edge of things. That was something we wanted to find in those days. I also introduced him to quite a lot of people that he liked. He went to stay in Menorca at a friend of mine's house – he painted a fresco. I don't know whether it's still there.★

'The sixties were a period when there was a feeling of hope around; it looked like there were some new ideas emerging, and we looked for them. Stephen influenced me a great deal – more than I influenced him, in his view of style. I've told you his remark, "The trouble with England, there's too much taste and not enough style." Which is absolutely true. I don't know whether he made it up. But I think one felt that.

'The latter half of the sixties was different, from "Waterloo Sunset" (1967) to "American Pie" (1972). I got a bit sick of the 1890s decadence, and preferred the twenties in terms of style: the Silver Age of Aesthetes. I was extremely keen on that, because I've always been keen on the poetry of Pound. In a way it's beyond understanding I think; it doesn't matter, it's so beautiful. Any man, who's written a line about gin, you know, in poetry – somewhere in section "Rock Drill" of the *Cantos* is the line, ". . . not gin in cut glass had such clarity".

★ A postcard from Catto to Ferry from this period includes the remark, 'This is rather the sort of mural I want . . . I meant to remind you that I would love you to cover the odd wall in deathless art . . .'

'The hard imagist style in Pound, struck me as more interesting, in the long run, than my more teenage cult of Decadence. So in a way, I have a feeling for the twenties . . .'

Stephen Buckley: 'Also very important was the Morden Tower Bookshop. It was run by a man called Tom Pickard, and it was actually one of the watchtowers on the city walls of Newcastle [between Westgate and Gallowgate on Back Stowell Street]. Basil Bunting, who had been this protégé of Ezra Pound, had been rediscovered working on the *Evening Standard*, and Richard [Hamilton] did the first cataloguing of Basil's work, in this brown paper package called "King Ida's Watchchain" . . .'

As a venue for avant-garde writers (Ginsberg and Ferlinghetti, of the American 'beat' writers, for example, came to read there), the Morden Tower was a further example of the importance of small, independent, embassies of 'otherness' in British provincial cities in the 1960s. As the tower showcased a range of American and European poets, so in their broader function such venues and their audiences would often comprise perhaps the only available information on new or 'alternative' movements – from feminism and veganism to the teachings of Wilhelm Reich or the publications of the underground press.

Mark Lancaster: 'Tom Pickard was this kid who was amazing in a way I never quite figured at the time. These things just happened. I went to all the Morden Tower things.'

Bryan Ferry: 'I remember being there at a couple of the Morden Tower poetry readings – people like Allen Ginsberg. But I would rather have been chasing girls around Newcastle.'

As his meeting with Jeremy Catto in the early summer of 1966 had presented Ferry with a personage whose friendship would continue to have a profound influence upon his sense of self, so the following year would include a pivotal musical experience, the impact of which would be vital to Ferry's personal and creative resolution of the processes of fine art and the world of music. The same encounter would also come to mark the beginnings of Ferry's move to London – where within just four years he would have become one of the most fashionable and critically acclaimed new figures in pop and rock music.

Bryan Ferry: 'I remember hitch-hiking down to London to see Otis Redding play in '67 – his last tour I think; he died a little later that year. I think it was at the Roundhouse where I saw them play, and it was a great moment for me – a turning point, a Road to Damascus situation.

'I had been convinced that I was going to be a painter, and that my music "thing" was just a bit of fun. But after I saw that concert, I felt that I really must do something in music when I graduate. And I realised that the only way I was going to make music and for it to mean anything, would be to write some stuff, and try and combine the two lives: one of working in this quite intellectual, fine art school, which is wholly different from the very physical world of music – a very earthy thing. How do you combine them?

'When I got to London I just started writing songs and finding people who could play them – putting together the band. There was me and Graham first, and then the next would be Andy Mackay . . .'

But Ferry's ultimate decision to pursue a career in music did not prevent him from working assiduously towards obtaining his final degree, and from showing his work in various exhibitions during 1967. Indeed, Ferry's respectable showing in gallery exhibitions during his final years at university suggests that he was on a perfectly acceptable trajectory to pursue his career as a visual artist at a postgraduate level. This, in turn, heightens the importance of his decision to try to find a way of resolving the worlds of music and fine art.

The slim guide to the 'Summer Exhibition of Students Work, 1967' held at the Hatton Gallery, lists work by Nicholas de Ville (*4 Corners*), Stephen Buckley (*Bamboo*) and Bryan Ferry (*Spray*). The Arts Council exhibition, 'Northern Young Contemporaries, 67–68' (a prestigious showcase for work by new artists) likewise includes a work in acrylic by Ferry from 1966. More spectacular, however, and subsequently of note because of its eye-catching poster, rather than the works exhibited, was the exhibition held of Ferry's work at Dunhelm House, at Durham University, between 25 November and 10 December 1967. A photograph of Ferry taken by Jane McNulty served as the poster for the exhibition – featuring his Studebaker car which would later make a guest appearance in the lyric for 'Virginia Plain' – asserting in Hamiltonesque fashion the influence and importance of pop cultural media.

Tim Head: 'Bryan had a metallic green Studebaker, and Eslington Terrace was a row of houses which looked out on to a line of trees with a railway line underneath. Bryan always had this beautiful car parked outside – I never saw it go anywhere. Maybe it never did. But it looked great. Bryan had a show of his paintings, as Stephen did as well, at Durham University – someone they knew there used to throw open a room and put on a show. So there was this amazing photo that Jane McNulty took for a beautiful poster, of Bryan leaning nonchalantly against this American car, against a background of trees – so it looked as though it could have been Melrose Avenue, rather than Eslington Terrace. It's a beautiful image, and pre-dates all the Roxy covers. Nick was in my year, and lived at 14 Eslington Terrace, which was just two doors along.

'Bryan's ambitions then were more to do with art. He was singing in the Gas Board, and obviously interested in music, but it wasn't until I re-met him in London, a few years later, that he said he was writing these songs. So at that earlier point, we all hoped that we would one day become famous artists.'

The *Northern Echo* covered the opening of Ferry's exhibition at Dunhelm under the somewhat dramatic headline, 'Angry Young Artist's Chance'. It is eloquent of the times and the place that this reasonably small show was reported with due seriousness as 'news':

> After four years studying art at Newcastle University, 22-year-old Bryan Ferry was last night given a chance to show the public his work at his first one-man exhibition. Held in the staff club at Dunhelm House, a private viewing was given for personal friends and members of the Press, and will be open to the public until December 10th. Son of a Washington miner, Bryan criticised the 'narrow minded' North East picture buying public. He said, 'It is sad that there's no market for the less conventional type of painting in the North East. The people with money do not want abstract paintings, but tend to prefer the pretty landscape.' He would be happy, he said, if his paintings could give pleasure to people of all levels. 'In any case, someone uninitiated in the art world would probably be more honest in his outburst of appraisal.'

Ferry and his peers were in a prime position to commence careers as a new generation of significant artists. Far from being the products of a provincial backwater, their experience at Newcastle, coupled with the relationship to New York enabled by Hamilton, provided all of the 'Hamilton group' with solid, lively ideas in their own work, and an impressive sophistication of cultural outlook.

By 1969, Stephen Buckley, Tim Head and Nicholas de Ville would all have spent time in the US, while Mark Lancaster, subsequent to a position as artist in residence at King's College, Cambridge, would settle in America permanently in 1972, as close friend and assistant to the artist Jasper Johns. For both Head and Buckley, their trips to America towards the end of the 1960s would be filled with heady experience and a chance to witness the American pop avant-garde at close proximity. For Head, his time in New York would also introduce him first hand to the musical avant-garde of LaMonte Young and Terry Riley, as well as their peers, the Velvet Underground.

Tim Head: 'I spent a summer in New York, in 1968, working for Claes Oldenburg, and had met a lot of artists. In those days, I guess it was much easier to meet people; they were more friendly and willing to open their studio doors to a mere student. And so I got to meet a lot of wonderful people: Robert Smithson, Eva Hess, Sol Le Wit. Robert Smithson's writings were very important to me. Richard Hamilton knew all these people and was connected to them. It wasn't like it was such a distant thing. Then we'd go and visit Richard in London, and see his studio. So, it just made you feel that you were in touch with things that were happening in the world of art.

'Oldenburg was still in that wonderful original studio of his on 14th Street. It was a vast loft that ran the length of a whole block, and so he used to say that his bedroom was up in the Eighties, the dining room was in Mid-town and the storeroom below Canal Street.

'He was about to have a retrospective at MoMA, and I was putting together all these plaster pieces that had got packed away at his studio, some of which had got damaged – so I was gluing them back together and repainting bits. I actually thought about staying in New York, but I had an extra year to go at Newcastle so I came back. My life might have been very different had I stayed; it was a good time to be in New York – a lot of things were changing and happening.

'Mark Lancaster had been there earlier, of course, helping Warhol, and he gave me some introductions which were very helpful. There was Billy Copley, the son of Bill Copley who was the big collector of surrealism and an artist – CPLY. Billy did the Terry Riley *In C* album cover – which is just these musical notes. He knew Riley and LaMonte Young; and I remember going to see LaMonte Young, although I didn't know who the hell he was at the time.

'I was working for a silkscreen printers to earn money, as well as working for Oldenburg, and next door to the printers it said "John Cale" on the entry. So one day I asked whether he was John Cale of the Velvet Underground, and we had a long conversation that ended in him giving me these tickets to a concert they were doing in Boston at this place called the Tea Party – which is since long gone. Nico wasn't there – she was in Europe that summer; but everyone else was there. They played songs off the first album, and then the second half was just "Sister Ray". Everyone was spaced out, and it seemed to go on for hours.

'Andy Warhol had just been shot, a few weeks before I arrived, and Billy Name took me around the Factory – they'd just moved to Union Square. It was a village feel, almost. SoHo was just a commercial district back then, with a few artists who had lofts. There were no shops and galleries and boutiques. I saw the Soft Machine playing in the Museum of Modern Art gardens – strange that I should have to go to New York to see the Soft Machine . . .'

Bryan Ferry would graduate from Newcastle University with a 2.2 in Fine Art in June 1968. His student dissertation was written on the academically highly respectable subject of Seurat, the tragically short-lived nineteenth-century French artist and inventor of pointillism – some of whose later work, such as his painting *Le Chahut*, made a year before his death in 1891, depict Parisian nightclub and theatre scenes of the sort which Ferry's later songs and image would also evoke.

A travelling scholarship from the Royal College of Art would provide Ferry with immediate funds – although his principal journey would be straight from Newcastle to London. But by this time, he would also have become friends with Susie Cussins – the beautiful daughter of a wealthy Newcastle family, whose fortune derived from building. Further photographs by Jeremy Catto, taken at the Cussins' house in the high summer of 1969, have a somewhat idyllic air: Bryan dressed in black playing croquet on a vast flawless lawn, a stately chestnut tree overhanging the wall; more daring – Bryan, topless, lying on his back with flowers crossed on his chest, as though Millais's *Ophelia* had been re-styled by Gerard Malanga; or Bryan appreciating the luxuriant cerise pink blossoms of a flowering rhododendron, Susie sitting at his feet, resting her head against his leg with all the lilting grace of an art nouveau figurine.

Jeremy Catto: 'Bryan had to write a dissertation for his degree, and so he asked me what he should write about. I said, why don't you write about society painters of the 1910s? He didn't – he wrote about something more modern; but he said, many years later, that he should have done. I thought he should do something on Baldini [a painter best known for his sumptuous portrait, in shades of dove grey, lavender blue and silver, of Robert, Comte de Montesquiou, a friend of Proust and Wilde] or someone like that. It would have been just the thing for him, in a way.

'Susie, indeed, was a very nice girl, and very intelligent. She decided to marry a man who became one of President Reagan's advisors, a person of high rank in the CIA . . .'

Bryan Ferry: 'I think I have probably always been interested in elites. I remember when I left school very much wanting to go to university rather than art college – and at that time there was quite a difference. There were only about three universities you could go to, to study fine art, and you felt you were going to be with people who were more interested in the thought and theory of it. Whereas if you went to art school you'd be with people who were good at drawing rather than good at thinking. That's how it seemed to be. It was more difficult to get into university, but I suppose that you'd meet "a better class of person". I guess I had a fairly elitist view of what I was interested in. So I suppose I've always been a bit stuck up; I liked being with smart people rather than those who weren't. I wanted to be with people who would get me going, and not only at university.

'I remember when I was living in Newcastle for those four years, and you'd want to go to the clubs where the best-looking girls or the coolest people were. And there were cliques and elites wherever you looked; and I noticed that when I came to London as well. Although I can't say that I ever graduated to becoming a part of any particular group. I've always felt outside, and that's one characteristic of me I suppose. I've always been on the outside looking in. Or the inside looking out.'

There was an Indian summer feel, perhaps, to the subcultural mood towards the end of the 1960s; the sense of an era reaching its end, deliquescent, at times violent, anticipatory of change – a new term beginning.

Mark Lancaster: 'In 1968, at the ICA, the Duchamps were present when Arturo Schwartz gave a lecture on Duchamp's work, including implications of possibly incestuous feelings between Marcel and his sister. Duchamp appeared to snooze throughout. This occasion was on 5 June 1968, two days after Andy Warhol was shot, and just hours before Bobby Kennedy was assassinated in Los Angeles. Duchamp died later that year, too.'

In such a climate, during a long afternoon of flamboyant styles and progressive attitudes, approaching the cusp of the decade, the friends and acquaintances from the department of Fine Art at Newcastle University would all be moving, or have already moved, towards London and the south, to Cambridge and to Reading. The network of their sensibility would not only remain intact, but begin to expand, acquiring sympathetic, convergent new spirits from the worlds of art, fashion, ceramics, photography, performance and music.

In the closing years of the decade, Tim Head would go to London to take a postgraduate qualification at Saint Martin's School of Art; Nicholas de Ville would work firstly as a studio assistant to Richard Hamilton, then with Anthony Donaldson, and so would also become immersed in the London art world of the late 1960s and early 1970s; Stephen Buckley had followed Rita Donagh to Reading, where he took his MFA in Fine Art between 1967 and 1969, prior to teaching in Canterbury. Mark Lancaster, as artist in residence at King's College, Cambridge, would watch the moon landings alone in a small Gothic room with the ninety-year-old novelist E. M. Forster, whom he recalls describing the event as 'an unnecessary adventure'.

Alert, now, to the demands of his vision of a new kind of pop group, quite different in temperament or style from anything that had gone before, Bryan Ferry would take his place in London with an eye to locating those artists and collaborators who might best realise this complex, vivid, fast, grandiose, erotic, romantically overloaded, modern work of art – its haunting shade a clash of jarring colours.

part 2

reading, ipswich,
winchester 1964–1969

'I was a teenage art school.'
Brian Eno, notebook, 1969

fifteen

Karl Stoecker's photographic 'postcard' portraits of Andy Mackay and Brian Eno, as they took their place in 1972 on the backdrop design of silver-blue quilted vinyl that ran across the inside of *Roxy Music*'s gatefold sleeve, show two hyper-stylised, imperiously aloof and intently peculiar looking young men.

Mackay, in a tight, black, silver-buttoned shirt, is stunningly handsome – a mascaraed rocker, greasy quiff piled high at the front and straggling in disdainful rat-tails down the nape of his neck. Chin resting on hand, each finger wearing a heavy ring, his image is that of the brooding, loner rebel: a one-shot amplification of the rock and roll style of fifties Americana.

Four years earlier, this same young man had been dressing as a European aesthete of the early Modernist period – complete with austere side-parted hair, a scholar's round-framed glasses, white linen jacket, high knotted cravat and a wild flower in his buttonhole. The common denominator of the two looks – the Wild One and the Wilde one – was their devout romanticism.

Brian Eno – abbreviated, like Mozart, to the single name Eno – presents in Stoecker's portrait a more sinister proposition. Finely and sensually featured, his look is less loner than other-worldly; in a blouson of blue-tinted leopard print, his shoulder-length hair swept back from his professorially high forehead, he is photographed gazing placidly down-wards, his inscrutability bringing to mind the pitiless sangfroid of a cruel yet highly cultured dauphin. Like Mackay, he looks less a pop or rock musician and more a time-travelling visitor from another planet, experiencing earth in the early years of the 1970s with an expression of tolerant disgust.

Sealed so successfully within their artfully recreated personae, where had these two young men – one a musician classically trained to degree standard, the other a self-confessed 'non-musician' – emerged from? Were they as effortlessly cool and aloof as their images suggested? What was the constitution of their curiously contrived-looking glamour? The answers to these questions lay in a further network of student friendships – for Mackay at Reading, and Eno at Ipswich and Winchester – and the formative resolution of fine artistic, pop cultural and determinedly flamboyant attitudes out of which Roxy Music would emerge.

Amongst the diaspora from Newcastle University's Fine Art depart-ment during the middle and latter years of the 1960s, Stephen Buckley, Rita Donagh and Tim Head would all acquire links, professionally, per-sonally, or both, to the equivalent department of Fine Art at the cam-pus-based, 'red brick' University of Reading. There was also a connection within the older generation: Terry Frost, the great abstract artist and lecturer in painting at Reading in the mid-sixties, was a Fellow at Newcastle, and had once been taught by Hamilton's former colleague Victor Pasmore, during the latter's period as a tutor at Camberwell School of Art, London, in the mid-1940s.

Meanwhile, over at Ipswich Civic College, Newcastle University grad-uate Roy Ascott would inaugurate in 1964 – the date of Brian Eno's arrival at the college – his highly controversial, cybernetics and behaviourism inspired 'Groundcourse' which he had first developed at Ealing Art College two years earlier. (Ascott had been photographed at work with his students by Lord Snowdon, who would subsequently include the image in his visual compendium of the swinging sixties, *Private View: The Lively World of British Art*, published in 1965.)

Rita Donagh in particular would become an iconic figure for the new generation at Reading. In her first appointment on leaving the centre of pop cool at Newcastle, where she in turn had been studio demonstrator between 1962 and 1964, Donagh was regarded at Reading as not just an inspiring teacher, but supremely modern, progressive in her thinking, and remembered by one former student, Viv Kemp, as being always impeccably dressed in an ensemble of grey, white and black.

Working alongside Mark Lancaster's friend Roger Cook (who, like Lancaster, was at this time represented by the Rowan Gallery), Donagh became an immediately energising presence in the Art department – crucially, with a pronounced interest in contemporary avant-garde music and performance. As a consequence, John Cage, Morton Feldman, Cornelius Cardew and other major modern composers would visit Reading University during the second half of the 1960s – their performances and events much admired by Andy Mackay. (From the mid-1970s, in a further connection with the musical and performance avant-garde, Mark Lancaster would work as first designer, and later artistic director (from 1980), for the Merce Cunningham Dance Company in New York.)

Donagh would also bring a political awareness to the Art department and to the processes of art-making – the work and example of Joseph Beuys being an important influence. (At this same time, the tutor in art history at Reading was Caroline Tisdall, likewise an authority on Beuys and later author of the survey volume of the German artist's travels, *We Go This Way*.) As a former student of Pasmore and Hamilton, Donagh would apply and develop the notion of the Basic Course, becoming interested in the processes of art-making, rather than the pursuit of an end product.

Both across the Reading campus, and within the wider community of contemporary British artists, endlessly interconnected by their various part-time, visiting or full-time teaching posts, there was the sense that the Art department at Reading was entering a period during which it was creatively progressive, actively trans-media and a venue within the university as a whole for those who aspired to intellectual and social cool. Such radicalism, however, would not be without its critics – as Ascott and Eno would also discover at Ipswich and Winchester respectively.

If Newcastle had seen a generational circle of art students in the early and middle years of the 1960s, for whom Richard Hamilton, Pop art, New York, Warhol, soul music, Duchamp, R&B, Mod styles, and a somewhat aristocratic sense of exclusivity had been the prevailing taste, then the arts scene at Reading – blossoming slightly later in the decade – would contribute a sensibility that was distinctly further out, aspirationally counter-cultural.

The milieu occupied by Mackay at Reading would be flamboyantly in tune with London's burgeoning underground culture; the vogue for sensory overload and the avant-garde being matched by the fashion for 'revolution' – the latter a significant aspect of British university campus attitudes at the time, and comprising an amorphous power-surge of counter-cultural and protest tendencies, covering a wide range of creative and ideological bases.

If this weren't enough, in their quasi-politicised engagement with the avant-garde, and as co-conspirators in what they saw as neo-Dada mischief making (via their Sunshine Group activities) Mackay and his friend Simon Puxley (subsequently Roxy Music's 'media consultant' and a close friend of Bryan Ferry) would also maintain a stance that was more than tinged with aesthetic movement poise.

These activities would be immediately succeeded by those of 'Moodies': a predominantly female group of Reading art students, whose glam-trash, pre-punk fusion of performance art and pop posing would comprise a complete blurring of the division between art and lifestyle, and eventually grant them a warm welcome in Germany – where they would be hailed by one magazine, to their amusement and alarm, as 'The biggest music sensation since the Beatles'.

Within this broadening network of friendships and acquaintances, it would be the Reading connection, ultimately, by way of Viv Kemp (who as a student at Reading between 1966 and 1970 would at one point be the girlfriend of Andrew Mackay, but later would marry Tim Head), which introduced Mackay, Eno and Simon Puxley to Bryan Ferry – who by 1969 would be based in Kensington.

Viv Kemp: 'Everybody in Newcastle and Reading had these big links, because they were the only two universities where you could study Fine Art. So a lot of people at Newcastle did MAs at Reading – like

Stephen Buckley and Tony Carter. And of course Rita Donagh taught me, so through her Richard Hamilton came down . . .'

As undertaken by Mackay (reading English and Music at Reading between 1965 and 1969), Simon Puxley (who would graduate in English and then stay on at Reading to write his doctoral thesis on Rossetti), Viv Kemp (who took a first in Fine Art), Polly Eltes (also Fine Art, a Moodie and later a model for Zandra Rhodes, married to Simon Puxley), Anne Bean (Fine Art, another Moodie, later a major British artist), and others, there would be a penchant for 'happenings',★ protest, raised political awareness, and the furthest frontiers of the musical and performative avant-garde; for activities which were aggressively radical in their sense of modernity, but steeped in a kind of stylistic game-playing that was simultaneously flippant and profound.

These tastes were further supplemented, in the case of Mackay and Puxley, with a determinedly English fascination with aesthetics, dandyism, and exquisite pose; a reclamation of the nineteenth-century romanticism of Swinburne, Coleridge, Aubrey Beardsley and the Pre-Raphaelite Brotherhood. As Viv Kemp would later remark to the author, regarding the aloof exoticism of her undergraduate milieu: 'But the whole of our group was *so* exclusive – and you were either *in*, or you were *out*. Proust's Paris absolutely sums it up. People like Simon and Andy, really, were such aesthetes.'

It would only be a matter of time before the activities at Reading – notably the enthusiasm for avant-garde performance and music – would forge a relationship with Brian Eno, by then an increasingly controversial figure at Winchester School of Art, and one whose role as an artist/enabler was already involving him in music-making systems as a non-musician performer.

Rita Donagh: 'It was amazing how Brian Eno's story at Winchester was almost parallel to my story at Reading with Andy Mackay. How for art students, at that time, music became almost *more* important – the ideas, I mean.'

★A 'happening' being a kind of free-wheeling, multi-media event – part party, part art fair, part '*tout déréglement des sens*'.

Once again, the generation of students who would subsequently meet at Reading, filled with revolutionary fervour, had mostly been born in the years just following the end of the Second World War, opening their eyes to rationing, drab streets, a purer countryside and the drive to rebuild.

sixteen

Coals from Newcastle . . . ; Andrew Mackay, born 1946, Lostwithiel, Cornwall, to move to Pimlico and a London childhood in the 1950s; the Festival of Britain, rock and roll, British Beat and the Promenade concerts at the Royal Albert Hall; the romance of London in the late 1950s and early 1960s.

If the Penshaw Monument, for the young Bryan Ferry, had come to represent the culture and finesse of a 'life beyond the coalfields' of Durham and Newcastle, then these coalfields in their turn had busily played their part in the fuelling of Britain's return to peace during the late 1940s and 1950s.

Some of the coal would be loaded on to long, low, sea-going coal boats, there to make their way south from Tyneside to the Thames estuary, along the Thames proper through the heart of London, to be unloaded in silvery heaps by the wharf on the southern side of Grosvenor railway bridge. It would then be fed on to trundling conveyor belts, up into the maw of Battersea Power Station – directly in view, as it happened, of the young Andrew Mackay, then a schoolboy living with his mother, father and brother in a new council flat in Pimlico, which faced the power station from the north bank. Andrew would spend his spare time watching the busy traffic on the river, or exploring the exotically scented wharves and warehouses downstream, in the old London docklands around Shad Thames and Rotherhithe.

Born in Cornwall, but removed to Pimlico when still a baby, Mackay would find his place as one of the last generation to grow up in what might be termed the 'old' landscape of central London, prior to the major reconstruction and route-planning projects of the 1960s. In Pimlico, still pitted with bombsites and opened into sudden expanses of cleared rubble, the Mackays were living in a part of London which seemed (then as now) a slightly obscure residential backwater, surrounded on three sides by the imposing ceremonial architecture and blank, high windows of Westminster, Millbank and Victoria Street.

For a child growing up in such a district, central London and its institutions – Buckingham Palace, Saint James's Park, the West End, Kensington Gardens – were intimate and walkable: an urban village. And this at a time – approaching 1951 – when the government's 'tonic to the nation', the Festival of Britain, was about to transform the southern bank of the Thames from Battersea to Waterloo into an illuminated pleasure park of edifying and celebratory attractions, championing the drive to rebuild the country subsequent to the devastations of the Second World War. Three of Richard Hamilton's immediate friends and colleagues in the visual arts, Hugh Casson, Kenneth Rowntree and Victor Pasmore, would be directly involved in the festival – Casson appointed its Director of Architecture, and Pasmore and Rowntree in creating a mosaic for the festival buildings.

For the young Andrew Mackay, music of all sorts – primarily classical, but also rock and roll, British beat, operetta, church choral – would be his dominating interest from childhood. His father (a gasman by trade) was also an accomplished classical piano-player, and the household was deeply musical.

Andy Mackay: 'I was born in Cornwall, but my father was a Londoner who lived in Pimlico. He had been stationed in Cornwall during the war, and six months after I was born we moved to London – so effectively I grew up in Pimlico. I went to a very beautiful church school called Saint James the Less – a lovely Victorian church just off Vauxhall Bridge Road. It was designed by G. E. Street, with a wonderful ornate interior, and a nice mosaic by G. F. Watts above the sacristy.

'We were aware of being poor – not that we were particularly poor, but an ordinary blue collar worker just didn't make that much money; enough to "get by" and a fortnight's holiday in a guesthouse somewhere. I remember that if I walked through an area like Kensington or Belgravia, I would think how incredibly smart they looked . . . I loved the river, and playing around there; we also used to play in bombsites quite a lot. The docks were still working, and beyond Blackfriars there were spice ware-houses; they used to unload corn at the Hovis building by Vauxhall Bridge, and the Power Station at Battersea was running off coal coming up from the Tyne on a coal boat.

'We moved to a council estate called Churchill Gardens when I was about eleven, and that was right opposite Battersea Power Station. We were the first people to live in that flat – people were just desperate to move into somewhere with a bathroom. But I remember everywhere as being very grey – there wasn't much colour in anything. If I see a colour photograph of London at that period it somehow seems faintly wrong. Apart from the Coronation and the Festival of Britain, which were both more colourful events, it was still pretty smoky; there were still smogs – right up until the mid-1950s. After the Festival of Britain, the festival buildings were there for the next few years. I remember the Skylon, and the Battersea Park structures.'

As a schoolboy living on a council estate in Pimlico during the central years of 'Austerity Britain', Andy Mackay would swiftly acquire a broad and deeply felt awareness of classical music – not as some remote, impos-ing genre, almost beyond aspiration, but as a territory in which he was quite at home, and eager to explore further. Music for Mackay would then be expanded by the arrival firstly of rock and roll, and then of British Beat music. This, for a young, romantically inclined Londoner, was at a time approaching the heady days of the Soho coffee bars as musical venues (the '2 Is' being the most famous for live music); vitally, however, for Mackay, the Royal Opera and the Proms would exert an equal pull to the liberations delivered by early rock and roll.

Andy Mackay: 'My father, who was a gasman, and never had any particu-lar aspirations career-wise, was a very good classical pianist. He had taken lessons in his late teens, having left school at fourteen. He had lived at home until he married my mother, when he was forty, and had bought a Steinway upright piano. He played Chopin, Beethoven – some odd, quirky pieces, like Brahms's *Hungarian Dances*, or little bits of Debussy.

'We had a piano before we had a record player, and we had a record player and hi-fi radio before we had a television – so it was always that priority. But I was never forced to listen to classical music, it was just what we listened to. I loved Brahms, Wagner, Berlioz, Mendelssohn – big, nineteenth-century stuff. Loosely "Romantic" music – Tchaikovsky, and so on; the sort of things that orchestras played a lot in those days. Whereas no one, for instance, was playing Mahler much at this time.

'My school wasn't a big music school; but I was lucky because I'd discovered that I could play tunes on a recorder, and could amuse my friends by playing them. This stopped me from getting bullied, maybe. When I subsequently went to Westminster City Grammar School I wanted to learn the clarinet, because Acker Bilk was a big star by that time, with 'Stranger on the Shore' [a soothing, amiable instrumental which took the number 2 spot on the UK chart in November 1961]. The school said they hadn't got any clarinets, but they had an oboe – which they said was much the same – and would I like to learn that? So I learned to play the oboe instead. I was a chorister, as well, and my school provided the choir for Saint Margaret's.

'The school was furiously streamed, and I was always in the "B" stream – I would hover between being near the top, and then sometimes falling back and almost being put in the "C" stream. For my oboe tuition, as the school didn't have a teacher coming in, there was some small sum of money left – the school had connections going back to the almshouses of the Elizabethan period – and this paid for me to have lessons at the Guildhall with a wonderful teacher. This was during the middle to late 1950s . . .'

As it had for Bryan Ferry, the arrival of Bill Haley's 'Rock and Roll Show' in the UK in 1956 would make an immediate impression on the young Andrew Mackay. A marker for the beginning of the pop age, subsequent to Haley's chaos-provoking tour of British theatres, pop music and rock and roll would open up as a lifestyle, as much as a musical genre. The other musician singled out for special mention as acceptably 'cool' is Humphrey Lyttelton – whose 'Bad Penny Blues' had so caught the pre-teenaged Bryan Ferry's imagination.

Mackay would later develop, musically, as a player of tremendous stylishness, collaging the heat and raunchiness of traditional rock and roll, with the sensibility of classical European romanticism, underpinned by a fluency in the creative freedoms authorised by 'happenings' and the musical avant-garde. In this he would assimilate and refine musical style with as much attention to nuance and detail as Ferry had paid to sartorial elegance and the study of the blues. Dandyism as an informant of creativity would be of paramount importance to both Ferry and Mackay.

Growing up to become the beneficiaries of sixties pop radicalism, in the time it took this immediately post-Second World War generation to reach their early twenties, the domain defined as, and opened up by 'pop' would have stretched from 'Mr' Acker Bilk and His Paramount Orchestra in their striped shirts and bowler hats, to the odoriferous mattresses strewn on the floor of Jim Hayne's Arts Lab, in Drury Lane. As for Ferry, the idea of pop music as a heightened lifestyle would be of interest to Mackay.

Andy Mackay: 'I was ten in 1956, and a teenager by the time the sixties started. So I picked up on rock and roll, mainly it seemed through the older sisters of my friends – they seemed to be the conduit for that. I remember a row of prefabs [temporary houses built in bomb-damaged districts, some of which became permanent homes] opposite where we lived, and hanging around outside one of them, where they had a record collection, and just listening. And I remember *distinctly* hearing what must have been Elvis records, and how amazing that sounded. Although when I was younger I was more inclined to classical music. My parents were Methodists, and so they did a lot of hymn singing – also Gilbert & Sullivan.

'From when I was fifteen, sixteen, that was the era of great modern pop music; and by then it was on the radio. You had to listen to shows like *Two Way Family Favourites*, which was for British forces stationed in Germany. It was a request programme, and one of the few places where you would hear rock and roll records. A lot of it was crummy old musical numbers, but then someone would request Little Richard.

'Tommy Steele, Cliff Richard, Marty Wilde, skiffle – it all sounded very exciting. And of course the first Bill Haley tour was a memorable thing. I remember him arriving at Victoria Station; he was such a funny, nondescript-looking person. And although I didn't like the British jazz scene, people like Humphrey Lyttelton seemed quite cool, and you imagined that they had some great *lifestyle*. One of the things about popular music was that you thought of these people hanging out in coffee bars in Soho, and I was very taken by all of that.

'I never thought that classical musicians had any kind of life, really; I thought that they somehow finished concerts and went home. I was a furious classical music listener. With my brother, we would get season tickets to the Proms and go virtually every night – it was very cheap. This was around 1963, 1964. When I was older, I also used to go to the Royal Opera, to see things by Verdi, Wagner. I would queue for the five shillings seats in the gods; and what was great was that I could walk home at midnight, across Saint James's Park. Nobody at that time found this a dangerous thing to do. I was very much a London person, and there were areas of London that I found fantastically romantic.

'1963, I felt, was the year of the Beatles, the Rolling Stones and Phil Spector. I loved the Beatles – I thought they were fantastic. It was my generation who were exactly the right age to grow up as these things were happening. So *Ready Steady Go!* was the television programme that changed the teenagers' view of the world; and before that *6.5 Special* – which always seemed to be introduced by very old presenters. Some of it was really good – Lord Rockingham's XI and the Vernon Girls were great.

'Importantly, I didn't see a conflict at this point between pop music and classical music: I used to play in school orchestras and then we would listen to pop music as well. After that, I think music teachers got terrified that everyone was going to become musically illiterate – which to some extent they have.

'But I think that around this time it crossed my mind that writing and playing pop music might not be a bad way of making a living. I could read music, and I could play reasonably well.'

seventeen

Eno I: Brian Peter George St John le Baptiste de la Salle Eno; born 15 May 1948 Woodbridge, Suffolk; his childhood and early exposure to creativity; his grandfather's deconsecrated chapel and pipe organ; why Eno is here; his Uncle Carl Otto; paintings by Mondrian in miniature; the decision to become an artist.

If Andrew Mackay's early education was dominated by formal training in classical music, then that of Brian Eno, with whom he would exchange avant-garde musical performances between Winchester School of Art and Reading University, as students in the second half of the 1960s, could not have been more different.

For Eno – in many ways the ultimate art student – education at art college would be a mixed experience, and one which he would regard with some ambivalence. Mentally and temperamentally suited to flourish within the demanding processes of Roy Ascott's 'Groundcourse' in Ipswich, he would then be frustrated by the traditionalism of some of his tutors at Winchester. At the same time, such confrontation would not be without its adrenalin, perhaps intensifying Eno's own sense of enquiry at a time, generationally, when the musical avant-garde was finding a home within art schools.

In his notebook, 'August–November 1976', Brian Eno would propose an observation about himself, to himself. Under the title 'What sort of person do I think I am?' the assessment included: 'I feel that my special talent is being able to put together diverse ideas, and sense what the new combinations can do . . .' Ten years earlier, in one of his first art school notebooks, he had rehearsed his ability to rearrange concepts; for example:

'. . . make some music to be heard and not listened to. Make a painting of a notice board . . .'

Suggesting an activity not unrelated to montage, this talent for reconfiguration would stand as an accurate summary of at least a portion of the creativity that Eno came to research within art, music, science and systems building. It would also describe an important aspect of his brief but pivotal involvement with Roxy Music – of which as a founding member he would attract considerable attention as both the contributor of a pioneering use of electronic effects, and as the perceived embodiment of a unique intellectual charisma and personal exoticism. (It would be Brian Eno who subsequently identified, crucially, that Roxy Music as a group and as an idea stood in opposition to the taste for musical and stylistic 'authenticity' which prevailed during the early years of the 1970s.)

As interested in numbers as he was in paintings (profiled by Richard Williams in *Melody Maker*, for the week ending 29 July 1972, Eno would be introduced as busily consulting a set of logarithm tables), and more interested in self-generative systems, perhaps, than anything else, Eno was defined by his boundless curiosity. In his notebook for 'Summer '68', he would write, 'a way shall be found before a why shall be found', adding: 'Where there's a will there's a way, and where there's a way there's a why.' The two maxims are punctuated in the middle of the notebook page by a statement composed in one of the Magritte-like reversals of cause and effect that would come to typify Eno's operational stance: 'Instead of light shining out of your window at night, darkness shone out by day.'

Eno specialised in – has subsequently become the leading exponent of – creative and deductive formulae which possess both their own poetic mechanism and the ability to reconfigure subject, concept, material, purpose and process. For example, again in his notebook for 1968, Eno would doodle the comment, 'THE EDGES AROUND NOTHING'; or, the following year, observe:

> . . . since process aesthetics revolve around repetition of similar themes (that's what Susan Sontag doesn't dig) what is dug after a while, is not the process/idea, for this is acknowledged anyway, but rather, 1) the elegance of execution, and 2) the effect of the process. Note that both of these qualities are judgeable in terms of 'aesthetic of beauty'. So maybe everyone agrees but their languages differ . . .

Eno's role as a questioner and intellectual adventurer would be vastly enhanced (at times by way of confrontation with the authorities) by his experience of what he records in his notebook for 'June '69' as, '*five long years of Art Education*'. It would also be within the process of art education that Eno developed the wit and conceptual swagger that became as much a constant in his work as his ability to transpose concept and theory into aesthetics of immense verve and elegance.

In his initial decision to work in the 'pop' medium – and there would be a conscious, noted moment at which he made this choice – Eno would share with Ferry and their art school peers a fascination with trying to resolve the differences between two opposing forms (in this case performed 'classical' music and recorded pop and rock music), and thus create a new approach to musicality.

There is also a sense of elitism in Eno's early stance – an attitude reflected by the refined, haughty expression, with raised eyebrow and faint, inscrutable smile, that Eno would sometimes wear in early press photographs. Aware from a young age of his precocious intellect and ravenous sense of enquiry, in his art school notebook for '21.12.67–6.5.68', he airily announces: 'Brian Eno will be conducting tutorials in his office today. Any staff member needing advice or guidance please feel free to come and see me.' He then proceeds to mime monomaniacal ennui in a note-to-posterity of some exasperation: 'Terry Riley, the cunt, picked up one of my seventeen-yea-old ideas and performed it at the Museum of Modern Art. Rauschenberg did, too. Ah, these vultures – Ah! The universal consciousness. The joke's on them, for I didn't even bother to do it. I never do anything. Nothing's good enough.'

From childhood, through the early adolescence in which he was befriended by eccentric, gifted relatives on the one hand, and a Thomas Pynchonesque crew of dissident beatniks on the other (in 1964, he would be photographed holding drumsticks as a member of a group called the Black Aces) Eno would seem to be living an almost perfectly scripted life. There was much of the English idyll about his early years, growing up in rural Suffolk at a time when the institutions of village and small-town life were still intact, yet abutted – for the culturally inquisitive – by the presence of American military installations through which one might hear authentic rock and roll and doo-wop.

In a notebook dated 'Sometime '72', kept in the few spare minutes between intense work with Roxy Music, Eno would note:

My self images are as follows:

1) poor boy made good against the odds.
2) artist in judgement not skill.
3) converter–ecological sub-unit, putting to good avail what others waste.

The 'poor boy' seems presented to the world as already exotic, self-aware of his originality, which Wilde-like he presents to the world in partially tongue-in-cheek and partially serious self-penned aphorisms – for example: 'I don't believe in trying to change the world (except as a hobby)' and, 'There are so many questions I'd like to answer. If only someone would ask them.' The business of questioning and re-questioning the nature of our relationship with the world, delighting in those interventions and collaterals of process which enable new perspectives, would thus occupy Eno from childhood.

Enter Eno, etymology first:

Brian Eno: 'My name is quite rare, and so it is fairly easy to trace. It goes back to Lincoln in the early eighteenth century, and coincides with an influx of Huguenot settlers. There is a well known Huguenot name spelt "Hainault" – in fact the world champion cyclist, when I was a child, was a Belgian called Bernard Hainault.

'So the theory is that Huguenots who had been expelled from mainland Europe came to the east of England and started a flax and linen trade there. And it is then assumed that my ancestor came over and Anglicised his name . . .'*

Like Ferry, Antony Price and others of the milieu from which Roxy Music emerged, Eno was one of the immediately post-war generation of

---

* Eno's fondness for composing anagrams and word games would lead him over the years to compose a sequence of anagrams of own name; jotted down in his notebook for 'Late '69' are: *Brian Eno = Ben o'rian, Bari Neon, Noa Brine and Roni Bean.* All have a fabular quality, like the invented names of members of some outlandish American punk group; at the same time, they carry more than a whiff of English surrealism – as does much of Eno's writing, both in the dreamscapes and witty wordplay of fragments in his notebooks, and, later, as a lyricist.

'working class' young people to benefit from the availability of grants for art school education. As for his peers, this modern education within the arts would keep pace with the introduction of rock and roll and black American music.

Throughout Eno's childhood and adolescence, up until entering a foundation year at Ipswich Civic College, there was a quality to his experience in which the quaint Englishness of an Ealing comedy was matched by a family history bejewelled with colourful detail and improbable event. The Sitwellian whimsy of some of his writing – lyrics and prose – gives expression to this.

Brian Eno: 'I was born into a working-class family – but it was rural working class, which is a little different from urban working class. So in fact I never knew that we *were* working class; that was an idea which was never in my mind until I went to art school, where I met other people who had had the same experience. But we didn't feel poor, or anything like that.

'My dad, being a postman, was quite a respected member of the community. He was proud of his job, and one felt that he had a place in things. Also, I was a Catholic, which made me slightly different from the other kids – there weren't so many Catholics around.

'In terms of an awareness of creativity, my grandfather, firstly, was an interesting character. He, like all of us, was a postman, but he also was a very broad-ranging musician. He played all sorts of instruments, particularly wind instruments – saxophone, bassoon; he had a tuba. He also loved organs, and would repair mechanical musical instruments; that was his hobby, but he did it quite seriously. In fact, one of the churches in Woodbridge still has one of his organs in it.

'My grandfather lived in a de-consecrated chapel – a chapel that a priest had committed suicide in, to be exact. Under such circumstances you can't ever reuse the building as a place of worship. So at the time he bought it very cheaply; it was a rather spooky place, with lots of creaky stone tiles. And he had it filled with all kinds of incredible things; he was rather like a rural version of Lieutenant General Pitt Rivers, who started the Pitt Rivers Museum in Oxford [a collection of archaeological and ethnographic objects]; he just collected things. He had great bundles of Zulu spears sitting around; or you would go around a dark corner and there would be a Japanese suit of armour. It was an incredible place for a child; and everywhere, there were keyboard instruments . . .

'Over the course of his life, my grandfather was often called to replace pipes in organs, and as a consequence he started building an organ in this chapel. After a while he ran out of structure to put it on, and so he started just putting the pipes up on the walls. So this instrument developed, with pipes everywhere – on the ceiling, wherever. Sadly, both that and everything else he had collected were destroyed when he died – except for a player-piano. You could pedal this piano quite discreetly, so that people couldn't see your feet, and so when visitors came over to our house I would pretend to be playing . . .

'I was familiar first of all with mechanical instruments, which were the synthesisers of their day, in that they were very sophisticated. They not only had musical sounds, they had rattles and shakers and bells – all sorts of things built into them. My grandfather also had a barrel organ, with tambourines and so on. He was a member of the Woodbridge Excelsior Band, as was my eccentric and very gifted uncle, his first son – who was called Carl Otto Eno.

'The reason I am alive, in fact, is that in 1906, when my grandfather would have been about twenty-six or twenty-seven, he wanted to be a musician – and so he joined the German Army. The German Army had huge numbers of bands, and you could join simply as a musician. So if you couldn't get a job as a musician in England, that was where you went.

'He stayed there for two years, and then came back to England. His first son he called Carl Otto, because he very much liked Germany and the German people. He maintained several friendships with Germans for the rest of his life – even through two world wars. The upshot of this was that he was seen as a German sympathiser – even though he wasn't politically a German sympathiser – and he spent the First World War in internment. It wasn't horrible; although I am sure it was somewhat humiliating. First of all he was kept at Olympia, in London, and then on the Isle of Wight. As a result he didn't go to the trenches – where 78 per cent of what *would* have been his regiment were killed. And I am here today because of that.

'So this was my grandfather's first son: Carl Otto – and he was also a musician and a very eccentric and interesting man. He was a postman – of course – at one point, a gardener and a painter; he loved painting, and

I think I got into painting through him. He was always doing tiny little landscapes in oils – quite beautiful. He liked the Dutch and Flemish landscape painters . . .

'I used to go and see him every Thursday evening. He only lived about half a mile away from us, and as he never had a son, I think he took me on as one. He was very nice to me and spent a lot of time on me. He would always ask me puzzling, mind-expanding questions, such as, "How big do you think the *Queen Elizabeth* ocean liner would be if you could squash all its atoms together?" later telling me, "It would be about the size of a cube of sugar, but it would still be the same weight."

'Uncle Otto also repaired china. He would fix up fine porcelain that had been broken, and so well that you couldn't tell . . . All of my ancestors were big *hobbyists*. They had the day job – postmen – and the rest of the time they were doing all kinds of other things.

'One day, Uncle Otto showed me a little book about Piet Mondrian; and it had all those fantastic Mondrian pictures in it, but reproduced at a small scale. And I was so knocked out by this. One, because they were so striking, visually, but secondly because they were so simple. I thought that this was amazing, that you could do something that simple, and it can have such an effect. And I decided then that I was going to be an artist. It was the closest thing to magic that I could think of. I must have been between nine and eleven; I'm pretty sure that it was before I went to secondary school.

'I remember him telling me about all the different varieties of modern art. I particularly loved the sound of "neo-plasticism". I loved all those names! "non-objectivism" – and another that had such a long name I told all my friends that that was the sort of artist I was . . .'

eighteen

Brian Eno: 'I wasn't as intrigued by science, as a child, as I have become. I liked numbers, and playing with numbers, but I wasn't *really* interested in science until I started reading about evolution theory – and that completely fascinated me. I would have been about seventeen by then, beginning to read cybernetics and evolution theory. Both of those things seemed to me connected.

'As regards the interests of the adult figures who were around me, it seems perhaps obvious that I grew to have the interests that I have. My next uncle, Douglas, who was the youngest, was a clarinet teacher. And he wasn't a postman – at least, not for very long. He was a peripatetic clarinet teacher, going around various schools.

'And he was very important in my life for one particular reason: he had a little film projector. He lived in Ipswich, which meant that we didn't see him that much – even though Ipswich was only six miles away. I remember on one visit – I must have been about four, I suppose – he had what I later discovered was a Disney film; so we were sitting in his living room, and he had the projector projecting on to the wall. I remember the colours were so intense, and so bright, that this experience of colour was something I never forgot. I thought for years that it was a dream I had had. *And I always wanted to remake that experience.*

'I remember when I was very young, experimenting with torches and toffee papers to project light – in the hope that I could achieve an effect as strong as that. It took quite a lot of forensic work to later recall what exactly I had seen which left such an impression on me. My parents later told me that he had borrowed the projector. I can remember nothing more about him, except for the fact that he used to make toffee by putting a poker in the fire until it got red hot, and then sticking it into a sugar bowl. He died when I was twelve – rather young . . .

'Then there was my dad, who was a postman from the age of fourteen to when he retired – with just a break when he was a soldier during the war. He had two hobbies: one was repairing watches, which he had taught himself to do during the war. He would mend watches for people on his post round, for ridiculously low prices; he did it out of friendship, I think, and he would spend whole evenings working on a watch. Then he would charge whoever it belonged to sixpence.

'The other thing that he was really good at was whistling. In Germany they have a category of whistler who are known as "art whistlers". These are people who are professional whistlers; and in the 1930s and 1940s they would have bands in which the lead instrument would be a whistler. So they used to have a whistling quartet in the post office, when they were doing night duty together. They would get into a rhythm, with my dad doing the percussion on the wire mesh of the sorting boxes. They were really good. They rehearsed to get things right, and worked out sections – just like a barber shop quartet, only whistling. It was real working-class art.

'I later asked my father whether he had ever played an instrument. And it turned out that he had been the drummer in a three-piece band that basically played at weddings. He had a motorcycle and sidecar, and the whole band, with all their equipment, would travel in this from engagement to engagement. He had never told me this – and probably never would have, unless I'd asked him.

'In Suffolk, during the 1950s, I also felt connected to rock and roll. We lived in this little town of Woodbridge which had just four thousand inhabitants; but within five miles there were two huge American airbases – Bentwaters airbase and Woodbridge airbase; and then there was HMS *Ganges*, the big training ship out at Ipswich. So there were airmen and soldiers around, which meant that there were cafes and jukeboxes – Woodbridge probably had more jukeboxes than any comparable sized town in the world. And of course the most interesting thing was that they all played American R&B and doo-wop and so forth; they got the records that most Americans wanted to hear.

'I was therefore in the very interesting position of hearing the crappy English versions on the radio – people doing English versions of songs that I then heard in their original, often black, form. I was in no doubt as to which I preferred, although I didn't necessarily know that the singers I liked were black. I built up a big record collection, of singles, and it was only much later that I found out who all the artists were. There was no pop press that I saw – I never saw *Melody Maker* or anything like that. And gradually it dawned on me that almost without exception these were all records made by black people – although being doo-wop there were a few Italians from Philadelphia, the Four Seasons for example. So I felt as though I had the edge on everybody else, in terms of what I listened to, because I felt that I had heard the real thing.

'I loved drawing – to the point that my mother would ask me why I never went out to play. But I also had an early obsession, which I think was the first time that I felt I was really making something of my own – and that was that I used to design houses. I would imagine houses that I was going to build in the future, and they all had strange ideas – like they were labyrinths, or they had a waterfall running through the middle; another, very impracticably, straddled a chasm – so the house was built as a bridge, and could be used as a bridge. Yet another was built entirely around a courtyard with a tracery of walkways – rather Arabic, I thought.

'I had a building set called BACO which was really sweet, in that it was only for architecture – you got doors, and bay windows, and chimney stacks, and things like that. All the parts were obviously designed on the basis of 1930s suburban brick housing – the kinds of houses you see alongside the M1 when you're leaving London. I liked to see if I could make them with strange additions – wings sticking out, or whatever.

'The feeling I like is the feeling of making a world of some kind, and that's what I still like; the feeling of being inside this world, and wondering what it would be like if everything was like that. And that was the first time I had that feeling. Creativity is always a very strong desire to make a world of your own, in some way, and that could very often, or very likely, result in wanting an alternative to the one you're in.

'I would do strange things to the "player-piano" – and so you could say that I made music as a child. We had a lot of rolls that my grandfather had collected, and I would make new holes in them – of course, this has been done much better! – but I would put a bit of tape over the some of the holes and so forth. I liked the *system* that the player-piano represented – and I liked performing some extra surgery on the rolls that nobody liked! But that was really the only musical thing I did when I was young – except for singing along with records, which apparently I was famous for. My sister's friends used to laugh at me, apparently, especially in the cinema. In those days when you went to the cinema, you would sit there for half an hour while they just played records. So I would sing along to all of them.

'I didn't enjoy school very much. The first was a Catholic convent, which was ruined for me by one very stupid thing: the food was atrocious, and they forced you to eat it. If you didn't eat it, you then had to stand on a chair in the refectory and eat it. Sadism of the most stupid kind. So a lot of my early time at school was ruined by worrying about lunchtime. I learned to vomit spontaneously. I can still do it. The only way you were allowed not to eat your meal was to prove that you were ill; and you could prove that you were ill by vomiting. I learned to make my stomach turn – which I did for what seemed like years. I remember sitting there all morning in a state of anxiety about lunchtime; and then when lunch was over, it was all great. It is more than possible that the whole path of my life depended on what subject happened to appear after lunch rather than before. Anything before lunch I couldn't pay attention to.

'This sounds fatuous, but these kinds of things *are what make a difference.* There was one record associated with this; at the point when this whole issue was at its worst, there was a record by Frankie Vaughan called "Green Door" – if I hear that record now, I almost vomit. It was played on Radio Luxembourg, which my sister used to listen to a lot, at the peak of this horrible experience I was having.

'I left school when I was sixteen, in the fifth form – so I did what were then called O levels, and then went to art school. By this time I had fallen in with a very interesting crowd. Woodbridge was a very funny little microclimate, because there was a lot of money around it from all these GIs; and there was a lot of not only pop culture, but culture in general – because they weren't all into doo-wop. I made friends with a woman called Janet Brown – she was a real bohemian, and she was older than me. I would have been about fourteen at the time, and she must have been in her mid-twenties – which seemed very much older. This was in 1961 or 1962 – Brian Hyland's "Sealed With a Kiss" was riding high in the charts – and Janet was a very funny character for a little town. She was a big, tall, outspoken, quite posh woman, who dressed fairly outrageously and had a son called Dickon.

'Janet had a council flat where she also held a kind of *salon* – a little meeting place of bohemian friends, many of whom had been to Ipswich Art School, and some of whom were gay Americans. So her place had become a haven for gay GIs. There was one called Gerry who taught me to play the theme from *Charade* [Henry Mancini, 1963] on the piano – they were into that whole culture, musicals, and films such as like *Breakfast at Tiffany's*, a genre which I had never been exposed to before.

'Janet, for some reason, and this crowd, adopted me as their mascot. They would take me for picnics and so on. Janet had a funny old convertible car and so all these beatniks would come by and I would jump in the back. They also knew this man called Ray Holland, and his exquisitely beautiful wife. They lived on a boat in the river, and they employed me one summer to repaint the deck. It was an old motor torpedo boat called *Viking* . . .

'While I was doing that I heard about an old wrecked boat that was for sale across the opposite side of the harbour – maybe half a mile away. So I bought this boat with a couple of friends for £10 – and then we had our own place. I lived there for a couple of weeks, living on baked beans . . .

'Everything about Woodbridge was very nice, and it was a lovely place to grow up. There was a vital culture of people making things around the harbour, and there was a lot of commerce in every sense of the word – a lot of movement. What I remembered most about the places I grew up in was the inviting mysteriousness of them – the way they hid themselves from you. This was in my mind when I wrote "On Land (Ambient 4)" in New York, years later. The whole feeling of Suffolk, to me, is taciturn . . .'

nineteen

Eno III: Background to Eno's foundation course studies in art at Ipswich Civic College, 1964–1965; Roy Ascott, cybernetics, behaviourism and the 'Groundcourse'; introducing Tom Phillips.

One day in 1955, a Royal Air Force staff car pulled up not far from the Fine Art department at King's College, University of Durham at Newcastle. Inside was a young man, commissioned within Fighter Control, who had ambitions to study as an artist. Within seven years he would have established one of the most controversial foundation courses in the history of British art education.

This was Roy Ascott, Brian Eno's future teacher at Ipswich Civic College, subsequent founder of Planetary Collegium (a research community concerned with creativity, technology and consciousness), and career-long advocate of the application of cybernetics (behavioural control, conditioned communication, feedback, participation and systemic relationships) to the processes of art-making. Graduating from King's in 1959, before spending a further two years at Newcastle as studio demonstrator, Ascott would be appointed in 1961 to his first teaching post at Ealing College of Art and Design, in West London. Once there he would create his own, radically progressive, version of a Basic Course: Ascott's 'Groundcourse' which comprised an unheard-of approach to the teaching of art. Based on Ascott's interpretation of cybernetics – a subject he had encountered while browsing in the library at Newcastle – the basis of the course has been retrospectively summarised by Emily Pethick:

Ascott has described the Groundcourse as 'a microcosm of a total process of art education'. Its curriculum was based on the stimulation of consciousness with 'behavioural' exercises, games and matrices that were aimed to shake up preconceptions and established patterns, where the student's disorientation is contrived within an environment that is sometimes unexpectedly confusing, where he is faced with problems that seem absurd, aimless or terrifying.

Coincidentally anticipating the '*tout déréglement des sens*' that would soon be mandatory in the sensory assault of any self-respecting 'happening', the Groundcourse aimed at reconfiguring the ways that students looked at the world, and, more controversially, their own personalities. These games and exercises were followed in the second year by students having to devise their own 'problems', '– working in groups to form self-regulating systems and acting out a new personality *contra to their own* for ten weeks, designing "calibrators" and "mind maps" to read off their responses to situations.'

Edward A. Shanken, writing on Ascott's career, further describes the central ethos on which the Groundcourse was based:

> According to Ascott, it was at the level of consciousness that the artist, artwork, and viewer exchange aesthetic information and alter their individual states, thereby transforming the consciousness and behaviour of the (social) system as a whole. The artist [Ascott] applied such concepts in the systematic Groundcourse he designed and directed at the Ealing School of Art in London (1961–4), where he introduced processes and methods such as inverted logic, chance operations, and behavioural psychology into the curriculum.

In such an atmosphere, needless to say, Eno would flourish – challenged, absorbed, delighted. Others were less at ease with the lack of convention and the intense emotional demands. As a consequence (as Eno recalls) the drop-out rate from the course was high. At Ealing, Ascott would put together a team of teachers that would include R. B. Kitaj, Anthony Benjamin, Bernard Cohen and Harold Cohen, as well as visitors such as Gustav Metzger (whose ideas on 'auto destructive art' would, famously, make an impression on The Who's guitarist, Pete Townshend, then a student on the course) and the cybernetician Gordon Pask – who would be treated to a banquet created by Ealing College's cordon bleu cookery students, prior to giving his after-dinner speech on cybernetics.*

Ascott also brought into play – in a manner resonant of a sociologist's appropriation of the Bauhaus model (with its motto, 'art and technology – a new unity!') – the employment of various non-arts teaching specialists. These would include a cybernetician, a linguist, a sociologist and a biologist. There was also, perhaps, some intersection between the methods and technologies to which Ascott had been exposed in Fighter Control, and his subsequent fascination with systems building. As with computers, robots, atomic bombs and jets, the technologies designed during the Second World War would become the futuristic emblems of the new pop/space age.

Roy Ascott: 'When I did my National Service, I was commissioned into the very interesting area of Fighter Control. That was around 1953, and I was based near Edinburgh. The work was to do with recognising patterns; but what I subsequently realised was that this was swiftly becoming a wholly electronic environment – utilising electronic signage and so on. So it was a very stimulating place to be.

'As an art student in Newcastle, I was completely taken over by Victor Pasmore's ideas, and by his work, which I thought was absolutely exquisite. I had turned up for my interview in a staff car, can you believe it? But I was engrossed at that time in the work of El Greco, and in particular in his painting of hands, and so I was probably allowed in on the strength of that. It was in my second year that Pasmore introduced the Basic Course – the year before we had still been drawing the shape between bottles – and I really *got* what the Basic Course was about. I loved the idea of a basic language – the idea that you could move in any direction. This suited me very well.

'They all thought that I was going to get a first. I had seen the first Jackson Pollock show at the Whitechapel [November, 1958], and had subsequently spent the summer making Pollock-style paintings – stamping all

---

* Stephen Willats, subsequently a major British artist, also studied under Ascott at Ealing. Willats's mixed media, text, 'found object', image and signage-system works would route cybernetics, semiotics and communications theory into often dramatic explorations of subcultural communities and their ideologies. One work, *Living Like a Goya* (1982) would be based upon his creative dialogue with a woman called Julie Sissons, *couturier* to transvestites and denizen of the post-punk/futurist Cha Cha club, who in the early 1980s would literally – and for her own good reasons – recreate herself as a work by Goya.

over boards and pouring paint and so on. These were all I had to put up in the crits [fortnightly assessments of students' work by the whole teaching body] and I have to say that Gowing was brilliant about them. I had been doing very constructivist stuff, and he recognised that these were still "constructed" paintings, but the other side of the coin, so to speak . . .'

Rita Donagh: 'When I was at Newcastle he [Ascott] was an older student, who was very dominating in the school, and who painted like Jackson Pollock. None of us had heard of Jackson Pollock, so to see this guy throwing paint on the floor was quite shocking. At that time in the 1950s, to be influenced by Pollock was quite progressive.'

Roy Ascott: 'Claude Rogers [who would be Professor of Fine Art at Reading] was examiner for my degree, and he wouldn't go for giving me a first. So they offered me the studio demonstrator post, which meant that you got a studio of your own, and so of course I went for it. The problem was, that I was interested in Duchamp, as well as Pollock.'

In Duchamp's construction of the *Large Glass*, Ascott identified what he saw as a concern with process – a self-surveillance – rather than an 'end product'. As antithetical to Pollock's intuitive, intensely soul-mining approach to making a painting, this created a tension of interests for Ascott. (Between Hamilton and Ascott there is no recorded exchange of ideas, although both were of course aware of each other's work within the Art department at Newcastle.)

The attempted resolution of seeming contradictions – between abstraction and figuration, for example, fine art and popular culture, performance art and personal style, frivolity and seriousness, populism and the avant-garde – that would be a constant within the interests of the circle in and around Roxy Music (and with which Brian Eno would find himself faced in the late 1960s, when considering his own creative path), would also provide Ascott with what he has since called his 'Eureka!' moment – the notion of relating cybernetics to art.

But in identifying cybernetics as a means of understanding and teaching art, Ascott was going out on a limb of some length. Others within the arts had read cybernetics and found the subject of interest – Hamilton, for example, had read and admired Norbert Weiner's *Cybernetics* (1948) but saw in it no connection to art. Similarly, Ascott himself was aware that his work at this time – some of which, based largely on 'diagram' forms, would be shown at the Molton Gallery, London, in 1963 – had no close relatives in contemporary art. Ascott was thus highly radical in his adoption of behaviourism and cybernetics as the model for an art school foundation course.

In the catalogue for his show at the Molton Gallery, Ascott's artist's statement anticipates later aspects of Eno's creative outlook: '... the intention to make movement a subtle but essential part of an artefact', for example, has its continuance in Eno's generative music systems and installations; while the statement: 'My independent enquiry is regularly reinforced with close reference to scientific publications and search into their methods of analysis and investigation' will be at the basis of all of Eno's subsequent thinking.

But would Ascott be radical, or simply isolated?

Roy Ascott: 'The work I was making in the early 1960s didn't relate to anything else being made during that period. It came from trying to resolve non-figurative work with conceptual work – how would that work? And trying to use cybernetics in the process? Those were the things that gave rise to all this . . .'

Behaviourism and cybernetics were regarded by many intellectuals, rightly or wrongly, as branches of an infant and not necessarily plausible science. The writings and methods of the American behaviourist B. F. Skinner, in particular, had been met with a certain amount of mistrust. Some of this was due to sensationalist mis-reporting of Skinner's creation of experimental 'conditioning environments' (not least for his infant daughter).

More understandable, perhaps, was concern over what seemed to be ethically questionable ideas: that human or sentient qualities such as free will and deep subjectivity could be over-ruled by feedback-controlled environments, for example, and tested in terms of 'measurable behaviour'. In 1971, there would be a sharp intake of breath when Skinner published the frighteningly titled *Beyond Freedom and Dignity*.

Drained of controversy, however, and as applied to the creation of an art school foundation course, the ideas within behaviourism and cybernetics would take shape as a set of games and exercises in which students would have to question their environment, their responses and their decision-making processes. In a state of constant self-surveillance and surveillance by one's peers, as to whether one sank or swam would be largely a matter of individual temperament.

Roy Ascott: 'In 1962 I got this job at Ealing College of Art. Over the summer I had spent a lot of time in the library at Newcastle, where I found a book on cybernetics. It contained all these phrases like "Black Box" and "retro action" – which I thought were like poetry, even though I didn't understand a lot of them!

'Now I had got this job at Ealing as Pasmore's protégé, to teach basic design, and I swiftly realised that this was too limited for me. But I began to understand how cybernetics, which is about systems, could replace anatomy or perspective as the main principle: it's about interaction, and about change. So I decided that I would make of Ealing an organism; we wrote a manifesto at one stage which said things such as: "You don't receive information without giving information" and so on. Really, I was trying to find my way from cybernetics to work *where the rules came from the making of it . . .*

'At Ealing, I established the course that subsequently ran at Ipswich. It was a two-year course, so I took the view that the first year was about changing preconceptions, but in very important ways: firstly, by dismantling the idea that you are either a good or bad artist, and that whatever you are is fixed – who you are, and so forth.

'There was a curriculum of sorts, which I described in my essay "The Construction of Change", published in *Cambridge Opinion* [issue 37] in 1964. The first year the course was structured around delight, surprise, shock, introspection, profound subjectivity, outrageous objectivity – *any-thing* that would get the kids out of a suburban, O level, schoolwork way of thinking.'

In recounting the second-year programme of the Groundcourse, Ascott's description of getting the students to define 'models' of identity, and then move between them, leads to his observation that this was rather like being 'on a stage', and that one's personality – who one is – could become malleable and transferable.

A somewhat unsettling concept, the notion of self-recreation will resonate in both Eno's description of Roxy Music presenting themselves as 'members of the intergalactic parliament', Nick de Ville's observation about the adoption and shifting of personae as a valid medium in which to work, and also (as detailed later) in Anne Bean's later account, when she was at Reading, of applying ideas from the writings of Gurdjieff – notably the concept of 'self-re-membering' – to the assumption of created personae: becoming a mythic, new version of yourself, moving between styles.

Roy Ascott: 'In the second year, there was no timetable whatsoever. The students spent the first phase considering, "How do you figure what a human being is?"; "What's your model?" And in a way it didn't matter *what* your model was, but could you make a "mind map" of that particular model?

'Of course from the thirty or so students on the course, you would realise there was no single model. Given that, presumably you could move *between* models. So we got them designing "calibrators", to measure and create situations, such as: in a small room, one other person, can't use string, cannot speak, must stand up. In other words, a number of behaviours and materials. The idea was that no single person would be able to do anything . . .

'They would then be given a task – to make a game, for instance – and to do this they would be put into six groups of five people. They then had to learn to negotiate in order to make anything happen – they had to interact; *plus*, it wasn't really "them" in the first place, it was their "model". So they could do no wrong, and they could do right – it was kind of like *they were on a stage*. Anything was permissible. You never quite knew who you were, or how you would behave. It was very behaviourally based. At the time I was extremely interested in B. F. Skinner, although of course I could see the dangers.

'The idea then was that the students would have to *draw* the process they had undertaken. Why? Because they had been conscious of the behaviour and intimately involved within the process.'

The resulting work, often in the form of diagrams and maps, would not always find favour with admissions tutors at the art colleges to whom Ascott's foundation students subsequently applied. Similarly, a project devised on the Groundcourse which took the form of a noticeboard, on which were pinned envelopes containing sets of instructions, was submitted anonymously to the Young Contemporaries annual exhibition, but rejected by the selectors.

For a young person such as Eno, with an interest already in thinking across ideas, ceaselessly testing their boundaries, the Groundcourse was like a playpen. Also, in his subsequent interest in contemporary avant-garde music, at Winchester School of Art, many of the scores for works would take the form of diagrams or maps that bore some relation to the 'mind maps' and systems that figured in Ascott's teaching.

It would also be at Ipswich that Eno would meet the artist Tom Phillips, with whom he would form a long association. A detail of Phillips's *After Raphael?* (1972–3) would feature on the cover of Eno's album *Another Green World* (1975), and Phillips's *IRMA: an opera* would be released on Eno's Obscure label in 1975. As Rita Donagh has observed, the same contemporary composers would visit both Winchester School of Art and the department of Fine Art at Reading University.

Roy Ascott: 'At Ipswich we had a slightly different team, but we also had the chance to set up our own Diploma of Art and Design course. Kitaj had introduced Tom Phillips to me, and so he came on board. Phillips was very interested in music, and because of this Morton Feldman [1926–87, an American avant-garde composer] came to Ipswich – I remember him staying at my house for a few days – and Christian Wolf and others. Then Paolozzi came for a little while, and Geoffrey Clarke, who was terrific.' [Clarke would become the snappily titled Head of Light Transmission and Projection, at the Royal College of Art, London, 1968–72.]

Brian Eno: 'I was very lucky, actually, because within my area – which was East Suffolk – there were two art schools that I could apply to. There was Colchester School of Art, that was quite well financed and quite respected. And there was Ipswich Civic College that was just a little tiny place that nothing much had been happening at for quite a long time.

'So I applied to Colchester, and was accepted. But it turned out that East Suffolk County Council wouldn't pay my accommodation, and so I very reluctantly went to Ipswich. And it just so happened that the year I joined the art school had been taken over by this guy called Roy Ascott, who had just been at Ealing School of Art, where he had been for two or three years – and that was a very interesting art school.

'Roy had three specific ideas: one was that art was the politically, socially and psychologically transformative activity of society; and second was that it had to be allied to an awareness of science: it was no use just saying that it all just "came out of your imagination". He wanted to set up a situation in which people were articulate about what they did, and where they were expected to be questioned about it: a critical kind of place, in fact, unlike what was going on in most art schools at the time, one might add. In 1964, art schools were just dissolving out of the rigid, pre-1960s idea of people drawing from life, but they were not resolving *into* anything – it was more a kind of "Do what you like".

'In my experience, Roy Ascott was the first art educationalist who came up with the idea that we needed rigour about different things. So the third strand of his activities was based in his interest in B.F. Skinner-type behaviourism. His notion was that part of what an artist could do was create a sort of different behavioural conditioning for society: how do you change the mental landscape against which people are acting, if your actions are always predicated on assumptions of where you are in the world, and what the world is? Retrospectively I can see that he wanted to say you could detach actions from context, and re-think them – he wanted to break that coupling.

'The first year I was at art school was pretty much like an ordinary foundation – deciding whether you wanted to do graphics or painting or whatever. But after that first year, the Ascott ethos set in. He had been at Ipswich for that first year, and had been carefully hiring some of the people who had taught with him at Ealing – so he had a very interesting group of staff. For instance, we had a full time cybernetician – unknown at an art school. We also had a mathematician who would come in. Then we had visiting lecturers – one of whom was an art dealer, which was very advanced. It was like saying, "This is the business you're in – so talk to someone who's in the business."

'Another very important figure for me was Tom Phillips, who was very much the link into what was happening in contemporary music in England and America. He was the person who first told me about John Cage – connecting me up with Cornelius Cardew, John Tilbury, Christian Wolf, this whole school. I met Morton Feldman at his house –

a beautiful-looking man, chain-smoking Lucky Strikes, who never took his hat off . . .'

As Eno recounts the intensification of the Groundcourse during the second year, one can see how emotionally demanding the various 'games' might be to young, perhaps insecure students. One is reminded of the scene in John Schlesinger's pitilessly bleak study of self-advancement in Swinging London, *Darling* (1965), in which Julie Christie is taken to a 'sophisticated' party in Paris where the revellers play a behavioural game, assuming each other's personalities in order to take turns to say what they really think of one another. For a student with a reasonably robust sense of self, however, the second year exercises could be genuinely inspiring and intellectually challenging.

Brian Eno: 'In the second year, we moved into a different building – and this was the building where Ascott reigned supreme. We all turned up with our boxes of paints and so on, and were effectively told that we might as well put them away. The very first project we had was for two weeks: there were thirty-six students and we were put into eighteen pairs; each pair of students had to invent and build a game of some kind. This could be a board game, a card game, a physical obstacle course – anything. But the idea was to be able to investigate people's personalities, and to see how people respond in a situation. The game would have different levels of risk and security, and you would watch what different choices people made. They weren't of course games in the sense that there was anything to win.

'Every member of the thirty-six students went through all eighteen games. As you went through the game, the two people who had designed it watched what you did and wrote up their observations of how you played. Thus you ended up with seventeen reports about your personality, written by your fellow students. These were then summarised – which were the salient points that kept coming up? You then had to design a personality that was exactly the opposite.

'For instance, if a person talked a lot and took control of things, we're going to think of a person who doesn't speak unless they're spoken to, and who does what they're told. Having designed this other character – it was based on work by Tony Bezan, called "mind maps" – the bombshell was dropped: they said now we're going to have another project with six groups of six students – and by the way, you all have to be the "opposite" characters in your mind maps. So we then went on to another project for the rest of the term. And I think this was something that everybody ought to try in their lives: *not being allowed to be who you are.*

'So because I was quite talkative, I couldn't talk unless I was invited to contribute to a conversation. The funniest part was that I wasn't allowed to move. I was very energetic, and so I had to sit on a goods trolley until someone moved me. Also, because I tended to like making plans but was hopeless about doing anything, I became the person who had to make things – actually build things. When something needed to be made, they would wheel my trolley into the workshop and I had to make it – and this went on for the whole of that first term.

'Not surprisingly, it was extremely stressful for some people. Out of those thirty-six students, three left, and two had nervous breakdowns. The school was an old Victorian schoolhouse, around a quadrangle, and one day we all came in and there was a notice saying that we should all assemble in the quadrangle at 9.30. So everyone went in there at 9.30, and suddenly all the doors locked – we couldn't get out. Then the staff appeared on the roof – there was a flat-ish roof – and they all appeared with chairs. They just sat there and looked at us. And it was so interesting what then happened – what sorts of things people did. You could have just sat in a corner and ignored it; but this sense of being evaluated, scrutinised, produced some very strange behaviour in people – shouting, demonstrating, banging things, threatening to smash the windows.

'Then Tom Phillips read this text out, I think over a megaphone, and it was a quote from Lenin; it said something along the lines of, "You are worse than chickens. A chicken will be trapped inside a chalk circle, but you have drawn your own chalk circle and entrapped yourselves." And that was the only thing they said. So this went on all morning, until lunchtime – four hours of being stared at by these people. It was so interesting to see how much electricity could be put in the air by this situation.

'But it wasn't one-sided: they were quite happy for us to turn the tables. On one occasion we, the students, said that as they were always watching us work, then we wanted to watch them work. We had this long common room – a Victorian assembly room – and set up canvases for the staff, and chairs for the students, and then we harassed them while they were trying to make paintings.

'I could tell that it was genuinely tough for them. It was a sign of their respect, that they took it seriously. They assumed that we could think badly of them, and they were worried that we would; they knew that they had taken us quite a long way, psychologically, using a policy of disorientation – that was a big part of the philosophy of the thing, that one way of getting someone somewhere new and interesting was by forcibly cutting their connections to everything they knew. And that was something that really didn't suit a lot of people's temperaments. And I think the staff felt quite guilty about it, in a way. Because nobody knew if this educational experiment was going to work, or if you were going to get a bunch of dysfunctional adults.

'I would say that in general the school had very good results. Another thread in this was that there was a general disenchantment with painting. I certainly felt that painting seemed so marginal at this time; so what we were doing was what now would be called performance art and installation art – conceptual stuff involving activity out in the community and so forth. Making tiny paintings and then hiding them. But the idea of making a painting to go in a gallery seemed very impotent.

'And this became the undoing of the whole thing. Ipswich Civic College was applying for degree status, and this meant that you had to invite this committee, called the Summerson Committee – after Sir John Summerson – to assess the college and say whether or not they could award degrees. And of course when they came to Ipswich, there was tons of stuff going on, but very little painting, so Roy just moved away. The technical college of which we were a part wanted the art college to have degree status, so that was that.'

Roy Ascott: 'I was only at Ipswich for a while; the course was refused recognition as a DipAD on the basis that if I left, what would it be? Which seemed very unfair, given that we had written it all out, as you had to. But they saw it as my instigation, and, effectively, I was fired. The man who fired me said he was "cleaning out the Augean Stables" ...'

Brian Eno: 'There was a magazine that came out, called *Control*, which was very much the heart of the philosophy of what we were doing. It was a very interesting art magazine, in the first place because it didn't have any pictures in it, or any writing by critics. It was simply artists talking about a new philosophy of what art should be in society, and it was very much intended as a revolutionary call to arms.

'Roy also wrote a brilliant article in *Cybernetica* magazine ['Art and the Cybernetic Vision'; *Cybernetica: Review of the International Association for Cybernetics*, vol IX no. 4 1966; vol X no. 1 1967] which would be very interesting to revisit now – because the vision at Ipswich was unfulfilled. The Ipswich diaspora went to various other places when the unit broke up. Tom Phillips, for instance, went to Wolverhampton, as did Roy [where, unhappily, he would be Head of Painting, Wolverhampton Polytechnic, between 1967 and 1971]. I went on to Winchester School of Art, because one of the Ipswich teachers, Anthony Benjamin, had said that he would apply for a teaching post there and we could try to start something similar to the Ipswich project.

'Some people went on to Watford where Peter Schmidt was – which is how I met him. (Schmidt and Eno would co-create the creative decision-making cards "Oblique Strategies".) George Brecht from the Fluxus group had also been connected to Wolverhampton, and to Leeds, where Patrick Hughes was partly based. So we all stayed in touch, and tried to keep going what had been happening at Ipswich – or tried to turn our new art schools into something with the same flavour.'

In his experience of the Groundcourse, one can see the basis of Brian Eno's interest in systems, creative problem solving and thinking pan-culturally across the arts and sciences. Hence Eno's career-long interest in music as laboratories for the testing of ideas.

Brian Eno: 'But I shouldn't glamorise Ipswich too much – a lot of it was a big mess and people didn't know what they were doing; but I had at least got used to the idea that *you were expected to be articulate*, and people would call you on it. You couldn't get away with just "art speak". You had to try, at least, to think out what you were doing. Ipswich made me become fascinated in the connection between intellect and intuition. Normally these things are seen as disconnected; but I came out thinking that they were part of a continuum, and that you had to know when to use them.'

After 'five long years of art education' Eno would make the decision (an act of apostasy for a neophyte of the avant-garde) to work at least initially within the broader arena of pop and rock music, rather than in the smaller world of the avant-garde – where, in Britain at this time, during the latter half of the 1960s, most of the audience at most performances were on first-name terms with one another. It would be at Reading that he made contact with two regular members of that intimate audience, Andrew Mackay and Vivian Kemp.

twenty

Andy Mackay arrives at Reading University to study music and english; the changing temper of the student body; 'private discussions over coffee' as the true cells of undergraduate intellectualism; flash-forward to a student dinner party in 1968; radicals and traditionalists; the importance of the Fine Art department.

The study of music at degree level, during the 1960s, followed a demanding and, for the most part, inflexibly conservative syllabus. For Mackay, the rigidity of his courses would match his passionate interest in classical music, but also serve to frame his increasing attraction to the possibilities suggested by the avant-garde. As Brian Eno would also experience, this was an era during which leading composers within the avant-garde would find their audience and venue at the more progressive art schools and departments of fine art. For the most part, significantly, these same composers were then barely acknowledged by music schools following the traditional syllabus.

The merger of avant-garde music and performance would provide an arena for some of the activities that Andrew Mackay and his friend Simon Puxley would subsequently pursue at Reading with some fairly serious intent − notably through their 'Sunshine Group' and 'New Arts Group' (an event organised by someone at Winchester School of Art in 1968 who would introduce Brian Eno to Andy Mackay). Uniquely, however, Puxley and Mackay would add a distinctly literary dimension to their activities − a delight in aphorism, paradox and pronouncement that came close to aesthetic pose, but was also dedicated to Dada-like disorganisation.

209

Mackay's seriousness as a student of music, coupled with Puxley's erudition as a student of Victorian art and literature (encouraged by the university's great expert on Beardsley and Pre-Raphaelitism, Ian Fletcher) does much to suggest the intellectual sophistication with which they and their small circle of associates were later approaching these semi-serious excursions into underground activities.

Andy Mackay: 'I read English and Music at Reading – and was the only person to do so. I had looked at two degree courses, both in joint honours Music and English, because I was never really a good enough musician to read straight Music. When I say "not good enough", I mean with regard to the more technical aspects of music degrees at that time. They weren't music history or musicology, but forty per cent practical, forty per cent music history and twenty per cent some area in between – performance and interpretation and so forth.

'As a child I had wanted to be a conductor – but to be that, I later realised, you had to be better than everyone else in the orchestra. You have to be able to hear the wrong note that nobody else hears; you've got to be able to memorise the whole score, and hear all the harmonies in your head. I can't do that; it's simply a level of music-making that some people have and some don't. It isn't an intellectual thing.

'As a consequence I was looking more for music history and musicology-type degrees. York University at that time had one, and also had a famous avant-garde department where Wilfred Mellors was professor. He was very much up on John Cage, Stockhausen, indeterminate music and so on; he had also written *Music in a New Found Land*, about American avant-garde music: Cage, Feldman, Charles Ives . . .

'I didn't know much about all that, being an ordinary sixth former who had vaguely heard of Stockhausen and had never heard of Cage. I thought modern music was Webern!★ But I did an interview at York, and they offered me a place. Reading University, on the other hand, did a degree in Music and English – the crossover element being mostly things like Handel's oratorios and word settings, Purcell, or twentieth-century English song – Vaughan Williams's setting of Stevenson's *Songs of Travel*, all

★ Anton Webern: 1883–1945; Austrian composer and follower of Arnold Schoenberg, whose ideas would become central to the development of serialism in modern classical music.

that sort of area. It was much less concerned with avant-garde music.

'But they offered me a place as well, and I thought that it was closer to London. York was miles away, and I didn't really know the north, and so I accepted the place at Reading. I did a kind of gap year, working in Brixton library, and then went to Reading – with no particular expectations save those that everyone had in 1965, which was to spend three years having a bit of a laugh and generally getting away from home, which was very important in those days . . .'

In the mid-1960s, Reading itself was a moderately sized shopping centre, surrounded by suburbs of varying gentility, and then the fields and woodland of the Berkshire countryside. It was near enough to London, however, to feel in reach of the centre of things. Arriving at the Whiteknights campus of Reading University in the early autumn of 1965, Mackay would find himself within a social environment that was entering a transitional phase in its sense of identity and purpose.

This was a shift which can be monitored over the three years that Mackay was at the university, by the tone, design and content of the Reading Students Union newspaper *Shell*. Between the middle and late 1960s, the newspaper exchanges the somewhat tweedy 'Varsity rag' notion of student life for a style and rhetoric much closer the underground press of *International Times* and *Oz*.

As mirrored by the pages of *Shell*, the influence of underground subculture, and in particular the politics of protest, would increase alongside a general sense of student disaffection – that student life itself has become compromised by the truisms of its own lifestyle, and that apathy has deadened the student body to a point where undergraduate opinion has become dangerously malleable.

At the same time, it is important to note that an equal number of students (as Mackay recalls) were more than happy to be identified by their college scarves and flannel trousers – even as the local celebrities of freak power were growing their hair and proposing a Home Counties version of the counter-cultural credo that John Sinclair pithily summarised as 'Dope, Revolution, and Fucking in the Street'.

The issue of *Shell* newspaper for 7 October 1966, for example (the beginning of Mackay's second year), contains the following announcement (note the forthcoming appearance by two Mod groups, the Action

211

– whose 'Baby, You've Got It!', produced by George Martin was released that same year – and the Profile):

> DANCE TICKETS FOR THE COMING UP DANCE will be on sale in the Union coffee bar from 8.00 pm on Friday evening, and on Saturday morning from 10.00 am to 2.00 pm. Appearing will be The Action and The Profile.

This is followed by an editorial on the (equally Mod) subject of 'individualism', as it might be shaped in student life, concluding with a few words from the President of the Student's Union, Graham Turner. The tone is simultaneously patriarchal, nuanced with anarchism, and in keeping with the urgency of what would later become know as agitprop:

> The University Halls, you will discover, are as full of sheep as the University farms. Be an individualist – not for its own sake but because both you yourself and the student body will be better for it. Do exactly as you wish, and not as you feel you ought or as the student society seems to compel you . . . At present, the most active cells of intellectualism are to be found in private discussions over coffee.

The call for individualism is followed up by 'Disillusioned post-grad' writing under the headline 'Don't come to Reading – it's dead': 'Wake up students of Reading! Shake off this apathy, conservatism and cobwebs of Victorian conformity!'

By March 1968 (two months before the Bonzo Dog Doo-Dah Band played at the Vice Chancellor's Ball), *Shell*'s editorial would have become decidedly more militant, fixating on the war in Vietnam: 'Surely the time has come for us all to use whatever means we can to stop this war. Whoever wins can never justify victory . . .' And by 1970, the underground tendency takes direct expression in the bald statement: 'FUCK UNIVERSITY EXAMS'.

In a flash-forward of twenty-four months after Mackay's first term, a photograph taken in 1968 shows precisely the kind of 'private discussion' that had been suggested earlier by Graham Turner. The lighting is intimate, disclosing the conversationalists in a dimly lit student kitchen. A cylindrically shaded overhead light hangs fashionably low over the small dining table, on which are crowded two wine bottles, a packet of cigarettes and a cake. On the three facing sides, are Andy Mackay (caught in profile), his friend Simon Puxley (blond, intent, lit like a film star in his open-necked shirt) and Viv Kemp – her hair centre-parted and her eyes fixed on Mackay. Behind Puxley's shoulder is a heavily bevelled, frameless mirror in an art deco style; more impressively, high on the kitchen wall above Viv's head, are six prints by Joe Tilson – then a visiting lecturer at the Fine Art department. Kemp's subsequent recollection of the evening, and of Puxley and Mackay as aesthetes, is offset by her account of how she converted the cake (of which she was the creator) into something of a pop age conversation piece:

Viv Kemp: 'Those are Joe Tilson prints on the wall, because he used to come down to Reading and teach. Andy and Simon weren't dandies as such, they were more *poseurs* . . . but such aesthetes! Andy would put on different looks – an Oscar Wilde look, a *Death in Venice* look. I was doing my thesis on Yves Klein, before Klein had even been heard of in England, and so we went on a trip to Paris. And then we went on a trip to Persia! We bought an old army lorry for one hundred and fifty quid, and ten of us went . . . And that was the cake that I had made for the evening, only it didn't rise, so I painted it like a moonscape.'

But the ideological landscape at Reading was not necessarily as flat and depressing as initially suggested by *Shell*, and would certainly, within the experience of Mackay, Puxley and Kemp's generation, become seriously engaged with an array of conceptually (and by extension politically) turned-on activities. The Fine Art department, too, would become a focal point of artistic and political radicalism – a phase which would achieve extraordinary results in the 'White Room' experiment established by Donagh and some students (including Anne Bean, Polly Eltes and Viv Head) in May 1970, and which would prompt Donagh to make her painting *Reflection on Three Weeks in May, 1970* (1971), referencing the simultaneous news of police violence against student protesters at Kent State University in America.

Rita Donagh had arrived at Reading University in 1964 to teach the first year Fine Art students – in effect to establish a Basic Course not dissimilar from that she had followed under Pasmore and Hamilton at

Newcastle. The Art department had its own sense of exclusivity, concretised by its position, at that time, half a mile from the main Whiteknights campus on the Bulmershe site. The department was overseen by the distinguished Bloomsbury artist Claude Rogers (1907–79), who even in the late 1960s (according to Stephen Buckley, who having taken his MFA at the university would ultimately become Reading's fourth Professor of Fine Art) was still using the brushes that once belonged to the great English painter Walter Sickert.

Stephen Buckley: 'Reading was the first MFA course in the country – a postgraduate MA course that didn't involve a thesis. And it was an old boy's catalyst, to some extent: Terry Frost had been a fellow at Newcastle, Claude Rogers had been appointed at Reading and started the MA, and he was a friend of Kenneth Rowntree [Professor of Fine Art at Newcastle from 1959] from the Euston Road School. Also, I'm pretty sure that Rogers wanted to break the assumption that everyone had to go to a London art school. I'm not certain, but that's a guess.'

A characteristic of the times would be the division within departments of Fine Art between (crudely put) 'traditional' and 'progressive' members of the teaching staff. This is not to suggest that the former were old and out of touch, and the latter engaged and enlightened; rather, that deeply held and intensely felt positions were maintained, the disagreements between them were bound to be heightened by the move towards experimentation and radicalism that flowered during the 1960s. At Reading, Ipswich and Winchester this situation would be particularly pronounced, and the sense of debate around 'What is an artist?' and 'What is an art school?' would enter one of its most interesting phases.

   Most of the 'traditionalists' were coming from a devotion to painting – the St Ives group (a mid-twentieth-century flowering of the abstract avant-garde, whose members would include Peter Lanyon, Patrick Heron, Terry Frost) or the Euston Road School (a group of modern realist British painters founded in the late 1930s around the art school in Euston Road; amongst the members were Lawrence Gowing, the young Victor Pasmore and Claude Rogers). It is significant that these ground-breaking painters would be the 'parent generation' under the eyes and opinions of whom the pop age and sixties avant-garde would establish their own enquiries –

Richard Hamilton, in many ways, being the first pop modernist to favour Dada and surrealism over the traditions of painting.

Rita Donagh: 'I was employed by the wonderful Claude Rogers; which is interesting because Claude was one of the founder members of the Euston Road School. I applied for the job and I think he must have had a fellow feeling for Lawrence Gowing, his old friend in Newcastle.

'It was absolutely incredible that he gave me the job; I was the one woman short-listed among four candidates, and they gave it to me rather than one of the men who had applied. There was always the feeling that I was there to teach the babies; because it was the first year Basic Course which I was teaching with other people – including Roger Cook and Terry Frost, who was a wonderful man. So in that sense there was a method. I taught them about Klee, through the *Pedagogical Sketchbook*. And what we call now "de-constructing" – the Bauhaus technique was just de-constructing – point, line and plain.

'There weren't many women teaching there – there was one woman teaching sculpture. And once the students were out of the first year they went back into the Euston Road thing – which was painting. It wasn't like Newcastle, which was a fierce hot-bed of modernism. Perhaps the "cool" thing was simply keeping your head up high amongst all the men. And it wasn't easy. I wasn't feminist, or pioneering women's rights, but I enjoyed the work and believed in it. I still think the great principles of the modern movement are what drives one along – pre-First World War: Malevich, Klee, Kandinsky. Of course, coming from Newcastle I also knew about pop music, so that must have seemed quite cool.'

Roger Cook: 'The Art department at Reading during the latter half of the 1960s was definitely progressive. One of the things that happened was that it had been based on the life room, with a Slade, Coldstream, Euston Road tradition; but Claude Rogers – although obviously one of the founders of the Euston Road – had a notion of progressive ideas about art education. I think that I was also responsible, in a way, for sweeping away that dependency on the life model. At that time, I was totally hostile to the Slade tradition.'

Tim Head might also have studied at Reading University rather than Newcastle, save for the intervention of Rita Donagh during his interview at the former. He would be destined to maintain links with the group at Reading, however, through his later relationship to Viv Kemp. This network of student friendships, filtered at the end of the 1960s through the coming together of the graduated art students in London, and their consequent connections to students at the Royal College of Art, would form the coterie out of which Bryan Ferry would assemble Roxy Music; it would also – as important, in many ways – comprise the devoutly modern attitude, poised artistic outlook, vibrant Pop art glamour and sense of exclusivity for which Roxy Music's first album would come to stand.

Rita Donagh: 'I taught Vivian [Kemp], in Reading. It's very Proustian, I always think, because Viv came to Reading, and then Tim [Head] came to Reading when I was teaching there. It was the first time I met Tim. When the students came for interview, Claude Rogers would sometimes come into the studio ask me to take them around the school. One day he opened the door, and there was Tim. I took him all around the school, and he told me that he had applied also to Newcastle. And I said, "Oh – I hate to do this, but I think that if you get offered a place you should go there." I felt very bad, you know, recommending him not to come to Reading. But in fact he got a place at Newcastle and went there, and Viv stayed at Reading.'

Viv Kemp: 'I was a year older than everyone else, because I had been in Manchester for a year on a *ghastly* joint English and History of Art degree. It was all Anglo-Saxon crosses, so I got in with the anarchists. I went out with Martin Jake who was head of the Young Communists and then editor of *Marxism Today* for what seemed like years. So by the time I came down to Reading I was a bit more clued up than the young people just out of school, who were into painting landscapes.'

Andy Mackay: 'As it turned out, it was a very fortunate decision to go to Reading. Because the thing that gave Reading an edge was the Fine Art department – as well as having a very good English department at that time, *and* a good Philosophy department. But having the Art department gave the hipness that you needed in the 1960s. Art schools were still the hippest places, and so the would-be cool people would mix with Art department people; so that also meant that those doing English, Philosophy, French would mix in that sort of area.'

216

twenty-one

Reading, 1965–8. Aesthetes and activists I; Simon Puxley; university opposition to the radical tendency; the Girl with Kaleidoscope Eyes; a 'happening' in Reading; tea with Michael X; advertising Pink Floyd.

The period between 1965 and 1969 would see a deepening (and darkening) of the lifestyle that could be opened up by the subcultures of and around pop and rock music. A consequence of this development – as demonstrated within the Art department at Reading – would be the chance to acquire not just new areas of knowledge, but entirely new ways of thinking. Art, aesthetics, process, conceptualism, trend and purpose were becoming focused on a notion of activity which was primarily political – either as metaphor, or as direct response, or both.

The Edenic phase of the pop experience – the colour, exuberance, glamour, wit, eroticism and delight in technology – was being matched by the growing psychedelic inclination: a social and cultural project that was as inward looking ('Live in Your Head', as the slogan went) as massage pop of the period 1955 to 1965 had been concerned with absorbing the accelerating processes of modern media and popular culture. Beyond 1970, a new hybrid of what some journalists would call 'pop decadence' would emerge, in which the resonance of the avant-garde no less than highly poised theatricality – androgyny and 'queerness' becoming a useful cultural metaphor – would play a formative part.

For Andrew Mackay and his immediate circle of friends and acquaintances at Reading, the dalliance with hippy ideals and the Revolution (as the ubiquitous term then being used to denote opposition to almost any form of establishment, institution or older methodology) comes across as both sincere and flippant, committed to the calling for an avant-garde and an exercise in the traditionally youthful romanticism of manifesto writing.

In his third year at Reading, with Simon Puxley (who at one point had been *Shell* magazine's jazz critic) and Dave Harvey (once saxophonist in an outfit known as Pat Brandon's Jazz Group), both of whom were also reading English, Mackay would co-found the 'Sunshine Group' – the tenets of which spliced championing the avant-garde with a form of English psychedelic outlook. Once again, the project would seem to balance personal philosophy and posed cool – an exercise in style and a genuine commitment to new ways of approaching art and culture. Certainly 'Sunshine' and the happenings and activities leading up to it, were dedicated undertakings with significant consequences for Mackay and Puxley.

Of all the figures within the 'inner circle' around Roxy Music, Simon Puxley (1945–98; later Dr Simon Puxley, usually known in Roxy circles as 'The Doctor') would be of particular importance, not least in regard to his subsequent relationship to Bryan Ferry, and the significance of that relationship to Ferry's creativity. Puxley was also, clearly, a fascinating figure in his own right: a devout romantic in the classic Swinburnian mode, for whom the cult of heightened personality – shock, wit, excess, style, a delight in words, imagination and erudition – was both enhanced and cursed by his attendant addictive tendencies. Tragically, his life would become dominated by long-term drug addiction, even as he continued to work closely alongside Ferry – who as Viv Kemp later recalled 'would have done anything to try and help or save him'.

In the years leading up to the success of Roxy Music in the early 1970s, however, Puxley emerges as a brilliant personality and a literary figure in the most profound sense – this brilliance and profundity being intensified, paradoxically, by his seeming inability to resolve the complexities and glamour of his personality into a creative expression and form of his own. His doctoral thesis, the gorgeously titled 'An Arduous Fulness: Rossetti and the Sonnet Tradition', submitted to the university in 1971 [R.2632], would read in retrospect as an intellectual underpinning of his own romanticism. And in his close student friendship with Andy Mackay, and their activities together, the contours of this vivid personality, with its

218

charm, poise and literary promise, might be seen coming in to fresh relief.

Andy Mackay: 'Simon was a room-mate of mine. We just happened to be in the same intake, and he had the longest hair in Reading. Which wasn't very long, just noticeably. Basically, Simon and I were really good friends during our first couple of years at Reading; then he stayed on and did a PhD about Rossetti's sonnets. I think that six years at one university is too long – especially when the second three years are on a very narrow subject. And in a way, I think Simon stayed too long at the university, by which time he was a very big fish in that particular pond.

'He had the most beautiful girlfriend [later wife] in Polly Eltes – who was a very glamorous art student and subsequently a model – they were the glamorous couple of Reading. But in a way, I feel that Simon never quite fulfilled what I think he had hoped he could do. Later on he wasn't involved in any music or performance type schemes; but he was in the early Dada things that we did.'

The 'early Dada things' would have been all the more audacious in the context of a British red-brick university in the middle of the 1960s. It is important to remember that just as Pop art did not exist as a known cultural area during the time when Richard Hamilton was making his first pop paintings and writings in the late 1950s, so in the mid-1960s the 'counter-culture' of psychedelia, happenings, the avant-garde and political protest was for the most part reasonably exotic.

Between 1967 and the early 1970s, the various members of the Reading 'faction' would create works and events both within the university and, later, in the London Arts Lab. Thus, Mackay and Puxley's 'Sunshine Group' activities would just precede the 'White Room' experiment at the Fine Art department – one consequence of which would be the formation of the Moodies, the theatrically glam, pre-punk performance art group whose founding members would include Polly Eltes and Anne Bean, and whose activities and sense of *raison d'être* will provide a further example of the evolving Pop-art/fine-art continuum.

In the meantime, however, the mainstream of the student body was obligingly aghast and amazed at the new radicalism within the arts at Reading. In February 1967 (the year that Mackay would host a 'happening' at the university, with guests including a variety of bona fide underground celebrities), one correspondent to *Shell* expressed their opinion of the Fine Art department, and in doing displayed a remarkable (and somewhat suspicious) awareness of some of the department's reference points:

THE ART DEPARTMENT – A LAW UNTO ITSELF: Opinions on the art student population vary from 'an interesting, colourful bunch', to, as one Letters Faculty lecturer was heard to comment, 'drug addicts' and 'idle morons', who 'exchange one uniformity for another'. The sixth form leaver is immediately thrown into a world of intellectual art, totally alien to what has gone before. The philosophies of Marcel Duchamp and Richard Hamilton are liberally quoted and applied, so that the bewildered art student finds that drawing string or marking the position of falling objects really do have some artistic meaning, but cannot understand why.

Andy Mackay: 'You have to remember that when I went to Reading in 1965, the majority of undergraduates were kitted out in a blazer and a pair of grey flannel trousers, would usually have a striped university scarf draped casually around their necks, and would go out drinking beer. *And* they would mostly wear a University tie. Only the Art department had people who wore blue jeans – which were very hard to get . . .'

For the young Viv Kemp, arriving at Reading University in the autumn of 1966, both her work as a student in the Fine Art department, and her subsequent friendship with Mackay and Puxley, would soon make for an invigorating academic, creative and social life. Not only did the 'pieces of string' and 'position of falling objects' have a meaning for her, she was also – like many of the art students – deeply interested in the meaning behind the meaning, and whether or not it might be rearranged.

Viv Kemp: 'I was going out with Andy Mackay, at Reading, where he was reading Music and English. I was studying Fine Art, and Andy was very into experimental music. Simon Puxley was Andy's best friend. Simon did English at Reading with us, and they were into *esoteric aesthetics*, but totally. They produced poetry magazines; and later Simon and Andy actually did a performance together at the Arts Lab. The thing about Andy was that he always had an amazing style. Even at Reading he dressed in a great way – pale-green shirts, and eau de Nil: Pre-Raphaelite things, in fact! It was stylish times. But this lecturer in the English department, Ian Fletcher, was also a big influence – in rather decadent things: Proust, Beardsley. And if you then combine that with the very avant-garde – with Duchamp, John Cage, Richard Hamilton, The Velvet Underground . . . Well!'

In many ways, 1967 – recalled by Kemp as the year of the Beatles' *Sergeant Pepper*, 'hippy times' – would see the flowering of Mackay and Puxley's English avant-garde psychedelic neo-Dada happening scene. With both serious intentions and an eye for a good time, the group's activities between 1967 and 1968 would see the formation of their 'Sunshine Group', the publication of the group's magazine (one issue only), a 'happening' arranged by Mackay at the university, and the beginnings of the group's involvement with the underground scene in London.

(Backing up Kemp's recollection of the importance of *Sergeant Pepper*, a squib in *Shell* reports, with reference to the lyric of 'Lucy in the Sky With Diamonds': 'Would anybody who sees tangerine trees in Whiteknights please let us know. There's a rumour going round that they're coming out in sympathy with Graham Turner's Marigold coffee bar. Also any girls with kaleidoscope eyes.')

As ever, Mackay's (and friends') activities should be seen in relation to the conservatism with which they were surrounded. Photographs from this period show Mackay as every inch the *fin de siècle* spa-town aesthete – a dress rehearsal for Dirk Bogarde as Gustav von Aschenbach in Visconti's *Death in Venice*, meets Erik Satie. In a passport-booth portrait from 1968 the auto-faction of the look is perfected: carefully side-parted hair, metallic round-framed glasses, an open shirt with a cravat with floral design, and a white faintly pin-striped jacket with a flower in the button-hole.

The portrait is in quarter profile, Mackay's expression posed, serious. There would possibly not be an equally poised portrait of a young man with a taste for avant-garde music until the members of Kraftwerk sat for a group portrait in a photographer's studio in Paris, their appearance more that of a shy quartet of university librarians, as opposed to the creators of *Die Mensch Maschine*.

Andy Mackay: 'To put all this in perspective, I was still singing madrigals

with a little choral group, and still playing oboe. I had started playing saxophone with this university group called the Nova Express – who were a
blues group really, and not particularly good. But there were a few jazzers
in it – I could never understand jazz, and I still don't.'

Mackay's sartorial aestheticism was the outward expression of the prevailing ethos within the 'Sunshine Group'. It is a look which seems to hark
back to both English Edwardiana, and the earliest days of modernism – in
the latter to celebrate a time when the 'new' framed its ability to shock
within a setting of leisured elegance and the last summers of nineteenth-
century grandeur: an attitude as European in temper as the fixation on
New York by Ferry, Lancaster et al. in Newcastle had been American.
(One of Roxy Music's most dramatic and defining numbers, 'A Song for
Europe' [1973], would later be co-written by Ferry and Mackay, and
Ferry would also speak of Simon Puxley's importance to the writing of
the superlatively romantic lyric.)

Occurring in the *Sergeant Pepper* summer of 1967, Andy Mackay's 'happening' would also bring him into fleeting contact with a leading figure
with London's counter-cultural scene – the subsequently discredited (and
executed) black rights activist Michael X. This encounter, and its ramifications as regards the university's suggestion to Mackay that he should
probably be more careful about the company he was keeping, is also an
indication of Mackay, Kemp and Puxley's proximity to the underground
proper.

Michael X was the protest name of one Michael Little – a half
Portuguese, Trinidadian sailor who had arrived in London in 1958, and
would be variously known as Michael de Freitas and Michael Abdul
Malik before settling on the politicised surname adopted by the
American activist Malcolm X. His career would begin as henchman to
the Notting Hill based gangster landlord Peter Rachman (who, as a friend
of Christine Keeler and Mandy Rice-Davies would later find himself a
scapegoat in the Profumo affair), and subsequently follow a shadowy path
between criminal activity, Black Power and the underground scene. As
Jonathon Green points out in his analysis of the relationship between the
black community of the 1960s and the underground: 'For the West
Indians the charm of the counter-culture, in a world in which so many
doors were closed to them, was its openness. There were whites who

seemed friendly. The initial bond may have been marijuana, but for a while there would be more.'

Michael X would become known as a leading figure within the organisation of Black Power in the UK, through his creation of a supposed black liberation front, the 'Racial Adjustment Action Society' – otherwise known as RAAS. (The less political meaning of which is nothing more than West Indian slang for 'arse'.) Widely condemned by his peers and subsequent historians as little more than a hustler, de Freitas/X would enjoy a couple of years as the radical chic darling of the British liberal bourgeois media.

In a manner identical to that detailed by Tom Wolfe, in his account of the fund-raising cocktail party held by Leonard and Felicia Bernstein for the Black Panthers, to finance the legal defence of those Panthers held on the charge of plotting to blow up the Bronx botanical gardens, de Freitas/X had the white intelligentsia utterly mesmerised. Green again: 'Like every hustler, he [de Freitas] was an actor, relying heavily on the credulity of his audience; that the era's white liberals found themselves emotionally paralysed in the face of an articulate, "revolutionary" black man, unable to essay the slightest criticism, merely boosted his success.'

It was shortly before the wave of this success would start to lose strength, in July 1967, that Michael X addressed a meeting in Reading. While a star turn for counter-culture conscious students, X would subsequently be charged with contravening the Race Relations Act for telling his seventy strong audience, 'If ever you see a white man laying a hand on your black woman, kill him immediately.' Michael X was jailed for twelve months. In 1975 he would be hanged for murder in Port of Spain, Trinidad.

Andy Mackay: 'We arranged a happening in 1967. I was in a hall of residence that was a separate building – it had once been a little private lodge in its own grounds, with a lake. Second-year students tended to live there. I said that I wanted to have a party, which you were allowed to do if you asked; but I then arranged for all sorts of happening type events: spontaneous painting, people playing music, big speakers playing *Sergeant Pepper*, and a very small amount of dope smoking.

'At that time I was also a member of a small anarchist group, who were very into films. I also invited David Medalla down, an artist who used to show at the Indica Gallery [and was editor, from 1964–7 of the *Signals Newsbulletin*, co-owner of the Signals Gallery on Wigmore Street – not far from where Roxy Music's principal couturier and stylist Antony Price would soon have a shop – and mentor of the Exploding Galaxy troupe of international multi-media artists].

Viv Kemp: 'David Medalla had the Exploding Galaxy, every Sunday afternoon in the Roundhouse at Chalk Farm; they had all these very wild, psychedelic bands and everyone just went and took drugs and danced. There were the light shows with oil bubbling under slides – every Sunday afternoon . . . This was before his very political era. David was from the Philippines, and very experimental; he was famous because of his kinetic sculpture – a box on the floor which produced thick, white soap bubbles that just filled the room . . . If you look at any books on kinetic art, he's always there. He was very important at this period.

'Andy, Simon and Dave would write poetry and do experimental performances. There was even one where Michael X came down and read poetry for them, and stayed the night . . .'

Andy Mackay: '. . . Through this vaguely political side of things we had met Michael X, the black activist – a Trinidadian who styled himself on Malcolm X. He was patronised by the white avant-garde – John Lennon gave him some support, I think. He was working for black rights, and there was quite a big immigrant population in Reading. Through him I used to go into the black community, and went to some very heavy ska dances with lots of Caribbean food and that sort of thing. Michael was in fact a total fraud and a very bad person; I remember my head of hall, who was a professor of criminology, calling me to one side and saying, I think you should be very careful of getting involved with this man – and Michael was subsequently hanged for murder in Trinidad. So I have the rare distinction of having had tea with someone who was later hanged for murder. In any event, I think he came to the happening.

'I got into trouble, because I had said that this was going to be a private party, and of course loads of people came from the town. Like all of those '67 things it was sort of pointless really, but at the time seemed really exciting. It could have done with more live music, and there wasn't really a great deal of good live music within the university itself. Although being when it was, a lot of fantastic groups played there: the Who, Pink Floyd, Alexis Korner . . . and Geno Washington was always popular with student dances.'

Shell had already forewarned its readers of the multi-media capacity of Pink Floyd. An announcement for the Pink Floyd concert at Reading in January '67 had brought home the vogue for avant-garde audacities. The wording is a further reminder of how remote the now iconic frontiers of rock culture were to the majority of their contemporaries: 'This Saturday's dance features the Pink Floyd, who claim to be the first psychedelic group in the country. During their act anything might happen – moving images from projectors, smoke bombs, fires. They have even hacked up a car on stage . . .'

Tickets were still available.

twenty-two

Aesthetes and activists II: *Sunshine* magazine – 'Man, we had fuzz raids all the time'; Ian Fletcher, art nouveau, Beardsley and new pop style; English music hall and Dada; Roy Saint Pierre's call for Revolution; first trips to alternative London.

In the autumn of 1967, the 'Sunshine Group' would produce (the one issue of) its eponymously titled magazine, which doubled as a ticket to a Sunshine event and was ironically numbered 'Vol. 12 No. 6'. The cover, with its group photograph of the four sulky looking editors and collaborators printed in a hue of tangerine sherbet orange, is like a premonition of the picture sleeves of post-punk singles that would appear a decade later. The four 'Sunshines' – Mackay, Puxley, Harvey and Kevin Costello – are photographed from above, looking up or, in the case of Puxley, with studied indifference to one side. Standing on a paved area near a flight of steps (shades of Mark Lancaster's 'Maxwell House' shoot at Newcastle), and flanked by an institutional-looking corner of fencing, the group exude fast, bored cool. No smiles; rather, hands clasped aesthetically in front of the sternum, or professorially resting on the chin. The lettering is hippy-Beardsley; the content, astonishingly sophisticated.

The university had already been alerted to the 'Sunshine Group' by a somewhat baffled report in the pages of *Shell*, earlier that year. Headlined 'SUNSHINE, FLOWERS AND NO DRUGS', the story did its best to convey the scope and intentions of the mysterious 'Sunshine' organisation. As expected, the ideas of the group are couched in a near unfathomable blend of seriousness and ambiguity. In conversation with the author forty years later, however, Mackay described their activities as 'not, actually, entirely to do with having fun – more a serious attempt to get into performance events and happenings'.

The *Shell* report commences with what might be the opening of a British sex comedy of the same period: 'I had arranged to meet four of the leading figures behind the Sunshine movement in their flat in Bulmershe Road. But the scantily clad girl who answered the door directed me instead to the public bar of the Star in London Street.' So far, so traditionally undergraduate. But Mackay's description of the group's purpose engages seriously with what were then the corresponding concerns of the underground movement:

> It's a sort of cultural co-ordination movement. We're between us interested in pushing the avant-garde aspects of art, which are generally inaccessible because the establishments that normally control performances are overpoweringly conservative. This is the case in this university. I helped disorganise a be-in last term in the garden of Fox Hill which was quite nice. This, and some encouragement from our friends in the London underground scene, led us to thinking more about this during the summer. We are now more concerned with the rapidly expanding artistic fields of spontaneous and semi-spontaneous audience participatory dramatic and musical events.

To which Kevin Costello adds, 'We're hoping that Exploding Galaxy will come down from UFO.'

There is also some useful game-playing at work, the intent of which is politically grounded. Asked by the reporter, 'Why do you refuse to exist as an official society, and have no constitutional basis?', Dave Harvey replies, 'Because we're egoists.' The emerging impression is that the 'Sunshine Group' is also concerned with a certain exclusivity – echoing Viv Kemp's pronouncement that as regards their particular scene one was either 'in' or 'out'. The journalist then asks whether the group are connected to 'hippies' or 'flower power' – to be rebutted with the comment that the 'Sunshine Group' is above mere fashionability: ' "You need sunshine before you get flowers, man," was the only answer, and Simon Puxley's only remark, in the whole evening.'

The report concludes with what would have been a fairly loaded reference to drugs, and their place within subcultural and counter-cultural activity – even that is hard to gauge as the seriousness of the 'Sunshine Group'. The group's answer, that 'We'd like to create a university where they are no longer necessary' chimes with the short-lived establishment by 'anti-psychiatrist' David Cooper; Allen Krebs and Joseph Berke, also in 1968, of the Antiuniversity – an alternative education centre housed briefly in Shoreditch, that would prove so 'anti' (despite the alluring utopianism of its 'courses') that it was eventually colonised by dossers and sunk by its own clamour for dismantling organised education. (Berke had been involved in the (in)famous Conference for the Dialectic of Liberation, held at the Roundhouse, London, in 1967 – an event at which, as artist Carolee Scheneeman subsequently told the author, it was widely believed that agents of the CIA had spiked the free sangria with LSD.)

SUNSHINE, FLOWERS, AND NO DRUGS

I had arranged to meet four of the leading figures behind the Sunshine movement in their flat in Bulmershe Road. But the scantily clad girl who answered the door directed me instead to the public bar of the Star in London Street.

There I asked them first what Sunshine was all about. "Well its a sort of cultural co-ordination movement," replied Andy Mackay, "We're between us interested in pushing the avant-garde aspects of art, which are generally inaccessible. because the establishments that normally control performances are overpoweringly conservative. This is the case in this university. I helped disorganise a be-in last term in the garden of Fox Hill which was quite nice. This, and some encouragement from our friends in the London Underground, led us to thinking about this during the summer. We are now more concerned with the rapidly expanding artistic fields of spontaneous and semi-spontaneous audience participatory dramatic and musical events."

My next question to Kevin Costello was: "What are you intending to do this term?" He replied that "Several poetry reading and musical happenings have been scheduled—and panties of course. We're hoping that the Exploding Galaxy will come down from UFO."

"Why do you refuse to exist as an official society with no constitutional basis?" I asked Dave Harvey. "This is impossible because we're egoists. We've been accused of audience alienation, but when this happens its not our fault. At least its not deliberate like the Mothers of Invention. I'd rather call it iconoclasm, a deliberate destruction of pre-conceived concepts—people can't often take this, that's all. They usually learn however."

Mackay disagreed: "Alienation might be the only way."

When I suggested a connection with the "Hippies" and "Flower Power," they were insistent that Sunshine is not simply a prevailing fashion. "You need sunshine before you get flowers, man" was the only answer, and Simon Puxley's only remark in the whole evening.

"And drugs?"

"We'd like to create a university where they are no longer necessary."

ANDY, Dave, Emily, Kevin, Liz, Miranda, Simon and their friends invite all freshers to the stars.

BULMERSHE INDECENT EXPOSURE

A man indecently exposed himself to two girls from Bulmershe College of Education, Woodley, recently.

The two girls were taking a Tutor's dog for a walk in the woods at the time.

This is not the first time this has happened at Bulmershe. Similar incidents took place on three occasions last year.

Police are investigating the matter.

This is not to say that the 'Sunshine Group' were themselves proposing a total dismantling of the university system; rather, as the free 'supplement' sheet with their magazine would announce, they had
fundamental reservations about the system on which their own university was currently run. (Jim Haynes, subsequently of the London Arts Lab,
had also been called in to run courses on 'media' at the Antiuniversity. The
whole project was in one sense a development of the earlier [equally
short-lived] Free School, established in 1966 in a basement in Powis
Terrace, Notting Hill, just down the road from David Hockney's studio.
Amongst the pupils there had been Emily Young – the 'Emily' of the
Pink Floyd song 'See Emily Play', daughter of the author of the sexolog-
ical survey *Eros Denied*, and later an artist who during the early 1970s
would contribute to the Penguin Cafe Orchestra, launched on Brian
Eno's Obscure label. In a further musical connection to Brian Eno, the
composer Cornelius Cardew had also given some courses at the
Antiuniversity.)

The *Sunshine* magazine was announced by way of another report in *Shell*
– and it is some testimony to either the originality or the outrageousness of
the 'Sunshine Group' that they would merit yet more coverage in the university newspaper. The story ran with the eye-catching headline:

MAN, WE HAD FUZZ RAIDS ALL THE TIME
Reading has its own Sunshine Group. Seen last Saturday creating
utter chaos and a magazine in General Office, were Simon Puxley,
Andy Mackay and Dave Harvey, all 3rd year English students.
Background to the Sunshine Group involves a decision to bring a
branch of Total Art to Reading. 'It's new art,' said Mackay, 'and that's
why it's important, because it's new.' The magazine costs nothing
and came out on Thursday. New editions will appear whenever the
editors feel like it. Dave Harvey, who some will remember as saxophonist in Pat Brandon's Jazz Group, believes that spontaneity is also
of vital importance. The creation of the Sunshine Group wasn't easy.
'Man, we had fuzz raids all the time,' said Puxley, one-time *Shell* jazz
critic . . .

In terms of manifesto or protest, *Sunshine* magazine's 'supplement' began
with a warning: 'You presumably have come here anticipating intellectual

MAN, WE HAD FUZZ RAIDS ALL THE TIME

READING has its own Sunshine Group. Seen last Saturday creating utter chaos and a magazine in General Office were Simon Puxley, Andy Mackay and Dave Harvey, all 3rd year English students.

Background to the Sunshine Group involves a decision to bring a branch of total art to Reading. "It's new art," said Mackay, "and that's why it's important, because it's new."

The magazine costs nothing and came out on Thursday. New editions will appear when the editors feel like it. Dave Harvey, who some will remember as saxophonist in Pat Brandon's Jazz group, believes that spontaneity is also of vital importance.

The creation of the Sunshine Group wasn't easy, "Man, we had fuzz raids all the time," said Puxley, one-time Shell jazz critic. They even have to spend their time trying to persuade Tony Marcel, respected member of the Reading Players, that they are right in producing anything at all.

Talking about Tony Marcel, it seems that "All That Fall" was a rave success at the Edinburgh Festival. Beckett's agent saw the play and was "thrilled." Beckett himself wrote a letter of praise to Nikki Chester-Lawrence, and asked for a programme.

That doesn't mean the Union is going to get its £600 "loan" back, though. According to Marcel, Reading Players intend to pay back about £350, which isn't a bad return considering the prestige value of the performances. Marcel has got that new car, however . . .

Kaftan and a new Marigold Bar

JOHN AYLETT, an ex-Editor of Shell, failed to get enough advertising to produce a private magazine he hoped to bring out this term.

As a result, it is reported, he's turned Hippie. Wearing a gorgeous kaftan, flowered shirt and policeman-type cape he was seen wandering through a northern industrial town at 4.00 a.m. one Saturday morning. Asked what he was at, he replied "I was looking for Cricket Lane." And Football Fields I suppose.

And now, a message to the readers. Would anybody who sees tangerine trees in Whiteknights please let us know. There's a rumour going round that they're coming out in sympathy with Graham ("It's not yellow") Turner's Marigold coffee bar. Also any girls with kaleidescope eyes.

excitement because you expect a university to provide an interchange of ideas, a participation in the growth of sensibility to life in general. You have to be strong to do this because the system as it is may well and probably will destroy your hopes and dampen your enthusiasm.'

There followed a criticism of the divisions maintained within the 'academic and social environments' – with the university departments and the halls of residence. 'The obsession with social discipline and an artificial, cloistered group has to be resisted to retain any individual, and this means intellectual, freedom.' Somewhat more punkishly, the supplement signs off, 'Shall we leave it at that?'

Sunshine gives an eloquent sample of two principal trends emerging in what might be loosely termed the revolutionary and aesthetic subculture of the middle to late 1960s: the rhetoric of protest and the rise of artistic revivalism. The latter, as evidenced by the pivotal exhibition of the work of Aubrey Beardsley (Victorian artist and illustrator in the 'decadent' style, and a friend of Wilde) held at the Victoria & Albert Museum, London, in 1966, would be of particular importance as regards the visual tastes of young designers during the latter half of the 1960s. Above all, this burgeoning interest in revivalism – whether for art nouveau, Edwardian children's book illustration, aesthetic movement decadence or the 1920s – was concerned with the conduct of modern style and stylishness, its agency as aesthetic influence extending from psychedelic underground graphics, through fashion and retail to tasteful posters (available in the late 1960s from 'Gallery Five', London W1) for fashionable domestic interiors.

Viv Kemp: 'There was this wonderful tutor [Ian Fletcher] who was a big authority on Wilde, the Pre-Raphaelites and Beardsley. Beardsley, of course, was very big at that time in the sixties, even in design, and a huge influence on Biba. The fact that Arthur Rackham [Edwardian artist and illustrator of children's fairy stories] was Antony Price's favourite artist explains everything . . .'

The opening two pages of *Sunshine* show Beardley's illustration for the Sixth Satire of Juvenal, 'Juvenal Scourging Woman' (a flagellation scene in which the woman is seemingly impaled on an ornate column); facing this, an editorial of sorts, written in reasonably breathless prose and taking the form of a manifesto on the importance of a somewhat aloof mode of individualism. Once again, the accent is on an aristocracy of cool – the re-creation of oneself as enlightened being, armoured by one's insight and sophistication: '– we are important: to you, because as you are now you are not sufficient . . .' pronounce Sunshine. 'We are no organisation but egoists'; 'Individuality is essential for a sympathetic response to much of the contents of this magazine'; 'The impersonal nature of the world, and the alienation of man within society demands a conscious retaliation on the part of the individual. This is possible through art . . .'; 'To burn always with hard gemlike flame is success in life.'

The editorial signs off with four numbered statements, each assigned (mysteriously) a corresponding animal. From these parting shots the cult of an individualist aristocracy underlines itself (typically) with aphorism. For example: 'Two. Not an outsider, but detached, and doesn't forget it: elusively articulate . . . Three. Sedate: a dilettante attitude even in times of great emotional crisis; this and an air of detached amusement belies acute sensibility. Crane. Four. Cool, deadpan facade, dramatically intense. Keen scout. Hawk.'

Even allowing for the forgivable affectations of undergraduate prose style, *Sunshine*'s editorial reads rather as the application of Mod exclusivity to aesthetic movement intellectualism.

The neurasthenic misogyny of Beardsley's drawing is also echoed in the editorial's ambiguously worded closing statement: 'Women our potential works of art; not our friends.' A sensational aspect of the Roxy Music image would be the intensely stylised glamour of the cover art of their albums; in these, women would become eroticised screen goddess figures, ravished glamour models, predatory sirens – a periodic table, in fact, of sexual availability. The somewhat Mod 'maleness' of the Roxy circle would be matched by the fetishistic enshrinement of beautiful women within the group's imagery. Like some febrile fusion of Pop art and Pre-Raphaelitism, the Roxy Music aesthetic might well have looked back to 'Women our potential works of art' as its founding creed. (The inside back cover of *Sunshine* is a line illustration of a young (topless) flapperish woman inhaling a flower as she fondles her bared breast. It is signed, simply, 'Sunshine Promotions'.)

As a bringing together of influences, *Sunshine* makes heady reading. The contributors include Dom Sylvester Hovedard – the artist, concrete poet and monk ('this monk who has discussions with god through an olivetti', as his contribution observes), whose work was represented by Nicholas Logsdail at the Lisson Gallery and who would have his own retrospective at the Victoria & Albert Museum, London, in 1971; also 'TWO POEMS' from the aforementioned David Medalla, with their recurrent exclamation: 'THE GALAXY EXPLODED'. (Medalla would define his works as 'Cosmic Propulsions', because – as he put the case in an artist's statement – they were like 'microcosmic seeds' that could grow into 'macrocosmic events'.)

From the quieter waters of the university itself, devout romanticism in one form or another prevailed. An anonymous essay on 'Jazz: Innovation and Experiment' is most probably authored by Puxley. In keeping with Ferry's tastes, by coincidence, John Coltrane, Ornette Coleman, Albert Ayler, the Modern Jazz Quartet and Charlie Parker are all championed. Jazz itself is identified at the essay's heartfelt conclusion as an art form through which the individual can express their freedom within an oppressive and indifferent society.

Two sonnets by Ian Fletcher exemplify such heightened romanticism, Rossetti-like in tone and style. The first, '*Un dieu meurt au nadir*', begins:

Those frugal solitudes we know too well
When twilight's leaden nimbus frets the air . . .

and the second:

Lost image and pure absent presence alone
By presence lost but absent still decline . . .

Viv Kemp: 'Ian Fletcher taught them all – and he was a very interesting guy. That's why there was all this Beardsley stuff, and nineteenth-century imagery . . .'

Andy Mackay: 'Pre-Raphaelites figured large in the Reading curriculum, because there were two academics in residence who were great enthusiasts for the second half of the nineteenth-century English arts – which were not particularly fashionable at that time. Then there was the famous Beardsley exhibition at the V&A in 1966, and that rediscovered Beardsley for the sixties generation.

'We were also big fans of the Pre-Raphaelite Brotherhood, and they were definitely a big influence. But it was the Dadaists who struck me as more fun, and more important as a group movement. Dada seemed more exotic – foreign! Not having travelled much when I was a student, I loved the whole idea of Paris, Geneva, Rome . . .'

Mackay's modernist *flâneur* image, as captured in photographs of the period, and his fondness for the European glamour of Dada, would sit alongside both his interest in the contemporary avant-garde and a penchant for specifically English uptakes of the romantic or Dada experience. Hamilton's interest in Dada, channelled through Duchamp and Picabia, had also introduced the movement to students at Newcastle: the phenomenon of social modernity, the hi-jacking of the processes of commercial world, spectacular clamour, and the opening of art to a technically limitless range of possibilities were all central themes.

There is also the sense in which the various cells of Dada activity – in Zurich, Cologne, Paris, New York – had the allure and glamour of an exclusive sect dedicated entirely to the modern, and to the general over-throwing by a small, enlightened in-crowd of all that seemed old and entrenched within its own comfort. And then there was the comic aspect of Dada – its ambiguous delight in the absurd, that would certainly be apparent in some of Mackay's early performance pieces (and in the activ-ities of his peers in performance – the Moodies, the Kipper Kids and a lit-tle later, in 1971, artist Bruce McLean's Nice Style Pose Band).

In its turn, the comic aspect of Dada would find an echo in English music hall – a form which, amazingly, Bryan Ferry would become increasingly taken with, and would later feature in his and Mackay's semi-humorous discussions about how best to present their image and perfor-mance. The Bonzo Dog Doo-Dah Band, articulate art students, for the most part, steeped in a sophisticated awareness of Pop art and cultural his-tory, were also partially inspired by Dada, and firm favourites on the col-lege and university tour circuit towards the end of the 1960s.

Andy Mackay: 'The Bonzos played at Reading, and they were terrific. There is definitely the English art school influences of Dada rediscovered – if indeed Dada was ever forgotten. I never know with the Bonzos whether they intended to be a comedy band from the start, or whether in fact they thought they might be doing something else, and then found that what people liked was their comedy.'★

In the meantime, 'Sunshine Group' protests in the name of individualism found their place within a greater swell of revolutionary fervour, the rhetoric of which was becoming both a prominent feature of student life, and seemingly more urgent in the face of the student demonstrations in Paris and the burgeoning anti-war marches. But there was also a broader

★ In conversation with the author in 1997, Mackay would ask the same of early Roxy Music: 'One of the things about early Roxy Music is that we all thought that we were doing something different to the end result. When we did a supposedly "difficult" song, like "Would You Believe", on the first album, we *thought* we were playing a very funky rock song . . .'

sensibility of disaffection, and one which would became a ubiquitous cultural metaphor. To dismantle the old order, was the principal intention – leading with the British art schools to the kind of revolts that occurred at the Slade and Hornsey School of Art.

Revisionist histories of these events – or even the recollections of their now late middle-aged witnesses and participants – tend to agree that much damage was done in the youthful desire for revolt, but very little was followed through or offered to replace the overthrown old order. The British artist John Stezaker, for example, has recalled how destructive he found the *coup d'état* that occurred when he was a student at the Slade:

John Stezaker: 'We were dismantling the structure totally, with nothing there to replace it. [At the Slade] we had William Gregory for Visual Perception, for instance – and all these things vanished after '68. There had been an amazing line-up of intellectuals involved in the Slade teaching at that time, and afterwards there was this emptiness, and it never really recovered . . .'

The ethos of protest was more than mere faddishness; and at Reading there were certain vociferous activists for whom the Revolution amounted to more than concern over the division of students within halls of residence or university departments. Roy Saint Pierre (subsequently a lifelong campaigner on environmental and peace issues) penned a somewhat more intense call for revolt:

BASH STREET: How many lessons will the student need? The first thing our kindergarten revolutionaries must learn is what the revolutionary project is. They must stop mouthing the theories that their ideologues say Lenin et al said Marx said. They must, and this is crucial, discard the crassest of all the spectres haunting the official left – the dichotomy between private and political life. To mouth clichees about the class relations of society, while reproducing the possession and domination which characterises them in our own personal relationships – 'my girlfriend', 'my friends'- and in our own lifestyle, exposes the bankruptcy of ideology and the real schizophrenia that it engenders – a graphic illustration of oppression.

For the student this means further vicarious identification with the proletariat, without, for one moment considering the implications for

his own life of Marx's definition of the proletariat as the living nega-
tion of the system. Social repression produces and is produced by individual repression. Social barriers and splits are the same barriers and
splits that render the individual ...

To despise the bourgeois means everything is permitted. Let nothing we hate, let no symbols of our alienation remain. We shall strike
against our oppressors whenever, and wherever we can. Slogans, sabo-
taging, squatting, arson, sheer delight ...

The call to arms was followed up with some direct action from members
of Reading University – and in two cases at a fairly spectacular level:

Viv Kemp: 'A female student in the year above me at Reading [who went
on to have a senior position within the British arts establishment]
chucked a can of red paint over Edward Heath – she was so angry with
the Conservatives ... And then there was another friend of ours from
Reading who went off and bombed cars – she put a bomb under a min-
ister's car at Hadley Wood, and was in prison for twenty-five years. I can't
remember what their group was called; they were a bit like the
Baader–Meinhof, only they were from north London ...'

Eno, meanwhile, over at Winchester, had been reasonably unimpressed by
the bombast of some of the student revolutionaries. Writing in his art
school notebook for '66/67' he records: 'How remarkably easy it is to be
anarchic, subversive and generally disgruntled when the powers that be
aren't around. And note the remarkable and clam-like facility with which
these same young rebels shut up when there is authority present.' Once
moved to a commune in London in 1969, he would get to the point more
directly; in his 'Late '69' notebook Eno will write, (in a sideswipe to the
practical issues underlying squat politics: '... we don't have a housemaid –
it's me. If a group can't handle itself at the level of washing up, then what
the fuck will it do with probability theory?'

twenty-three

Fine Art and the musical avant-garde at Reading and Winchester; the Scratch Orchestra; the Maxwell Demon; soloing on a signals generator; Brian Eno and the further contemplation of creative opposites; meeting between Mackay and Eno; the New Arts Group; 'Piece for Upright Piano and Polythene', UK premiere at London Arts Lab.

The importance of the relationship between art schools and contemporary avant-garde music lay also in its intellectual authorisation of rule-breaking and experimentation. As set against (for instance) the more traditionalist faction in art education or music, the creative world opened up by the avant-garde would empower all manner of connections between artists, musicians and students involved in different activities, but stemming from similar sensibilities. As Ascott has recalled of composers and musicians coming to Ipswich, the visiting lecturers and performances by leading members of the avant-garde were as totemistically indicative of radicalism as they were instructive and artistically forceful.

Rita Donagh: 'The teaching we did at Reading was very much involved with music by then – John Cage and so on. The Music department in Reading was very traditional, and we were very unorthodox and progressive in the art school. Viv used to bring this friend of hers down, from the Music department, called Andy Mackay, and he was amazing. He was incredibly quiet – very, very charming and nice, and would come to anything that we did.

'One of the great events was Cornelius Cardew coming down. Cardew liked going to art schools, and he used to collect his Scratch

Orchestra [an open membership orchestra frequented by Eno, in which all the members were of greatly differing musical ability and would play together at their individual levels of technical competence]. Cardew was a disciple of Cage at that time – he was breaking away, but he had been very close to John Cage. Then the Cunningham ballet would come over, and Morton Feldman . . . And in a way this was more exciting and interesting than going to exhibitions at that time.

'Feldman had a lot of friends who were artists, and he liked to meet art students. These musicians and composers used to find the art students more responsive than the music students – which was the certainly the case in Reading. At Winchester School of Art, Brian Eno was very involved with contemporary music, as we were, and introduced the same composers down there: Cage, Feldman, Cornelius Cardew. It's funny; it's like a web growing across the country.'

Brian Eno: 'I was very interested in what was happening in the English avant-garde; so I was regularly making trips to London to visit Tom Phillips – who lived in Camberwell – and to go to concerts of experimental music. These were usually attended by the same thirty-one people – it was such a tiny crowd. Michael Nyman was always there, Christopher Hobbs, Gavin Bryars, Tom Phillips, John Tilbury, John Cage. Cardew and Feldman were incredibly important.

'In the mid-1960s, the English art schools were the place where all these composers could get a job. It wasn't at the music schools – who were absolutely uninterested in them. When I was at Winchester College of Art, I used to hire these people to come down. Winchester was quite a moderately sized art school, attached to a huge music school. And I would get really the top names – who were very willing to come down – Christian Wolf, David Bedford, Tom Phillips, Frederick Shevsky. We paid them ten pounds to visit, I think. And art students would be there, but no music student ever came to anything that we did. *They were never even curious!* And it was only one hour – and it was music; it was their job!

'At art school I would make behavioural scores for making paintings – a set of instructions that I would then give to four people, all of whom would interpret them in their own way, and then I would put together the four finished works as one. This was somewhat similar to the ideas going around in the Scratch Orchestra – which had a lot of overlap with

238

the Portsmouth Sinfonia [with whom Eno would play the clarinet]. The Scratch Orchestra was started by Cornelius Cardew, who was teaching at Morley College – this was before he became a Maoist.

'When Cardew started the Scratch Orchestra there were maybe eighty people – mostly people from art schools. They also made publications, which brought together these very interesting people – composers, maze makers. Tom [Phillips] had this idea, for instance, where he would send a postcard and ask you "to write the musical of which this was a scene".

'George Brecht was heavily involved, and a brilliant person; I worked with him at Wolverhampton Art College at one point. It was part of Scratch that music came out of the whole orchestra, and nobody took particular credit for things. A piece of music, in one major way, is a little personal or social experiment.

'My very first recording was with the Scratch Orchestra – a Cornelius Cardew piece which became for me very important, "The Great Learning" [1968]. At the same time, Gavin Bryars was teaching at the art school down in Portsmouth, and he then formed the Portsmouth Sinfonia, with quite a few art students from Portsmouth and

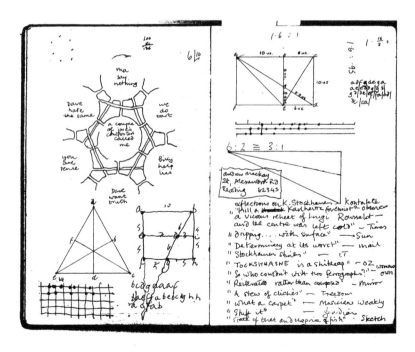

Southampton. And I also joined that. [Gavin Bryars's unforgettably mournful piece, 'The Sinking of the Titanic' would be the first release on Eno's Obscure label in 1975.]

'The one thing that was key to the Scratch Orchestra was that you had to go to rehearsals, and you had to take it seriously. Once a guy turned up and started playing deliberate musical jokes, and it just ruined everything. But something very magical happened when people tried their hardest to play things that they often had no hope of managing. There was something so touching about this. It was like flocking behaviour in birds: following the melody was a cloud of misinterpretations. Tom Phillips said, "I think being a member of the Portsmouth Sinfonia is possibly the best musical education you could ever have."

'We had people of all levels of musical competence – some were very good. Anyone could join, was the rule. It was very beautiful; you could sometimes hear somewhere in there the fine silver line of a melody, and then surrounded by this cloud, this halo, of everybody else.

'Later, the Portsmouth Sinfonia played on my album *Taking Tiger Mountain (By Strategy)* [1974]. It was also on that record, on the track 'The True Wheel', that I wanted to get a feeling like a school assembly; so I invited a bunch of friends who weren't particularly singers to sing the chorus . . .'

For Eno, avant-garde music had presented a medium in which all his ideas about systems, chance, randomness, feedback and cybernetics could be further explored. As important, however, to his experience of music and music making at art school was his interest in rock music and song writing. Eno was far from being aridly highbrow in his musical tastes – doo-wop, for example (so untethered and exotic-sounding in Suffolk in the late 1950s) and black R&B music had been amongst his earliest enthusiasms. The boy who sang along to the records at the cinema was never too distant from the intellectually inquisitive young art student.

At Winchester, the two sides of Eno's musical interests would confront one another, leaving him effectively with a choice as to what the form of his involvement in the making of music was going to be. At the heart of this decision, as Eno perceived it, was the need he felt to resolve within a new form of activity the differences, strengths and failings he had perceived in the respective genres of pop and the avant-garde.

Through his involvement with an art school band – Merchant Taylor's Simultaneous Cabinet, later to become the Maxwell Demon – Eno would begin to experiment with the application of electronics to 'group' music making, primarily through the super cool role of playing 'signals generator'. With Anthony Grafton, a fellow student, playing the guitar, the Maxwell Demon would record one song on Christmas Day 1968 entitled 'Ellis B. Compton Blues'.

Brian Eno: 'When these composers came down, I thought there were so many ideas there that were ripe for plucking. But it worked the other way around as well: for there were so many practical approaches to music that *pop* musicians knew about, that the avant-gardists didn't. And I really thought that my mission was to get these two separate bodies of knowledge melded together in some way.

'A very good example was the fact that pop musicians knew about studios; they knew about recording – they knew that listening to a record was a different experience to a live performance. They realised that the record had to be a distinct, separate and satisfactory experience; it couldn't just be a memento of a performance. So pop musicians were way ahead of the avant-garde in terms of thinking how do you make a successful work of art on a piece of vinyl.

'You had Steve Reich, for example – who made both a record that changed my life ['It's Gonna Rain' (1965)] and some really bad ones, as well – I think through not understanding what recording was about. Some of those very diagrammatic pieces of his, like 'Drumming' [1971], just didn't work as a record. It was like seeing a sketch of a musical event; you didn't really want to listen to it more than once.

'I was doing these semi-happenings, in music, at Winchester and in other colleges. I couldn't *play* anything; and I had started out in music using tape recorders, and playing Christian Wolf pieces. At the same time, I was just starting to play with a friend of mine at Winchester called Anthony Grafton, who was a guitarist. I had some tape recorders, and we recorded a few songs.

'At art school I played signals generator in a band called Merchant Taylor's Simultaneous Cabinet, which then became the Maxwell Demon. The latter is a creature from physics. James Clark Maxwell invented this creature, in relation to entropy, that could separate hot molecules from cold molecules – an anti-entropic. Playing signals generator was basically playing a device for testing equipment: it generates a pure sine wave that sweeps through the frequency, and is thus very hard to play because it's not precise at all – not like playing a keyboard. But I would play solos on my signals generator – which sounded a bit like a theramin.

'Incidentally, the electronics break – that squeal – on "Virginia Plain" is the early EMS synthesiser – out of tune, as always. Because that was before the synthesiser came with a standard keyboard – because they thought it would be great to tune the keyboard any way you wanted, so you could make an octave wherever. Which is fine, in theory, but it also meant that every time you wanted to play you had tune the keyboard so that the octave was true. Which was very difficult to do, because as the thing warmed up the oscillators would all drift.

'So I was straddling the two areas at the time, and not knowing how to resolve them; they had such different *intentions* these two kinds of music. It wasn't until 1968 that I started to think that I might be able to do something in pop.'

Worthy of mention is the fact that Thomas Pynchon, the enigmatic American novelist with whom Simon Puxley would become so fascinated, had written a role for the Maxwell Demon in his eerie pop novella *The Crying of Lot 49*, published in the UK in 1966. A study of paranoia and conspiracy theory, *The Crying of Lot 49* includes a scene in which a hippy scientist inventor called John Nefastis believes the Maxwell Demon is an actual entity, sifting molecules, capable of passing on messages. 'It connects the world of thermodynamics to the world of information flow,' says Nefastis. 'The Machine uses both. The Demon makes the metaphor not only verbally graceful, but also objectively true.' (Which is of course pure Eno.)

The novella also features a bar called the Scope, where electronics assembly workers from the Yoyodyne corporation gather to listen to electronic music:

A sudden chorus of whoops and yibbles burst from a kind of jukebox at the far end of the room. Everybody quit talking. The bartender tiptoed back, with the drinks.
'What's happening?' Oedipa whispered.

'That's by Stockhausen,' the hip greybeard informed her, 'the early crowd tends to dig your Radio Cologne sounds. Later on we really swing . . .'

As had been the case with Dada nearly sixty years earlier, the instigators of the revolutionary avant-garde in music comprised a tiny number of people. A student of music with rebellious inclinations, Andy Mackay found his own routes to confronting the establishment. While course requirements remained largely traditional, his increasing attraction to, and involvement with, the notion and practice of avant-garde performance would render him largely unpopular with the faculty staff. His fondness for Dada, mingled with the fact that he had already become – through Viv – a regular visitor to the Fine Art department (which, as reported in *Shell*, was already under suspicion as an outpost of radicalism) – would ulti-mately lead him to follow his own course, firstly in collaboration with Puxley as the 'New Art Group' and later, after leaving Reading, with his own 'New Pastoral Music' projects.

The extent of Mackay's commitment to the avant-garde was thus con-siderable – and would make his subsequent decision to join a rock group, for reasons relating in no small part to his considered assessment of his musical abilities and ambitions, all the more determined. In many ways, Mackay – like Ferry – was an artist who was looking for a medium in which to fuse seemingly opposed, or at best culturally separated, areas of interest.

As Bryan Ferry would find in the creation of Roxy Music a means of reconciling the differing emotional and artistic demands of pop music and fine art, this was an act of synthesis with which Mackay no less than Eno would readily identify, and for their own reasons. The common denominator, for all three of the young musicians, prior to working together as Roxy Music, would be the creative and cultural parity that they saw between art and pop.

In Mackay's case, pupillage within the avant-garde would serve to open up the potential of pop and rock as a medium; but it would also persuade him – rightly or wrongly – that he was an artist who needed the instantaneous, visceral response that came from a rock audience, and which one was unlikely to find in the rarefied, much smaller world of the avant-garde. In one sense, it would be Morton Feldman who opened up the possibilities of music to Mackay, in much the same way that Hamilton had opened up the possibilities of art to his students.

Andy Mackay: 'The Music department hated me, because I discovered some serious avant-garde music and this gave me a weapon with which to attack their incredibly academic teaching – which was not unlike what was taught thirty or forty years earlier. You wrote counterpoint in the style of Palestrina, or set chorals in the style of Bach. You'd bring in your harmony, and then they would draw lines through it, saying, "You can't possibly have a diminished chord there!"

'So I knew that I had to find a way out of this. Then Morton Feldman came to give a talk – that the Music department had paid for, oddly enough; I don't know why, he must have been giving a tour of the universities. But he gave this totally mind-opening lecture, in which he destroyed the classical basis of music-making: that it doesn't *matter* what order you put the notes and the beats in – all of that.

'I'd also made friends with some of the more avant-garde people, and so we set up a little performance group – which was how I met Brian Eno. We were called the New Arts Group, and our only reason for existing was to be provocative – much more going back to Dada than anything actually thought out. In fact, anything that annoyed the academics and seemed modern was okay. We would just go and be provocative, in that old-fashioned, early twentieth-century way. We would play, for instance, totally discordant music – but with no intellectual reason behind it . . .

'This found a sympathetic audience at Winchester, however. Eno was there, and so he then came back [to visit Reading]. At that point he was rather more widely read in this area: he had actually made some LaMonte Young performance pieces, for example.' [LaMonte Young; born 1935 in Idaho, USA, is an American composer and musician whose work is concerned with duration. In rock music circles, he is best known for his influence on John Cale and the Velvet Underground.]

Eno's notebook, 'Late '67/68' marks the meeting – Mackay's address, '28 Alexander Road, Reading', is written between a graph ('6:2 ≡ 3:1') and a list of imagined 'reflections on K. Stockhausen + "Kontakte"', including 'So who couldn't with two ferrographs? attributed to *Woman's Own*.'

A handbill/poster produced for the New Arts Group's historic visit to

Winchester School of Art announces 'Reading University New Arts Group will perform for one hour and a half "Mona Lisa Five" in four parts. In the Refectory, Winchester School of Arts. Sunshine Promotions.'

Eno would then repay the visit.

Brian Eno: 'I met Andy Mackay in Reading when I went over there to do a performance. I was at that time doing these long delay echo pieces: there are two machines, and you're recording off one and playing back on the other, so the length of the tape in between is the length of the delay. And I remember doing this concert at Reading where I had the tape leaving one machine, and then going way out into the hall around all these aluminium chairs, and back to another machine. So it was a very long delay – about four or five minutes before any sound you made repeated. And so I did a piece that just built up over the length of the show; and that was somehow connected to Andy's activities, and that was where we met – in around 1968.'

Andy Mackay: 'Subsequently, I arranged some things at Reading. We did a performance of John Cage's *Variations 4* in the Great Hall – basically you drop points on a map of where the performance is going to be, and you perform whatever you like at those points.

'I had also met Hugh Davies, who was an assistant of Stockhausen and ran a magazine for the Electro-acoustic Music Society – the *EMS*, it was called. He was in touch with Cornelius Cardew and other figures in the British avant-garde, and so *he* came down to Reading and gave a talk. It wasn't that often, or that serious – but it was there; and at that point we were trying to go out and do things. We used to go up to the Arts Lab in Drury Lane that Jim Haynes ran and I did a performance there with Simon . . .'

The Arts Lab was one of the venues of London's underground scene in the closing years of the 1960s, occupying two former warehouses at 182 Drury Lane, in what were then the somewhat shabby, still virtually Edwardian streets of Covent Garden. Since the mid-1950s, Haynes, an American, had been a kind of Poundian figure within new British theatre, visual arts and literary debate. Based in the 1950s and early 1960s in Edinburgh, where he established the Paperback Bookshop and later the

245

Traverse Theatre, he had also become friends with gallerist Richard Demarco – a similarly energetic and iconoclastic figure who would later work with Joseph Beuys.*

Haynes also worked with the avant-garde publisher John Calder, the dramatist and critic Kenneth Tynan and the auteur of mime (and supremely important figure in the high aesthetic cult between art, theatre, fashion, posing and pop in the 1970s) Lindsay Kemp. In 1967 he moved to London and set up the Arts Lab – a venue matched only by the Roundhouse as one of the central headquarters of 'alternative' London. There was a cinema in the basement, famous for the large foam mattress which comprised its communal seating, a gallery upstairs and a cafe ran by Sue Miles. There was also a connecting theatre space. Most important, however, was the way in which the Arts Lab had become the very embassy of the underground scene, and Haynes its resident ambassador.

Ultimately, the Lab would triumph in providing the blueprint for what became, nationally, a new generation of multi-media arts centres; at the same time, as with the Free School and the Antiuniversity, the fine line between pioneering a communal arts space that was hip to the radical discourse of sexual revolution, and setting up an easily abused venue for itinerant gropers and dossers, was all too quickly broken. In 1969 the Arts Lab would close – the energised idealism of its momentum worn down, and, more importantly, Haynes taken to court by Camden Council for unpaid rates.

To the students from Reading (and likewise for Brian Eno), the Arts Lab would have seemed for a brief while the Mecca of their sense of alternative identity. It provided cultural authority for their excursions into avant-garde performance; at the same time, it represented the whole, simultaneously seductive and aspirational trip of underground lifestyle.

Viv Kemp: 'It was more like squatters at this point; they took over this whole building, and the basement just had mattresses on the floor and they projected films, like all night – American prison camp movies,

---

* A decade later, in 1974, a superbly elegant photograph – turned into a signed edition of 400 – would record the meeting of Beuys, Buckminster Fuller and Lady Rosebery as part of Demarco's 'Black and Whites Oil Conference'. Seated in vast wicker chairs, in a hothouse cacti garden, the scene the trio present is both iconic and, somehow, determinedly chic.

Warhol, things like that. And you just lay on these mattresses in this dark basement . . . Upstairs they had exhibitions – but crazy exhibitions – or performances. The Arts Lab was where Simon and Andy did their big wrapping up a piano in polythene performance. It was a Yoko kind of thing to do.

'It was just around the time Christo was starting off. It was a totally musical piece – this was all around that John Cage era. It was fabulous; it was called *Piece for Piano*, and it consisted of Simon and Andy, with an upright piano in the middle of the room, which they wrapped up in polythene with string and sellotape. They had little microphones on the polythene which picked up the sound. And that was it. It took quite a long time – they did it very carefully. So it had nothing to do with the piano *keys* or anything, it was just actually wrapping up the piano – with the sounds of them walking round, carefully doing it.'

The typed handbill to accompany the performance (held in the early summer of 1968) reveals the extent to which the avant-garde milieu frequented by Mackay and Eno had found a useful (and all too rare) home at the Arts Lab. Billed under 'THE ARTS LABORATORY PRESENTS: THREE CONCERTS OF EXPERIMENTAL MUSIC – first programme', the evening began with 'Piece for upright piano and polythene FIRST LONDON PERFORMANCE' by Andrew Mackay and made by 'Andrew Mackay, Simon Puxley'. This was followed by Hugh Davies (the assistant of Stockhausen), with a first performance of his *Shozyg I, amplified stereophonic instrument for live electronic performance*; and then the wonderfully named Hugh Shrapnel, with the first performance of his *untitled work for any number of instruments* – the musicians including Paul Rutherford, a leading figure in the then burgeoning British 'free music' scene.

By the time he left Reading University in 1969, Mackay would have known his way around the underground scene in London, from the middle waters of which he, Brian Eno and Puxley would emerge to contribute to the creation of Roxy Music. As the 'gathering' (to use Jonathon Green's term) of the mythic sixties began to teeter on the brink of deliquescence and dispersal (the come-down after all that dope, revolution and fucking in the streets), so London's art, fashion and subcultural scene would become increasingly dense, multi-layered and conducive to new

247

ideas of modern style, routed through knowing revivalism. The avant-garde of contemporary music, so important to the more progressive factions within the British art schools, was taking its place within such a context.

Andy Mackay: 'And so we used to go up to London. The great thing about Reading was that you could hitch to London on the A4, and on a good night you would nearly always get a lift. I went to the original "14 Hour Technicolor Dream", at Alexandra Palace; and to the UFO at the Roundhouse, with liquid light projections by the Boyle family. There was a lot of acid around, but I was too scared to ever take it. I saw a lot of people who had gone too far with acid, and decided to give it a wide berth . . .'

Viv Kemp: 'It was like "doing funny things" because that's what you did – it was the sixties . . .'

twenty-four

Eno IV: The Faculty vs. Brian Eno.

In the spring and summer of 1968 – that season of student protest – Brian Eno would find himself being the subject of what amounted to a heated 'test case', at Winchester School of Art, in a debate between the old school of painters and the progressive faction. Refined to its core issues, what was being contested and discussed was the nature of art education, in relation to painting in particular.

In one sense, Eno was experiencing the slipstream of mistrust that Ascott had met from his peers, and which had subsequently resulted in his removal from authority: that experimentation with process, routed through cybernetics, systems, games playing and so forth, bore absolutely no relation to the study of painting, and very little to the broader study of art. This, in its turn, raised the more sensitive issue, 'What is an art college for?' and 'What should an art student study?' Behind all of this, needless to say, was the more practical question of whether or not Brian Eno would continue to receive his County Council bursary of £330 per annum – no small sum in the mid-1960s.

It is evidence of Eno's charisma and persuasiveness as a ringleader that matters got even this far. Doubtless, there was a portion of his stance that owed the rigour of its contrariness to the traditional inclination of students to want to kill off what they regard as the patriarchal authority of their teachers. (Just as Andy Mackay and his colleagues were determined to simply irritate the authorities with their musical happenings and neo-Dada performances.) Doubtless, too, the heady scent of revolution was in the air, fashionable and intoxicating. But there is also, clearly, the fact that Eno's activities within the college were genuinely questioning methods of art education, and raising significant issues regarding creativity.

Brian Eno: 'I went to Winchester School of Art in 1966. It was a very far cry from Ipswich. By the time I had left Ipswich, I was really thinking "We can change the world, and we must!"; whereas at Winchester – it wasn't Victorian, by any means, but it was very much in the St Ives, English, slightly parochial, modern art kind of territory. John Hoyland, for example, was one of our visiting teachers. The head of painting was Trevor Bell, from the St Ives School, and head of sculpture was Heinz Henghes – who was actually a very nice man; a fiery German Jew with a very strong accent, who had come to England as a child in the 1930s.

'But for me, the teachers at Winchester weren't doctrinaire enough. I had found that what matters is strong statements – it doesn't matter whether they're right or wrong. If you have a teacher who says, "This is what I believe, and this is right", and if that is well articulated, you can find your own position in relation to that. It makes you articulate your own position, even if you disagree. The valuable people in any situation are the ones with strong statements. But a lot of the teachers at Winchester – whom I am not putting down – were very easy and fluffy.

'One of the mottos of Ipswich was "Process not Product"; and when I went to Winchester it was all to do with product – the picture at the end. So at Winchester I was looking for anything that would keep me involved with process; it's hard to think of music, certainly, without thinking in those terms. The other idea about process was "process within a community" – which again made music and "happenings" appealing, because they involved rules and ways of tinkering with systems. Plus, there was an emerging trend within the arts that you could point to, in music, to prove that you weren't completely mad.

'But this was not particularly respected at Winchester, where they were very into things like colour theory – which seemed to me at the time to be unbelievably unimportant. I felt that we should be asking much more fundamental questions than that. And in fact I had a very interesting vindication on this, because I was constantly in arguments with the staff about that way of teaching art. I would say when I thought that something was irrelevant, and I wouldn't take part ...'

250

```
FINE ART DIPLOMA STUDENTS          RECORDS SHEET

         H. HENGHES
Tutor :  ------------------------------------ (Painting/Sculpture)
                            DECEMBER 1966
.... Period covered by return ---------------- to -------------------

    Student :     BRIAN ENO

    Attendance :

    Work :     A promising student. Difficult to pin down to work
               Hampered by intellectual considerations, but certainly
               worth the effort made for him.
```

In his 'Late '67–68' notebook, Eno wrote a summary of his opinion of the art school method as he perceived it:

Art schools are not quite destructive. Art schools manage to balance themselves on the fence between telling you what to do step by step, and leaving you free to do what you want. Their orientation is basically towards the production of specialists, and towards the provision of ambitions, of goals, and identities. The assumption of the correct identity – painter, sculptor – fattens you up for the market. The identity becomes a straitjacket; it becomes progressively more dangerous to step outside of it. As Desmond Morris writes, 'The answer is that there is a serious snag in the specialist way of life – everything is fine as long as the special survival device works, but if the environment changes then the specialist is left stranded.' The environment is unstable, and, what is more, we cannot avoid being involved with all men, all the time. These two conditions are not conducive to experts, specialists, and professionals.

By way of contrast, in his notebook for 'Spring 1973', written shortly after his departure from Roxy Music – his appearance, by this time, that of an androgynous exquisite, part Garbo, part Dr Strangelove – Eno would note: 'More than any other art form, rock music appears to have made evident the fact that now there is room for the non-specialist, the non-virtuoso, the amateur. It is possible that this could only happen in a particular form that refused to be analysed into stasis and self consciousness, and where novelty for its own sake is acceptable.' Hence Eno's immediate sympathy, six years earlier, with the principals of the Scratch Orchestra and the Portsmouth Sinfonia.

Brian Eno: 'On the other hand, the things I was doing at the college they regarded as nothing to do with the painting course – which was true, really. I wasn't making paintings, I was doing all sorts of other things, and a lot of the staff didn't think that I should be at an art school. They thought I was an interesting character – but that I was taking up the place of someone who could be a proper painter. And that was a fundamental disagreement as well. Because I thought that art schools should just be places where you thought about creative behaviour; whereas they thought an art school was a place where you made painters. So there were many levels of disagreement.'

Eno's art school reports from Winchester, between 1966 and 1969, reflect the gathering difference of opinion between the staff over his activities, and the establishment of 'pro' and 'anti' Eno factions. The Scottish painter William Crozier, assessing Eno, set out the terrain: 'Progress: Poor', he decreed, adding: 'He does not compare well with his contemporaries, but this comparison I feel is somewhat unfair as I do not think he should have pursued this *course* to this stage. I do not know what activity he is best suited to, but I hold that it is not painting.'

Anthony Benjamin, on the other hand, championed Eno's corner – to the extent of proposing him to be a valuable resource to the art school, and comparing his artistic eclecticism to that of Leonardo and Michelangelo. He wrote:

> His involvement in ART has been an example to many other students, who have benefited from his enthusiasm and from the ART ACTIV-ITIES that he has sponsored and organised, and which otherwise would not have been available to the Fine Art students. Much of what he does is not limited to painting as such, but much of what Leonardo da Vinci, Michelangelo, Marcel Duchamp etc. did was not limited to painting as such. He is a most suitable and good student, and should undoubtedly be retained. The only reason to do otherwise would be that the course is inadequate, not the student.

And there you had it. The very sanctity of painting was being brought into question, and with it the entire *raison d'être* of the course, and, by extension, the college.

Brian Eno: 'The paintings that I did make were very much like music – in the sense that they had scores, quite often: a set of things that you had to do, just like in a piece of music. One of my pieces had a score which involved ways of dividing up the canvas into areas, by combination of measurement and randomness, and ways of deciding the colours that were to be used. This was done by numbering all the tubes of paint that I had, and devising a system that would decide the amount of each to be used. So the colours were basically arbitrary.

'Now we had one teacher who used to visit who was the hero of the Saint Ives School – a very smart man called Harry Thubron, who was also of course a famous art educationalist. He went around and looked at everybody's work, and then called us all together for a talk – up until then he hadn't really spoken to any of us. So he said, "Well, I've looked around, and there are some quite interesting things going on. But there's only one student who is doing anything interesting with colour, and that's Brian Eno." And I could see Trevor's face drop, because I had fought so strongly about this issue.

'But Thubron was right, in a way. There *was* something very weird about the choice of colours because of the method by which they had been arrived at. Whereas the people who were into colour theory were doing somewhat less good versions of the things being made by the older people who were into colour theory.'

In this instance, Eno may have won the battle, but he hadn't won the war. By 1968, an increasingly heated and exasperated internal correspondence – subject Brian Eno and his eligibility to stay on the course – was passing between the members of the faculty, the head of department and Eno himself. As early as June 1967, one astute tutor in the pro-Eno lobby had reported:

> I believe that at the moment we cannot expect him to develop very far on his own steam, because we have not the facilities he needs and which may not be in line with this course. His world is much more to do with sound, words and colours – a combination which is theatrical in so far that he always demands an audience for everything he says and does. Nevertheless, an interesting student.

M. Harrison, on the other hand, took the opposing view – Eno's idiosyncrasies, far from being of value, were:

> a bad influence on other students. Brian is one of those people whom

253

other students seem to follow, merely because he can theorise. To most students at art school discovery is made through the doing; when someone like Brian comes along and discovers something without doing anything (plastic), it acts as a brake on others' development.

It was the 'process versus end product' debate, caught in a deadlock. Harrison concludes with the now standard trump card of the 'anti-Eno' faction, that Eno is 'Not a painter.' Yet another tutor, David Troostwyk, summed up the situation: Eno was, 'An individual here at Winchester because of the lack of similar contemporaries. Interesting for us, but not so good for Eno.'

Brian Eno: 'There was a period when they tried to throw me out of the college – because I used to try and stir up all the other students into a "process not product" way of thinking – and with some success. The feeling was that I was a disruptive element, which was most probably true – in that I wasn't helping other people believe in what they were doing. Because I kept questioning the ethos of the school, a lot of people who might have made quite acceptable mediocre painters were dropping painting and getting diverted into other areas. And for some of those people I was probably not a very good influence. They slightly abandoned what they were doing – which they had a feeling for and were good at – without getting hold of anything else. This was at the time of the Hornsey Art School sit-in and so on; and I, certainly, wanted to join in with all that.'

Matters reached a head on 6 March 1968, when the head of department, Heinz Henghes, wrote to Eno stating that he would have to formally demonstrate a commitment to painting, or accept that he would most probably fail to gain his diploma:

> You will be required at the end of your third year to mount an exhibition displaying an adequate number of paintings and prints, by which your ability to deal with these aspects of the visual arts is competently demonstrated. I urge you to re-evaluate your cosmology and to realise that there is as much benefit and virtue in the practice of painting as there is in any other creative activity, and to come to terms with it from now on.

A very chilly brief, demanding two paintings – 'canvas or hardboard and paint' – was attached.

In April, head of painting Trevor Bell (a distinguished artist described by the Tate catalogue as 'celebrating the act of painting') contributed to the correspondence with a long memo, headed 'Summary of tutorial'. This took the middle view, that there was 'a very strong difference of philosophy' between Eno and the faculty, but that his ideas were *completely valid*. Were Winchester a different kind of institution, he maintained, specialising in broader research, then there would be useful work to be done, following through some of Eno's ideas.

Throughout the spring and early summer of 1968 the battle raged on, culminating in a formal interview with David Pare, the overall college head, who stated that he would be unable to recommend a renewal of Eno's County Council bursary if the situation went on unresolved. Having seemingly agreed to reform, Eno then declined to back this up in his working methods, and was subsequently placed on probation at the college, until December 1968. During this time he had to satisfy the staff of his competence as a painter, by successfully completing a painting brief. It is significant that a special point was made of telling Eno that the paintings in question must be his own work.

In a memo to Trevor Bell, written on 3 July 1968, Henghes identified what was in effect the stand-off between Ascott's 'cybernetic' approach to art-making, and that of the painting department of an art school: 'He continues to produce work which is not a personal style of painting, initiated by himself, but depends on the production of a painting on the enlistment of the time and talent of other people, students and staff. He sets a pattern and is more properly to be described as a "games master" than a student of painting . . .'

Had Eno studied at Reading – where Rita Donagh, in the spirit of Hamilton, was directly urging a concentration on process, rather than end product – he may have had a more rewarding experience. As it was, by Christmas 1968 – when he was recording the one track by the Maxwell Demon – Eno had agreed to satisfy the demands of his tutors that he make a painting, and would go on to obtain his diploma the following summer. His interests, however, were drawn increasingly into the world of electronics and music; and his real debate – beyond issues of process and end product at art school – lay in which kind of music he was going to devote himself to.

twenty-five

Politics and Pose Bands: Reading University Department of Fine Art in the late 1960s and early 1970s; the 'White Room'; *Reflections on Three Weeks in May, 1970*, Polly Eltes, Anne Bean and the Moodies; a crucial dialogue between Anne and Polly, also regarding Simon Puxley: 'An Arduous Fulness' and 'Notes for Up-to-date Revivalists'.

Andy Mackay had graduated from Reading University in the summer of 1968, soon to leave for Rome, where he would spend most of 1969. In the meantime, Simon Puxley, remaining at the university, would commence work on his doctoral thesis on Dante Gabriel Rossetti and the sonnet tradition – 'An Arduous Fulness'. As Viv Kemp was completing her own degree in Fine Art (she would ultimately be awarded a first and carry off five university prizes) the new intake of first-year students would include the extraordinarily striking Polly Eltes, who would in turn become a friend and collaborator with another young woman in the Fine Art department, Anne Bean, newly arrived from South Africa.

Polly and Simon, as Andy Mackay mentions, were due to become Reading University's most glamorous couple. They would also, individually and collectively, become two figures richly eloquent of the shift in style and sensibility that occurred in the exclusive, intimate and supremely modern demi-monde between art, fashion and music in London in the early 1970s. It was at Reading, however, that the basis of the new glamour for which they would stand began to cohere.

Polly Eltes: 'I met Simon during my second year [1970]. I was reading Fine Art, and he was an English department postgraduate – there was some dialogue between the two departments at that time. He was doing his PhD on Rossetti; and I think that he was also the first person, ever, to get a linguistics degree.

'Simon approached everything from a literary angle – there was always a sort of wit to it. I think that it was to do with personalities and people; and this crossing between the artistic disciplines. He was interested in music, and absolutely committed to jazz. He could play quite nice jazz piano, which he did at parties.

'You also have to remember that Reading is in Berkshire, somewhat rural. In our last year, for instance, we had a little semi-detached cottage that belonged to the Berkshire Hunt; and they were *enraged* by us. The Master of the Hounds would gallop through the back garden, but was horrified to hear that we were arriving and leaving after 9.30 at night. The university was big on agriculture, and the estate management students shared the site with the fine artists . . .'

Viv, Simon and Polly would all play significant roles in the densely networked code of sensibility – the approach to art, aesthetics, 'pose', exclusivity and personal style – that would exist within the 'inner court' around Roxy Music, and which through the group would be channelled into the mainstream of pop and popular culture, to reach the damp high streets and new brutalist shopping centres of Edward Heath's Great Britain.

At Reading's Fine Art department, the cusp between the 1960s and the 1970s would see the recognition – and in some senses resolution – of a further tension of opposites. This tension comprised on the one hand what became known as the 'White Room' experiment, in which Donagh and her students created for three weeks in May 1970 a temporary working environment that enabled both intense concentration on artistic process (the distinction between student and tutor, for example, was dismantled), and also a venue for discussion and debate. The ethos of this experiment (inspired in part by the example of the politicised, democratic notion of teaching being put forward by Joseph Beuys) was summed up by the very image of the 'White Room' – the idea of whiteness suggesting refreshed modernity, newness and cleared space: a laboratory of perception.

Donagh's own work as artist would become increasingly political during her time as a tutor at Reading. In this she would pursue, on one level, an enquiry into the possibilities opened up by the dialogue between figurative art and abstraction – her art enfolding the viewer in its progressive questioning of its own representational capacity.

This process found early expression in her transposition through successive media of an image found in *Life* magazine of young gay men taunting police surveillance on 42nd Street, New York. From its source as a documentary 'human interest' photograph, through the mapping and blocking of its figures on to a prepared grid, their subsequent outline would then inform a sculptural piece, *Contour* (1967–8), comprising fluorescent argon tubing. Donagh's deconstruction of this particular image would be pivotal to the development of her art. For in addition to furthering her artistic enquiries, the process of this work established a thematic link between documentary evidence of a situation, its subsequent mediation, and its eventual reconstitution, in art, as a form almost of cultural pathology – at once commemorative and diagnostic.

Rita Donagh: 'In the early things I did when I went to Reading, you can see the attempt to resolve figuration and abstraction. To take this extraordinary photograph from *Life* and then to refine it into what became *Contour*. And in a way it does go back to the dilemma they posed back in Newcastle to all the students. It seems a kind of madness now; but that's what we were taught to do; that was the problem they set us.

'The one thing that Richard always insisted upon, always, was that he wasn't teaching how to make art. He was almost against that. So when you entered his classes you were not concerned with art at all. Victor Pasmore of course was the opposite; and so it was interesting. But the way of Richard's thinking engaged one with the *processes* of making; and in the 1960s and 1970s process became the defining thing in art, after the minimalist movement. One was very sympathetic to the way certain artists were working – for me, that was people like Michael Heizer, Barry Le Va – the Californian land artists; it was all process, and eventually there was no end product at all. But in a way Richard was against end product as well in his teachings.

'And that was maybe why, going back to Reading, one was attracted very much to someone like John Cage – to this idea of process and not production. I think that's why, when I got to Reading, it was as though Beuys and certainly Cage were giving one a way of thinking about the problem without worrying about an end product – which is a tremendous release, if you've been schooled in the practice of making art . . .'

Viv Kemp: 'Everyone who knew Rita was totally in awe of her, as they were with Richard Hamilton. She always looked wonderful and wore fabulous clothes; she only wore black or grey, very loose, and she had wonderful hair.

'Her reference points were totally Duchamp, and the people associated with him like Picabia. Also the Pop artists – she knew so much about Richard's work and the goings-on at the ICA, and it all sounded so exciting. Being aware of Richard and Rita was like being directly plugged in to the modern.

'But what was equally extraordinary were the number of people who rejected her approach. At Reading it was big paintings and lots of thick oil paint all over the floor – gangs of serious painters. There was one wonderful guy who taught us, who did these great big six feet canvases – landscapes – and he'd take his easel down by the canal, and he'd work so furiously that it would fall in, and then he'd pull it out again, and put it back on the easel and off he went. So you can imagine how the people who were into Rita and Richard – with the cleanliness of his mark – were so extremely opposite to what was going on.

'Claude Rogers was the professor, you see, and he was a very sensitive guy who was into Euston Road, Sickerty type painting; but he absolutely *adored* Rita, and knew that she was so special. Roger Cook was another tutor of mine; he'd been to the Slade and did very hard-edged shaped canvases. He had lived with Patrick Procter at one point, and was an incredible success by the time he was about twenty-two. He adored Rita, too, and was a big pal of hers. So in the department at Reading you would have these big discussions that were virtually Roger and Rita versus the rest of the department – these huge debates, with everybody – everybody . . .

'Every summer, everyone in the art department had to produce two paintings; and at the beginning of the summer term they would all be put up in the studio and the whole of the Fine Art department would cram in – the tutors and everyone. And Claude Rogers would go around making comments about each one, and it either made you or broke you. This was in front of all four years, and the postgraduates . . .'

In such a context, what became the 'White Room' was an event of fundamental importance to those who took part. It might now be seen as an example of both 'revolutionary' intervention, and the process that Richard Hamilton has described as 'wiping the slate clean'.

Anne Bean: 'Rita was really a very seminal figure at my life in Reading. Early in 1970 we had a life-drawing session, and Rita instigated with a small group of us that we'd get this life model into a room, and that we would do drawings from life rather than life drawings – that she'd be like this meditation point in the room. And we ended up living in this room – the White Room.

'It became very important to Rita as well. A core group of us lived together and kept creating from this life figure outwards. I recently re-created a piece from then, which was blindfolded life drawings. We made grids out of string from the model; we made the floor into a grid and played games; we dressed the model up. She was obviously a very co-operative model; but that was very much Rita's piece of collaborative, experimental installation . . .'

In a letter to the critic and art historian Tim Hilton, written in 1972, Rita Donagh described the 'White Room' in relation to a painting which she made as a consequence of the experience, titled *Reflection on Three Weeks in May, 1970*: 'On the first day a room was painted white throughout, including the floor. A student devised a grid as a means of regulating movement within the space. Crosses were put on the grid to mark squares where movement was prohibited. The studio became a stage – action/performance being a natural expression of group creativity.'

Rita Donagh: 'We had a typewriter in the room, and so the students wrote quite a lot. The project began to be called the "White Room", because we painted the whole studio white. It was a bit of a clique – it was a small group of people, and other people were a bit suspicious of us . . .'

This refinement of process would find one form of expression during the 'White Room' experiment, in what might almost have appeared its opposite: the formation of a troupe of students who called themselves the Moodies. Their complete fusion of fine art and 'glam' pop entertainment – performing covers of pop, rock, and cabaret songs – took the form of dedicated self-recreation as mythic, cartoon-like ambassadors of a pure pop sensibility. It was somewhat like the principles of the Scratch Orchestra, applied to the glamour and verve of being a pop performer.

Revelling in artifice, concept and sheer flamboyance, the Moodies were not simply a dress rehearsal for amateurist punk performance (although they were later courted by Malcolm McLaren), but also a vivid example of the fine-art/popula-culture synthesis that would so inform the creation of Roxy Music. (Anne Bean would later co-author the post-punk single 'Low Flying Aircraft' with Paul Burwell – another Reading student with whom Bean and artist Richard Wilson would later co-found, in 1983, the highly influential performance art group, Bow Gamelan Ensemble.)

Under such banners as 'revivalism', 'nostalgia' and 'decadence', the early 1970s would see the rise of a new form of pop/art lifestyle. This took the form of a cocktail of attitudes, drawn from Warhol, Hollywood, pop art, kitsch, nostalgia, Wilde, music hall, cabaret, science fiction – above all from a celebration of artifice. Examples would include *The Rocky Horror Show*, Andrew Logan's *Alternative Miss World*, and the ballet mimes of Lindsay Kemp – which were also influential on catwalk fashion shows.

A sub-strand, somewhat closer to performance art, would also feature: the anarchic performances by Anne Bean's associates, Martin von Haselberg and Brian Routh (aka the Kipper Kids), and Bruce McLean's Nice Style Pose Band. Even the early 'living sculptures' of Gilbert & George (specifically *The Singing Sculpture* and *Underneath the Arches* – the earliest performances of which, in London, were witnessed by Hamilton and Donagh) were related in sensibility – excursions into heightened states of identity, making artifice synonymous with romanticism, alternately feckless, disquieting, funny, cool, without purpose, compelling and clever.

Anne Bean: 'The Moodies would happen to overlap quite substantially at the Garage Gallery, London, with Nice Style – the Pose Band that Bruce McLean was doing then. We knew Bruce, but not very well. Those sort of things were in the air – *taking the sculpture off the plinth* . . .'

The Moodies were all female save two, Martin Kaufman and Rod Melvin – the latter a pianist who would subsequently play with Ian Dury in Kilburn and the High Roads, as well as with Brian Eno. Photographs of an early Moodies performance show an ensemble dressed in leopard print, vinyl, mini skirts, dark glasses, leather jackets, soul hats and heavy make-up. The effect is a kind of absurd reclamation of Warhol's 'superstars', filtered through all the monomania of rock music as a performed event. The troupe also played with politicised gender and sexuality – one of their various names would be Moody and the Menstruators, chosen more in the spirit of punk outrage than feminist identity art.

The Moodies' Sha-Na-Na-like delight in high theatricality was matched, crucially, by the utter division within the group between those members who saw their purpose as performance art (as did Anne Bean), and those like Polly Eltes who saw it more as an elevated form of 'showing off' – exquisite posing and dressing up. Once again, in the lineage of sensibility leading to the formation of Roxy Music – it would be a collision of seemingly opposed intentions that would create a work and an attitude that was unique, modern and utterly new.

These two phenomena, the 'White Room' and the Moodies, would represent the radical faction of the Reading Fine Art department in 1970, with the Moodies becoming a form of mascot group – later highly successful in Germany – in which the blueprint for what would become known in the early 1970s, by some journalists, as pop 'decadence' could clearly be perceived.

The tang of exclusivity related to the 'White Room' was matched by the way in which the Moodies would emerge from the experiment to take place as an artists' project wholly devoted to blurring the line between art and entertainment. In one sense, the Moodies – no less than the attitude to art making being simultaneously put forward by the artist and ceramicist Carol McNicoll (who also happened to be Brian Eno's girlfriend at this time) – might be seen as an echo of the ideas that Richard Hamilton had been formulating a decade earlier, and reiterated by Nick de Ville in his identification of playing with 'personae'. That art had the capacity to take shape within a virtually limitless array of media. In contemporary terms, this attitude represented the total rearrangement of the fixed containers of 'high' and 'low' culture – 'art' and 'pop'.

Rita Donagh: 'Anne Bean and Polly Eltes and the others, in their second or third year – Anne particularly – understood how *anything could be art*. That was the important thing; and it went right back for me. When I first encountered Klee, he says this wonderful thing: that it doesn't matter how small a thing is, so long as it's your own. And the idea going through all of this was the feeling that anything could be art – it was just how you did it, and what you did.

'Anne really understood that everything she did was her creative work; she was able to somehow bring that power with her. So with the Moodies, when they did their concerts or whatever you might call them, they might have been *received* like a pop group; but it was an art performance. It was art *and* life – and that was what was special about them.

'And I think that that's what we were trying to work towards in the "White Room"; so that even though we were engaged in this rather strange ritual, which was not like normal life, it was still part of the process. You didn't need to have the theory or write the theory, because working it out empirically one arrived at the theory more clearly . . .'

One will see the continuation of this idea and its practice within Bryan Ferry's concept of Roxy Music, and in his applying what he will term his whole 'artistic conscience' to overseeing the combined creation of the music, the image and the packaging of the group's first record. This would express in the medium of pop music the entire approach to living life as a form of art – the pursuit proposed by Tim Head as having been perfected, near enough, by Mark Lancaster.

It was also put forward as the social theory in Peter York's (simultaneously celebratory and satirical) magazine essay 'Them' (1976): that a generation of art students in the 1960s, raised on Pop art and an exposure to popular culture and revivalism, reinvented the applied arts as a form of multi-allusive *vie aesthetique*, and in a spirit which was simultaneously fashion conscious, and maintained with fine artistic seriousness.

The thread running through all of this – connecting the capacity of art to the adoption of personae, placing oneself as a character on a stage – is the notion of self-recreation. Touched on by Nick de Ville, Roy Ascott, Rita Donagh and Anne Bean, in relation to art education, this would be the central idea in the cult of posing and auto-faction that would grow up around Roxy Music.

Polly Eltes: 'The Moodies were all the people who wanted to be on the stage who were in the Art department. Some of them thought the band was actually fine art, and did a performance for the degree show . . .'

Anne Bean: 'Moodies had a write up in *Shell*, which was the student magazine; and there was a poster which said "Moodies Aren't Just a Dirty Rumour". I did an advert in *Shell* which just said "Too Hot to Handle – Moodies"; and every page had a burn. I was a painter who had got into sculpture, which very organically led into performance. Just the whole process of making sculpture became more and more important to me, and I became involved with the Bernsteins – a performance group. Martin from Kipper Kids got this old chemist's shop in the East End called Bernsteins, in 1970, which is what we got the name from. That then started ed ACME – cheap housing for artists.

'The Moodies were called Moody and the Menstruators, and we were going to reform as Moody and the Menopause. But I think we flummoxed the tutors of the Art department when we did Moodies as one part of our degree show.'

Polly Eltes: 'I wasn't a part of that, because I didn't actually think it was art – I thought of it as showing off. In fact, I wasn't even allowed to watch the degree show performance.'

264

Anne Bean: 'Nobody was. It was Claude Rogers, Lawrence Gowing, and two others – four people sitting very stiffly on a settee. That must have been later, in 1973. We got no marks – it was refused. They likewise refused my dissertation on "What is an Artist?" – mostly because it was presented in an old herring box, so it stank so much. Caroline Tissdale was my tutor, and she loved it . . .

'I suppose Moodies began with us just playing around with Rod and the piano. It was one of those things which was meant to be a one-off, and suddenly seemed to catch people, and carry on, and expand. And it could have expanded indefinitely, really. I don't know why, looking back, because most of it was pretty dreadful stuff. From my point of view I was interested – and I'm articulating something post event – in the whole Warhol thing, and although it sounds pretentious there was also that whole Gurdjieff [1866–1949; Armenian philosopher and mystic] notion of "being anything" – you can just grab anything.

'Gurdjieff was a seminal influence, strangely enough, in a lot of Reading thought. His disciple, the Russian writer, Ouspensky [1878–1947] wrote a book called *In Search of the Miraculous*, in which he recounts that everything is *artificial*, everything is *unreal* – that you're being recreated all the time. This sounds pretentious in relation to the Moodies, but it was something that grabbed me very much; it's a pre-punk thought, in that you don't to have to have particular talent in any direction, you just have to have real desire and verve. And I think that idea did excite me.

'*In Search of the Miraculous* doesn't seem to have been so in other art schools, but for some reason it was very much in the ether in Reading. Simon Puxley was interested . . .'

Polly Eltes: '*Very* interested; it was very important to him.'

Anne Bean: 'Gurdjieff was a philosopher who combined Eastern and Western thought and basically said "everything's unreal", "everything's an illusion" – you can create your own being. It's called "self re-membering".'

The writings of Gurdjieff would also exert an immediate and profound influence on the young Kevin Ayers – Soft Machine co-founder and future collaborator with Brian Eno. Ayers would describe the effect of Gurdjieff's ideas as 'even more devastating than my first joint', and write, in 1968, 'Why Are We Sleeping' in response to their effect on him.★

Through the Moodies, the evolution of a concept was summarised: as Hamilton and Donagh had presented an idea through their teaching, via Duchamp, that, 'art can be anything', by way of the Moodies this concept was expressed in the most open means – blurring the distinctions and intentionality between performance art, personal style and entertainment. For Anne Bean, this would represent a profound act of auto-faction or 'self re-membering', which had significant ramifications with regard to her thinking as an artist; for Polly Eltes, the activities of Moodies were more secular, so to speak, and concerned primarily with assuming a pose and being exclusively 'cool'. (Antony Price, fashion designer, style guru and friend of Bryan Ferry would later tell the author that fashion, 'is nothing more, or less, than the seriousness of frivolity' – a similar notion to Eltes's concept of the pose.)

But the terms of this debate, while expected in relation to the history or theory of art, in this case became extended to the arena of personal conduct and self-concept beyond the gallery. The sculpture has not only come down from the plinth, it was taking its ease in the modern world – mannered, elegant, the embodiment of aphorism. For Bean (who in one piece made at Reading in 1971, *Conversation Between Thought and Expression*, would simulate the dress, pose and expression of a shop mannequin), the perhaps harmless act of 'posing' – of playing games with your presence – could then be linked to a form of magic, and the undertaking of certain assumed roles to enable a particular result. (One has the

---

★ In 1973, Kevin Ayers would release his seductively laid-back album *Bananamour*, the inside artwork of which would feature a photograph of Ayers in white tuxedo and black bow tie, playing chess in the amber-lit opulence of a London gentlemen's club. The scene is ambiguously aristocratic – at once tongue-in-cheek and meticulously styled. A year later, Eric Boman would photograph Ferry wearing a white tuxedo and black tie for the cover of *Another Time Another Place*. The shift in attitude between the two images is palpable: for by that time, Ferry would have very nearly crossed the divide between proposing *la vie deluxe* through pose, and taking his place as a genuine member of sophisticated 'high' society. *Bananamour* also features the song 'Decadence' – a term much in use to describe a particular pop sensibility in the early 1970s, and in this instance, more specifically, a valediction of sorts to the increasingly drug-confused Nico, erstwhile icily beautiful blonde chanteuse with the Velvet Underground.

intuitive sense that there is a whiff of this same magic, deep in Duchamp's notes for the *Large Glass* – a combination of eroticism and action, circling around his term, 'cinematic blossoming'.)

In the early years of the 1970s, through Moodies and a more general school of deportment, playing games with pose and role-playing would heavily inform the tone and temper of Simon and Polly's burgeoning relationship with the fashionable demi-monde. Once again, the ramifications of the game would be balanced on issues of greater significance, as identified by Bean.

Eltes to play:

Polly Eltes: 'Going back to that idea of blurring art and life, of performing in some way, another example would be the bridge games. You see, Simon loved to play bridge, and we would play all through the night, until it got light. Then Paul Burwell got really angry, because he thought that we were trying to be a *real* bridge circle. But there is no doubt, with the bridge, that Simon was doing it at one remove – in a sense that it *wasn't* real; he was exploring a parallel universe of people who play bridge – enacting a bridge game, but it wasn't real . . .'

Anne Bean: 'It was very magical, in that there were certain things you could do, but it was in order to bring *something else out*. And this, I suppose, exists very much in the sense that all these things are games that one chooses to play.'

Polly Eltes: 'And posing and playing go together.'

Anne Bean: 'And not just in terms of playing bridge, but beyond, in all things; so rather that everything is a game. You make certain choices, and "who one is" is *not a stable place*. This idea affected me very deeply; that I could do Moodies but do something very, very different the next day. And I really enjoyed that dynamic crossover of activity. It was brilliant; it was an astonishing education; passionate . . .'

In a further flash-forward to 1973, shortly before the group disbanded, we will find the Moodies heavily profiled in the *Sunday Times* magazine. The feature opened with a double page photograph of the Moodies, ranged on banked wooden steps (the seating of a small German theatre, perhaps) with clusters of empty lager bottles behind them. Unsmiling, threatening even, they resemble nothing less than the surly female orchestra at the KitKat club in Bob Fosse's film of Weimar Berlin, *Cabaret* (which had just been released), crossed with what might be rejects from an amateur kabuki troupe – or even (if such a thing were conceivable) rejects from the New York Dolls.

As captured by Hans Feurer (who would subsequently become a leading fashion photographer, creating the Pirelli calendar for 1974), the ambiguous intentionality behind the Moodies is made strikingly articulate: that here are neither satirists nor mere purveyors of mere camp; rather, the five young women and one young man appear withdrawn behind their masks; in their green fishnet tights, cheap floral boas, teetering silver platform shoes, and, in the case of Eltes and Melvin, full white face paint; the stance is aloof, separatist – part unsmiling clown, part dress rehearsal for punk at its most disaffected.

The *Sunday Times* journalist, Meriel McCooey, identified in Moodies a debased version of the trend for glamour and nostalgia that would dominate the pop style exemplified by Roxy Music – and which was later retrospectively analysed, with no small degree of acuity, by Howard Schuman in the first series of *Rock Follies*. McCooey describes a Moodies performance in Hampstead:

> 'Ah yes! I Remember it Well!' from *Gigi* and some of the more aggressive Presley songs are performed, but they interpret these rather than imitate the originals. They make no announcements and use no words. 'Thank You for Being an Angel', sung with melancholic grace by Rod Melvin, became farce as the angel who drifted around the stage shedding sequins at every step turned out to be a cross between Mae West and Jayne Mansfield.

Anne Bean: 'But then the Moodies started to be taken terribly seriously. Not just critically, but in terms of people saying that we should be choreographed, and have our hair done.'

Polly Eltes: 'Island Records miked us up at the Bush Theatre, through Richard Williams, and they couldn't do anything with us . . . He said it was impossible.'

Anne Bean: '*Time Out* called us "The Menstrual Seven".'

Polly Eltes: 'Malcolm McLaren sat with us, but because we were "Art", we didn't speak. So I remember being in the house at Ladbroke Grove, where Simon and I were living then, and poor Malcolm sitting in the corner – perfectly acceptable, being interested, and no one would talk to him because *it was very uncool to speak.*'

Anne Bean: 'Malcolm wanted this great big pink Cadillac to drive us down Oxford Street – or something.'

Polly Eltes: 'He did. And this was *pre*-Sex Pistols. Very shortly afterwards he found what he was looking for in them.'

Anne Bean: 'Which was much more suitable. And then *Barry Flanagan* of all people [UK artist] was interested – and he, actually, would have been the most interesting person to have done it. He would have done something quite, quite quirky.'

Polly Eltes: 'And didn't we go to tea with George Melly?'

Anne Bean: 'He was *terribly* excited about us. He thought we were all lesbians. I think he just loved the ambience – he wanted to put us on at the Chislehurst caves. I mean, Led Zeppelin had played there, and so George Melly wanted us to do it as well.'

Polly Eltes: 'Did he pretend to be more deaf than he was? It was after he'd had a sherry that he seemed to make more sense to me.'

Anne Bean: 'I think, in fact, that we generally disappointed everybody.'

Polly Eltes: 'Well I remember that by the time George Melly left he was deeply disappointed by us – perhaps because we didn't speak.'

Through Moodies, one can read a summary of the pop subculture of 'decadence', androgyny and artifice that would dominate the early 1970s – from the rise of David Bowie to the emergence to prominence of *The Rocky Horror Show* and Andrew Logan's *Alternative Miss World*. Games with gender, intentionality, fashion, artifice, kitsch, camp, irony and paradox abound. In addition to which, the scene would create direct social links between different areas of the arts.

Anne Bean: 'I think George Melly had assumed that we were much more seriously *showbiz . . .*'

Polly Eltes: 'And we were so *anti*-showbiz!'

Anne Bean: 'Even though the whole thing was a take on showbiz – which was the funny thing. And when it started to be *deeply* boring was when people started to think that it really *was* showbiz.'

Polly Eltes: 'And then later on came people like the Sadista Sisters – women who were being political; and we really had nothing to with that – we were apolitical.'

Anne Bean: 'We liked playing with a gender issue – but in terms of just throwing it completely off-centre. I loved the fact that we did a benefit for *Spare Rib*, for example.'

Polly Eltes: 'And that women's art festival in Rotterdam.'

Anne Bean: 'So I loved the fact that we could go into that arena, but we could also be deeply politically questionable in other contexts.'

Polly Eltes: 'I was so bothered by our fakeness – and I did feel that we let everybody down around us. And they were so enthusiastic and believed in us. But then backed off because they weren't sure whether or not they were being laughed at.'

Anne Bean: 'They weren't sure where we were coming from, because basically *we* weren't sure; and Rod, for all his conceptualisation, was very enthusiastically showbiz in one big part of himself.'

Polly Eltes: 'Richard O'Brien, Andrew Logan, the *Rocky Horror* people – all those people would have seen us . . . Some Moodies were more able to choose material for themselves than others. Anne had an album called *Down to Eartha*, and we did perform nearly every track off that album. It was only later that we started sending up numbers by Captain Beefheart and Yoko Ono.'

Anne Bean: 'In other words people whom we really liked [Anne quotes from press cuttings]: "They take the hit song's feeble wit at its word and vamp the music so affectionately that the parody ends up better than the original"; "I found the dreamy all-girls-together atmosphere pleasantly erotic on a damp night"; "An alarming mixture of technical breakdown and excruciating visual and musical jokes. Hooray for the Moodies!" –

you see we were covered with *acres* of press. "A zany and more embarrassingly embarrassing group of performers it would be hard to find – the Moodies quite unexpectedly stole the show.""

Polly Eltes: 'Lindsay Kemp was an important influence – and in fact we supported him at the Bush Theatre at the time of *Flowers* and *The Maids*. He was also involved in fashion shows. When I started modelling in the Italian collections, Lindsay would help choreograph the shows. It spread from fashion to film to music – the interconnectedness was extraordinary. So we had thematic and personal links to Lindsay Kemp. So the link to fashion was very important. When Zandra Rhodes did her show at the Roundhouse, it was hugely ambitious – mixing dancers, models, using powerful black-outs and lighting.'

Anne Bean: 'In a sense I still have that feeling that we had back then: that if you've really made it, you've somehow given something up. Although I think it held us back, that philosophy. We were very, very suspect of being known . . .'

In the relationship and subsequent marriage between Simon Puxley and Polly Eltes one can see the twinning of intellectualism and a faintly eccentric glamour that would be common to the 'Roxy' circle, as they took their place in London at the beginning of the 1970s, and entered the imperial phase of their particular milieu.

In Moodies, Polly et al. had identified the commuting between models of identity, and 'high' and 'low' art forms, that was as conceptually sophisticated as it was theatrically engaging. Simon Puxley, at the same time, was writing from the point of view of an English studies academic, with an eye for what would become known three decades later as 'media studies'.

Puxley's contribution to a university magazine, *New Signature* (entirely more respectable than the crypto-underground publication put out by Sunshine), would be titled 'NOTES FOR UP-TO-DATE REVIVALISTS', and would discuss the burgeoning trend for 'nostalgia' – including cinema, medieval architecture, and Twiggy modelling fashions based on the styles of the 1940s. A little less than two years later Puxley would write the iconic sleeve note for *Roxy Music*, in which the thrilling slippages of time ('what's the date again? (it's so dark in here) 1962 . . . or twenty years on?') would be a key feature, and in a curious, associative manner, set the tone for a subcultural teen style that was both archaic and modern – a sartorial pronouncement and resolution of contradictions.

Likewise, Puxley's doctoral thesis – a hefty two volumes – would comprise a highly detailed and elegantly written analysis of the sonnet form in relation to Rossetti and Victorian romanticism, with much concentration on literary style as the mirror of feelings and identity. Puxley's subsequent, tragic, addiction to drugs serves to heighten, retrospectively, his insights. Class, creativity, identity and self image would collide in him in ways that were both empowering and destructive. As evidenced by the subsequent intensity of his relationship with Bryan Ferry, not least as a vital creative catalyst, there was a deeply literary quality within Puxley that underwent its own at times unbearably painful contortions in trying to find expression. Charm and disaster walked side by side within him – this supremely unlikely future 'Media Consultant' of the world's most glamorous rock group.

Polly Eltes: 'There are a lot of links between this whole group of people and the nineteenth century. I remember one of [the German rock group] Can – Micky – saying to me, "I would be absolutely happy to live in the nineteenth century – I can't be bothered with today." And Simon was also a nineteenth-century figure. Somehow it fitted – style wise. It was terribly Romantic – and Simon was committed to Romanticism in a way; that was one of the wonderful things about him – one of the frustrating things, too.

'I saw a picture recently of Simon standing with his butterfly net – something totally out of the nineteenth century. And his attitude to living in England and travelling – "*venturing forth*", west or east, were very much in the spirit of the nineteenth century. He was bubbling over with originality and ideas. It's difficult in hindsight, you can't say what caused what; but I would say that Simon's downfall was that he was absolutely enraged about his background, which was an ordinary one: a working-to-middle-class background, with very good, church-going parents. He always blamed his background for not getting into Oxford. He said, "I got to the interview, but I came from a house where there wasn't a single book, so I just didn't get through." I think he was quite bitter about that; I don't know how far that went, because he loved his family too. And then there was the addiction. The addictions had already set in when I met him, but I came from a background where I didn't recognise that. He was already knocking himself out with this or that, way back when he was doing his PhD.'

In the opening quotation of his doctoral thesis – a Rossetti sonnet, 'As Day or Night Prevail' – there is a hint of portent, transcribed before the knockings out had taken over, but chilling, none the less:

A sonnet is a coin: its face reveals
The soul, – its converse, to what Power 'tis due: –
Whether for tribute to the august appeals
Of Life, or dower in Love's high retinue.
It serve; or, 'mid the dark wharf's cavernous breath,
In Charon's palm it pay the toll to Death.

Later:

Viv Kemp: 'When Simon was taking heroin, Bryan would have done anything in the world to help him. He was beside himself, and he couldn't operate without Simon. Some years ago he had spent two years writing all the music for an album, but he didn't have any words – and it was because, I think, Simon wasn't there. And I remember saying, "You should get in a big car and get someone to drive you around London at night; and just imagine you've got Simon there beside you – and the words will come."'

part 3

london 1968–1972

'The world we are talking about was a world obsessed
with things clever, and with spotting things clever ...'
Antony Price to the author, 2003

twenty-six

The cast assembles; a nod to the 'New Bohemians'; re-routing Pop art through the prism of London; introducing Juliet Mann, Antony Price, and Keith Wainwright.

Bryan Ferry: 'The first night I ever spent in London was in David Hockney's studio in Powis Terrace. I remember thinking that this was just fabulous: it seemed enormous to me, and I just remember sleeping in the middle of this huge studio . . .'

It is significant that Bryan Ferry's residence in London would begin by his spending the night at Hockney's flat in Notting Hill: both the district and a particular, more exotic milieu within its community would be central to the world between art, fashion, rock music and the applied arts, which flourished as the sixties gave way to the seventies. It was a world with which Ferry would swiftly become intimate, and whose creative values he would add to his formative palette.

By 1969, the principal people who would be involved in the making of Roxy Music, or who would witness aspects of its creation at first hand, were either already in residence in central London or had sufficient contact with the capital to regard it as their operational headquarters. These would include all of the figures whom we have encountered so far en route. In London, these relationships would extend, re-form and entwine – particularly by way of the Royal College of Art, and fashion – to complete the creative chemistry out of which *Roxy Music* would emerge in such a spectacular manner, just a little under three years later.

As London's underground culture had had a particular affiliation with what were then the decayed stucco terraces between Notting Hill Gate and Westbourne Grove, so in lighter mood some of those within Roxy Music's initial milieu had also been drawn to west London. Their social terrain might be mapped as connecting the Royal College of Art and its environs, around Cromwell Road, Knightsbridge and Kensington Gore, to the largely gay scene that then existed around Ladbroke Grove and Notting Hill – its magnetic north, so to speak, being taken from David Hockney's flat in Powis Terrace.

As later described by Jack Hazan's quasi-documentary about Hockney, *A Bigger Splash*, made between 1970 and 1974, the Notting Hill side of this landscape was simultaneously obscure, lively, and shabby – the tall white mansions broken up into countless flats and bedsitts, and the damp streets appearing delicately drab in dirtied shades of white, grey and pale pink.

But a certain social strata of creative people felt at home in the edgy, bohemian ambience. Affordable and exotically eccentric, Notting Hill had been the residential base since the mid-1960s of Ossie Clark (fashion designer by appointment to the pop aristocracy of the high sixties), his wife and collaborator, the fabric designer Celia Birtwell, Hockney himself, his then partner and muse the young American artist Peter Schlesinger, and his friend and confidante Mo McDermott – Salfordian to Clark's Mancunian, an artist and early Hockney model who made highly fashionable, free-standing wooden silhouettes of trees and flowers.

The writer Duncan Fallowell – who graduated from Magdalen College, Oxford, at the end of the 1960s to become the first rock music critic on the *Spectator*, a collaborator with the German avant rock group Can and a friend of Simon Puxley – would later recall, in an autobiographical essay, the flavour of the district as he found it in the early 1970s:

Newton Road was off Westbourne Grove. A poky bedsitter, at the very top of a narrow stucco house, was my official address. I'd found it in an accommodation agency in Notting Hill Gate. The house was administered by a homosexual with a tall haircut who was very proud of the rubberised mackintosh he wore for going out. In the room opposite mine was Joel with two-tone hair, a professional shoplifter and rent boy. He wasn't much good at being either because he had a sweet, non-criminal nature, but he did his best. His room was lined with leopardskin wallpaper and a huge stock of wave machine lamps hypnotically tilting backwards and forwards; they were on twenty-four hours a day.

Within the maze of streets, squares and crescents descending towards Westbourne Grove, various intimate communities – some later labelled 'alternative', others closer to the underworld proper – thus created a scene of their own which had direct links to the worlds of pop music and fashion, as well as creative industries from set design to advertising. Amongst the main characteristics of this urban village, as experienced by the milieu who would become friends and collaborators with Bryan Ferry, would be a propensity for amusement, camp entertainment and pleasure that was more concerned with fun and style than the suffocating decadence described by the quasi-occultist gangster film *Performance*, then being filmed in the same neighbourhood.

Indeed, there would be a marked absence of both cynical negativity and 'heavy' drug culture within the predominantly fashion, art and theatre crowd whom Bryan Ferry would get to know during his first years in London; a mood prevailed of seamless but unexhausted partying – to old-fashioned hi-jinks, almost – which, despite a certain amount of drug use by some, was vastly distanced if not in time but in temperament from the lifestyle of the immediately preceding underground scene.

The new generation, importantly, would be defined by the strength of their work ethic as much as by the flamboyance of their somewhat camp, almost quaintly English hedonism. It was a mood – part infantilist, partly art student bohemian, part young urban dandy – retrospectively summarised by one of the scene's most striking members, the designer and early muse to the fashion designer Antony Price, Juliet Mann, in her retrospective pronouncement: 'Oh, dressing up! Dressing up! Always! Really, any excuse.'

This would be a period when androgyny and 'queerness' would become far broader metaphors of identity and outlook – filtered through fashion and music to become public statements of otherness and fashionability.

Juliet Mann: 'I suppose that we must have looked like things from another planet – it was a very fashion, art school crowd. And it was quite a closed circle, I felt, in those days. We were very much into American soul

– I remember going to see Aretha Franklin at the Hammersmith Odeon, and Stevie Wonder; it was more that sort of thing we went to than going to see other English pop groups . . .

'We used also to go to a gay club in Kensington High Street called "Yours and Mine" – there were very few women who went. There was a glass dance floor, and a friend of mine recalls dancing with David Bowie, although quite by mistake. At that time, around 1970, the only other gay clubs one knew of were in Soho, and sordid. Yours and Mine was a more acceptable, sympathetic place to go . . .

'At this time, for us, fashion and pop were all part of the same thing – although the fashion seemed more important. What you looked like was very carefully planned. There was a real love of Hollywood glamour, which was very important to Antony. For instance, I remember having a blonde wig and a red wig. The idea was to look like Rita Hayworth – a very film star idea. But importantly, even with all the "glamour" things that were going on, I *always* worked at a nine to five job as well . . .

'I can't believe I ever got into some of those outfits! One of Antony's was an off-the-shoulder frilled top on a piece of elastic, in black spotted crêpe, and shorts with *frills* around the legs – and that was a normal thing to wear on a night out.'

Adrienne Hunter, who had been Ossie Clark's PR during the late 1960s and would become in 1973 – by way of her pre-existing friendship with the Old Harrovians John Gaydon and David Enthoven (the founders of EG management) – the PR to Roxy Music, would similarly witness the shift in focus – a rearrangement of energy, almost, subtle yet significant – that occurred as the sixties gave way to the seventies.

Adrienne Hunter: 'I had experienced the latter end of the sixties, and was perhaps a bit Sloane in the beginning; then, through Ossie Clark, I had connected to the really full-on sixties. And the seventies were very different – you had to be much more together. In the sixties you just sort of ambled along; and amazing things happened and nobody really thought about tomorrow. You simply lived for the moment. But the whole energy of the seventies was more focused – and of course the sixties people just had to grow up a little.

'Something happened between the end of the sixties and the begin-

ning of the seventies, to do with art, fashion, music, and, sort of, Chelsea
– and I think that something was Roxy Music, actually. Roxy brought in
a new era, of people who could *dress the part*.'

So how might we best describe this gathering of participants, as they took
their place to evolve into an intimate, self-promoting and tirelessly inventive subsection of metropolitan society? In keeping with their inclination
towards nostalgia for earlier glamour, one answer to this question is usefully supplied by a journalistic account of a precursing, remarkably similar group – identified back in 1950 by a lecturer in history from Columbia
University, New York, Charles J. Rolo, and published as 'the first in a series
of social studies' in the first edition of *Flair* magazine, edited in New York
the same year by Fleur Cowles.★

Titled 'The New Bohemians', Rolo's essay, for all its somewhat self-
satisfied elitism, describes what will be, in effect, a rehearsal for the aspirations, constitution and participants of the world expressed by Roxy
Music – and, by the middle of the 1970s, the beginnings of the exchange
by Bryan Ferry of a fantastical *vie deluxe* and vision of 'high society' for
personal access to the real thing. As Rolo pronounces, one can almost
match his list of 'New Bohemians' point for point with members of
either Roxy Music's founding circle or their subsequent sphere of influence:

> Of course, members of Cafe Society and members of the interna-
> tional set, and people who are neither noticeably blue-blooded nor
> remotely Bohemian belong to this sizeable new coterie. In addition
> to the socialites, writers, artists, actors and actresses, it includes dress
> designers; decorators; fashionable photographers; editors (senior and
> junior) of the fashion magazines; a sprinkling of fashion models; a
> few literary agents and literary journalists; recherché craftsmen who
> have made a name for themselves with avant-garde ceramics or
> avant-garde cinema; rentiers with artistic leanings; and a somewhat
> incongruous company of officially accredited camp followers – the

★ In *Flair* – with its first editorial printed as gold handwriting on midnight-blue tissue –
we can also find a direct rehearsal for the 'punk glossies', *Deluxe* and *Boulevard*, published
in London during the last years of the 1970s: a fusion of art, fashion, 'society' and trend
watching, presented from the point of view of a small, super-fashionable coterie of in-
crowders.

petits amis and petite amies of the members in good standing. Prominent members of this group in which a great deal of talent is concentrated, are ipso facto members of the corresponding elite in London and Paris.

For the youthful ancestors of this glittering tribe, as we monitor their initial progress through the capital during the Indian summer of the 1960s – art students or former art students, designers, stylists, musicians, writers – London will be the prism through which the ideas formed during arts education can be refracted into a realised and commodified form – not just as art, but as applied arts, music, fashion, pop product, and perhaps most importantly, lifestyle.

In one sense, these vivid manifestations of artistic talent might also be described as completing a circuitry between fine art and commercial-industrial popular culture, the diagram of which had been sketched out by Richard Hamilton and his fellow members of the Independent Group nearly twenty years earlier.

For as Hamilton and his colleagues had identified the new world of mass-produced, mass-mediated popular culture, and in some cases made its vibrant components the subject of their art (leading the British neo-Romantic painter John Minton to wonder mournfully whether the future of culture would be 'ton-up boys and bubblegum wrappers'), so many of their students – not least the updated 'New Bohemians' involved in Roxy Music – would now quite strategically re-route Pop art back to its social and industrial sources. Pop art became art pop, fashion, magazines, style, social outlook and – vitally – fandom. For both Bryan Ferry and Brian Eno, moreover, there would be the deeply held conviction that the initial manifestation of Roxy Music was both an art form and, on one level, its own 'school of art' – defining a particular creative and ideological stance.

As fashion historian Marnie Fogg will describe the fashion and lifestyle store Biba as 'the democratisation of style', so Roxy Music would enable for their fans, through their music and image, the paradoxical proposition of an exclusivity that was open to all – as with Mod in its purest form, you knew when you belonged, and you could read the style codes.

Seen from the other end of the social telescope, the writer and biographer Fiona MacCarthy, who had been presented as a debutante in 1958, was subsequently in the rare position, eleven years after her 'coming out' season, of comparing Biba's fantasy notion of archaic, 'aristocratic' elegance, with what remained of the real thing. In her memoir, *The Last Curtsey* (2006), MacCarthy paints a vivid and insightful picture of the fashion at the end of the 1960s for nostalgia and vampish elegance, and how the popularity of the style related to the gradual deliquescence of actual 'society':

> The point about Biba style was that it was pastiche High Society, replicating the etiolated glamour of debs of the year in *c.*1930. Biba clothes were not expensive. Teenagers from the suburbs raided Biba every Saturday, returning home with carrier bags bulging with their spoils. Once the style of the elite was taken over by people once regarded as an underclass the mystique of the debutante was undermined.

With this mind, Baudelaire's observation about dandyism's 'new kind of aristocracy' occurring 'in periods of transition, when democracy is not yet all powerful, and aristocracy is only just beginning to totter and fall', could not have been more accurate. On a more general level, within London's fashion scene in the late 1960s, there was a connection between the street style of Mod (which the founder of Biba, Barbara Hulanicki, had studied first-hand when watching Mod couples queuing outside the Lyceum Ballroom in Wellington Street, Covent Garden) and the development of a modern style and attitude which created 'new imaginary worlds' in rather the same way that Eno would define pop music as doing.

Whether Biba's all-conquering fantasy melange of twenties flappers, forties cigarette girls, Pre-Raphaelite curls, sequinned skull caps and art nouveau, in wild shades (summarised by fashion historian Marnie Fogg) such as 'browns, maroon, orchid, amethyst and plum', or the Pop art designs created for Mr Freedom, many of the cutting-edge fashions of the late sixties and very early 1970s could be credited to former Mods who became fashion visionaries and icons.

In the exuberant *salons* of Notting Hill, Bryan Ferry would thus encounter some of the people who would be vital to the original styling of Roxy Music 'above all as a state of mind' – to anticipate his own assessment of the group. This was a clique that would include, in addition to Juliet

Mann, two of the people whose influence would maintain an imperial presence within the metropolitan demi-monde throughout much of the 1970s and beyond: the fashion designer Antony Price and the hair stylist Keith Wainwright, increasingly known as 'Keith from Smile', after the name of his salon.

The names of Keith and Antony Price would be added, in a stroke of conceptual brilliance, to the list of credits printed on the inside of *Roxy Music*'s gatefold sleeve. An echo of those listed by Richard Hamilton for the creation of *Self-Portrait* on the cover of *Living Arts 2* in 1963, these declared that a work of art could take the form of a magazine cover or a pop record, and that, moreover, it could be made with the same meticulous attention to detail and delegation of technical expertise that was once paid to the making of a Hollywood musical. In terms of their lifestyles no less than their art, this idea would be central to the milieu out of which Roxy Music would emerge.

twenty-seven

London, 1965–1968, with a backwards glance to the mid-1950s: Designers, stylists and taste makers 1: the arrival in London from Yorkshire of Antony Price, his personal style as a style manifesto and his further education in fashion; the importance of Professor Janey Ironside; the social importance of the Royal College of Art; introducing Eric Boman and Peter Schlesinger; a glance towards Redesdale Street, Chelsea – Malcolm Bird and Margot Cox; the arrival from Sussex of Juliet Mann; Jim O'Connor's motorbike; Pop art and the high-fashion London lifestyle of the late 1960s – first nod to Biba; Antony Price's gradua-tion show in 1968.

Come take a walk in sunny South Kensington
Any day of the week.
See the girl with the silk Chinese blouse on,
You know she ain't no freak.
Come loon soon down Cromwell Road, man,
You got to spread your wings.
A-flip out, skip out, trip out and a-make your stand, folks,
To dig me as I sing . . .

So sang Donovan on his infectiously cool celebration of the burgeoning Chelsea scene, 'Sunny South Kensington', recorded in 1966 – the year after Antony Price had arrived there from four years of art studies at Bradford Technical College, to study Fashion at the Royal College of Art under the college's iconoclastic first Professor of Fashion, Janey Ironside.

As recounted by Janey's daughter, the journalist and author Virginia Ironside, in her memoir *Janey and Me* (2003), the appointment of her mother to a professorship at the Royal College in 1956 was national news.

As an event within not just the British fashion world (as such a thing existed in those days) but also within the broader current of British cultural life, Janey Ironside's professorship represented a real sense of change – threatening to some in its modernity (simply by the new professor being female), but immensely welcome to others. As Ironside recalls: '. . . the same year that Bill Haley released "Rock Around the Clock", my mother became Professor of Fashion at the Royal College of Art at a salary of £1,800 a year, considerably more than my father could earn in two.'

In order to appreciate the impact that Ironside would have on not just the Royal College, but on the opening up of arts education in fashion design to students such as Ossie Clark and Antony Price, it is worth considering the metropolitan context that existed at the time of her appointment – a whole decade before Donovan invited his listeners to come loon soon down Cromwell Road (where, coincidentally, the Fashion School of the Royal College would be located during much of Price's time there).

In his book *Burning the Box of Beautiful Things*, which examines the shift in sensibility within the Royal College of Art towards the end of the 1950s, with particular reference to the college magazine *ARK* as a showplace for work by the students of graphic design, Alex Seago recounts the drabness that existed in London in the middle of the 1950s, and in which the radicalism of new approaches to art and design was thus vastly heightened:

> *ARK* 12 (Autumn 1954) captures this feeling of frustration and longing for new stimuli in an article entitled 'Londres la nuit', by Cyril Ray, a *Sunday Times* columnist, who describes the dreadful mediocrity of night life in contemporary London and the poor impression it left on foreign visitors to the capital: 'Along Fleet Street to Leicester Square and the champagne supper that was to be the highlight of our tour. Five tables were occupied in the restaurant that was to be that evening's high spot and there was plenty of room for the floor show – four girls in top hats and fishnet stockings. There was a table laid out for the night life party and we had not one but *two* triangular sandwiches containing the meat from old, cold chicken legs and margarine . . .'

A version of this desultory scene (which must surely be forgiven, in part, as the concussion caused to the capital by what were still the recent events of war) would also await the newly appointed Professor of Fashion, two years later. Hence Janey Ironside's immediate intentions were to modernise and internationalise the teaching of fashion in England – initially to the bewilderment of those who failed to see why this was necessary. As Virginia Ironside recounts:

> When a journalist from the *Daily Mirror* asked her what her aim was, she boldly replied that she wanted 'to promote an internationally accepted new English look'.
> 'How do you mean?' he asked.
> 'Well, French, Italian and American clothes all have an individual good look,' she said. 'But the general view of the English look at the moment is of rather dowdy tweeds and cashmere twin-sets worn by horse-faced women.'
> 'And you want to change that?' he asked.
> 'Yes.'
> 'Hmm,' he replied. 'Well, thank you anyway.'

In many ways, the British media had been quite correct to respond as broadly and loudly as they did to the appointment of Professor Ironside; for her arrival at the Royal College of Art in 1956 was as much a starting point for the modern pop age as that same year's release of 'Heartbreak Hotel' or the opening at the Whitechapel Gallery of 'This is Tomorrow'. Inaugurating a new age in the teaching of British fashion design, Ironside promoted modernity of style and modernity of outlook – the latter, crucially, enabling a system at the pinnacle of British arts education in which such future stars as Ossie Clark and Antony Price would be able to complete their training, and immediately establish themselves within the fashion centre of London.

As Janey Ironside would write in the late 1950s about the opportunities since the Second World War for previously excluded, working-class young people to study art and design by way of new grants, so she would bend rules in order to encourage those with exceptional promise. Her daughter recounts the alarming prejudice in fashionable London circles towards people from northern Britain, in particular, that her mother did much to dismantle within the selection procedure for new students.

Again, this welcoming of northern, not necessarily middle-class talent is a mirror of the new pop sensibility which, within ten years, would have championed new pop stars from the north, the working classes, or both.

Roxy Music, and in particular the deluxe elegance of the 'Hollywood' style designed for the sensibility of the music by Antony Price, would notably achieve some of their greatest triumphs with working-class audiences in northern industrial towns and cities. It would be a charming irony, therefore, that this most exclusive and glamorous of groups would propose through their music a new, classless aristocracy, based entirely on personal style. And this was an ethos which had begun, in one sense, twenty years before at the Royal College of Art. Virginia Ironside writes:

> If my mother could see some kind of spark of originality or energy in the scruffiest portfolio, she insisted on interviewing the student who had sent it in. She picked rough diamonds with talent, not girls from finishing schools. People from the North in those days were considered beyond the pale and were never given the chance, but my mother welcomed the likes of Antony Price, a farmer's boy from Yorkshire, and Ossie Clark from Salford, and gave them the opportunity to use the College as a showcase.

Lady Henrietta Rous, in her introduction to *The Ossie Clark Diaries*, describes how: 'Bernard Nevill and Janey Ironside had been on the interview board. Nevill remembers that Ossie and fellow student Antony Price stood out for their chutzpah, confidence and vitality. Ossie recorded, "I was interviewed by Janey Ironside, later to become a dear friend. She was a truly startling woman, like a magic person."'

Like Simon Puxley, the fashion designer Antony Price would be a supremely important contributor to the creation and sensibility of Roxy Music – he might almost be described as the Cecil Beaton to the group's *My Fair Lady*. And Price, like Puxley, was steeped since childhood in a deeply English romanticism. As Puxley had been drawn to Swinburne or the Pre-Raphaelite Brotherhood, so Price's artistic vision had at least some of its roots in Victorian and Edwardian children's book illustration – specifically Arthur Rackham (1867–1939). He was also a great admirer of the neo-Romantic, supremely heightened Englishness of the films of Powell & Pressburger, in particular *I Know Where I'm Going* (1945) and *A*

Matter of Life and Death (1946). In these he would have identified some of his favourite things: a dream-like Englishness, touched by the supernatural, and inhabited by beautiful young people wearing military uniforms.

What Price admired so much in the work of Rackham, however, was the organic fluidity of the form – the unravelling, spooling, fantastical quality; there is also a pronounced elegance in Rackham's drawing, and a profound understanding of not simply the female form but the sexuality of the female nude – both qualities of Price's own drawing.

If one then *adds* to the sensuous, blue-green dream world of Rackham, Price's equal passion for Hollywood cinema of the 1930s and 1940s (itself so often likened to a dream factory) and the meticulously constructed eroticism of female stars such as Rita Hayworth and Marlene Dietrich, one begins to see how he conveys in his own work, uniquely, a fusion of technical brilliance, *l'heure bleu* glamour and erotic romanticism. In this, Price is foremost a craftsman and technician – sharing with Richard Hamilton and Marcel Duchamp a fascination with the design of sexuality and glamour, but always with an eye to beauty, above all.

Antony Price: 'I was born in 1945, in the Yorkshire Dales, at the head of the River Ribble between Dent and Hawes and Ribblesdale. My mother was from Keighley; my father, Peter, was a Spitfire pilot during the Second World War. He was a wonderful artist – just wonderful. When I was a child, he painted an image of a charging bison on the front of my Red Indian smock, using just furnishing colours – blues and greens; he made beautiful balsa wood pistols to go with my pirate costume. I know full well my talent comes from him.

'It was just the most idyllic childhood, of animals and wild flowers and mountains – heavenly. At that time we were living near the Leeds to Carlisle railway line, which went into Bleemore tunnel and on to Dent. In the winter we would be snowed up for weeks. I was the eldest, so I would be sent into Settle to get provisions; they actually stopped the trains for us to be able to get on, in order to get food. They also used to use the line to test out exotic trains. At the centre of our village was the signal box, containing a Mrs Sedgwick – the last signalwoman in England. It was beyond "Famous Five". I was transfixed by the *technology* of the signals – all those levers and wires.'

Juliet Mann: 'When Antony Price gave a lecture to fashion students at the Odeon, Marble Arch, somebody asked how he had got so good at pattern cutting. To which he replied, "By learning how to make dry-stone walls in Yorkshire."'

Antony Price: 'In some ways it's funny that someone like me ended up doing fashion. I only went to art college because I could draw, and I was making paintings from childhood. A childhood dream book for me was *The Wind in the Willows*; and I'm obsessed with Rackham, and the drawings of Kay Nielsen. I have a book of Rackham's illustrations for *Das Nibelung*, and his Valkyrie are simply fabulous. It's that screamingly organic thing.

'It's very romantic I suppose; and Eric Boman [photographer and fellow graduate of Royal College of Art] used to say that I was *so* romantic – and possibly he was right. Romantic in an artistic, Pisces, dreamy kind of way – the only person I knew who was like me was Gala –' ['The mysterious and eccentric Gala Mitchell was a cult model and favourite of Ossie Clark and Antony Price,' writes Peter Schlesinger; Mitchell appears on the back cover of Lou Reed's album *Transformer*] '– and she was a Pisces too; it's the curse of the fish person. The turquoise, lilac-blue world ...When I used to drive down to Arundel with Juliet [Mann], we would go through Leith Hill, or up to Chanctonbury Ring – which was all pure Rackham. Old man's beard; bluebells, ivy ...

'Later still, there was a scene in my Camden Palace show in 1983, with these sea queens all in cross-pleated lilac dresses, with golden galleons on their heads; and it was all done underwater to Eno's track "Backwater". It was so beautiful – these three girls with wonderful Judy Blame jewellery ...'

The extravagant, sexual elegance of Price's design would be enabled by its sheer technical inventiveness; for as eroticism thrives on illusion, so Price – like the artist technicians of Hollywood whom he admired so greatly – was concerned in his work with the nuts and bolts of how seemingly effortless glamour is achieved. In this he would be one of the great anatomists of artifice – a designer obsessed with what might almost be termed the mechanics of style. At the same time, he would develop a distinctive appeal in his designs which was based on a bravura blurring of gender and flamboyant sexual fetishism. Both of these devices would be deep in the signature of Price's work; conflated they would be astonishingly far sighted.

Antony Price: 'My design style is born out of the fact that I possess the ability to cut extremely complicated patterns. When I went to Bradford College of Art, in 1961, everyone had a chance to do all the different things – commercial art, sculpture, and so on – I was very good at sculpture, because I can make excellent shoe lasts.

'I did four years at Bradford – one year of general art, and three of fashion – and then three years at the Royal College of Art. My main influences were Balenciaga and Givenchy – both, by the way, highly contructional designers. Balenciaga was an architect before he became a designer, and his clothes were like moving buildings. I preferred that pure, technical design – the perfect seam.

'When I did my college show at Bradford I showed a coat made out of one piece of cloth, with one seam. If you did that now they'd think you'd run out of fabric. But I was trained as an industrial designer and industry is what I'm in. It's akin to factory whistles blowing and people sitting down at machines. Had I made vacuum cleaners, I'd have been Dyson.'

Price would go to the Royal College of Art in 1965, arriving a student generation after Ossie Clark and David Hockney. Even as a student, Price's appearance was extraordinary – an alarmingly coiffured man whose appearance was part warrior chieftain, part swashbuckling adventurer, part disoriented time traveller, part androgynous film star, and part Notting Hill bohemian of the psychedelic era.

On moonlit nights during term-time, anyone strolling along the Cromwell Road towards the French Lycée might well have been struck by what could seem a visitation from some parallel universe of bizarrely costumed comic-book super villains. Already driven by a tireless work ethic, Price would ascend an external fire escape of the Fashion School after the caretaker had turned out the lights, in order to break back into the building and work through the night on the department's machines. Should he have turned towards a street light on the way up, however, he would present a formidable sight.

In those days – around 1966, 1967 – Price would be dressed in an ankle-length, black fur coat, under which was a flounced shirt – with the collar turned up high in the style of a Regency beau – some extremely tight trousers and a pair of thigh-high black leather top boots. His hair – which featured extensions, nearly fifteen years before they became the house speciality of the Antennae salon – would later be described by its owner as 'way beyond mullet – more like Atahualpa, the Inca chieftain'. And then there was his make-up, subtle yet apparent: a mood enhancer, lifting his features into sharper, more declamatory definition, as though Elvis had tutored with Rudolph Valentino.

The overall effect, needless to say, was one of a massively amplified presence: a dizzying act of self-recreation, through which Price became a kind of mythological version of himself. Having worked in the college holidays for the theatrical costumiers Berman's & Nathan's, Price had acquired much of his outfit – shirt, coat, and thigh boots – from the costumes worn by Albert Finney in Tony Richardson's 1963 film adaptation of *Tom Jones*. But worn with make-up and hair extensions, as streetwear, the dandyism of Finney's original costume was given a profound twist: one of those slight refractions of intentionality, but one which might now be taken as eloquent of Price's pivotal importance to not just British fashion, but to the entire conceptualism of modern styling.

Price's appropriation of theatrical costume suggested the male wearer as heroic, but sexually ambiguous and other-worldly – eroticised and extravagantly poised; not a man dressed like an actor in a period costume drama, but – vitally – as though an actual film character had stepped down off the screen, in all his romantic energy, to walk the streets of London in the middle of the 1960s. Streets, moreover, that were still peopled by citizens adjusting to even the boutique and psychedelic styles of the sixties, and who would have regarded Price's flamboyance as little more than deranged – threatening, risible, not-of-this-world.

Ascending the fire escape, piratically garbed, Price, incredibly, was beginning the importation of a new sartorial sexuality; and as he later remarked to the author, in one of his many aphoristic asides, 'Fashion is a principal weapon in the armoury of sex.' Underpinned by such an insight, his work would revolutionise the erotic lustre of modern glamour.

As a style, Price's montage of exotica could also be read as the beginnings of a manifesto, calling popular culture to the service of a meticulously crafted look, in which uniforms, fetish-wear and period costume drama were fused into wearable fantasies. By his own admission, Price would usually reach the Royal College from his flat in Lansdowne Road, Notting Hill, at around one in the afternoon, simply because his hair and make-up had taken so long to prepare. He was a night person – hence his nocturnal returns to the Fashion department – and his day would begin, as it would end, with a total dedication to appearance.

Antony Price: 'I arrived at the Royal College of Art in 1965, under the last year of Janey Ironside. She was a bizarre woman in some ways, but all we cared about was what she looked like – because that's what we were into: looks, looks, looks. At the point at which I was mid-College, Ossie was cruising up and down the Kings Road in a silver Buick Riviera, and Hockney had that fantastic flat in Powis Terrace.

I did my exam at Kensington Gore, but we were actually based in a building in the Cromwell Road – near the French Lycée. They moved the Fashion School over to there, and then moved it back again when Sheila Brown took over. One of the most fabulous things about the Royal College for me was that it was on the flight path – I had never seen a civil airliner. To watch a Boeing 707 coming in to land was for me a wonderful thing – I was obsessed! It was probably because my father was a Spitfire pilot that I became interested in the shapes of uniforms. I was surrounded by pictures of someone in a uniform: a very romantic figure.

'Movies were also very important for me. At Bradford Art College I remember seeing Eisenstein's *Ivan the Terrible*, which was just spectacular – I goggled in amazement at the hard, stylised photography of it. *Extremes* of design fascinated me. I like to remind people that the entire Hollywood dream is pretty much a Jewish dream, and it should be remembered that many of the men who made Greta Garbo, Rita Hayworth and so on – with all that *incredible attention to detail* – are displaying a Jewish attention to detail. That sense of perfectionism has always been incredibly important to me. I love movie clothes; I was born out of period. I should have been Travis Banton [Hollywood costume designer, 1894–1948] doing Dietrich's stuff.

'The 1935 version of *A Midsummer Night's Dream* was another major film for me. I saw it first in 1969, at the Electric Cinema, stoned out of my head. Jimmy Cagney plays Bottom. But fine art was less of an influence.

When I got to college I saw all the painting students sitting around in the bar, smoking roll-ups and going to the odd lecture – while we were up fucking sewing all night!'

During his time at the Royal College, Antony Price would be part of a group of fellow students that would include the designer and contributor to *Petticoat* magazine Margot Parker, the illustrator Malcolm Bird (who would subsequently contribute his distinctive, faery-fantastical style to the decoration of Barbara Hulaninki's store, Biba), and fashion students Jane Whiteside and Jim O'Connor, who with his subsequent partner, the wonderfully named Pamla Motown, would design for Tommy Roberts's cartoon and pop inspired Mr Freedom boutique, as well as making some stage clothes for Andy Mackay. Juliet Mann (who was already working as a designer, and who had not attended the Royal College) would also be the link between Antony Price and Keith Wainwright.

Andy Mackay: 'The crucial discovery of Roxy Music would be that you could be serious and have a lot of fun without compromising either. Whereas other "glam" rock bands, like, say, the Sweet or Slade, went too much for simply being glam rocky – Bowie was somewhere in between – and we would start off expecting to be kind of serious. Thinking back to the UFO performances and the Soft Machine quietly bent over their instruments – making a lot of noise but not responding to the audience; that was the sort of group I thought I'd be in. Likewise the Velvet Underground were a quiet band – they were all hunched over the instruments. And I'm never quite sure how Roxy Music ended up being a totally up-front performance band.

'Somehow, we came out differently. Maybe it was the influence of the fashion friends around – Antony Price, Jim O'Connor, Pamla Motown, Carol McNicoll, Wendy Dagworthy, Keith at Smile, Malcolm Bird – but we moved towards that image and performance style.'

The Royal College of Art during the latter half of the 1960s would ultimately play a pivotal role in the network of personalities, cliques and talents out of which Roxy Music would ultimately emerge. For in a timely conflation of early careers, both the group from Newcastle University *and* the group from Reading University would become closely acquainted, firstly by way of a shared house in Redesdale Street, Chelsea, in which

Malcolm Bird was then lodging, along with Tim Head and Margot Parker; and secondly by way of the popular student dances which were then regularly held at the Royal College. Juliet Mann would be the unifying figure within the metropolitan cast of this fusion, and Viv Kemp – soon to become Mrs Tim Head – would unite the Reading and Newcastle factions. In such a manner, during 1969 and 1970 Bryan Ferry would be introduced to both Andrew Mackay and Simon Puxley, and to the Ladbroke Grove scene of the Royal College fashion students. Chronologically, the beginnings of this latter coterie can be found in the arrival in London from Sussex of Juliet Mann.

Juliet Mann: 'I studied fashion at West Sussex College of Art & Design, in Worthing; and there was one boy in our department – which was very unusual in those days – and he got into the Royal College of Art to study fashion in the same year as Antony Price. I didn't apply for the Royal College, but I moved to London when he went there and would turn up in the evening with sandwiches and things . . . Which was how I met Antony.

'I was doing childrenswear – which didn't really exist in those days. People like Antony at the Royal College were doing very individual menswear and so forth. When I was at college people were doing things like ball gowns and evening wear – that was considered very elegant and desirable. I had a work placement in one of those fashion houses on Conduit Street, where you used to dress the models in beaded evening frocks, with silk and chiffon and lace – that's what we aspired to, that's what we thought was happening. The designers we looked up to were Alice Pollock, Mary Quant, Tuffin & Foale, and later Ossie Clark. Basically we went down Carnaby Street, or pressed our noses to the window of Mary Quant's boutique in Knightsbridge.

'So the Royal College crowd became kind of my crowd, and I ended up going to a lot of the parties in Ladbroke Grove – wearing some sensational outfits by Antony, to say nothing of various wigs . . .'

The photographer and illustrator Eric Boman, who would take the photographs for several of Bryan Ferry and Roxy Music's most iconic album cover images (notably Ferry's *Another Time Another Place*, and Roxy Music's *Country Life*), and would subsequently work with the legendary shoe designer Manolo Blahnik amongst others, was a contemporary of Price's at the Royal College, and renowned for his flamboyant style as much as his stunning looks.

Boman would subsequently become the partner of the Californian artist and photographer Peter Schlesinger, who during the earlier 1960s was in a relationship with David Hockney, and would inspire some of Hockney's most important work of that period – the great sunshine and swimming pool scenes, with their visceral sense of stillness, heat, reflectiveness and time. Schlesinger's own photographs, later published as his *Visual Diary of the 1960s and 1970s*, would be a remarkable record of their particular period and society. Between them, Schlesinger and Boman would define a visual style which was as insightful as it was glamorous, achieving vibrant, brilliantly poised effects through a seeming lightness of touch.★

Eric Boman: 'I went to the Royal College with Antony Price, although not in the same department – he was the year above me. I was there from 1966 to 1969, doing graphics. Nobody taught you as such. You just went in and talked to your friends and smoked a lot of cigarettes, and then you all went out in the evening. Antony was friends with Juliet; he would doll her up, doing the false eyelashes and everything – and she would look like a painting by Sargent or something, just fantastic.

'In my own case, I was an illustrator and very influenced by Pop art. So that came into your work and into your environment. We're talking about people who were very visual, very smart . . . I spent a couple of weeks in Spain one summer with Mark Lancaster, staying in Marcel Duchamp's apartment. Richard Hamilton and Rita Donagh were also there . . .'

Peter Schlesinger: 'In the 1960s, I think there was a very small Kings Road set – a group of people who typically would hang out at the Casserole,

★ In a flash-forward to 1973, Bryan Ferry recalls: 'We filmed the videos for "A Hard Rain's a Gonna Fall" and the other was "These Foolish Things", both in the same afternoon and evening with Jack Hazan (maker of *A Bigger Splash,* 1974). They were shot in the Roundhouse, I think. Antony Price did the make-up, Polly Eltes was one of the backing singers on "Hard Rain", one of the others was Eric Boman in drag. "These Foolish Things" is just me in a white suit standing beside the piano, with Eric Boman in black drag as some Billie Holliday, Diana Ross character pretending to play the piano. He had a gardenia in his hair. It's ironic because *Bigger Splash* featured Peter Schlesinger who became Eric Boman's boyfriend, and still is.

which had a gay club underneath called the Gigolo, where Ossie Clark used to go.'

Eric Boman: 'When I first came to London in 1965, I stayed in a bedsitter off the Kings Road, and at that time the Kings Road had Sunlight laundries and butchers and bakers on it. And there were three boutiques – Top Gear and Countdown, owned by James Wedge, and Bazaar, owned by Mary Quant. Other than that it was a normal high street.

'A year later it all changed. I did an article for *ARK* called "Monkey Parading", which was a title from Savile Row: when people went out promenading to be looked at in their finery. And that is in a way what people were starting to do in the Kings Road. And if you knew what *I* would wear to go up the Kings Road! For instance, I had taken with me from Sweden a robe that my grandmother would wear, made of old Liberty silk paisley. I wore this over a T-shirt with leopard-print pants, *tons* of make-up and *tons* of jewellery – this would have been '68, '69. By the early 1970s it had cooled down . . .'

Antony Price's other contemporaries, Malcolm Bird, Jane Whiteside and Jim O'Connor, would all become significant figures within the explosion of new creativity which occurred in the London fashion world towards the end of the 1960s. In many ways, the pioneering figure in the creation of this new scene had been Ossie Clark, not only as a designer whose clothes many fashionable modern women adored, but also as a celebrity representative of British pop's imperial in-crowd. Like his Royal College contemporary David Hockney, Ossie Clark was adopted by the wider media to represent the phenomenon of a new era.

For the immediately following generation of Royal College fashion designers, such as Antony Price and Jim O'Connor, vampishness, pop playfulness and radically heightened style statements were there to be amplified. If Clark had revisited the soft elegance of thirties tea gowns, then Price created garments that at times referred back to the forties, but with an edge and energy of futuristic fetishism. For Jim O'Connor, the reference point was Pop art – and more specifically to applying the visual wit and emblematic power of Pop art back to its sources within commercial, artisan popular culture. O'Connor had been a London Mod – as had Keith Wainwright – with the Mod dedication to modern style.

Jim O'Connor: 'To me, as a person who was working class, the sixties were art school and the chance to do some real art. Antony and I were in the same year at the Royal College – I was doing menswear and he was doing womenswear, and then in the last year he came and joined us doing menswear. It was fun. We had these big tables and we worked opposite each other. I think he thought I was a bit odd – we were probably a bit suspicious of one another at first. But then we got on well – encouraging each other, exaggerating ideas.

'Pop art was the big thing for me. Later, when I saw *Easy Rider*, I decided that I wanted a bike like the one Peter Fonda has in the film. So this guy in Battersea built it for me – beginning by going over to Belgium to buy a derelict old army bike, one of the last of the spring forks. This thing had a stick shift, and foot clutch; and I painted Keyhole Kate on the fuel tank [original artist, Allan Moreley] and the backrest was a chrome bar that came up in this keyhole shape. So it really was Pop art . . .'

The re-appropriation of Pop art by non *fine art* cultural production would be intrinsic to the London fashion scene at the end of the 1960s and the beginning of the 1970s. Indeed, all three versions of the Biba fashion store would in many ways be increasingly extravagant affirmations of the modern relationship between applied arts, revivalism, fashion and lifestyle. Once again, there is a resonance in this development of the totally styled life which refers back to the ideas which Duchamp, Hamilton, Lancaster and Donagh had refined within the fine arts.

By way of example, Jim O'Connor's 'Pop art' motorbike exemplified the trend that Tom Wolfe had examined as far back as 1963, in his famous essay about the Hot Rod & Custom Car Show held annually at the Coliseum in New York – 'The Kandy-Colored Tangerine Flake Streamline Baby'. In this Wolfe proposed a direct correlation between the enthusiasts who devoted their lives to creating extraordinary, retina-enlarging cars and bikes, and the traditional cultural perception of the fine artist. Describing one builder of custom cars, Wolfe wrote:

He was a very serious and soft-spoken man, about thirty, completely serious about the whole thing, in fact, and it soon became pretty clear, as I talked to this man for a while, that he had been living like the *complete artist* for years . . . Creativity – his own custom car art –

became an obsession with him. So he became the complete custom car artist. And he said he wasn't the only one. All the great custom car designers had gone through it. It was the *only way. Holy beasts! Starving artists! Inspiration!* Only instead of garrets, they had these garages.

Writing at a time when Andy Warhol and Roy Lichtenstein were developing some of their great early Pop art works, Wolfe was analysing the dialogue between Pop art and total Pop art lifestyle, based on a new form of applied arts. For the young art and design graduates on London's fashion scene towards the end of the 1960s, the proposition was subtly but significantly rearranged: educated within the fine arts establishment, to a very high level, the intention was to infuse personal style with the energy and impact of art – to take serious artistic ideas to the terrain of music, fashion and lifestyle, without compromising the individual values of either.

David Enthoven [co-founder of EG – Roxy Music's initial management]: 'The brilliant thing about the latter part of the sixties was that you had that wonderful Pop art movement which had really flourished with Hamilton, Jones and Blake, but *then* went over to Mary Quant, Biba, Zandra Rhodes. An extraordinary flourishing of fashion, art, music and film – and they were all intermingling. And people were *dressing up*. It was definitely a period when twenty-year-olds had kicked over the traces.'

This was certainly the case with Antony Price's designs at the end of the 1960s and the beginning of the 1970s – as described by his crucial contribution to the styling of *Roxy Music* – and was a relationship to creativity which fed right back to his obsession with the designer technicians of Hollywood. Extravagant, sensual vision, technical brilliance, dazzling effect, a triumph of artifice – these were major points within Price's brilliance as a designer and style guru.

Judith Watt [author, fashion historian, biographer of Ossie Clark]: 'Roxy Music were "art college" in the same way as Ossie. Specifically, the idea of the group was from that kind of modern liberal education, where you can do anything you want, and you will be fed images, and you will be

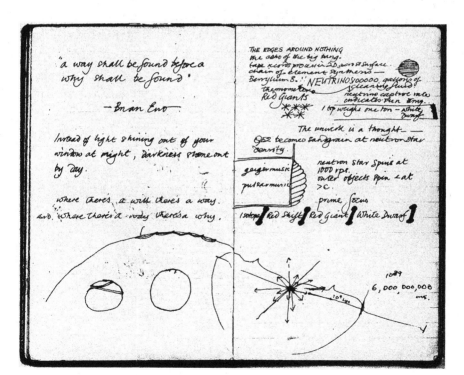

12 Andy Mackay as Modernist aesthete in the *Death In Venice* style, late 1960s. 'It was stylish times'

13 Viv Kemp in Venice, 1969

14 Brian Eno notebook entry, 'Summer '68' – aphorisms and geigermusic

15 Andy Mackay, Viv Kemp and Simon Puxley, Reading, late 1960s. 'Such aesthetes – but totally . . .'

16 Rita Donagh (photograph by Ugo Mulas). 'Everyone who knew Rita was totally in awe of her, as they were with Richard Hamilton . . .' (Note portrait of Andy Warhol in background, who would be a major influence on Donagh's art and thinking)

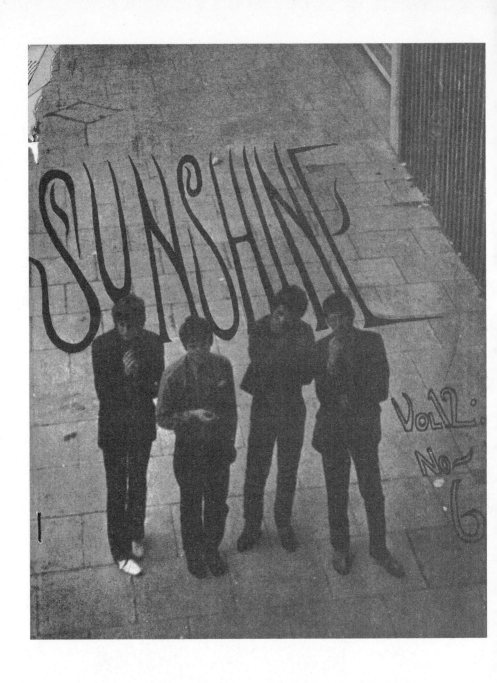

17 Cover of *Sunshine* magazine, published by Puxley, Mackay and members of Sunshine Promotions, University of Reading – 'neo-Dada happenings'

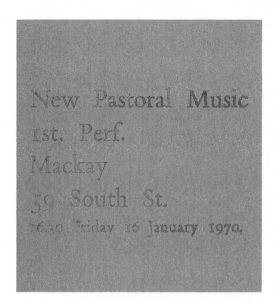

MALCOLM
BIRD
5 Redesdale St SW3
Phone: 01 352 3439

18 Announcement card made by Viv Kemp for Andy Mackay's 'New Pastoral Music' performance, July 1970 – 'a set-up of music playing machines, run by little electric motors which I
bought from a shop in Bloomsbury'
19 Malcolm Bird *carte de visite* – in Pop elfin style and featuring the address of a house shared
in Chelsea circa 1970 by Bird, Tim Head and Margot Parker
20 The first promotional 'flyer' for Roxy Music, by Malcolm Bird, 1971

21 Antony Price, circa 1970 – 'more like Atahualpa, the Inca chieftain'. Note gold-banded Saint Moritz cigarette, also favoured by Bryan Ferry, and which would subsequently become the smoke of choice for all Roxy Music fans

22 Antony Price, circa 1969, in the entrance of the 'dragon's mouth' staircase at the Stirling Cooper shop, Wigmore Street, London

23 Juliet Mann in dress designed by Antony Price, holidaying in Sardinia, 1970

s sketch and the real thing
y-and-white polka-dot cot-
shoulder, ruffled, and cut
shoulder straps. $20. . . .
triped cotton top, white
front-slit skirt. Each, $17.
shiny black ciré jumpsuit.
-shoulder blue cotton top
s. $18. Figure-fitting side-
rap skirt. $17. All these
ns at Che Guevara, 23-25
reet. . . . The perfect shoes
oe high heels by Manolo
49, Old Church Street. . . .

24 Bryan Ferry on stage with Roxy Music, early 1972. 'We *are* rock and roll'
25 Designs by Antony Price for Che Guevara featured in American *Vogue*, early 1970s. Note
the High Priest of 'Them', Andy Warhol, in background of right-hand photograph

26 Brian Eno wearing the iconic 'feather collar' costume made by Carol McNicoll, 1972. 'You could make things that were serious art, and they could also be popular – that was the ideal'

made to think; and you can challenge the status quo – you can question anything, and you can look eclectically at an image, it doesn't matter where it's from, it will mean something to you visually.' In all of this Price is seriously interesting. He can make anything – sheer, brilliant body sculpting; and he's very good with fabric. He can cut brilliantly, too. I think some of the ideas were a reaction against the mini-skirt – if Ossie was doing the thirties, Price takes the forties look and vamps it beyond belief. And I also think that somewhere in there it's looking back at one's childhood.

'With Antony and Ossie, maybe the design style was also something to do with the sexual politics that were going on at the time – with strong women figures. I think they were reacting against all that Carnaby Street horror, and I would bet that the drugs they were taking were very different. These boys were buzzing, and partying with lots of interesting people . . . I mean look at Gala Mitchell – isn't she much more interesting than Twiggy? Or Sandie Shaw? There's no comparison. So later you've got some feminists of the time reacting against Roxy Music's album covers – well, you want to meet someone scary? Meet Gala! It's *complete artifice*! The absolute antithesis of hippies and dungarees.'

By the year that Bryan Ferry graduated in Fine Art from Newcastle University, soon to be interviewed at the Royal College of Art for a travelling scholarship, the 'cool' young fashion stars on the Ladbroke Grove scene were taking their place in an era of style that would be dominated by revivalism on the one hand (a gathering of enthusiasms from art nouveau, Beardsley, aesthetic movement Englishness and Orientalism, through to a major obsession with art deco), and by a much more American, modernistically Pop art sensibility on the other.

As defined on the one hand by Biba's various incarnations, and by Stirling Cooper and Mr Freedom on the other, this would be the fashion context for the young designers – Price, Whiteside, O'Connor, Motown – who contributed to the earliest style of Roxy Music, and which in some ways reflected the time travelling sensibility of the group's initial music.

Other vital contributors to Roxy Music's look would be Wendy Dagworthy – who in 1971 designed stage clothes for Phil Manzanera and Bryan Ferry – and Brian Eno's girlfriend, the artist and ceramicist Carol McNicoll. The flamboyance of these outfits is somewhat a continuation of the idea, within performance art by Anne Bean, of 'taking the sculpture off the plinth'.

Wendy Dagworthy would be introduced to Bryan Ferry very early in the group's career, by way of an old friend – Ferry's new lawyer Robert Lee, who had just been immortalised in 'Virginia Plain'. Dagworthy, a graduate of Hornsey College of Art, would be responsible for the clothes worn by Phil Manzanera and Bryan Ferry in the group photograph on the inside gatefold sleeve of *For Your Pleasure*, the second Roxy Music album.

Wendy Dagworthy: 'I met Roxy Music very early on, through an old friend of mine – Robert Lee – a solicitor. I had just left Hornsey College of Art, and had a job designing. But I used to make clothes for friends as well. Bryan had mentioned to Robert that the group were looking for stage costumes, and Robert recommended me. Bryan said the kind of feeling he wanted, and I came up with some drawings. I think I made him some trousers, first of all; then I made the bell-boy outfit, and the toreador. From that Bryan asked if I would be interested in doing some clothes for Phil Manzanera – the rhumba number. Sadly a lot of those outfits were stolen after a concert.

'Bryan knew exactly what he wanted – he was very specific. I then did the research, made drawings and found fabric swatches and so on. But he knew what image he wanted to project, definitely. Likewise Brian Eno – whose girlfriend at the time, Carol McNicoll, was then at the Royal College.

'At the beginning of the seventies, we were all into art deco furniture and buildings – we collected things like Clarice Cliff ceramics. The Biba Rainbow Rooms [the upstairs cabaret at 'big' Biba, in Derry & Toms], were very much the feeling of that time. I was using a lot of evening wear fabrics for daywear – sequins, panne velvets, lurex bomber jackets, things like that. In the context of the more politically radical late sixties, I think that we were probably more into glamour . . . It was that Hollywood glamour, linked in to art deco – Busby Berkeley and so on. My menswear maybe had a slightly feminine touch; I used bright colours – a suit in pink, for example – and tried to push it as far as I could. Polly Eltes used to model for me.

'Again, this was the time of silver snakeskin shoes – quite eccentric looks. There was Mr Freedom, and all of that going on. I suppose "flam-boyant" is a good word to describe my work. Although I can't remember getting big publicity from designing some of the early Roxy clothes. It was a time and a group of people committed to a very profound idea of style. You used to dress up – a lot. Also, it was "style" rather than what we now call "labels" which predominated. It all seemed new at the time – there were no set formulae; you just did it your own way.

'During the late sixties and the early seventies there was very much a relationship between rock music and fashion, and all of the groups had their own style – the Stones, for instance. Also someone like Ossie Clark was very friendly with the Stones and the Beatles; likewise Antony Price was very connected with Roxy Music – so I think that the fusion was beginning as a movement. Antony's style was very glamorous; whereas mine was never glamorous in that figure-hugging way. The clothing reflected the 1930s and the 1940s – hence the collectable furnishings and mirrors on Portobello market at the time.'

In 1968, however, at the height, arguably, of the underground scene in all of its multi-directional revolutionary fervour – London's fashion 'in crowd' of Ossie Clark's imperial era were mingling trippy bohemian car-nival ('the happiness explosion' as Tom Wolfe heretically identified an era more often described by its own pundits as consumed with oppression and paranoia) with the creation of new styles.

In his *Style of the Century*, Bevis Hillier details the chronology of revivalism in the 1960s, with precise reference to the museum shows and publications which did much to inspire its fashionability. In itself, such a close relationship between art history and fashion, producing such imme-diate, pervasive, hybrids of style – the absolutely up-to-the-minute by way of a pop reclamation of the design styles popular between the 1890s and 1940s – was eloquent of a modern reassertion of aestheticism. Hillier to play:

> . . . the art nouveau revival began with the Mucha exhibition (May–July 1963) and the Beardsley exhibition (May–September 1966) at the Victoria & Albert Museum, London. The decadent sin-uosities of both artists were as captivating as in the 1890s; and Beardsley in particular – 'the Fra Angelico of Satanism', as Roger

Fry had called him – appealed to the Permissive Society. It is difficult, today [1983], to recall how shocking were the phallic drawings
of the Lysistrata series by Beardsley, first reissued in a portfolio
which was on sale among the clothes at Granny Takes a Trip.

Hillier – whose own survey, *Art Deco of the 1920s and 30s* was published
in 1968, and who would co-curate an exhibition of art deco at the
Minneapolis Institute of Arts in 1971 – dates the deco craze (and its title)
from, 'a commemorative exhibition staged at the Musée des Arts
Décoratifs, Paris, in 1966, titled "Les Années 25". It was the subtitle of this
show – Les Arts Deco – which gave the style its modern name of Art
Deco.'

Janet Street-Porter: 'Barbara Hulanicki, who owned Biba, would hold parties every Saturday night where there was a huge cross-over of people. We
knew a lot about art deco, and when the foyer of the Strand Palace Hotel
was demolished, we bought bits of it and saved them from wreckers or
dealers – we donated the entrance to the Victoria & Albert Museum.
Although I got some ceiling lights. Barbara was a serious collector of art
deco as well – people would go to Paris to buy it mostly; you didn't really buy it in London.'

As Jeremy Catto – a former customer of Granny Takes a Trip (on the
shopfront of which was inscribed the Wildean pronouncement, 'One
should either be a work of art or wear a work of art') – had observed that
the decadence of the 'Yellow Book Nineties' was less to his taste than the
'silver age of aesthetes' in the 1920s, so for London's fashionable
cognoscenti between 1969 and 1973, art deco would be the revivalism of
choice. The taste for revivalism would then follow a loosely historical
course through the vogue for the war years of the 1940s: Glen Miller,
WAAFs, and the sleek eroticism of Vargas Girl pin-ups.

Nostalgia for the elegance of art deco, and the rise of so-called (by
some journalists of the time) 'decadent' pop stars such as Lou Reed and
David Bowie, revelling in extravagant artifice, would also mark time
between the late 1960s and the early 1970s with a worsening economic
depression in the UK – culminating in the three-day week of early
January 1974. Arguably, the thirst for glamour, elegance and *la vie deluxe* in
pop and fashion – for worlds as fantastical as Malcolm Bird's designs for

Biba – could be likened to the scenes described by Florine Stettheimer's *Cathedrals of Broadway* back in the actual 1920s: a desire for escapism at a time of depression. In the late 1960s, however, for the Notting Hill clique of Royal College students and their associates, the style party was just beginning.

Antony Price: 'My degree show was in 1968 and the studying had taken seven years in all. It was all menswear – one of the models was a mad boy who married the model Gala Mitchell; another was Gervaise, a boyfriend of Patrick Procktor at the time. I made six outfits in all, and they were all pretty stylish. I won just about every competition I entered at college. My menswear collection included a long brown leather coat, quite narrow cut, lined in beige and chestnut herringbone tweed; underneath was a waistcoat and big trousers in the same fabric – with a big cap. It looked quite twenties. Then there was a beautiful short jacket, with points at the front – waiter-like, with blocked shoulders, in burnt orange snakeskin. A black shirt with it and cream trousers. And there was a beautiful dark green overcoat. They were all beautifully tailored, wonderfully shaped . . .'

twenty-eight

Designers, stylists and taste makers II: The road to Smile, Stirling Cooper and Mr Freedom – fellow travellers from Mod to Pop art cool – Keith Wainwright and Pamla Motown; fashion as art as style.

With the release of *Roxy Music* in 1972, Antony Price and Keith from Smile would be noted by a generation of music fans for whom the glossy cardboard album sleeve was both a glamorous agent of the group whose music it packaged, and a treasure trove of insights (at its best) into the creative outlook, interests and message of the musicians involved.

Never before within the pop and rock mainstream had a group so self-consciously, and for obvious stylistic effect – building their 'new imaginary world' – listed credits for not just their hair and clothes, but also those of the model who graced the cover to such memorable and epoch-defining effect. To some extent, the success (and for some, notoriety) of *Roxy Music*'s sleeve was due to the games with sexuality and gender that ran deep within the image and sensibility of the group.

In the early 1970s, 'serious' rock albums were entrenched as a male form – even when recorded by female artists. *Roxy Music*, with its (Hamiltonesque) credits for a named model (a high fashion, Antony Price and Ossie Clark catwalk model, moreover), hair, clothes and make-up was determinedly feminised – yet at the same time unmistakably heterosexual. In powder blue, pink and gold, the world suggested by the sleeve conveyed male swagger, lush sexuality and heightened cool. Its brilliance lay in the ambiguity of its sexuality, and the translation of this sexuality into a manifesto on modern glamour and primary Pop art source material – the pin-up girl.

The credit to Smile for Kari-Ann's hair on *Roxy Music* slipped a chic, in-crowd name to the wider world. Keith had been the hair stylist of choice to fashionable London since the early to middle sixties, and in the early 1970s his reputation would be joined with that of Price as the imperial arbiters of modern style, 'by appointment' as it were to Roxy Music. As with Antony Price, Wendy Dagworthy, Jim O'Connor and Pamla Motown – all contributors to the early Roxy look – the ethos of Keith and Smile described the development of a new approach and attitude to personal style and outlook – the roots of this approach and its subsequent form being deep within their creators' formative experience as Mods.

In keeping with the glamour and exoticism that Roxy Music would present from their earliest outings, Keith came from a background in which style, pop cool, and being a well-known member of fashionable London society were all commingled. As first an apprentice, then a stylist for Leonard at Grosvenor Square, and finally the owner of Smile, Keith would occupy a position in the swiftest current of metropolitan pop fashionability.

By the early 1970s Keith would have become an avant-gardist within his own profession – not just by experimenting with styles and colours that were still considered more peculiar than adventurous by many of his peers, but also in creating, by way of Smile, an embassy and venue for his own approach to personal cool. To have your hair cut by Keith at Smile (during a period when the ubiquitous consumer industry of style culture was yet to have assembled, and 'otherness' was still highly visible within a largely conformist society) would be something of a personal mission statement – it placed the client as a person of high fashion and progressive taste, tuned in to the latest style codes.

Keith Wainwright: 'I became an apprentice hairdresser; and in those days you did five years – three years sweeping the floor and washing hair, then two years when you actually got to do people's hair – mostly colour, perms and ancillary work to the stylist. When I very first started I was actually told *not* to speak to the clients – because my accent was too broad. And so I used to practise my elocution – but fairly soon I reverted to type.

'I was a Mod, and the Mod scene in London was very, very localised. We used to go to the Embassy in Welwyn, or sometimes off to other venues. You'd get your clothes looked at, and your scooter looked at; but whatever you did, you didn't ask a girl to dance, because you'd be on foreign ground. This was in the middle of the 1960s. At this time, me and my mates had all seen *Breakfast at Tiffany's* – we had the suits, we were cool. I remember being desperate to get a suit from Austins, which became Cecil Gee in Shaftesbury Avenue.

'I've always liked pop – I never liked jazz. The very first record I bought was by Doris Day, and after that my dad took me to see Frankie Lyman and the Teenagers at the London Palladium. I loved Fats Domino, the Everly Brothers, Buddy Holly, the Platters. The boys who liked Eddie Cochran were too rockerish for me. I didn't think at the time that I liked specifically black music – these were just the things that appealed to me. At the time it was all Val Doonican and crooners. When I used to go down to Brighton on my scooter, we used to go to the Aquarium – where they always had a live group. I was more interested in musicianship than music, and purple hearts [amphetamines] weren't our thing. Later, when I worked for Leonard, we used to take what were called "slimming pills" – and those weren't even thought of as "drugs" in those days.

'When I finished my apprenticeship I had what is now termed a "year out", because I wanted to educate myself and travel. I was just twenty, and took a job on a boat going to South Africa. I took a quick commission and then got work on a cruise liner, going around the Mediterranean; from there I went back to South Africa, and then to Rio de Janeiro. On this trip I spent an extra day in Naples, and a guy I had been working with asked me to go to Rome – so I just got on the train and went.

'In London I did Mary Quant's hair for a while, because she lived around the corner from the hairdressers where I worked before I worked on the boats. At that time I also did Lady Annabel Birley's hair. I liked Roy Orbison and all the same popular music that she liked, and when I told her that I was leaving to work on the boats she asked me to be a DJ at Annabel's [Mayfair nightclub, founded by Mark Birley in 1963, and named in honour of his then wife] – and my life would have been quite different if I'd done that.'

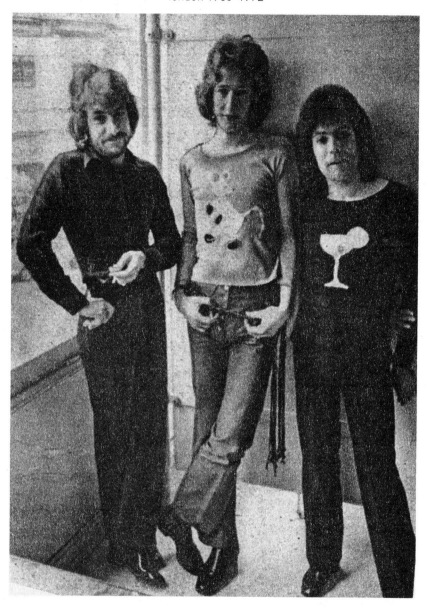

In this particular chronology of style, Keith Wainwright would be a direct link between the elitism of Mod – and Mod's influence within the new creative industries of television, fashion, advertising and media, almost more than pop – and the 'new kind of aristocracy' that Roxy

Music would come to represent.

The individualism and style consciousness of Mod, however (all acceleration and clean, straight lines) prior to its commercialisation and evolution into different strands of music and fashion – psychedelia and northern soul, primarily – would be at odds with the more inward-looking hippy counter-culture of the later 1960s. Former Mods such as Keith, Janet Street-Porter, Jim O'Connor and Pamla Motown were rooted in both a working-class work ethic and a sharp, fast, outward-looking attitude. As such, the drug culture of revolution and inner exploration were anathema to their sense of cool.★

Throughout the late 1960s and early 1970s, Keith would radically dismantle the formality and traditionalism of salon hairdressing as it had existed in Mayfair and Knightsbridge since seemingly for ever – a hushed, middle-aged, conservatively feminine world of fluttery handed deferential service – and create a new approach to his profession which acted upon and encouraged the opening up of entrenched English boundaries of gender and class. In short, as a key agent of pop modernity, Keith used a unisex approach to hairdressing – then a statement of substantial originality. In this, he would share with Antony Price the recognition that changing attitudes to gender and sexuality were key to creating a modern style, and combine this new approach with technical brilliance as a stylist. Suitably enough, television and pop music would assist him in this process.

Keith Wainwright: 'I worked at Leonard, in Grosvenor Square – it was an off-shoot of Vidal Sassoon. If you were a bit hip, you weren't so much a Vidal Sassoon person because you knew about Leonard – you'd go there.

'Because I'd done my five-year apprenticeship, I had phoned Leonard after I'd finished on the boats. They didn't need a stylist, but they asked if I could do tints and perms. I then had an interview with Daniel Galvin and got the job. And *because* I'd done hairdressing on the boats, I'd also

---

★ Such unease in the face of full-on tuning in and dropping out was not uncommon amongst the seriously stylish. In a flash-forward to the early 1970s, Duncan Fallowell recalls his friendship and collaboration with the members of the German avant rock group Can, and their approach to relaxation:
Duncan Fallowell: 'I think that the whole Can scene was a bit far out for Bryan – it unnerved him. We used to take drugs and talk very frankly and strangely about our inner selves. Well that's not really *Bryan*, is it?'

learned men's hairdressing a little, as well.

'Now at that time – the middle of the sixties – you either did men's hair or women's hair. And I was getting asked to cut the hair of the male hairdressers at Leonard because I wouldn't do it like a barber. I'd cut it how they told me, and leave it that little bit longer. So then the *female* clients started saying that they wished their husbands or boyfriends had these kinds of haircuts, and Leonard saw an opportunity. So I would finish work as a colourist at five, and then take three appointments between 5.30 and 6.30 doing men's hair. And people like David Puttnam – who was then a hot-shot in advertising – would be offered a haircut if they came in, and it would be done by me, rather than Leonard, because he wasn't a men's hairdresser.

'So then I cut hair for the Move and Tony Secunda [the husband of Chelita Secunda, socialite, muse to Marc Bolan and Ossie Clark's first PR.* He secured the Move's residency at the Marquee, London, where their stage act included hacking up effigies of politicians as well as television sets], and I did Roy Wood – Long John Baldry, Elton John, the Steampacket. So I was working with the high flyers and the pop following that was getting up; because they didn't want "normal" kinds of haircuts.

'This was all at Leonard in Grosvenor Square; and Leonard then opened a men's salon. He wanted me to sign a ten-year contract with him, but a lawyer I consulted advised me to certain matters that would arise if I signed, and suddenly the offer went quiet. I went on holiday, and when I came back, Leonard said that he thought it was best I leave.

'So there I was with a male clientele, and in the meantime doing hair for Jane Birkin (when she was married to John Barry and in *Blow Up*), Sarah Miles, those sorts of people. For a while, during the summer of 1969, I filled in with a job at Scissors in the Kings Road; and then I

---

* In a brief aside to Chelita Secunda, the artist Duggie Fields has written: 'It had been sometime in the late 1960s that I first got to know Chelita Salvatori – Secunda when I met her – and she had ever since played an enormous part in my life. She had been one of the first to buy my work, and to introduce it to many others including Zandra Rhodes, who as well as buying my pictures went on to become one of my greatest friends and supports. Chelita was a muse to both the fashion designer Ossie Clark, and the pop star Marc Bolan. Indeed being the instigator of Marc's addiction to glitter and women's clothes, she can be held responsible for much of the look now referred to as Glam Rock.' Tragically, Chelita would die in 2000, aged fifty-five.

opened Smile in the November.

'I shared a flat with my business partner, Leslie – and he used to do Cathy McGowan's hair (co-presenter of *Ready Steady Go!*); they had both come from the suburbs together. As a consequence he would do Sandie Shaw's hair, and Cilla Black. So Leslie had a female clientele, I had a male clientele and the other employee, Paul, also had a male clientele. We soon realised there was a market for *not* setting hair – because the girlfriends of the men whose hair I cut, rather than having to set their hair, just wanted a blow dry.'

As noted by Marnie Fogg, Cathy McGowan became a transmitter of style by way of her appearance on *Ready Steady Go!*, and this in turn was a major boost to the Biba mail order catalogue, which gave all the young women who didn't live near London the chance to get the look:

> . . . Cathy McGowan presented the show, having been offered the job as a typical teenager of the time. She rapidly achieved iconic status as 'Queen of the Mods' and her hair and clothes were copied widely by the audience of teenage girls. A viewer remembers: 'I was transfixed with envy, all the girls were. I used to iron my hair to make it straight like hers. I thought, if she can get close to all these pop stars, then so could I. All I needed was the hair and a dress from Biba.'

Keith Wainwright: 'The concept at Smile was, that because we wouldn't use rollers, we'd do men and women in the same place, and we'd set the salon out on a grid system; we had blinds rigged up so that it could be private if you wanted it to be, or open. But it never got private – it was always open.

'For fourteen years we were based in Knightsbridge, and during that time of course Covent Garden took off and we were on a direct line. And if you went to the Royal College of Art, you walked down to Knightsbridge tube station to go to Covent Garden; well it wasn't so difficult to go to Smile while you were on your way. And that was instrumental in our success, as well . . .'

Towards the end of Bryan Ferry's first year in London, the members of the Ladbroke Grove set would all be establishing themselves at the forefront of the capital's newest fashion scene. In addition to Keith opening Smile in the November of 1969, the following month would see the opening of Tommy Roberts's new boutique, Mr Freedom.

Roberts would first take over the premises of Hung On You in the Kings Road, and subsequently move to Kensington Church Street. His previous shop, Kleptomania, in Kingly Street, around the corner from Carnaby Street, had specialised in vintage clothing, ephemera and polyester voile Victorian dresses – which he has recalled selling out faster than they could make them. As a key fashion location in the late 1960s, Kensington Church Street would be the site of the penultimate Biba, prior to the final, short-lived but epoch defining residency of the store, from 1973 to 1975, in the former (but genuinely art deco) Derry & Toms department store on Kensington High Street.

Jim O'Connor's degree show at the Royal College of Art would be written up in *Vogue*, and along with fellow former Mod Pamla Motown he would be recruited to design for the new store – one characteristic of which was the use of Pop art and infantilist kitsch imagery in its garments and look. As recorded by one of Biba's historians, Alwyn Turner: '... revelling in Pop art and kitsch [Mr Freedom] dealt in spangly hot pants and dungarees and adult sized boy scout uniforms. Unsurprisingly it was Elton John's favourite boutique. Thomas [Steve Thomas of Whitmore-Thomas, the designers of choice for Biba] remembers taking Barbara [Hulanicki] to lunch there, with all the food coming in bright primary colours.'

Juliet Mann: 'Bryan would always have clothes by Antony; and Jim O'Connor and Pamla Motown who worked for Mr Freedom also made things. Jim's look had a tang of Teddy boy about it. Mr Freedom was very Pop art, and Jim and Pam also did things for Andy Mackay.'

Andy Mackay: 'Looking forward a little, I think you would then have to put it [Roxy's initial Pop art image] down to that particular year, eighteen months, between 1971 and 1972, by which time all of those really strong designers and fashion people would have been setting up their shops and doing things. Jim and Pamla were designing for Mr Freedom, and that cool look was taking over from Biba as the previous style. It was a harder, more American style. And Antony Price was designing for Stirling Cooper and doing an amazing range of clothes. So the encouragement of all those design-conscious people was very important.'

In Pamla Motown, the classic stylistic lineage leading from suburbia, to art school (at Harrow School of Art) to Mod to London's fashion scene is utterly intact. In this, her early career – like that of Duggie Fields, whose parents moved from Tidworth, in Hampshire, to the north London suburb of Boreham Wood when he was a teenager – keeps pace with the period of British Pop art, and in many ways is directly aligned to the key features of the London Pop art scene. As a supremely pop figure (beginning with her adopted name), Pamla Motown's experience as a student in the late 1950s and early 1960s mirrors that of Mark Lancaster, Stephen Buckley and Bryan Ferry. Her recollections begin with the formative fixation with style, and the possibilities of self-recreation.

Pamla Motown: 'Us grammar school girls were, at that time (in the late 1950s), keen to wear wide skirts below the knee with crinoline petticoats. We had beehive hairdos and wanted to look like Brigitte Bardot, or Audrey Hepburn. We liked listening to Elvis Presley.

'Down the road from my grammar school in Harrow, I noticed people attending a college, and dressing like I wanted to dress. They looked interesting and I was intuitively drawn to the place. I had a burning desire to go there. Harrow Art School. I went in one day and found they had Fashion as a degree class and was determined to get in. I was accepted and got a small grant, supplemented by the fact that I still lived with my parents.

'I had no idea school could be so much like the world of my fantasy. Most of the students were "beats" and wore black-leather or duffel-coats. Trad jazz was the thing and we would traipse up to the common room and dance to the latest 45s by Long John Baldry, the Temperance Seven, Big Bill Broonzy, Cy Laurie, Chris Barber and Acker Bilk. At one time the Rolling Stones played the local Railway Arms in Wealdstone with Long John. It was the start of the trad boom giving way to the rise of American R&B, and blues. This was the influence on the Beatles and Merseybeat.

'The old fashions gave way to the Mod look (though some kids retained a kind of Rocker look) and the NYC ad man look. The music in the common room changed to hardcore R&B, rock and roll and blues.

Bo Diddley, Chuck Berry, Muddy Waters, Howlin' Wolf and Buddy Guy – the same influences that the whole evolving art school youth culture was throbbing to.

'A lot of this influence came to us through the visiting lecturers. These were our favourite teachers, as they seemed to like the same cool things we did. They were more in touch with the "real" world than the more staid professors who were full-time teachers and seemed to be part of the decor of the old building we occupied.

'I was allowed two "majors" (leading subjects for degree) as the fashion school was a bit too traditional for my taste, and the graphics department had all the cool teachers – such as Peter Blake, Tony Messenger and Derek Boshier. I liked them because they weren't really interested in boring traditional work, only creative stuff. We would cross the street to the Havelock Arms after class and talk with these teachers for hours about goings on of cultural interest . . .'

In the subsequent course of her own career, and the network of friends amongst her art school peers, Motown would be a connecting figure to Jane Whiteside and Antony Price within the Royal College circle, as well as to the whole Ladbroke Grove scene. The distinctions between creativity, profession, social and personal life were almost wholly blurred within this community, creating a densely networked and intimate collection of people.

Immediately following his degree show in 1968, Antony Price and fellow graduate Shelagh Brown had been recruited by his friend Jane Whiteside (who had graduated the year before) to design for a new fashion label, Stirling Cooper. Co-founded by Whiteside and two cab drivers, Ronnie Stirling and Jeff Cooper, the label was destined to join Biba and Mr Freedom as one of the hip new successes on the London fashion scene of the late 1960s and early 1970s.

Price's early menswear designs for Stirling Cooper – soon to be seized upon by the teenage stormtroopers of glam rock – would declare his interests in applying sexuality and fetish to fashion. As summarised in a picture caption by Marnie Fogg: 'Trousers designed by Antony Price for the Stirling Cooper label in 1971. The overt sexuality of the crotch displaying trousers is mitigated by long hair and the use of cosmetics.' Price would design menswear for Stirling Cooper, but was also directly involved in the concept and appearance of the actual shop, Stirling Cooper. In the early 1970s Price would open a second shop, Che Guevara, on Kensington High Street. Juliet Mann recalls them working all night to shop-fit the new store, possibly somewhat under the influence of hallucinogenics, and watching the sun rise over Barkers department store directly opposite.

Antony Price: 'The first Stirling Cooper shop on the corner of Wigmore Street in the late 1960s had a dragon's mouth staircase connecting the upper and lower floors; the clothes were hanging on black pagodas. The logo was the rose in the ring. It was done out in black lacquer, with a painted wave and a Buddha seated downstairs; it was beautifully done. Jane Whiteside and I designed it, as soon as I left college.

'In those days, it was considered totally cringy to *copy* anything that was successful; the whole idea was to start something new – fuck the money. Which you didn't really need, anyway, because you could have a fabulous flat for about £3.50 a week. You didn't need that shit. And at Stirling Cooper I was earning very good money. We called it the "wedge".

'Quite frankly, I didn't mix with the sort of people who worked hard all day and bought normal dresses; everyone I knew was a total nutter and lived down Ladbroke Grove. But a few of my things hit it by accident. The look was epitomised by my "spiral zip" dress and the menswear was very sexual and erotic – verging on fetish-wear.'

On the threshold of the 1970s, Antony Price and Juliet Mann were at the centre of a fashion community who were pushing the absolute limits of personal style. The sole *raison d'être* of their enterprise, and that of O'Connor, Motown and Keith Wainwright (the latter three staying true to their Mod creed) was quite simple: it was to look as good and as inimitably cool as possible. Hence their immediate attractiveness, around a year later, to Bryan Ferry.

Juliet Mann: 'At the time, if you went out, you wouldn't have to think what to wear because Antony would immediately have an idea – a sample he had hanging up, something off the production line at Stirling Cooper. Antony could go from a polka-dot fifties look, to lamé, to faux leopard skin. I remember at Barkers department store, in Kensington High Street, there was a Fabric Hall – as we called them in those days –

in the basement; and you could get the most surprising things there. You would probably only find such a weird selection somewhere in the outer suburbs.

'We always used to buy remnants – oddities – from Barkers. Antony found *green lurex snakeskin print* at Barkers – which being a genius pattern cutter he made into the most amazing outfit.* He made a piece at Che Guevara, his second shop in Kensington High Street, that was a black motorbike dress in *cire*; it was later featured in some flip-book of Amanda Lear wearing one and getting undressed. When you laid the dress out, it was like a snake; then, when you fastened this single long spiral zip, the whole thing zipped into the dress. It was art. No question.'

---

* One version of the sleeve image for *Roxy Music*, not used, would show Kari Ann dressed in a fifties style, figure-hugging, pedal-pusher jump-suit, made by Price from said green lurex snakeskin print.

twenty-nine

London, 1969. Designers, stylists and taste-makers III: an overview from Duggie Fields; a journey through the sixties: how Pamla Motown got to Notting Hill; a flash-forward to 'Them' (1976) and a few words from its author; Wendy Dagworthy's outfits for Roxy Music; a few words from Janet Street-Porter, Mod, model, *Petticoat* journalist; the Zandra Rhodes connection; Carol McNicoll; and an invitation from Brian Eno.

In the period between the opening of Smile, Stirling Cooper and Mr Freedom in 1969, and the first rehearsals of Roxy Music in 1970 and 1971, the essentially gay male Notting Hill scene would become a venue for intense social and professional exchange. Somewhat resembling a private club, but with a constant stream of new arrivals and connections between different small groups of friends and acquaintances, this would be the milieu in which, in the early 1970s, Bryan Ferry would first meet Antony Price, Juliet Mann and Keith Wainwright.

In part through the Ladbroke Grove set, and in part through the Royal College of Art, the scene into which Bryan Ferry would arrive would create both a social link and a link in sensibility for those whom the cool of Pop art, and a capacity for complete individualism, had become a personal style by way of cutting-edge fashions and a particular metropolitan vision.

Duggie Fields [artist]: 'Style didn't get separated off from the other interests – music, literature, movies, art; it was all part of the same thing. There was definitely an "us" and a "them", and that's how you could have an underground scene in the late sixties. The "us" would come from visual recognition symbols – which needn't necessarily have been about fashion; *it was more a way of being in the world that you could recognise in somebody else.* Their style would tell you that, but also the vibe that came with it. Some people could have very confused vibes; or very fucked-up vibes.'

Pamla Motown's further career would be concerned almost entirely with her (continued) reading of the 'visual recognition symbols' to which Fields refers. As her involvement with fashion and a fashion crowd deepened, so she would become intimate with the Notting Hill circle immediately around David Hockney, and most importantly with the artist-designer Mo McDermott. McDermott in turn was friends with the set designer Brian Morris, then based in Ladbroke Grove, who was also a friend of Juliet Mann and Antony Price. It would be at a party held in Brian Morris's flat that the historic first meeting between Price, Keith, Mann and Ferry would take place.

Motown's journey through the 1960s, firstly to Notting Hill of the Ossie Clark era, and then to becoming a designer for Mr Freedom with Jim O'Connor sets the scene. With regard to living a Pop art lifestyle, Motown's – then highly individual – dedication to skateboarding would match O'Connor's, fascination with creating the 'Keyhole Kate' motorbike.

Pamla Motown: 'My best friend, Jane Whiteside (later to start Stirling Cooper as their designer), was going to the Royal College of Art – as was my new boyfriend – and so I decided to apply. It was a ticket to move up to London.

'Then I met someone who offered me a job with a bunch of other young hip artists from the London set, working for Adam Pollock, who designed sets for Glyndebourne. Through this job I met Mo McDermott, a friend and model for Hockney, and he moved me into the room next to his at the top of the notorious 74 Ladbroke Grove. Jenny Rylance lived downstairs. She was dating Rod Stewart and later married Stevie Marriot, lead singer of the Small Faces. [Marriot supposedly wrote 'I Feel Much Better', released in 1967 on the Immediate label, for Jenny Rylance.]

'The chance to earn a living won out over more school, and I found myself in Notting Hill Gate and made friends with Ossie, Celia, and

David Hockney, all through Mo. By the time my friends from Harrow [art school] were ready to move up to London to find housing to go to the Royal College, I had secured an amazing flat. This was in the summer of 1964, and I just seemed to follow my interests and ended up in the right place with the right people at the right time. Portobello Road was an important part of the Notting Hill style and weekly trips on Saturday were a must in order to decorate our flats – Mo was so good at this.'

Motown's experiences at this time exemplify Adrienne Hunter's observation about the easygoing, ambling nature of fashionable life in bohemian London in the 1960s. At the same time, Juliet Mann had first moved to Paddington Street, in Marylebone, and been able to get a flat and a job in pretty much the same afternoon. At this point it was still possible to live cheaply in central London, particularly if one was socialising through the art school and Royal College network. Mann would recall how across the space of a month one could save enough from one's wages to have dinner at the fashionable restaurant Odin's, just off Marylebone High Street.

In the immediately ensuing link up of art student factions out of which much of Roxy Music was about to be formed, the dances at the Royal College of Art would be of central importance. Motown, too, attended these dances – slightly earlier in the sixties – and her experience becomes part of a lineage of connections, which, dizzyingly, would link Mark Lancaster and Viv Kemp to the visiting tutors who taught Motown at Harrow.

Pamla Motown's tutors had included, in Derek Boshier and Peter Blake, two of the four young artists featured in Ken Russell's *Monitor* documentary on British Pop art, *Pop Goes the Easel*, first screened by the BBC in 1962. (The others were Peter Phillips and Pauline Boty.) The final sequence of the film shows what appears to be an art school hop (presumably at the Royal College, given the students who appear, including Hockney in full ceremonial blond regalia), but filmed in fact at the Bath Street studio of Richard Smith – who would subsequently pass the studio on to Mark Lancaster.

Pamla Motown: 'Through my college friends I went regularly to the Royal College dances, which were a hotbed for new fashions and showing them off. By now we were listening to Motown, Stax and all the great soul dance music coming out of Philadelphia and Detroit. I made a new out-fit for each dance and got myself on *Ready Steady Go!*, as the only girl skateboarder on the credits. I skated to the music of the Who's "My Generation" with Steve Hiett, my boyfriend Neil and Roy Giles – all Royal College students. Skateboarding fascinated me as it was very American and we made our own boards and attached roller-skate wheels to the bottom. There were some great slopes at the Royal College, where Steve, Neil and I regularly went to practise. We became "known" and that's how we got the *Ready Steady Go!* gig.

'By now I had moved into a basement flat on Elgin Crescent with Neil, Jane and her boyfriend. I worked dressing windows at Jaeger on the edge of Carnaby Street and left there to start my own business making and selling clothes bags, visors and other Mod clothes. Pauline Fordham, an avant-garde lady with a boutique near Tuffin & Foale off Carnaby Street, bought my mini-dresses made from Union Jacks, along with Courreges inspired plastic visors and other Mod dresses. Through the grapevine I heard about Kensington Market and realised I could have my own boutique, as the smaller spots were, I believe, only £5 a week. I made crochet dresses and knit tops and skirts. This was a good income but even more so, it was "the place to be". The market was mostly occupied by hippies coming back from the drug runs to Marrakech and Nepal. There were amazing clothes and artefacts, long embroidered dresses and fine Indian cottons but not really my style . . .

'By the summer of 1967 drugs began to influence the music and clothes and I began to lose interest in keeping up with that hippy scene. I liked Mod and Pop art and girl groups – I liked futuristic rather than ethnic. I wasn't interested in dropping out or getting high on drugs. Life itself was a high and designing and wearing clothes and showing them off were fun for me. We weren't really rebels or professionals; rather we had a kind of total, deep-in-the-gut understanding that we were the reality and the future of the emerging youth culture. We knew who we were and who wasn't one of us. We knew our people by what they said, how they dressed, where they went and what music they listened to.

'The sharing of ideas and style that came out of the art school atmo-sphere spilled over into everyday life and work. That was a large part of what made it dynamic. That was a large part of what being part of that art school scene was all about. I could say more about the upper classes and their rather naive interest in all these novel happenings; but it was really when the working-class kids got into the art schools, previously available only to the rich or middle class, that the movement took wings and flew.

'Finally, around 1968, Tommy Roberts, an East End rag trade guy, and Trevor Miles, a cute young wide boy with a gift of the gab and a large circle of friends, knew of me and I was invited to design a collection for their new store, Mr Freedom. They wanted to do a Pop art style and I was thrilled to go and help them. A new chapter unfolded, as it was through this that I met Jim O'Connor – who came and worked for Mr Freedom – Keith, Malcolm Bird and Duggie Fields.

'Much publicity followed as our designs gained popularity and the shop became famous. It was wonderful in that it was all very innocent compared with today. Jim and I became the spokespeople for the company and eventually left to work on our own. At that time making custom clothes for Andy McKay of Roxy Music, Verity Lambert [television producer] and Keith Wainwright – Keith always loved to have cool clothes.'

Having travelled this far in the accounts of the principal designers, stylists and taste-makers – separate from the musicians and fine artists – out of whose sensibility Roxy Music would emerge, it seems a good moment to flash forward to Peter York's essay 'Them'. In her account of her early career, Motown describes the precise milieu of art-school educated, post-Mod street aesthetes whom Peter York would later examine. Theirs was an ambiguous condition, to say the least, particularly as regards the relationship between class and elitism. It is entirely within its spirit of exclusivity and stylistic elusiveness that the 'Them' faction, with their post-Mod (and perhaps postmodern) sense of created identity, should be so clear – as already stated by Price, Motown and Fields – on the central issue of how one recognised a fellow member of the style in-crowd.

Written in 1976, at the time almost as an explanation for aspects of punk and post-punk, 'Them' was the only essay to be written outside of 'the scene' (as Polly Eltes will describe it) of which Roxy Music would become the house band, house style and imperial ambassadors. It is essentially a thesis on the effects of montaging style at a dizzying rate, pulling together everything (as we have seen) from Pre-Raphaelitism to science fiction by way of Warhol, Biba, and fifties pin-up magazines.

York's breakdown of the scene is precise: 'Them Venues' include both the Royal College and the ICA while the 'Them Hairdresser' is Keith, and 'Art School etc. Influentials in the Them movement' include Price, Ferry, Zandra Rhodes, Duggie Fields, Carol McNicoll and Brian Eno. 'Them Couturiers' include Jim O'Connor and Pamla Motown, with Ossie Clark mentioned as 'then and forever'. The absence of Antony Price from the list is clearly an editorial error.

Central to York's essay are two notions. Firstly:

> Art school people and quasi art school people, post art school people, fashion business people and Applied Art media stars were of course in the forefront of this merging of sensibilities (the montaging of revivalism and camp, primarily); and secondly: Camp and Pop put together produced what I call Art Necro: a quick change revivalism which became very big business around the turn of the decade [1960–1970] when, as John Lombardi says, people were looking for something *silly* to take their minds off depressing things ... The Necro industry gave employment to many Thems: designing old/new record sleeves, doing jackets for books about Forties film stars, working in Antiquarius in the Kings Road, and so on. Send-ups or fun-clothes – fried egg appliqués etc. – gave us the Mr Freedom/Paradise Garage/Tommy Roberts look ...

In the midst of all this, Bryan Ferry – described by York as 'the best possible example of the ultimate art-directed existence' – is defined as 'the most important pasticheur in Britain today'; with the closing line, 'He should hang in the Tate, with David Bowie.' For York, at that time, Bryan Ferry might be claimed as the living embodiment of postmodernism – an utterly contemporary work of art.

Peter York: 'At the time that was written, it seemed an important observation to make – that Ferry was an art object. Because he *was* an art object.

'Before writing that article, I'd noticed these people around. They were superannuated art school and very noticeable. And in their extreme London form there was a style to them. And one of the things you noticed was the Japonaiserie of them. How could you knock around and not be aware of Andrew Logan? [Artist, designer and craftsman, founder of *Alternative Miss World*, first held in 1972.]

'Then I found people who knew these people – people at *Harpers&Queen*. One of the absolute codes was having an Andrew Logan broken glass brooch. Once you got the hang of it, they were a very easy group to identify. It was a small group of people who lived in Earls Court sort of places; or, in the case of Andrew Logan, he was one of the *earliest* converters of a riverside warehouse at a time when the docks stood empty, and all those warehouses were huge, looming places – you wouldn't know where you were going.★

'If you try to trace the stylistic *embourgeoisement* that followed the sixties, there wasn't *that much* of it, because there wasn't much money around – and all that blanding out was what "Them" set Themselves against. Very few of Them were poor kids from poor places, that I can think of; they were mostly nice kids who might otherwise have become nicely spoken churchmen – quite a polite, British mode of artiness.

'They were important in the sense that there was a strong dose of irony, a huge dose of camp, and most of the key men were gay. It was art school, art school, art school. They would be very important in the introduction of punk, and Malcolm McLaren, but they weren't very cause driven – as, say, was Caroline Coon [Brtish artist, journalist and activist]. The Clash world would be a very different world. What most movements do is make way, in their early days, for their predecessors. And there would be a lot of Themness in the post-punk and New Wave period, which gave jobs to Themish people.

'Zandra Rhodes had gone before in that aesthetic, and was a recognised success and sold to rich American ladies – and was a patron of her former art school friends. Early Notting Hill – she was in Saint Stephens Gardens then, which was chic-rough in those days but rather more rough than chic.

'The one great event in Their universe was *Alternative Miss World* – it was a masterpiece of camp.† And if you didn't like new camp you might find it pretty heavy going. They had a camp comedienne, Fenella Fielding, who was a great friend of Andrew Logan; and a fellow traveller in that world was Richard O'Brien – and you can see how that sensibil-

★ Keith Wainwright recalls that he used to refer to the street in which Logan was living as 'Drown'em Rd', because the building leaked so much.
† Which in 1985 would be won – in a vaguely Duchampian way – by a robot beauty queen called Miss R.O.S.A. Bosom, built by artist Professor Bruce Lacey.

ity infused *The Rocky Horror Show* [London premiere, 19 June 1973].You think of all those themes, which were then so new – camp fifties, cross-dressing, recycled teen and girlie group. The *Roxy Music* album has all of those things to some extent, but it's far more sophisticated. It's sort of camp, but it's hetero-camp. But if Themness had a residence band, Roxy Music would most certainly have been it . . . They were always at the epic, early Roxy Music concerts . . .

'Now where did Roxy Music come from? Well, we know where Bryan came from, and it wasn't Earls Court; Eno – the education system kicked in, and made it right for him. Neither were metropolitans in the first instance – but they wanted to be. And they were not gay. But the huge influence of Antony Price is there; that he *made* Bryan be more daring in his gestures, because Bryan didn't want to be that daring. So it is very important for people like that to have an Antony. But if you were to say, "the gang's all here", as regards the original Thems, you'd be talking about a group of no more than ten or fifteen people.'

The importance of 'Them', as a retrospective focus in considering the broader constellation of people around the initial circle of Roxy Music, lies in its acuity as a summary, as well as a specific analysis of a change in trend between the late 1960s and the early 1970s. On its first publication in 1976 – by which time Roxy Music possessed superstar status – the essay would be written up in the London *Evening Standard* ('Are You a Them or are You an Us') with a photograph of Antony Price dressed 'in a silvery grey uniform he designed himself'. A 'Them' ball was also held in the (by then) newly fashionable Covent Garden.

As a cult that refers back to an earlier moment, from the mid-1970s to the earliest 1970s, the idea of 'Them' (a term seldom, if ever, used by the people whom the essay described) brought together several key people and phenomena in the tinting of an era's mood.

The designer Zandra Rhodes, as York notes, had become a colourful, central presence in London's fashion scene, and both former Moody Polly Eltes and Janet Street-Porter (in the middle years of the 1960s a writer for *Petticoat* magazine) would model her clothes. A graduate of the Royal College of Art herself, Rhodes would also be one of the first to recognise and collect the work of Carol McNicoll. Likewise Caroline Coon, who had studied painting at Saint Martin's School of Art, would also model in a Zandra Rhodes show. Once again, there would be a direct link to Pop art and revivalism. Like her fellow Mods Pamla Motown and Jim O'Connor, Janet Street-Porter would reject the deeper hippy movement in favour of a far more urban aesthetic, concerned with pop culture, futurology and glamour.

Janet Street-Porter: 'I was a Mod between 1963 and 1965, which was when Mod started in Chelsea and Fulham. Then when I was studying at the Architectural Association in 1965, I was making a lot of clothes and selling them down Carnaby Street – silver plastic, that kind of thing.

'I always wore a lot of Ossie Clark clothes, and then Zandra Rhodes opened her Fulham Road shop. Her early stuff was derived from comic strips, and don't forget there had been a huge exhibition of comic book art at the ICA around this time – in the early 1970s ['AAARGH! A Celebration of Comics' – ICA, December 1970]. Also Mr Freedom was very influenced by comic strips.

'So there was this cross-over between comic books, the future, the Archigram group – it was a real melting pot. Interesting projections of what the future might be like, but also a huge rejection of the hippy culture that was Indian and ethnic – although a lot of people smoked dope. People like Keith Wainwright and myself came from pretty working-class backgrounds, and all that stuff seemed quite weird.

'I think the look was – and this was before punk – all to do with *superiority.* We felt that we were so clued up about the scene, that there was this innate sense of superiority. Every night of the week we were going out; you knew the way you looked was right; and even though everyone else laughed at it you just thought they were wrong. I think it comes partly from a background where parents sneer at you, but partly from a ruthless sense of self-improvement. I mean I wrote lists of all the movies I went to, the books I read, the clubs I went to, and who I saw from the age of fourteen. I went to see the Russian *Hamlet* when I was fifteen! All the French new wave stuff, and Fellini, obviously. And I know that Zandra felt the same.

'Through Zandra we met Carol McNicoll, who at that time was going out with Brian Eno. Her work was sensational (ceramics) and Zandra bought a lot of pieces, and that's how we met Brian Eno. The first thing I remember is being roped into performing the *1812 Overture* with the Portsmouth Sinfonia at the the Royal Albert Hall. But Carol definitely got his look sorted out.'

The relationship between the created image and the created lifestyle would be the tenets of the milieu defined by 'Them'; and in its most extreme and intense variation – as we will see in the ideas being discussed at the Camberwell commune where Brian Eno and Carol McNicoll were living in 1970 – the idea was to actively and profoundly fuse together art and life into a kind of Pop art, avant-garde reclamation of the Arts and Crafts Movement. As with the ideas being pursued and debated by the Moodies, there was a much shorter distance between the 'high' culture of fine art and the 'low' popular cultures of fashion or pop music – a distinction which (to use the term chosen by Carol McNicoll and Polly Eltes) could be refined into the single act of 'posing'.

It has become a truism of cultural studies to remark that Susan Sontag's *Notes on Camp* (1964), reveal above all that 'camp' is a term so slippery and ambiguous that its true meaning lies in its avoidance of a fixed definition. But the same elusiveness can be said of the cult of the 'pose' and 'dressing up' and 'superiority' that was simultaneously a fixed point within, and an amorphous, atomised colouring of, the sensibility amongst the Royal College fashion clique of the late 1960s and early 1970s, and their immediate circle of style-aware acquaintants. Certainly, this cult was the product of a conflation of ideas and attitudes – the decisional aesthetic underpinning to the more technical, problem-solving demands of creativity and art-making.

As 'Them' proposed an elite, so the proposition held true in the early adult experience of many whom the essay purported to describe. This was the sensibility – call it an evolved form of Mod cool, if you want – that would be included within the range of ideas that Bryan Ferry brought together in Roxy Music, and which then would become democratised through the pop music mainstream. The brilliance of Roxy would lie in the intense, immediately vivid and eloquent world that the group seem to both describe and represent, and in the simultaneous absence within their music or appearance of any single, delineating image.

Simon Puxley, writing under the archaic, gentleman journalist pseudonym (chosen for him by Bryan Ferry) Rex Balfour, would convey the originality and energy of this balancing of opposites in an anecdote. Describing a very early set by Roxy Music, at the party of 'a top glamour photographer' in 1971, he relates: 'That night, when one of the partygoers, driven to distraction by this unprecedented musical farrago, aggressively demanded that they "play some rock and roll", the singer just smiled and replied in cool, measured tones: "We *are* rock and roll."' The *détourne* relationship between verb and subject says it all.

thirty

London, 1969–1970. Meetings 1: Bryan Ferry in London, songwriting with Graham Simpson; 'Pop Art Redefined' – Mark Lancaster's jukebox; Tim Head in London; Viv Kemp in London; the Reading and Newcastle connection; a party in Ladbroke Grove.

Bryan Ferry: 'After I'd graduated, and moved to London, I found myself living in a house along Kensington High Street and getting Graham [Simpson, with whom Ferry had played in the Gas Board] to come down from Newcastle, where he was still living. And I said that I'd been writing songs, and he started working with me. I was writing things – I didn't have a piano, I had a harmonium. And so I was pumping away on this harmonium playing these first Roxy songs, and he was playing along. So first of all there were just two of us.

'Graham was a fabulous player; very unusual. There's a lovely thing of his on "Chance Meeting", on the first album. He had all this jazz in his head. His mate was Evan Parker [b.1944], who was this wild, avant-garde player, and he lived some of the time with Evan; and so I'm not sure whether he felt that what we were doing was not serious enough, or jazz enough. But once again, there was somebody who, if he hadn't been there, I don't think my career would have taken off.

'I'd received a travel scholarship from the Royal College of Art, and it paid for my year after university; it supported me, really, so that was quite an important thing. I was supposed to go and live in Rome or somewhere, but I didn't get that far. I wonder if I was supposed to hand any work in? It's a bit late now I suppose ... But it was great – maybe £1,000 or £500, but it seemed like quite a lot. But it paid for a year. Then I started teaching, two days a week [art and ceramics at a school in Hammersmith] and that was enough to support me.'

Between his arrival in London in 1969 and Roxy Music's audition at the Granada, Wandsworth Road, London SW8 for David Enthoven of EG management in January 1972, Bryan Ferry would begin to resolve the collision of artistic drives that he had identified within himself during his last term at university. He was caught in an unyielding tension between his commitment to becoming a fine artist, with all of the creative possibilities that such a vocation – in 1969 – was beginning to explore, and an equal desire to pursue his career as a musician, singer and songwriter.

The originality of his situation derived from the way in which he did not so much want to choose *between* these two careers, as blend them together – in effect using pop music – pop stardom, even – as a medium in which to make art. While such an ambition would fit precisely with the ideas being explored by a small faction of progressive thinkers within the art schools, Ferry's approach to the dilemma heightened the individual qualities of the two seemingly irreconcilable elements. The idea was not to create a rarefied art band, but to harness the pure pop energy of his greatest musical loves – black American blues, soul music, rhythm and blues, the Velvet Underground – and route such musical intensity through a meticulously created artistic statement. And this at a time when most music journalists were deeply suspicious of any form of music which deviated from the roots authenticity of blues-based American rock.

Bryan Ferry: 'I'd dabbled with singing when I was in the college band. But at that point hadn't thought of writing anything at all. Mainly because I couldn't play an instrument save for harmonica and a few notes of saxophone. It wasn't until I'd managed to string together a few chords, that's when I thought I'll make a go of this if I can put my whole artistic consciousness into it. And instead of creating paintings, I'll make – *and I really did think of it like this –* "pictures in sounds". I thought, how amazing if I can put my enthusiasm for music and my skill as an artist together.

'I knew I wanted the music to be very eclectic, stylistically. I wasn't really conscious of wanting to create a style; I wanted the music to be very emotional – which some people never found it to be, but I did; and to take things from all the different kinds of music I was interested in, which was a completely open book. It ranged from, on the one hand, experimental music – people like John Cage – through all the different strands of American music, which was the development of black music in America mainly.

'But what made me different from a lot of people from my time – from a lot of those musicians who were also influenced by the blues, like Van Morrison or Eric Clapton, who are the same period as me – is that I was equally interested in Fred Astaire and Gene Kelly and all of let's say "the white music" of America from that period. Tin Pan Alley, Cole Porter – that kind of music from the great musicals, which was more European-based music. It wasn't based on the cotton fields; it was more from Vienna – the number of the Jewish émigrés from Austria, Germany and so forth meant that a lot of wonderful music drifted into New York in the 1930s. And so you get that whole other Broadway sound – or whatever you want to call it. I liked all that as well.

'So there was a lot of music jumping around in my head, and when I started writing songs there was all manner of weird influences coming up, juxtaposed. And so yes, the word "collage" does spring to mind; of taking bits from here, there and everywhere, and hopefully creating your own stuff from it. And you have to bear in mind that I had five other people in the band whose strengths I was trying to play to as well. In the same way that Duke Ellington, with his band, always tried to write to the strengths of his band. He had a fantastic sax player in Johnny Hodges, he had Harry Carnie the baritone player . . .'

At the same time that Antony Price was noting how many of the artist technicians within the styling of Hollywood musical were Jewish, so Ferry had identified the genius of European Jewish émigrés to the American entertainment industry of the 1930s and 1940s. Some of Ferry's earliest attempts at songwriting – notably his '2 HB' – in reference to his long-standing admiration of Humphrey Bogart, and in particular his best-known starring role as the white dinner-jacketed Rick, of Rick's Cafe in *Casablanca* – were inspired in part by the glamour and mystique of Hollywood.

In the late 1950s and early 1960s, when Richard Hamilton had been rediscovering and examining the great Hollywood movies, the genre as a whole was hopelessly out of fashion within intellectual circles, who favoured the newly emerging social realism and 'new wave' European cinema. The tenets of Pop art, however, recognised in Hollywood key strands of stimulation – mass-market, mass-produced, meticulously constructed, mechanistic sex appeal.

Pop art, as the 1960s progressed, would come under continued scrutiny, even as the pop 'style' was being re-routed and diffused into other media. But in its fine artistic form, too, pop maintained its significance. During Bryan Ferry's first year in London, an exhibition at the newly opened Hayward Gallery, in its brutalist building on the South Bank of the Thames, would be titled 'Pop Art Redefined' – which was an audaciously advanced title, given that Pop art was hardly, at that point, a forgotten or outmoded artistic idea. A contribution to the exhibition would come from Mark Lancaster, who was asked to install (or to 'curate', in twenty-first century terms) a jukebox within the exhibition space, playing what he considered to be key a selection of Pop-art related tracks. At this point, Mark Lancaster was in the enviable position of being artist in residence at King's College, Cambridge, where he began to make work responding to the various architectural splendours of the buildings.

Lancaster's jukebox selection describes a pure pop sensibility, occurring at the same time Mr Freedom was opening; Pop art and its sources, even at the very end of the 1960s, would remain constant themes for Hamilton's former students. The relationship of these songs to revivalism or early 1970s camp is apparent; but more important, by far, is the way in which Lancaster was presenting the selection entirely free of nostalgia or irony, and as the elemental spirit of the pop age.

Mark Lancaster: 'When the Hayward Gallery exhibition "Pop Art Redefined" was being curated in 1969 by John Russell and Suzi Gablik, they asked me, as the person they knew who was into pop music, to provide a jukebox in the exhibition. Now, the very title "Pop Art Redefined", as early as 1969, seems both advanced, as it seemed then, and kind of weird.

'But I went to places in Soho where they had the latest jukeboxes, playing 45 rpm 7-inch records, of course, and arranged to rent the most glamorous one, which was delivered to the Hayward and installed on the top floor. It was a real working jukebox, which only played when somebody put the shilling or sixpence or whatever into it. I think I got the attendants to feed it now and then.

'I was criticised for my selection by one critic for what I thought were archetypal pop songs. Whoever it was said they were lightweight or a poor choice or camp or something. I had one Elvis and one Beatles, just to show I knew they had to be there; but I had more odd things, that I liked and that I associated with Pop art: the Everlys, Roy Orbison's "Crying", Bryan Hyland's "Sealed with a Kiss", Bobby Vee, Lesley Gore's "It's My Party", the Marvelettes, some Supremes song, Smokey Robinson's "Tears of a Clown", and definitely "God Only Knows" by the Beach Boys and "In My Room". Also probably an Adam Faith song and a Dusty Springfield. At any rate it was mainly "light-hearted" pop and no heavy stuff, and I put half of my own 45s in it and they got very worn out.'

Bryan Ferry: 'I told Mark that I was writing some songs, and he said what they are called? So I said that there was one called "2 HB" and he said "Oh that's so great – writing a song about a pencil." Which is a very Pop art concept really – except that I was writing a song about Humphrey Bogart.'

The 'Hamilton' generation from Newcastle University – Lancaster, Buckley, Head, de Ville – had all remained committed to their careers as artists, which was a prospect in which becoming either a postgraduate student or a teacher within an art school was wholly unavoidable. As Bryan Ferry secured work teaching art and ceramics at a girls' secondary school in Hammersmith, Tim Head would come to London to take a postgraduate course at Saint Martin's School of Art, and Nick de Ville would work for both Hamilton – who was now also resident in London once more, as both a major artist and a major pop celebrity – and then for the artist Anthony Donaldson. Both Head and de Ville would be important to the creation of Roxy Music, in a variety of ways.

Rita Donagh: 'I always think that Roxy Music was like the coming together of Reading and Newcastle through Tim and Viv.'

Viv Kemp: 'The second I left Reading after graduating, I went to a hop at the Royal College of Art, where I met Tim with a bunch of these

Newcastle people. Tim was living in Redesdale Street in Chelsea – he had this bedsit there. Malcolm Bird lived on the ground floor, and Malcolm's best pal from the Royal College was Antony Price. Antony was just starting out then as a designer. So it was Tim on the top floor, and Margot Parker in the middle – who was also a designer; she'd been at the Royal College and her best friends were there, too, who made these leather and feather outfits. She was friends with Duggie Fields, and so we all went to his exhibitions.

'Then Malcolm Bird on the ground floor did these Rackhamesque illustrations and some amazing interiors for Biba – elfin things, mushrooms and toadstools. He wore big black platform-soled boots, and had black hair, and was *very* into fashion.

'When I met Tim at the Royal College dance, his best friend was Nick de Ville, and they had of course all lived with Bryan Ferry at the house in Eslington Terrace in Newcastle. I first met Bryan through Tim, because they were big chums, but I was also friends with Stephen Buckley. I had a studio at Old Street – one of the first Space studios – above an old hat factory, right next to Bath Street where Stephen had his studio; and he'd taken it over from Mark Lancaster and Richard Smith. The lease had been won in a poker game from the film director John Schlesinger, who would have been making *Midnight Cowboy* around this time. They'd filmed some of *Pop Goes the Easel* there, and it was incredibly cool. It was like a New York loft. It had this big white room, and then the kitchen cupboard was just like a pile of white cups – which was *unheard* of in the sixties. It was pre-Conran, pre-everything. It was *so* cool.'

Tim Head: 'Do you know how Roxy Music formed? When I came back to London, I did a year at Saint Martin's; and a lot of people – like Stephen Buckley – went to Reading because Rita Donagh was teaching there. I'd been to Reading for an interview for the BA course, and Rita had said "If you get into Newcastle, go there, because Richard's teaching there" – which was very good of her. But a lot of people then did a graduate course – they went off and did another two years at Reading from Newcastle. So there was a big cross-over. I got to know these people, Simon and Elaine, who knew people at Reading, and through them I met Viv Kemp, whom I later married. And Viv of course had known Andy Mackay.'

Viv Kemp: 'It was the Reading and Newcastle connection; because when we all finished at Reading, my best friend John found a house in Battersea that he wanted to rent, but needed some extra people.

'Then Mali Morris [abstract painter], who had read Fine Art at Newcastle, and then like Stephen Buckley did her postgraduate at Reading, said that she'd got these two pals from Newcastle, Simon and Elaine, who were looking for somewhere to live. So they teamed up with John and got this house: and that was Reading and Newcastle in one house! And that's how I met Tim, because Simon and Elaine were amongst his best friends from Newcastle.'

Tim Head: 'When I moved to London in 1969 I saw a lot of Bryan – he was living in Kensington with Susie Cussins, who was also from Newcastle. And Bryan had said he was writing these songs, and was wanting to get in touch with other musicians – particularly experimental people. So Viv said "There's Andy" – who used to do these avant-garde music events at Reading with Brian Eno, who had been at Winchester. So Viv introduced Bryan to Andy, and then to Brian Eno. That's how it happened.

'Viv had witnessed Andy doing these Cageian performances at Reading, and had brought in Brian Eno to do things. So if Viv hadn't made that connection, who knows what would have happened . . . Bryan had said that he was looking for people who were into experimenting with music, and who had synthesisers and things like that. This was quite radical if you were thinking of going into the pop business.'

As the early music elements of Roxy Music were largely enabled by these meetings between art graduates from Reading, Newcastle and the Royal College of Art, so this same remarkable conflation of people would assist in the encounter between Bryan Ferry and the Ladbroke Grove crowd. If a specific occasion could be claimed as the first meeting between Bryan Ferry, Antony Price, Juliet Mann and Keith Wainwright, it would be the party held by Brian Morris, who was a friend of David Hockney and Mo McDermott. Morris was also a friend of Juliet Mann, who would flat-sit for him in Ladbroke Grove.

In this final constellation, therefore, the Newcastle, Reading and Royal College factions would all come together – creating, as it were, the social

frame in which Roxy Music would be set; as all the while Bryan Ferry –
at this time still working on songs with Graham Simpson – was simultaneously recruiting and rehearsing the musicians for his group.

Bryan Ferry: 'Tim was very cool – he still is – and always ahead of the
game a bit; a year younger than me. Anyway I saw him, and said that I was
starting to write some songs – he was then doing his postgraduate at
Reading University. I said that I wanted to do something with a synthesiser – there was an element of avant-garde music that I wanted to bring
in to what I was trying to do, and he said that he knew this guy called
Andy Mackay, who had a synthesiser – and that he'd get the two of us
together. He introduced us.'

Tim Head: 'I was living in Redesdale Street at the time, in Chelsea – the
first flat I got in London, for thirty bob a week or something. Malcolm
Bird who also lived there was a graphic designer – very fashionable at the
time, and would do these quite fey, wonderful drawings of magical things
like mushrooms . . . And he actually designed the first flyer for Roxy
Music, with a little aeroplane spelling out "Roxy Music" in the sky. He
was a big friend of Keith and of Antony Price; so I suspect that Malcolm
might have introduced Bryan Ferry to all those people. Malcolm was into
the 1920s and 1930s, but he also lived in his own world – a magic world;
it fitted in with the whole Arthur Rackham thing . . .'

Antony Price: 'We all first met Bryan Ferry at Brian Morris's party. Brian
Morris is a major art director for Hollywood cinema. There were two
very stylish queens who lived in a fabulous basement flat in Ladbroke
Grove, and they would have huge parties on Saturday nights. It was a time
when everyone was listening to the Beach Boys. It was very much the
Ladbroke Grove crowd – David Hockney, Ossie Clark, Mo, the whole lot.
Brian Morris had a huge home cinema system in his flat – this was pre-
video remember, and we would have *42nd Street* showing on the wall . . .
So we all met at this party. And then we met again at the Speakeasy in
Mortimer Street . . .'

Bryan Ferry had come to Brian Morris's party with another friend of
Juliet Mann's called Paul Macbeth – who at this point was working as a
private secretary for a friend of Elizabeth Taylor. Macbeth would subse-

quently work for the owner of Legends – a fashionable nightclub on Old Burlington Street, where much later in the 1970s Juliet herself would become well known as the glamorous hat-check girl.

Juliet Mann: 'It was all parties, parties, parties . . . Brian Morris was a friend of Hockney and Mo McDermott. Mo looked after Hockney's flat and had access to it; so we'd sometimes go round there on Saturday nights and marvel at these Helena Rubinstein dining tables . . .

Antony Price: 'Mo was famous for making wooden trees. As an innocent young student from the north, Mo's flat was my first experience of a giant sound system, lapsang souchong tea, and "Reflections" by the Supremes at full whack. My first gay sound system, in fact . . .

'I was a rising star behind Ossie, so I had met all of his models. At this time, I would do shows with Ossie as the "warm up", so to speak – so the models got to know me, as well, and some of them – like Kari-Ann and Amanda Lear – ended up on the Roxy Music album sleeves. I was also working with the photographer who later shot those covers, too – Karl Stoecker. And Bryan would have met all of these people through me.'

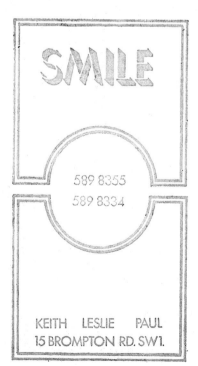

Juliet Mann: 'Bryan must have thought that all his weekends had come at once; because Keith and Antony Price were at the same place. So all of us met on the same night.'

Keith Wainwright: 'I knew Eno when he used to come to Smile on the tube – dressed how he dressed! That was when he was going out with Carol McNicoll.

'I remember that Juliet had told me about this band who wanted their hair done, whom Antony had met. And then we went to a party at Brian Morris's house in Ladbroke Grove . . .'

In one sense, the density of interconnectedness between these different, mostly highly flamboyant people, and their further outreach – by way, for instance, of Eno's relationship to Carol McNicoll and Zandra Rhodes, or Simon Puxley and Polly Eltes, and so on through the cast so far – would soon comprise Roxy Music's first audience of their peers; and one who would immediately recognise the modern sensibility of montage, pastiche, visual glamour, arts reference points and musical wit, quotation, punning and audacity that the group represented and conveyed.

For this initial audience, who would be stunned, delighted and thrilled by Roxy, the total Pop art lifestyle – the soundtrack to 'Them' – would take expression within the group and their image, into a glorious simulacrum of high society. For Ferry and the succession of individual musicians in the front line of actually making the music – and in Ferry's case working equally hard again in attempting to secure the best representation and record deal – the experience was equally urgent.

thirty-one

London, 1970. Meetings, 2: Brian Eno, Carol McNicoll and the Camberwell commune; Brian Eno says 'yes' to pop; Andy Mackay's black-out; resolving contradictions; first meetings and rehearsals in Kensington of Bryan Ferry, Andy Mackay and Brian Eno.

Deep in the unofficial constitution of dandyism, it is said, lies the importance of details. In such a system of belief, a detail of considerable importance would be the black cockerel feathers which extruded from the costume made for Brian Eno by Carol McNicoll, and which would acquire almost immediate iconic status.

Eno's black feather collar, however, was the agent of a far more profound aesthetic, and one which would be key to the resolution, in and around, Roxy Music, of what had been identified within the fine arts as the Pop-art/fine-art continuum. In short, this was the artistic intention to release fine artistic ideas into the mainstream, without jeopardising their 'seriousness', beauty or meaning. It is vital to the history of Roxy Music's formation that both Brian Eno and Bryan Ferry would see the group as directly related to this process – in terms of both the lineage of ideas and the creative direction of the music. Carol McNicoll, who would subsequently become a close friend of Polly Eltes, by way of her involvement in Roxy Music's and Polly's relationship to Simon Puxley, was in the very early 1970s making ceramic pieces which were at once domestic – a dinner or tea service – yet at the same time were wholly linked to surrealism and Pop art. She also considered the costumes which she made for Eno to be works of art, with complete parity with her other work.

McNicoll was born in the suburbs of Birmingham, in Solihull, and like Eno was from a Roman Catholic family. An indication of her artistic range as a student in the Fine Art department at Leeds Polytechnic, during the late 1960s, can be taken from a film which she made with three other students in 1968, inspired by a visit to see *The Sound of Music* and titled simply *Musical*. A still from the production reveals a large group of students, the men all dressed in dinner jacket and black tie, watching another man similarly attired (with white gloves) dancing with a naked young woman who is wearing a wig of long blonde plaits.

In her biographical essay on McNicoll, published as a monograph on the artist in 2003, Tanya Harrod writes of *Musical*: 'It reads as a lexicon of postmodern practices. The conventions of the classic musical were sent up, alternative happy endings were offered, the soundtracks of existing musicals were collaged and big set-pieces defiantly tackled on tiny budgets. The comedian Roy Hudd was invited to open the premiere, unaware that he had wandered on to a minefield of irony, parody and camp.'

Coming to the Royal College of Art, McNicoll had applied to both the film department and the ceramics department – an act which in itself defines the approach to creativity within her milieu. The commune in Camberwell where she would live with Brian Eno, as Roxy Music were forming, was dedicated to an all-embracing approach to creativity – to the total artistic lifestyle, with the different members engaged in all manner of creative activity, the collective intention being softly political as a statement on how to change the world.

Carol McNicoll: 'I was a student at Leeds, studying Fine Art, and there was a group of people who were a year above me, and who then set up a sort of artistic community, or commune, if you like, in south London. They got a house in Camberwell, next door to Tom Phillips, the painter, and it was shared between people who had been at Leeds and people who had been at Winchester. So one of the people who was living there was Brian Eno. And then there were the two other people from Leeds – Rob Johnson and Rob Neely.

'They were all going to start a band, and they also had an idea that they would start selling people's work. They had premises off Brick Lane, which was their studio. I had been making some things in ceramics, and Rob Neely – who was at that point working for Zandra Rhodes – showed some of my work to Zandra and sold some to her. Which was a part of their entrepreneurial thing. When I left college in the summer of 1970, I moved down to live with Brian in Camberwell, and worked for Zandra through the summer, before going to the Royal College.

'This group of people were supposed to be putting a band together; but it never quite happened. Then Brian Eno met Bryan Ferry – who was a person with whom I had friends in common. Bryan had of course been at Newcastle, and I had had a previous boyfriend who knew people there. Bryan Ferry had already had the idea for Roxy Music; and I think that at that point Andy Mackay was already involved.

'Brian Eno was I think quite torn, at first, as to whether or not to ditch this embryo group in Camberwell and go for the new idea. Because Bryan Ferry, from the very beginning, knew where he was going with this, and had an idea of how to get the band known, and get management and so on. So he was the one, as I remember, who was most professional in his attitude.

'Brian and I would trail around the Tottenham Court Road, looking in electronics shops; he was interested in electronics, and systems, from the moment I met him; and he was interested in all those people like Terry Riley and John Cage, Cornelius Cardew, and that whole area of music – which was in absolute contrast to what Bryan Ferry was interested in. So the combination was extremely interesting, because they were coming from different places; and also, of course, Brian Eno wasn't a musician – he was somebody who was interested in electronics, but he wasn't a musician in the sense that Phil Manzanera and Andy Mackay were musicians.'

McNicoll's formative year in London in 1970 exemplifies the often ignored dialogue, or at least sympathy, between a generation of art students who had been educated into a concept of art that was completely open-ended – the Duchampian, Warholian, Beuysian notion of working in any media – and those outside of the institutions of fine art, such as fashion designers, musicians, retail designers, jewellers, models, stylists, whose crafts and professions were in pursuit of the same ends. The common denominators of these mutually sympathetic approaches to art-making would be technique, experimentation and sensibility.

As Roxy Music were being put together – running through various early personnel changes★ in the gradual coming together of the core members who would record *Roxy Music* – it would become increasingly evident that this entire dialogue, between the fine arts and popular culture, was at the heart of a project which would soon bring the avant-garde to the mainstream, and would have a massive effect on not just popular music, but the coordinates of popular taste.

Between leaving Winchester School of Art and moving to London in 1969, Eno – like Ferry – had been giving a considerable amount of thought to precisely where his ambitions and artistic inclinations truly lay. Once again, the predicament was how to resolve the seeming contradictions between 'serious' or fine artistic approaches to making art, and a career within pop and rock music.

A series of entries in Eno's notebook for this period ('June '69') give an indication of his sense of liberation on eventually making the decision to work within the broader arena of 'pop'.

> Yearnings and burnings. Starting to learn music at a fearful speed. Oh, what shall we do? Insomniac I am with worry and worry. Money? Ideas? Workplace? Nuthin. Stick to Pop unless necessity weans one away. Is the dictum, these days.

And then on 25 June 1969:

> Here are me on my way to Leeds, and Peter J has just laid it to me that Pop is where it's at which is what I thought anyway.

Then, finally, on 23 July 1969:

★ These personnel changes in the initial formation of Roxy have been usefully dated and summarised by historians of Roxy Music and King Crimson (their established prog rock colleagues within the EG management stable, for whom Ferry would at one point audition as a vocalist) historians. The comings and goings of note were – Dexter Lloyd, drums, left June '71; Roger Bunn, guitar, left September '71; and more significantly, David O'List, formerly of the Nice, who made compositional contributions and played guitar in the early line-up of Roxy Music between October 1971 and September 1972.

Extremely happy
to tears again now.
At last!
Pop looks like
becoming my container,
not to mention contingent.

Bryan Ferry, Brian Eno and Andy Mackay would all, independently, prior to meeting one another, find themselves having to decide between 'serious' artistic activity (in fine art or music) and the call of pop music. For Ferry, as we have seen, the epiphanic moment occurred when he travelled down to London to see Otis Redding perform at the Roundhouse in 1967. For Brian Eno, whose artistic activities had, even as an undergraduate, been conducted at an exceptionally high degree of intellectual and emotional sophistication, the decision to attempt a 'pop' career was inevitably couched in the condition of enquiry and conceptualism with which, artistically and politically, he approached everything.

For Andrew Mackay – the classically trained musician and literary aesthete – the decision would be similarly balanced: whether to remain within the arena of classical music and the 'serious' avant-garde, or whether to pursue pop and rock music, as offered to him by Bryan Ferry and Roxy Music. For Mackay, this decision would be further sharpened by his assessment of his own abilities and confidence. For all three of the young artists, however, the choice between 'high' and 'low' forms of creativity would be less concerned with siding with one or the other, as finding a resolution of their disparities.

For Mackay, as for Eno, the music and performance avant-garde scene was far closer to his experience than the world of rock and roll. Of the three, Bryan Ferry was the only one who had worked as a pop musician playing on the small clubs and dance circuit. Thus, as 1969 became 1970, Eno and Mackay would be recruited to Roxy from a world which was highly rarefied, even by the standards of the contemporary art world of the time. Mackay, for example, was already experimenting with somewhat surrealist music-generating machines.

Andy Mackay: 'I went to Italy for a year and subsequently became a schoolteacher for a year or two. I was on the edge of the serious London avant-garde scene, going to performances here and there. And I was also working on a project which I called my "New Pastoral Music" ideas; this was a set-up of music-playing machines run by little electric motors which I used to buy from a shop in Bloomsbury. One was a mandolin, which I had bought or traded off somebody, with a rotating motor on top of it with strings hanging off it that brushed the strings as it went round to create a little tinkling effect. Another was a Chinese toy squeeze-box, that I then put inside another box and it made a little squeaking noise.

'But I wasn't serious enough about that – I didn't have the self-belief that you need to be that type of artist. I wanted instant reactions from people – which was why I started playing rock and roll. I couldn't stand seeing people looking at something and not knowing whether they liked it or not, or even whether it was working or not. So when I was in Italy I didn't do any music to speak of. Cornelius Cardew did a performance of the *Great Digest* when I was in Rome which I went to, but that was it. Christopher Hobbs and Gavin Bryars and so on, were more or less my exact contemporaries, and I suppose that if I had wanted to I could have chosen a career in the serious avant-garde.'

Viv Kemp would design and print some small announcement cards, pale-blue, for 'New Pastoral Music 1st Performance', held on Friday 16 January 1970. Almost exactly a year later, under extraordinarily dramatic circumstances for Mackay, he would be asked by Viv to contact Bryan Ferry about the group he was putting together.

Andy Mackay: 'I had advertised in the *Melody Maker* for a job, before I went to Italy. It said something like "Sax/oboe player seeks progressive band"; and the only feedback at all was from total jazzers, whom I couldn't relate to at all. I then gave up. In Italy I had tried to write a few songs, but didn't find it very easy on my own.

'Back in London, I started teaching at the south side of Clapham Common, in a Catholic boys' school called St Gerard's; also at a comprehensive school in Streatham called Thomas Grant. I did a term at each. Then a friend of mine from Italy came over, and I went to see her in Brighton – it was around 1st January, and a very cold day. I was travelling down by train, and when I was walking along the side of the station I completely blacked out – I don't know whether it was the cold weather or what. I woke up in hospital with an injured back – it's something that has never happened to me since. However, I was in hospital in Brighton for about two weeks.

'After this I went to stay at my parents' flat in Pimlico, and as you might imagine it made me terribly nervous about going out – I didn't want to walk along the streets on my own for fear that I would fall over again. So I actually didn't go out for three weeks – or I would maybe walk just a little bit around the block.

'Then Viv Kemp called me, and said that she had this friend called Bryan Ferry whom she thought I ought to meet, because he was trying to put a band together. By that time, I had bought a little synthesiser, and was sitting in my old bedroom twiddling around with various things, setting up little patches and programmes, and still writing faintly serious bits of music. I was listening to the radio a lot, as well, as there were all sorts of pirate stations by then which were quite interesting.

'So Viv had explained that Bryan was living in Kensington, and said that we really ought to go round and meet him. So I rang him, and suggested a meeting. So the first time I went out, for any distance, after this strange black-out, was to go to Susie's flat in Kensington High Street where Bryan was staying. I drove over in my dad's car, taking my bits and pieces with me – and he had a few instruments set up: an amp and a guitar and a harmonium. Graham Simpson was involved, and John Porter sort of came and went. So I went over and we worked on maybe two songs – one of them was the "Bob Medley". Then we started rehearsing regularly.'

Bryan Ferry: 'Andy came round to this place in Kensington High Street to see me and Graham, and he had this synthesiser – which was great – and an oboe; he didn't have a sax at that time. I loved the oboe; oboe, cello, French horn: I love those instruments. So he started playing along with Graham and myself, and it started to sound like something.

'After a few months or so, we wanted to tape ourselves. Everyone in the world has recording equipment now, but we didn't have anything like that – I don't think even cassettes were invented then. We didn't have a tape recorder, and we wished that we could tape some of this stuff that we were doing. So Andy says, well I know this lad called Brian Eno who's got a tape recorder. I think that Brian had come up to do something at Reading where Andy was, and they had met at some art performance.

'So Eno came round with this *huge* tape recorder – the heaviest thing in the world, like a tank – and set it up one night, here in Kensington. Then he taped what we were doing and said "Oh great! A synthesiser!" And so Andy started playing the oboe and Eno took over on the synth. When Andy came, he stayed as part of the group; when Eno came, he stayed. It was like the Magnificent Seven in that sense; the group was growing in a very natural and organic kind of way.'

Brian Eno: 'Andy Mackay and myself may have written to one another a couple of times; but the next time that we met was one of those moments in life when things could have turned out completely different to the way they did.

'I was waiting on Maida Vale tube station [Mackay recalls that it was Earls Court] and when the train came in I was equidistant between two carriages. But in the one I chose was Andy, and we recognised each other. He asked what I was doing and I told him that I was playing around with tape recorders.

'He told me that he had just joined a little band, that had just started – three of them – and they wanted to make some demo tapes. He asked if I would record them, and so I arranged to come over to Warwick Gardens, where they were rehearsing. I took a Revox machine, and met Bryan Ferry, Graham Simpson and Andy – they were the three. So I set up to record, and there was an EMS synthesiser there – which was perhaps the second commercial synthesiser. There had been the Mini Moog first, and then the EMS.

'Andy had planned to do electronics in the group, but hadn't been getting on too well and decided to stick to saxophone and oboe. So while I was there, they asked if I could possibly work with what they were doing. So then I was in the band.

'I enjoyed the process of working in a band very much. It is so surprising how an idea absorbs and infects everyone, and comes back so much better than it started out. Essentially, Bryan Ferry wrote everything – in the sense of the beginnings of things. He would write a chord pattern or whatever, and a melody and the lyrics. They weren't always completely formed, but they would be pretty much formed. And then what the band did was arrange them, basically. So these things would start with Bryan and a voice, and the arrangement came from the band.

'But I can't think of anything on those two albums that was actually originated by anybody else; all of those pieces were originated by Bryan; he was definitely the writer and he stayed the writer. But also we were all contributing.

'I think that we were quite self-conscious in a way. First of all, Bryan and I were both big admirers of the Velvet Underground. We very much liked the idea of a band sitting on that line between fine art and performance art and happenings, yet co-opting the pop audience – we thought that was a very good position to be in. The other part of it was that we felt, then, that there were so many ideas in the Velvet Underground that hadn't really been looked at – certainly in this country, but also in America as it turned out; and that there was a lot of opened territory.

'As we started to work, we were basically rehearsing, playing the same dozen or fifteen songs over and over for a year and a half – we rehearsed for a long time. And during that time we had various drummers and various guitar players before we settled on our line-up; so what was interesting was that those songs sounded *very normal* to us at the end. My biggest worry when we made our album, was that it sounded so conservative – so predictable. And as a consequence I was really surprised when it came out and people were saying it sounded like nothing they had ever heard before. We had played it so much by then that it sounded completely obvious – just like modern music, nothing especially radical about it.'

The principal idea of Roxy Music, as a montage and resolution of many different musical and stylistic ideas, would thankfully survive the birthing process – its consolidation into an utterly unique, new musical form, prompting many further ideas and questions about the nature of music-making, and, very quickly, the making of stars.

thirty-two

London 1971–1972. Introducing the band: Paul Thompson; Phil Manzanera's early musical background; Roxy Music as a revue; 'grand purple guitar arpeggios'; notes preserved by Simon Puxley on Bryan Ferry's early lyrics; 'The Eversley Brothers' – Bryan Ferry and the music hall tradition.

In his notebook titled, 'Some time 1972, general', kept as Roxy Music were beginning their remarkably swift ascent to commercial success, Brian Eno would write a statement titled, 'SERIOUS MUSIC BACK-GROUND/ROCK MUSIC BACKGROUND' in which he addressed directly the formative collision (as he found it) of musical styles within the group:

> . . . we deliberately set out to construct music that wasted no facet of our different musical backgrounds. We wanted to operate primarily in the rock music context – that is, we wanted this music to be available through extended channels open to rock music which are not open to the more esoteric musics. We regard the rock idea as a system that can be programmed in many different ways – we choose to program me it with not only the jazz, rock, blues tradition, but also with the less familiar 'serious' music tradition. We want to handle the visceral/physical as well as the spiritual and conceptual. As regards our musical backgrounds we split equally between the two areas.

The musical background was further enriched by the arrival from Newcastle of drummer Paul Thompson – a devotee of Bo Diddley who would bring a crucial physicality to Roxy Music, as well as exceptional musical finesse. In many ways, Thompson's brilliance lay in his equal sensitivity as a player (his favourite Roxy Music number would be 'For Your Pleasure', with its measured, trance-like pacing) and his capacity (like Mo Tucker, of the Velvet Underground) to provide an unwavering solidity and chassis to carry the other musicians. Brian Eno would later pronounce: 'If it hadn't been for Paul Thompson, Roxy Music would just have been another art rock band.'

Thompson was from the Jarrow district of Tyneside, but had had a very different experience of Newcastle from the students at the university. An apprentice plater in the Newcastle shipyards, he had both a keen interest in visual art and an obsession with pop and rock music, specifically as a drummer. His enthusiasm was such that as a boy he made himself a drum kit out of cardboard boxes and Meccano parts.

Thompson would play in a local group called the Urge, who later changed their name to the Influence and became Billy Fury's backing group. The demands of working as a musician in northern clubs proved also to be the end of Thompson's career in the shipyards:

Paul Thompson: 'What happened when you worked in a shipyard was that you worked as an office boy first, and you went to college one day a week – learning a trade. But I got sacked before working in the yard, for falling asleep. I think I was sixteen, and I auditioned for a local band who were working a lot – the Urge. They were playing seven nights a week; so I was earning £3. 2s. 6d in the shipyard, and about £35 a week playing in the band. I tried to keep both going, because I thought that the band thing might not last; but I used to get in from gigs at five at morning. If we were playing somewhere like Carlisle, it wasn't that far away in today's terms, but on the roads back then it used to take hours and hours. So I remember coming back one morning at five and having to get up again at seven, and I just collapsed at work and fell asleep. Which made me a professional musician.

'In the early days, I'd hear about the acts that were playing at the Club A-Go-Go, but I couldn't afford to see them. I actually stood outside the City Hall hearing the Beatles doing a sound-check – but it was something like eight shillings and I just didn't have the money; it was a lot of money if you were earning three pounds a week. We played at the Quay

Club – it was a tiny little place, and the room that bands used to play in was very long and narrow, a cellar room. The stage must have been about six foot square.

'It didn't really come into the equation, for me, that most of the others were art students. There was an advert in the *Melody Maker* – "Wonder drummer wanted for avant-garde rock group". I'd played in the Influence, and then I got more interested in progressive music. The places we played in weren't so interested in that – we were playing working men's clubs. So the work was fizzling out, and the band fizzled out. John Miles, the vocalist, went off on his own and did a club act. I went off with another band, which was only working once or twice a week, and then that fizzled out totally. So I thought I'd go to London, and try to get a job in a band.

'I wasn't doing it to try and make the big time. It was because I wanted to play. And on previous trips I'd seen bands play in the Marquee, and even that was great. To play stuff you like, and make a living out of it. So I moved to London and into a flat with some friends of mine in Shepherd's Bush. I signed on the dole, and they offered me £4 a week, which wasn't great. So one of the lads was working on a building site, and I got a job there working as a labourer. There was me, this other Geordie guy and about three hundred Irishmen.

'In the meantime, I was looking for jobs and saw these adverts in the paper. One of them was for a band which was playing all the little clubs around London, the other was "the avant rock group". So I phoned, and it was Bryan who answered. He immediately picked up on my Geordie accent, and said he was from Washington and so on. Of course, he didn't have a Geordie accent. We kind of hit it off from there.

'I went up for an audition, and there were Brian Eno, David O'List, Graham Simpson, Andy Mackay and Bryan. We ran through some songs, and it all just happened spontaneously, the way things sometimes do. It just worked straight away. It was a bit of a panic that day, because I'd done a session in Denmark Street and I'd thought I would be able to get my drum kit out of the studio that day. It was a Saturday, and there was nobody there – so I had to borrow a drum kit off Matthews Southern Comfort. One of the guys I was sharing a flat with was their roadie, and had the kit in a van.

'They had this little rehearsal space up in Chalk Farm which belonged to some theatre group. So okay they were all art students, but it didn't really matter. It was the music I was interested in – and the line-up. The first band I'd played in with a synthesiser and a sax – and I knew David O'List from the Nice. I haven't got a degree and that, and there is a big intellectual difference between me and the rest of the boys. But that doesn't matter so long as the musical chemistry is right.'

Bryan Ferry: 'Guitar or drums? I can't remember which came next. The first drummer we had was an American guy; and he was an orchestral drummer. He was escaping the draft. He had played in something like the Cleveland Symphony Orchestra – he was very good, a percussionist, really. Dexter Lloyd – military drums, really. He had a handlebar moustache. And there was another guitar player called Roger Bunn, who was like long-haired, a hippy guy. But I think there's a tape where he's playing on it as the guitarist. I'd love to hear those tapes . . .

'Then we auditioned for guitar players, and that's when I first met Phil Manzanera – he came to the audition. But he didn't get the job because I chose this guitarist who I'd seen some years before, playing in a group called the Nice – at a student gig at Newcastle. He was a guitar player called David O'List who I thought was really brilliant – kind of wild, Hendrix-ish, feedback, unusual . . .

'David O'List had been like a child player almost with the Nice – a teenager maybe. Years later he played for me on "The In Crowd". He was with us for a few months, but then that didn't work. I still had Phil's number, and so I rang him and he came back and joined. Paul Thompson I got through the *Melody Maker*. There were several people we auditioned, and I suppose the fact that he was a Geordie and played with such passion – he seemed such a normal, regular guy. He was covered with brick dust from this building site where he'd been working. He came to the audition covered with dust. He just seemed to have this way of playing which I really responded to, so I gave him the job. It was definitely the right decision.'

While O'List played in the early line-up of Roxy Music until February 1972, he would subsequently be replaced by the young Phil Manzanera – whose real name was Philip Targett-Adams, and who had been raised between Latin America and Dulwich College, south London – the alma mata of, amongst others, P. G. Wodehouse and Raymond Chandler. As a teenager, Manzanera had also absorbed an encyclopaedic knowledge of music, making it his business to listen to anything which came his way, and he and his friends Ian MacDonald (subsequently a highly acclaimed writer on rock music) and Bill MacCormick would all discuss precisely their feelings about each new musical discovery.

As a consequence, perhaps, of such advanced musical knowledge, by the time that Manzanera came to audition and play for Roxy Music, he was steeped in a mixture of free jazz, Latin American music, psychedelia and progressive rock. And as a further consequence of such eclecticism, he possessed the ability – as Bryan Ferry immediately noticed – to play with equal virtuosity in almost any style at all.

As important to the world which Roxy Music would convey to such infectious and pervasive effect – and Manzanera, photographed by Karl Stoecker for the inside sleeve of *Roxy Music*, would appear manic, his eyes hidden by Antony Price's unforgettable 'compound eye' wrap-around dark glasses – was the exoticism of Manzanera's background. As a further musical colour within the palette of the group, his playing provided a vibrancy which was clearly not entirely English – too joyously unre-strained – yet at the same time was steeped in the same somewhat stately sense of presence that distinguished Mackay and Eno. As he recounts his early life, commuting between South America and an English public school, his experiences possess all the heightened romance of a song by Roxy Music.

Phil Manzanera: 'My father worked for BOAC. In the thirties he had worked for the British Council in South America. He went out there in 1929, to the Caribbean coast of Colombia, and my mother was one of his students. From there he went to Argentina, then Buenos Aires; he was always in places where there was a revolution, so we think he was a spy.

'He was in six countries where there were revolutions – we were in Cuba, for instance, during the Cuban Revolution. We lived opposite the Chief of Staff of the Dictator, and there were gun battles from our house and so forth. Our house was given to a student leader at the end of the Revolution. But there were a lot of nights spent on the floor as shooting was going on.

'I first learned to play the guitar in Cuba – Cuban folksongs; and so I was brought up listening to South American music – going to the Tropicana Club in 1957 and 1958. So my journey, that ended up in Roxy, was quite weird. I came from a totally different background to the rest of the group, and had been at an English public school, Dulwich College. South America was great, and I used to go back there every holiday because my father – working for an airline – got free travel. So four or five months of the year I was in South America, and the rest of the time in Dulwich. But I wanted to be in London, because the sixties were so exciting. I used to listen to *Pick of the Pops* on the World Service from Venezuela, and simply want to be in London. I thought of myself as British, because initially I was at the British school. My mother, as a Colombian, would try to bring out the South American side in me. My father was very British – he might have been "Our Man in Havana"; and in fact that book was written during the very time he was there.

'So my English public school world collided with the total bizarreness and anarchy of Latin American culture. I always think that it took a long time for rock music to have any impact in South America, and I think that's because they had a strong rhythm orientated form of dance music that appealed to all generations – so when fifties pop music tried to make an impact the groove just wasn't there. It wasn't that useful for teenagers – until things toughened up in the rhythm department with Tamla Motown and so on in the sixties.

'At the same time, being in London in the 1960s was incredible – I was twelve in 1962, left school in 1969–70, and joined Roxy Music a year later.

'I was trained up in English psychedelia, and also of course in the middle sixties there was the way that the Velvet Underground and all that New York scene related to the explosive art going on in psychedelia – the freeing of everything, supposedly.

'As a boarder at Dulwich, I managed to get to all the key events in London in the sixties: I was at the Doors and Jefferson Airplane at the Roundhouse, I was at the Lyceum for all the key things, I saw Hendrix supporting the Who . . . Myself and Bill MacCormick (brother of Ian MacDonald) were all at school together, and we had our own little music university up at their house. Also, they were friends with Robert Wyatt,

who was just starting then, and my brother was friends with David
Gilmour. So when I was fifteen I met Wyatt and Gilmour, who were both
very influential on me. We used to get records out of the library and just
go through the whole history of music – everything – Satie, jazz, avant-
garde, everything. We'd analyse them, discuss them – everything.

'For instance, I found out about Charles Ives because Frank Zappa
mentioned him; and then one thing would lead to another – what does
Schoenberg sound like, what does Terry Riley sound like? When I eventually met the people in Roxy, I would meet them at Steve Reich concerts and so forth.'

As the Newcastle students had enjoyed an exceptionally intimate relationship with the burgeoning stars of British and American Pop art, so
Manzanera's introduction to two of the key musicians in the English
psychedelic scene would imbue the growing nucleus of Roxy Music with
a particularly heightened sense of context and inspiration. But it would be
the mix of elements in Roxy, musically and visually, which, somehow,
would create a group sound and image which would defy their initial
detractors on the music press and become an actual pop mainstream teen
sensation.

Bryan Ferry: 'I thought that there was a highbrow element to our music,
and a physicality – more so than in the Soft Machine, or Pink Floyd or
Tangerine Dream; there was an electronic, atmospheric side but there was
also a groove or a pulse to it. I liked what Pink Floyd did in terms of the
picturesque, but there was no sense of joy in it, particularly; I wanted bits
of Ethel Merman in there, or Otis Redding – bits of humour even. So I
wanted it to be quite comprehensive, in the way that when you look at
Picasso's work, some of it's very tragic and then there are other bits which
are playful or amusing. Which I think, ideally, we would want to convey
different moods.

'If you look at a Lucien Freud show, it all seems to have the same
mood – certainly over the last twenty years or so. But I didn't want to
have one look; I wanted each sleeve, or each album or each song to have
a different mood – almost like a revue: here's the sad song, here's the
happy song, here's a thoughtful one. I certainly wanted to have a lot of
variety, and compared to most bands, there was an awful lot of variety in

the colours of Roxy Music. Because you had oboe, you had the whole range of saxophones; you had Manzanera, who was playing quite unusual bits of guitar – and it wasn't just one style that he played. I suppose that underneath it all there was an earthiness; even though I had these quite airy-fairy ideas, I had this northern roots thing, and Paul very much had it – this solid, earthy beat. So all in all it was quite a lot to take in – sometimes too much for people.'

The extent and, as important, the precision of Roxy Music's earliest palette, in terms of the playing and staging of their music – comprising songs mostly written for their first album – can be gleaned from Brian Eno's notes (in his notebook, 'Roxy, early, 71–72') for the lighting of their performances, following Ferry's vocal. For example:

'If There Is Something'
Friendly yellow lights – cf 'Oklahoma'
'I would do.' – dark and more dramatic
occasional reds in torrid section,
grand purple guitar arpeggios – lights on player
Sax solo – fade to morose deep green and violet
'Shake your head girl' – pink spot on Bryan
2nd verse spot on Andy and Eno
guitar solo.

or (tantalisingly):

'Beauty Queen':
Bryan and Eno return into pools of light. Spots on each at stage side – others slink into place lightless – drums in on second verse. Bryan and Eno lights cut and Andy and Phil freak out. We move off and return with guitars . . .

or:

'2HB'
Tape Gongs Stereo
fade in treated piano
lights go through flickers and shimmer
to greenish tint.
'OH I WAS MOVED' – spot on (palm tree)

Bryan's face – going through colours
Sax solo/ trick lighting (sequinned background).

The extent to which these reasonably elaborate settings would have been followed in the earliest Roxy Music concerts – remembered by several of the friends who attended them, as being loud, rough and ready – is of less importance perhaps than the degree to which they had been thought out.

Bryan Ferry, too, was giving deep consideration to what, exactly, he was trying to convey in his lyrics. His earliest lyrics are in many ways the most abstract – word pictures of intensely vivid and unorthodox mood, and playing with mood, ideas and identity in a way which matching eclecticism and vibrancy of the music served in turn to massively heighten. As a lyricist, too, Ferry could not have been more singular and unique within the context of lyric writing in 1971 and 1972. In his earliest lyrics, as revealed by some notes preserved by Simon Puxley (with the annotation 'inscribed on yellowing papyrus'), Ferry was giving immense thought to the temper of each song. For example:

'Chance Meeting' (Quiet delicate simple plaintive)

voice & drama classical lovers chance meeting [inspired by the film *Brief Encounter*]

Narrative one mood through it'
or:

'Sea Breezes' – soft delicate meditative brooding on being alone – self pity and sense of hopelessness lead to passionate outburst – faster louder.

Too many times: soft but intense 'soul' brooding narrative/last night's dream about idealised love – : analysis of failure etc faster lilting beat – : philosophical summing up soul resignation of fate, etc.

The ways in which Roxy Music explored, musically and stylistically, a determinedly romantic – melodramatic, even – sense of mood and atmosphere, added to what Ferry has described as the simultaneous 'pulse' and 'groove' of the music, would grant them a formidable fusion of robust pop and rock rhythms, underpinning a high theatricality which touched almost on the seductions of parody and self-parody. There was a vivid sense of fun in the music – a vaudevillian, Hollywood musical form of showmanship – which made of each song a celebration and a carnival ride – be that the Ghost Train or the Tunnel of Love.

Ferry's vocal style, crucially, was uniquely suited to precisely this re-routing of the matinee idol or musical star, through a montaged history of musical styles. To follow the comparison to Hollywood musicals, it was rather as though Ferry could sing in the styles of both Gene Kelly *and* Georges Guétary, as they took their respectives roles as penniless American painter Jerry Mulligan, and celebrated cabaret singer Henri Baurel, in Vincente Minnelli's 1951 classic *An American in Paris*.

But vaudeville and music hall were also close to Ferry's interests and imagination – a form and process of supposedly populist entertainment, the potential of which had also been recognised by artists such as Gilbert & George, and of course the Moodies. Indeed, Ferry would share with Gilbert & George an enthusiasm for the music hall number 'Underneath the Arches' – an aspect of his musical background and career as a singer

CALENDAR 1972

357

which is somehow more revealing of his tastes and intentions than the fact that he auditioned for King Crimson.

Andy Mackay: 'Bryan and I always joked about the fact that rock and roll was basically music hall. When we lived together in Eversley Road in Battersea [in late 1971, subsequent to Ferry's departure from Kensington], we would joke about having an act called the Eversley Brothers, like a music hall duo. Bryan is very influenced by Flanagan and Allen and all those people. We used to sing "Underneath the Arches" from time to time, and I know that Bryan and Stephen Buckley would go around singing songs from film musicals – "On the Town" was a popular one.

'I think Bryan, somewhere, could almost be a reincarnated British music hall performer who loves the audience, and will always give a fantastic performance, even when he's down. It's part of a great tradition, and it's an American tradition as well. Bryan's musical taste is much wider than mine; I didn't really have a record collection, but he had a whole range of things from musicals to Ink Spots records, King Curtis, Drifters, Motown, and a lot of really good soul music.

'It's that thing of wanting the audience to tell you that what you're doing is good – which is why I could never be a serious artist. I think that's why I ended up being a sax player rather than a composer or a performer in some other area; I needed to know whether it was working or not. Which again goes back to that rather music hall tradition, and doubtless much further.

'My speculation is that Bryan Ferry is someone who was born to perform, and needs to perform – needs feedback. By contrast, I think that Brian Eno comes from the other side – that he has the confidence and self-belief to do something that isn't getting an instant feedback, and can carry on doing it.'

thirty-three

Earliest concerts and help from Charlie Ware, with a sideways glance to Juliet Mann becoming chauffeur-for-a-day for Kevin Ayers; Bryan Ferry attempts to interest record companies in Roxy Music, auditions for King Crimson, meets David Enthoven and John Gaydon, and sends a cassette to *Melody Maker* writer Richard Williams; Brian Eno on Roxy Music as a school of art and a champion of 'artificiality'; a flash-forward to the sociology of 'decadent' rock, circa 1973 and 1974.

Andy Mackay: 'Things were happening quite quickly. I was working; Bryan was working; and we had to rehearse in the evenings. I took on the Holland Park job, and we put ads in the papers for other musicians and auditioned guitarists – in a church hall on the edge of Battersea Park which is no longer there, just in Prince of Wales Drive. And we got lots of people – there must have been about twenty guitarists. We used to move the equipment around in my father's car or my brother's car – both of which began to lose their suspension because of the weight of the speakers.

'I don't quite know how we financed it – because we managed to buy a PA by the end of the year, and started getting some gigs. The very first was at a party, of an Italian friend – the name Gabriel Pantucci comes to mind – in Wimbledon; and the second was at the Hand and Flower in Olympia. By the end of 1971, we were gigging fairly regularly in a semi-professional way, and we recorded our demos in Eno's flat-cum-studio in Camberwell.*

---

*Brian Eno's notebook for 'Christmas '71–Spring '72' contains a list of twenty-seven different university and club venues where the group were due to play, including the 100 Club, London, the Hobbit's Garden, Wimbledon, and the Tate Gallery. The other venues are widely spread, nationally, from the Redcar Jazz Club to Essex University.

'In Roxy "Mark One" – pre coming to an agreement with EG management – we finished our demos in Camberwell around the summer of 1971; and then Bryan started on his furious and ultimately very successful tour of full-time hustling. I was still teaching, and we would play whatever dates we were given. The furthest away we played was Liverpool. We bought a transit van in the Old Kent Road, which Bryan and I were licensed to drive, and then we would use my dad's 1100.

'We used to be paid very small amounts; I think that once, in Potters Bar, we played support to someone and they weren't going to pay us anything at all. So we asked if they could manage anything, even for the petrol. And I seem to remember being given some coins . . . We used to have a funny lock-up in Hampstead where we had to unload the gear, which I should point out we were all much too weak to carry, and then go home to bed . . .'

Help for Roxy Music's transport had in fact come by way of Juliet Mann and her circle of friends in Notting Hill. Charlie Ware – whose sister Jill would become one of Roxy Music's first major fans, attending all their concerts in extravagantly chic outfits – was a property tycoon who had bought houses in Islington and Bath, at one point owning two houses in Bath's Royal Crescent. Tim and Viv Head would later live in a house owned by Ware in Lonsdale Square, Islington, where Jill – who was also an early and dedicated minimalist, according to Tim Head – occupied an entirely white room.

Juliet Mann: 'A friend of mine, Roy Pearson, went into business with Charlie Ware – who later put money into Roxy Music at one stage. They opened a car showroom in Notting Hill and imported American cars – PearsonWare Motors. We had a huge party there, and everyone was paralytic, draped over the bonnets of these huge American cars.

'I remember that I was absolutely besotted by Kevin Ayers, and Roy Pearson rang me up one day saying that they'd had a job from Ayers's management company, wanting a big American car to drive Ayers from his office to a concert in Hyde Park. Did I want the job? But of course I did! So Antony made me this fabulous grey chauffeur's suit – very severe . . .'

Bryan Ferry: 'We did some early rehearsals in Susie's house in Kensington High Street – very appropriate. And then when Brian Eno joined the band we did some in his house in Camberwell. I dedicated the first album, *Roxy Music*, to Susie. She was incredibly helpful, and supportive of the whole project.

'As was this man Charlie Ware, who lent us some money to buy the first group van. So, again, Roxy Music probably wouldn't have happened without Charlie Ware and Susie.'

By this time – between the spring and autumn of 1971, Roxy Music comprised Bryan Ferry, Graham Simpson, Brian Eno, Andy Mackay, Paul Thompson and David O'List. Ferry had made the acquaintance of the Ladbroke Grove clique, and had remarked to Juliet that he was putting together a band he believed could be very big. In the meantime, Ferry's vision of a new kind of pop group, replete with all of the art school and avant-garde ideas that had already been brought to it, was being tested by the unyieldingly blunt processes of small concerts, looking for management and attempting to find some interest from influential journalists.

Bryan Ferry: 'I felt that I was learning very fast, and that there was so much to learn, as well. How to make a record? Because we were floundering a little bit at the beginning, trying to make the first album.

'In my doing the rounds of Tin Pan Alley [Denmark Street, off Charing Cross Road, London – at this time, still London's traditional home of pop music recording and management], with people saying, "Yeah, great – it's the sound of the future. Come back in two years' time"', I would always insist that I stayed in the room while they listened to the tape, rather than just leaving it with them. I'd say it was the only tape I had, and I just sat there while they took phone calls with this weird music playing in the background . . . I'd have been playing them "Chance Meeting", "The Bob Medley" and "2 HB" – the

version with Roger Bunn and the American drummer playing on it.

'But while I was writing the songs for the first Roxy Music album, I read something about King Crimson auditioning in North End Road, in West London, for a singing bass player – the original being Greg Lake who had left to form Emerson, Lake & Palmer. I don't play bass, but I went along anyway. I think they liked me, but they wanted someone who could do both things. The fact that I had met them, however, and them saying just how good their management was, ultimately led to me going to EG. I had been to lots of other record companies with the Roxy Music tape, but the most positive response I got was from John Gaydon at EG, who was David Enthoven's partner. Mark Fenwick was also there, but I think that he was more the junior partner at that time.

'Just after we arrived there, John Gaydon left. He and David were two old Harrovians – ex public schoolboys with Harley Davidson motorbikes. A lot of bikes in fact – they had a whole mews full of them off Gloucester Road. And there always seemed to be loads of beautiful blonde women there – it was all incredibly glamorous to me. They had this *Easy Rider* mentality, with fringed leather jackets and cowboy boots up on their leather partner's desks, with these blondes floating around and American cars and everything. But then with these public school voices. But EG were managing King Crimson, one of the weirdest of English bands, so weirdness was right up their street.'

In the UK, the two labels dealing with 'underground' music and the heavier end of rock were Vertigo (with its trip-enhancing op art album label) and Chris Blackwell's Island Records. David Enthoven of EG would through his management of King Crimson become friends with Island's production and distribution manager, Tim Clark, who would subsequently (in 1994) become his business partner at i.e.music – representing first Brian Eno, and later Robbie Williams.

Between them Clark and Enthoven would witness the growth of the 'underground' music scene in the UK, and the almost parallel emergence of the new, mass-market teen glam acts, such as T. Rex. (Indeed, David Enthoven would recount to the author how he turned the cosmic, Notting Hill Tolkien weirdness of Tyrannosaurus Rex, into the hip-flicking, tin-foil, futuristic boogie of T. Rex by basically telling Marc Bolan to stand up, rather than sit on the floor, when he played live. If he stood up, the already sizeable audience would follow suit; likewise it was near impossible to play an electric guitar sitting cross-legged on a cushion. Combined, these changes would radically alter the mood of the band. In addition to which, 'T. Rex' was easier to spell.)

In hindsight it is easy to forget that Emerson, Lake & Palmer's rock orchestral virtuosity and vast technical repertoire was in full flow at the same time as the rise of 'futuristic' acts such as David Bowie and the Spiders from Mars. Roxy, however, would defy all such categorisation.

David Enthoven: 'EG was actually a management company, and Island Records was a record company. We had artists, and Island gave us creative freedom – we would come in with the sleeves, and we would generate "the look". Tim would be involved from the very beginning.'

Tim Clark: 'EG were really the A&R centre; they found the acts, signed the acts, developed the acts and sold the acts to us and through us to the fans. So I suppose in many ways what we at Island were was the marketing and selling arm – clearly working closely with EG and the artists themselves.

'I was at Island Records, and at the time when David signed King Crimson to the label I was in charge of production and distribution. We were then a very small company, and still largely selling West Indian music, and ska. In 1966 we had signed John Martyn – who was the first of Island's "white" acts, if you like, and then '67 and '68 was the period of expansion into the underground. We then had groups such as Traffic, Free, Jethro Tull and King Crimson and so on. So that was Island's real period of expansion away from its roots in Jamaican music.

'At that time, this was an area universally known as "the underground", and Island was the pre-eminent underground label in the UK. We had this extraordinary roster of artists that cut across different genres: folk musicians, such as Fairport Convention and Nick Drake – who certainly fell into that bracket then. Then we had ELP, and a little later Roxy Music, who opened up a whole new category.'

David Enthoven: 'We also had the out-and-out rock like Mott the Hoople, and the really bizarre – like Quintessence. The "Island Samplers" from this period were fantastic: *Nice Enough to Eat*, *Bumpers* and so forth.'

A little later, by the early 1970s, underground weirdness in British pop and rock music came in many different forms – one of the most successful being the then burgeoning progressive rock scene. This, or its alternative – guitar-driven blues-based rock – were in no way related to what Roxy Music were attempting. And neither, in fact, were the records being made by Marc Bolan or David Bowie – despite the fact that both were former Mods with a highly developed penchant for style and individualism – looking to make a futuristic sound. The principal difference – out of many – was that Bolan (who was represented, during his vital translation from Tyrannosaurus Rex to T. Rex, by David Enthoven and John Gaydon), and David Bowie had both worked their apprenticeships through Mod groups and hippy psychedelia. Both – in all their fabulousness – were by comparison with Roxy Music, old troopers.

The music press of the period, too, vehemently reflected these entrenched tastes – and with a degree of seriousness which is difficult to imagine in the twenty-first century. The reverberations of opinion were strident and heartfelt; and it was Roxy Music's lack of traditional, rockist apprenticeship – their precocity – which would most annoy their detractors. To arrive from nowhere, with what seemed a fully formed sound, image and identity, was somehow heretical. It was all too fast – a quality which, in fact, seemed to endorse the group's swaggering modernity and stately disregard for the traditions of the business.

They would now be helped on their way, however, by two powerful admirers – prior to auditioning for Enthoven and Gaydon in the spring of 1972. These would be the hugely influential music writer on the *Melody Maker* Richard Williams, and the disc jockey John Peel.

Bryan Ferry: 'I thought that there would be some people who would like it – who would like it a lot. And I suppose I thought that some people would hate it. Luckily, not that many people put it in print that they hated it. I remember targeting one particular person – Richard Williams – who I thought would like it. He was a real champion of our cause. I think I put a tape through his door – I was quite obsessive. Anyway, he telephoned me the next day and said, "I love this", and wanted to do an interview. I used to read the papers, and I thought that if anyone was going to like it, then it was going to be him – sure enough, he did like it.'

Richard Williams: 'I should say first of all that even then, in the very early

1970s, there was quite a lot of competition between writers to discover new bands. It wasn't careerist; it was more to do with sheer excitement. Because other than your own pride and a bit of status, the writer wasn't going to benefit in any way; you were simply championing something that you believed in, and I found it very exciting to champion things that on the face of it were unpopular – or at least unsuited for popularity.

'People didn't generally send you tapes out of the blue in those days. Normally it would be a PR or a manager who would ring you up – and much of the time it would be rubbish, of course. To this day, I don't know how Bryan found my home address. But there is a note in my diary for March 1971, which states, "Brian coming to drop off tape" – and that was Bryan. He must have rung, because my girlfriend had taken the call and he had dropped the tape off with her on a Saturday. And it was a standard 7.5 IPS reel-to-reel in a plastic box in a cardboard case, on which he had written the titles and his phone number. And it had a paper sticker with a Roxy logo – a propeller-driven aeroplane sky-writing the group's name [drawn by Tim Head's flatmate, and future Biba children's department designer, Malcolm Bird].

'So I played the tape, and thought it was pretty extraordinary. I have sometimes wondered, subsequently, whether I was playing the tape correctly or listening to two tracks at once . . . Which would have made it sound even more extraordinary. But it had "The Bob Medley", "If There is Something" and "Re-make/Re-model". It was very rough, and very striking. It was a collage of things that I like. And you could tell it was by someone who liked certain things about fifties pop music, who liked electronic music – all sorts of things; and with this strange singing voice, which also appealed because it was interesting to hear a voice that wasn't trying to be American. It was different . . .

'Can's "Monster Movie" was perhaps the only record that seemed to be coming from a similar sensibility, and I was interested in that first generation of German groups. Also perhaps Burnin' Red Ivanhoe – they were a Danish group, who were terrific, who happened to be on at the Berlin Jazz Festival in late 1970. They were bass, lead guitar and horns – they were like a much more appealing version of the Mothers of Invention, without that relentless cynicism of Frank Zappa. So a lot of free jazz influences and a powerful pop rhythm section. They were like

Roxy without the art-school influence, and were perhaps the nearest comparison. So all of the music sympathetic to Roxy, with the exception of the Velvet Underground, was coming from mainland Europe rather than America.

'I rang Bryan Ferry having listened to the tape, and said that I thought it was extremely interesting and would like to speak with him. He came to the *Melody Maker* office, and we went as I recall to the Golden Egg on Fleet Street – there was little choice of where to go in those days. I then wrote our conversation up in the "Horizons" page of the *Melody Maker*. I found him a very sympathetic person and enjoyed talking to him. He was more restrained and more intellectually inquisitive than most people one met in a rock critic's day.

'When I was seventeen or eighteen I had hung around with art students and knew what they were like – I enjoyed that attitude that art students from the sixties had. His sense of style was so against the grain of what was going on, and I had always rather regretted the end of Mod – would have preferred a nice mohair suit to a kaftan any day of the week. So I think I thought that Bryan was someone who could revalidate the Mod attitude to style.'

Headlined, 'New Names that Could Break the Sound Barrier – Roxy in the Rock Stakes' – Williams's article for the *Melody Maker* Horizons page was published on 7 August 1971, and began:

A curious feature of modern rock music, is the way it's taken potential artists away from other spheres. Men who might have become poets, painters, or even classical musicians have instead found an outlet for their creativity in the new medium, which also offers the chance of wide exposure – not to mention bags of loot.

Five years ago, for instance it would have been unthinkable for Bryan Ferry to have entered rock and roll. Fine Arts graduates from Newcastle University just didn't do that sort of thing. But now, in 1971, Bryan is leading a band called Roxy which has produced one of the most exciting demo tapes ever to come my way. Although it was recorded on a small home tape machine in what sounds like a Dutch barn it carries enough innovatory excitement to suggest that Roxy may well be ahead of the field in the avant-rock stakes.'

The quality which Williams had identified in Roxy Music, and found so appealing, was an example of precisely the sensibility that was causing a division amongst music writers of the time – between those who were interested in that which seemed almost wantonly opposed to rockist authenticity, and those who believed that same authenticity to be almost sacred, denoting in musical form the constitution of one's personal politics. For those with an eye to cultural boundaries, one can detect in the unease with which Roxy Music were greeted, an unsettled awareness of the beginnings of a popular postmodern condition – in which authenticity, authorship, content, style and meaning become an elaborate crosshatching of styles, history and intentions.

Richard Williams: 'It was of course in part a relatively straightforward reaction against hippydom and post-hippydom: against the very relaxed, free and easy vibes represented by most of the Californian bands from the Grateful Dead to the Eagles, and also by the singer-songwriter tradition in America and Britain, from Carole King to Cat Stevens.

'It was also the fruition of something that had begun with the Velvet Underground and Nico album, which had caught the attention of initially a small number of people – who found in it something that they probably didn't even know they were looking for. It came out in March 1967, and having read about it in the *Village Voice* I got hold of a copy and reviewed it for the local paper I was working for in Nottingham – and gave it a page. It just seemed so different and so exciting, and that darkness that it had seemed very appealing.

'I must confess that my interest in that was very dilettanteish; I didn't want particularly to act out what "Venus in Furs" or "Heroin" or "All Tomorrow's Parties" expressed; but I was intrigued, partly by the subject matter, but by the kind of music that the investigation of those subjects encouraged them to make – which was a more adventurous, extreme music which touched on other things I was interested in: Terry Riley, LaMonte Young and free jazz. You could hear at times in Lou Reed echoes of what John Coltrane, Cecil Taylor or Albert Ayler were doing.

'As the good vibes and embroidered denim scene got bigger and bigger, and the "muso" approach became more pervasive, I think a growing number of people were ready for something else. Now I have nothing whatsoever against musicianship – my interests come out of jazz, after all

– but there was a rather dull-witted dedication to technique in the early 1970s, largely in what we now call progressive rock or "pomp" rock.

'The *Melody Maker* was particularly identified with ELP, Yes, Genesis, and there was a very strong tradition at the paper of giving those groups sympathetic coverage – mostly because of the very wonderful Chris Welch. I didn't like any of that music, and wanted to see something new happen; so it was great to discover, not least in Roxy Music, some music after the Velvet Underground that had a pop veneer, but also a potential for the kind of experimentation that I was interested in.

'In this much, Roxy Music became notorious before they became famous. Almost everybody in the *Melody Maker* office hated them. As soon as I started writing about them, people took against the idea of glamour without dues. They could tolerate the idea of David Bowie because he'd been David Jones and hanging around the scene for what seemed like decades; so he had some kind of background that gave him some credibility in their eyes.

'I liked the idea that Roxy appeared to have sprung out of nowhere; I found that absolutely thrilling – even though of course they had some background. Bryan for instance had been in a couple of soul groups in Newcastle, rather like Lou Reed had been in The Shades or whatever they were called. But their absolute look of "breeding" really told against them in the *MM* offices; and it took quite a long time for even the more open-minded people to come round to them. But it was interesting that when they did, they absolutely latched on to them . . .'

Brian Eno: 'I liked very much the idea of synthesis – artificiality. A lot of what Roxy was about was a rebellion against the rather maudlin sincerity of the blues movement – which, by the way, I have come to appreciate far more. But at the time we disliked that whole stance – "really being inside the music" seemed old fashioned, actually; and the other thing we stood against, in our minds, was the New Orchestralism that had infected pop in the early seventies – which was partly based on multi-tracking, but also based on a few people getting into pop music who actually knew complicated chords and a few clever time sequences. So we were trying to . . . not be either of those.

'When you are just starting something, it's much easier to know what you don't want to be than to know where you're actually trying to go. We thought about ourselves in the negative quite a lot, I think. This was most articulated by Bryan, Andy and myself – we were very opinionated, very snobbish even, about what we were doing. We treated Roxy Music like an art movement that had set itself up in contradiction to what was going on at the time.

'In my case, this was very much to do with having been at an art school where I was continually fighting with tutors whose whole attitude to painting was that you had to really "get lost inside" the work. I just didn't like that attitude, which I took to be bumbling incoherence, and that way of presenting yourself as an artist. And I think that we all felt that we wanted to be something smarter and more articulate than that.'

Roxy Music's celebration of artifice and synthesis were qualities which, in their rejection of naturalism, would drive some critics and pundits to include the group within a new pop cult dedicated to all that was actively and toxically decadent. The criticism would be pervasive and lingering, extending from the music press through to the pages of *New Society*.

In a flash-forward to an article published in *New Musical Express* in April 1973, under the memorable title 'Ultra-Pulp Images on the Video-Cassette of Your Mind', John Ingham – in a thesis reminiscent of that given to Nigel Norris in *Rock Follies*, with regard to reviewing pop music like any other art form – took issue with the ways in which his peers found 'intellectualism' in pop and rock music to be ideologically offensive.

'That people attack Roxy Music and David Bowie's intellectual postures is cause for considerable concern,' wrote Ingham, 'because there is an enormously large distrust among the young for intellectualism of any sort . . . These attitudes extend to a lesser degree to Roxy Music, who are accused of being dilettantes, too computerised, pretentious, and, of all things, frivolous.'

He concludes with an accurate summary of Ferry's career to that date: 'Bryan Ferry studied under the English equivalent of Warhol, getting a good education in Pop art. When he realised that even a famous artist could reach only a relatively small part of the mass audience, he turned his attention to music, bringing his art training with him and thus creating "Pop" music.'

Bryan Ferry: 'The art world is quite small – the art world of picture-making, sculpture, video, and event-based art. And I was asking for trouble really, I suppose, to try and work in a bigger world than that, and one which is less special, and where you have to try and sell your art to a mass public. It's quite a nice thought, to think of making your work for a small and more discerning kind of audience again. But once you've sold in large numbers to a mass market, it's very hard to go back the other way.

'At the time, more than to sell vast numbers of records – I hadn't thought about that, really, at all – it was a case of just making a record, and thus making a statement, which could make some kind of mark and make people think. Especially smart people; we thought that maybe if it's going to appeal to anyone, it's going to appeal to people who are bright, smart, with it. That's the crowd we wanted to touch. The first record was really exciting to make, because it had so many different flavours. And I just thought, well it would make me think if I heard it.'

thirty-four

London, late 1971 to New Year 1972: Phil Manzanera auditions for Roxy Music – 'Quality Musicians Only'; rocking the Hobbit's Garden, Wimbledon; Tim Clark and David Enthoven; auditioning in Wandsworth and related events; Roxy Music as a school of art; the recording dates of *Roxy Music*; *Shell* catch Andy Mackay on his way to the Lincoln Festival.

As a critic to whom new challenging musicians could turn for at least some chance of getting heard more widely (or heard at all), Richard Williams would be of supreme importance, finding himself with a role discovering and encouraging young artists which would soon be formalised by his joining Island Records in 1973 as an A&R man. In the autumn of 1971, however, he would hear from Philip Manzanera's first group – the adventurously improvisational 'Quiet Sun' – as well as from Bryan Ferry.

Manzanera's admiration for the Soft Machine – whose music would evolve through English psychedelia to an intoxicating melange of improvisation and progressive rock, as related to the intense, avant-garde frontiers of free jazz as anything – would within a year be contributing a vital fusion of technical virtuosity and sheer musical wildness to the already potent (and on paper seemingly unworkable), musical mix of Roxy Music. The Shirelles and the Soft Machine, or Gene Kelly, Ethel Merman, Duke Ellington, Captain Beefheart and John Cage, laced with a shared regard for the Velvet Underground . . . As a psychedelic public schoolboy, tutored subculturally in the breaking down of generic boundaries, Manzanera would find such a heady combination entirely plausible.

Phil Manzanera: 'We had a couple of bands at school with Bill MacCormick and Ian MacDonald, very briefly. Ian subsequently went off to Cambridge and then dropped out again, immediately. We were starting a group at school, with Charles Hayward [who would later play in This Heat] – who was the drummer in Quiet Sun – and Bill, and myself. We also knew one pop star, Robert Wyatt, who had just done a single with Soft Machine. We adored what they did, and went to all their early gigs with Kevin Ayers and so forth; we also liked a lot of West Coast bands – Spirit, Jefferson Airplane.

'The Soft Machine and Pink Floyd were huge influences, and I had met David Gilmour through my older brother, who knew him. At the beginning of the whole movement of new bands, post the Liverpool bands, our antennae were up, and if it was happening in London we were out watching it. Music like the Soft Machine and Pink Floyd was considered experimental, and the whole concept and context at the time was that all the boundaries were being changed, and all the barriers were coming down, and anything went – you could mix and match anything, so your palette was suddenly enormous.

'So we made a positive thing in our band at school – we had live shows there, and a lot of people were doing drugs, basically: acid and cough syrup, all sorts of things. I must say that I wasn't, but people slightly older were – I was just sixteen. We had light shows, and our thing was improvisation – you would just start somewhere and head off for an hour . . .

'So we became a mixture of those ideas; and when we left school, the year after leaving and before joining Roxy, we did Quiet Sun – the three of us and another guy from Dulwich on keyboards. We did some demos, and even got a little bit of development money from Warners. But eventually we sent our tape, with the write-up to it by Ian, to Richard Williams at the *Melody Maker*. And our review came out one week, and the first one about the embryonic Roxy Music the following – and that's how we found out about Roxy.

'Robert Wyatt then asked Bill to play bass in his new band, Matching Mole, and I said that I didn't want to continue Quiet Sun without Bill. At this point they suggested that I follow up the advert that Roxy Music had placed, looking for a guitarist.'

The text of the advert, placed in the 'Musicians Wanted' columns of the *Melody Maker*, ran as follows:

'The Perfect Guitarist'
for Avant Rock Group
Original, creative, adaptable,
melodic, fast, slow, elegant, witty
scary, stable, tricky.
QUALITY MUSICIANS ONLY
'Roxy' 223 0296

Phil Manzanera: 'So I went for an audition at the small house that Bryan and Andy were then sharing in Battersea. It was a tiny place, a working-man's cottage, with the railway line at the back. In the living room, which was minute, were set up the drums, Eno, Graham Simpson, Bryan and Andy. And my audition comprised a two-chord Carole King number, which I found strange having just come from Quiet Sun stuff – so I was over-qualified in one sense, but it was wonderfully refreshing in another. I just felt instantly that these people were great.

'We then went upstairs and had a chat, and I played them a Quiet Sun tape which they hated. And they played me their stuff – which I loved. And I also had a terrible cold that day, so while I was playing I was continually blowing my nose. It was the worst possible condition in which to play an audition. But I went away thinking that I really liked them all, as people.

'In fact, Dave O'List got the job [in October 1971]; but I got on very well with them, and bumped into them all over the place. A friend of mine did a light show for them – the same guy who did our light shows at school – and I went along to help him. His name was Dave Price, and this would have been when they played at the Friends of the Tate Christmas party, just off Tottenham Court Road. So we were in there waiting for the band to turn up, and then they arrived and started unloading the equipment – I think Bryan was driving. Bryan was carrying in the Turner PA stacks, and so I decided to help.'

With Manzanera as the group's roadie, Roxy Music were now playing a succession of small concerts. One would be at Reading University Art department; the other – witnessed by John Peel, who subsequently invited the group to record a set for his influential BBC radio show *Sounds of the Seventies* – would be on 7 December 1971, supporting Genesis at the Hobbit's Garden club, in Wimbledon. (Which despite its funky Tolkien name was in fact a low-ceilinged room in an Irish club which one day a week gave itself over to the weirder end of rock music.) Juliet Mann would in fact drive Bryan and Roxy Music's drum kit to the venue.

Polly Eltes and Simon Puxley had been instrumental in suggesting that Roxy Music played at their departmental Christmas party, and it would be at this time that Bryan Ferry and Puxley would begin to become friends. (Puxley would write his famous sleeve note for *Roxy Music* in the late spring of the following year, and swiftly be recruited as the group's personal PR or 'Media Consultant' – a role in which his complete lack of suitability was regarded by all involved as being his greatest qualification for the job.)

Polly Eltes: 'I was still at Reading when Roxy Music started – we gave them a gig, in fact, at our Art department party. I remember Brian Eno had to lie on top of the amplifiers in the old ambulance that we had, and which we used to pick them up in. I was dressed as the Snow Queen that night. I would have met the group just before they signed to EG, who were of course based in the Kings Road.'

Richard Williams: 'Bryan then asked me to a couple of gigs – the Friends of the Tate was one, and then at the 100 Club. In those days, the distance from the stage to rear wall was not so deep; so you had Bryan, David O'List, Graham Simpson and Paul Thompson on stage, and Brian Eno at the back wall with his mixer and VCS3.

'The song I remember very vividly from that was "Re-make/Re-model", which just had such impact – a great opening track, with tremendous immediacy, because it was founded in a pure pop sensibility. "Re-make/Re-model" is a manifesto – all the little instrumental breaks are a cute way of saying "We cover these bases."

'Bryan was wearing an ice hockey jacket – a reference back to the fifties. I subsequently had dinner with Bryan and Andy and various girl-friends – I may have met Susie at around this time. Bryan subsequently lived in Redcliffe Square. The next stage was getting the John Peel broadcast – and I remember sitting in a car listening to it.'

Brian Eno: 'Richard Williams was a major contributor to our success. He had already given us this wonderful write-up in *Melody Maker*, and you have to remember that we were really unknown at this point, so it was a huge act of faith on his part. We were then asked to play, supporting Genesis, at the Hobbit's Garden in Wimbledon and John Peel was the DJ and compère that night.

'I had to do a lot of the changes on stage. My early role in Roxy was very peculiar. For my first concerts I was mixing as well – I'd be at the back of the hall, and the band were on the stage. At the back I had my synthesiser, the mixer and a microphone; so I was trying to mix the band – which I was really bad at, I have to say – as well as playing and sometimes doing backing vocals. This was very strange for the audience. They would all be watching the band, and suddenly this sound came from behind them; or there were noises occurring on stage and nobody knew where they were coming from.

'So we came on first, and I was at the back of the hall, as usual. Almost immediately there was a total crisis, because Andy – wearing huge platform boots – stepped backwards, right on to the plug of Bryan's vocal mic, crushing it. So I ran to the stage, and found that by holding the plug in a particular way I could keep the connection going; but if I moved a fraction it went. So I knelt for the whole show, in this one position – looking not dissimilar, most probably, to a hobbit myself. We didn't have a spare mic, or a spare lead, or a spare anything. And so I had left the mixing board, for the whole gig, set as it had been at the beginning.

'We left the Hobbit's Garden thinking what a total disaster the concert had been, but John Peel liked it, and he invited us to appear on his show [*Sounds of the Seventies* – producer John Walters, first session broadcast 21 January 1972]. This meant going to his studio and recording six songs for broadcast. We were quite looking forward to this, because it was a chance to get some proper recording done; all our recordings up until that time had been done in my bedroom – they were okay, but there was no chance of rebalancing anything.

'And so we came out with some decently recorded versions of the songs – recorded and mixed in about two hours.'

Andy Mackay: 'It was when we were on *Sounds of the Seventies* that Graham Simpson started cracking up. I don't know whether he was someone who just couldn't take pressure – this was such a big deal, and we were about to do the first number, which started with bass, and Graham just didn't play. He was just standing there. We all got more and more nervous, and then, eventually, he did start playing and it was a great session . . .'

Bryan Ferry: '. . . incredibly sad; I think he had some kind of psychedelic brainstorm, and seemed to break down. A few months later, we'd made the first Roxy Music album and we were trying to get it signed up by Island. EG paid for us to make it, and they brought some of the Island top brass – not Chris, but David Betteridge, who was Chris Blackwell's second-in-command – down to hear us. And there were a few of them there.

'Graham had already started going through this strange thing with us all, for several months, where he didn't speak to us. He would just come in, not say anything, play the bass and then leave. And this went on and on. That day they came, I think he just sat on the floor, and played with tears running down his face. It was awful; and I guess we didn't really do enough to try and . . . It's easy when you look back: why didn't we just grab hold of him and shake him and say what the hell's the matter? But we just let it go on and on, and the managers said that he had to leave. It seemed to be a strange, long breakdown. I think it was acid . . .'

At the beginning of February 1972, the combination of Richard Williams's enthusiasm for Roxy Music, a tape that Bryan Ferry had delivered, and the accolade of their having recorded a session for John Peel, brought David Enthoven of EG management to hear the group audition at the Granada bingo hall in Wandsworth Road. Richard Williams was also in attendance, his passion for the group having grown subsequent to seeing some of their smaller concerts the previous autumn.

Writing about their appearance at the 100 Club the previous November (where, bizarrely, a children's party had been in progress), Williams had noticed a young woman (he doesn't name her, but Jill Ware, Susie Cussius or Juliet Mann might all be contenders for the role) whose appearance was prophetic of the band's imminent image: 'Except for this . . . creature, who floats to the bar. Slinky pencil skirt below the knee, pill-box hat, bright peroxide spiky hair-do, and a good stab at an hourglass figure. Like Jayne Mansfield in a Buster Keaton movie. The children cast sidelong glances. Who is this person? "She's with the band . . ." Ah.'

It would be at the audition for David Enthoven that tension between Paul Thompson and David O'List would surface in somewhat dramatic form, with the result that O'List would resign from the group almost immediately, to be replaced by Phil Manzanera. Within three months Graham Simpson would also have retired from Roxy Music, the victim of a nervous breakdown. Rik Kenton would then be recruited to play bass in Simpson's place.

Phil Manzanera: 'I ended up at Roxy Music's audition for EG in the bingo hall on Wandsworth Road. There were Richard Williams and myself sitting there, and then David Enthoven came in. The group came on, and then for some reason Paul and David had an altercation on the stage.'

Richard Williams: 'The audition was in fact very good. Phil was roadying at that point and I knew him from Quiet Sun. It was more like a rehearsal than a forty-five minute set.'

Williams would later recall accompanying David Enthoven back to the Kings Road, in his Aston Martin, and the manager not being sure. The indecision was short-lived, however, and Williams could report to the readers of the *Melody Maker*, as a postscript to his account of the audition, that Roxy Music had now acquired management from EG.

David Enthoven: 'Roxy Music were not to everybody's taste, I have to say; and they had been round the record companies and had a fairly tough time with that tape. I got it because of Richard Williams and a man called Willie Robertson. Bryan had gone to Willie because he knew that Willie had insured King Crimson and T.Rex, and I think Bryan had gone there for equipment insurance. But when I stuck the tape in it was the first time I'd been moved since I heard King Crimson. It was just blindingly obvious. They were taking good, straightforward songs and treating them, and doing something quite madly avant-garde with them. It appealed to my sense of humour, too – it was "fun" music, which people also regarded as serious, but it was a ray of light – so fresh and new.'

Tim Clark: 'And some really cool dance music, too.'

David Enthoven: 'And lyrically brilliant, of course. It was "art school avant-garde" – I can't describe it any other way than that . . .'

Phil Manzanera: 'After the audition Bryan rang me and asked if I would mix the sound. I said that I knew nothing about how to do this, and they said that Eno would teach me – he had been mixing the sound and singing out at the front.

'So I went along to learn how to mix the sound, in this derelict house in Notting Hill, just off the Portobello Road, where they used to chop up the landing for firewood. Eno starting showing me the mixing desk, and they said that David O'List hadn't turned up, and would I help them out on guitar – sort of giving me an audition without knowing it. I had secretly learned all the numbers, the material that would eventually appear on the first album, and so I could play them all immaculately – which of course seemed amazing. I joined on the 14th of February 1972, and two weeks later they signed the contract with EG.'

Andy Mackay: 'At which point I gave up my teaching job, at half term.'

Almost exactly three months after he gave up his teaching job, Andy Mackay would be tracked down by student reporter Peter Nomis, from Reading University's *Shell* newspaper, just as he was leaving to play with Roxy Music at the Lincoln open-air rock festival – the Great Western – which was hosted by Lord Harlech and the actor Stanley Baker over 26th and 27th May 1972, and which, owing to the hurricane-like conditions which prevailed through-out, would soon become known as 'The Great Wet Western'.

Before the weekend was out, in fact, 7,000 feet of fencing would have been pulled down by bedraggled and disconsolate music fans attempting to either enter the waterlogged site without paying, or to leave it as quickly as possible, and the dormitory tents erected to house at least some of the sodden audience would have actually blown away . . . Reporting the festival for the *New Musical Express* (issue week ending 3 June 1972), Roy Carr would observe that during hard rocking Nazareth's opening set on Saturday morning, the rain was 'coming in at such an acute angle that it was possible for a line of eight or nine people to stand on the western tail-end of a hotdog van and keep reasonably dry.'

But all of this – despite which Roxy Music would play a triumphant, uproariously received set, for a group barely known as more than a name – was in the near future, as *Shell's* correspondent Peter Nomis grabbed a few words with Mackay:

'Although the group sport a whole library of degrees and diplomas between them, their music is anything but academic and dry. "We just want to play rock 'n roll" – that was just about all Andy had time to say when I called at his massive Edwardian house in South London. He was off – in a beat-up Mercedes – for Roxy's gig at the Great Western Festival. "Rock 'n' roll – we're a very hot band. But we are very cool people. I learned to be cool at Reading. The university was very cool in those days."'

thirty-five

London, Oxford, Croydon, I March to 25 June 1972: Having become Roxy Music; Bryan Ferry as a work of art.

Roxy Music's acceptance into the mainstream of fashionable rock management, and as a consequence subsequently acquiring a deal with Island Records (on 2 May 1972), would be the commercial validation of an artistic project which had no real precedent. The originality of the group derived from Ferry's vision of a montage of styles, which at the same time, seemingly through the very incongruity of their constitution, became one single, massively amplified style. Such an achievement could not have been entirely foreseen, however clever its original author, Ferry, and the young men involved in its realisation. Acquiring physical form in the shape of the album *Roxy Music*, however – recorded between 14 March 1972 and 14 April 1972, financed by EG and produced by Pete Sinfield – this style statement would trigger precisely the process that Eno ascribes to successful pop: the creation of a new, imaginary world, which beckons to the listener to join it.

Brian Eno: 'I always felt like a pop star! That's funny. Even when I was at art school I used to dress as though I was something fairly special; I dressed very strangely, and used to have my clothes made and so on. I had the attitude, if not of a pop star, then of someone who could do whatever they wanted.

'In Roxy our look was proud and future looking – not introvert. One of the things about the blues movement that we especially didn't like was that it was all backward looking – to do with roots and realism and sincerity. And we didn't want anything to do with that – roots just didn't interest us.

'We were postmodernists in that sense: we thought that anything out there was there for the taking – it's just a palette. The whole history of music – you don't have to have any reverence for it; you can take what you want from it, stick it with whatever else you like, and see what you get. That's why those records were so quixotic in their changes . . .'

Bryan Ferry: 'I was the author, if you like, and it was my vision; but having said that, the various parts of it were very important to the overall make-up. Therefore the fact that Eno was there was supremely important, and also Andy and Phil, and not forgetting Paul Thompson. However, I didn't know exactly what I wanted, at all. It was just a case of having a vague vision – which I couldn't define, obviously, until the music was made; but the vision, such as it was, was for the music to be very eclectic and to follow my musical tastes – to be based on my songs, my words, and to some extent, my design.

'I think that the thing about Roxy Music is that there was quite a vast – or bigger than usual – musical range in the group. We might not have been the best players in the world, but the palette there was quite extensive to work from. And I think that that's what made some of the early Roxy stuff so satisfying: there was a richness to it . . .'

Andy Mackay: 'I think Bryan Ferry had a vision, but I don't see how even someone as prescient as Bryan – and never underestimate Bryan's vision, imagination or ambition – could quite see what would happen when myself and Eno and Phil and Paul came together.

'Bryan had a major part on deciding in Paul as a drummer; which is much to his credit. Charles Hayward [later of This Heat] was initially up for the job – who was one of those far more English "nervous-style" drummers; which tied in with my idea of Roxy as a more "arty" band. But Bryan, I think, had a better view of seeing it as something that could be commercially successful – although that wasn't foremost in his mind. So in a sense, the vision was Bryan's – but what came out of it has to be considered in some ways a strange accident . . .'

A video made of Roxy Music at the Royal College of Art, performing 'Re-make/Re-model' – their musical 'manifesto', as Williams has described it – gives us a good indication of just how extreme musically, lyrically and stylistically Roxy Music were on their emergence in 1972. Bryan Ferry is wearing eye shadow of emerald green glitter; Brian Eno plays his stack of electronics rather as though he was bringing a light aircraft in to land in turbulent weather; the performance is simultaneously deadly serious and wildly exuberant, creating the hugely seductive impression that the viewer is witnessing representatives from a somehow more heightened world, somewhere in the near or distant future, from which their alluring, eccentric glamour derives. It seems almost as though, in fact, Roxy Music – as a group, and as an artistic activity – are in one way Bryan Ferry's artistic alibi for carrying out another, less quantifiable creative act: that of converting oneself into a work of art.

Phil Manzanera: 'When I came to Roxy a lot was already in place. But I was in tune because a lot of my influences were the same – I would imagine I was Sterling Morrison, or, when I was required to play something mad, I would draw on my psychedelic enthusiasms. But it wasn't thought out – it was totally intuitive.

'We used to say that we were inspired amateurs, and I suppose I could compete with them because their training wasn't essential to being in a rock band, or an art rock band, or whatever was being created there. Even though they may have studied more elevated theories of art, when it came down to the nitty gritty of performance and performance in recording, it required energy, ability – whether it was raw or not – and sheer drive to mesh it together.

'And I was part of that "glueing" process, my sounds creating a link between the individual styles of Bryan's playing, or Brian Eno's sounds, or Andy's sax. My use of echoes or feedback, for example, created a context for the other sounds; it became another ingredient in what I think now was primarily Bryan's journey intellectually, and we created a musical context, a vehicle, for him.'

Television footage from *London Tonight* shows Roxy Music performing 'Ladytron' – the title alone being a pure pop conflation of romanticism and technology – and in this we see the unique intensity of Ferry's singing style. As he starts to sing, his face assumes a theatrical and pointed grimace – an almost grotesque amplification of a cabaret crooner's seductive leer – which in its turn gives way to a stunned, effeminate, unblinking stare. He appears to caress the microphone with the space just before his face, preening, smirking, deadpan – one moment Dietrich, the next Johnnie Ray. The effect is reminiscent of the exaggerated acting style required of silent cinema.

Vocally, he was utterly original and distinctive – vibrato, impassioned, suave, manic, breathless – his genius lay in collaging vocal styles while retaining an inimitable singularity.

Roxy Music's performing style supports the theory that art which is radically new, whether in pop music or painting, has a quality to its unmistakable urgency and clarity that touches upon awkwardness or ungainly peculiarity. It is rather as though, in order to be truly new, a work needs a vital, enlivening strangeness. Eno would be greeted as the very embodiment of strangeness, his treatments and interventions sculpting the already dense layers of Roxy's musical styling to provide a Tardis-like acoustic chamber of filmic and atmospheric effects. (He would amuse himself by suggesting to interviewers that he was in fact an inhabitant of the planet 'Xenon' – spot 'eno' between the 'X' and the 'n' – a yarn which, in some cases, the reporters very nearly believed.)

Musically, his contribution was an immediate hit with the pundits. After Roxy's set at the Lincoln festival, the *New Musical Express* – never easy to surprise – reported:

> The outrageously attired Roxy are something quite original in a world of samey bands, and what they are attempting is quite remarkable . . . Many groups – especially Pink Floyd – have used taped sounds to advantage in their acts, but none so ambitiously as Roxy. The tape recorder is an integral part of the instrumentation . . . Does it work? Immaculately! . . . the taped sounds fitted into the group's fierce, semi-revivalists-with-electronics-edges music.

These taped effects had been created and conceived by Eno for a specific purpose, however, in which he designed both a practical and an aesthetic use for the technology.

Brian Eno: 'The other thing, of course, was that I came up with the idea of using pre-recorded tapes. I like the idea of scene setting – so a piece wouldn't just start with a count in. But there was also a very important functional reason. Because our songs were quite different from one another, they required, often, nearly everyone to change their instruments or the sounds they were using. So Phil might have to change guitar and engage five different pedals, and Bryan would move from one instrument to another, Andy would change to sax from oboe, and so on. So there was a possibility of there being a lot of fiddling around between songs, and we didn't want that. We wanted to be cinematic, in a way, so you weren't too conscious of the physical details of how the music was made. Most of these tapes were things that I had made before Roxy, actually – as separate existing pieces of music . . .'

With their debut album recorded, Bryan Ferry then turned his attention to its packaging – calling in assistance from both his former fellow Newcastle graduate, Nick de Ville, and from his new coterie of high fashion friends in Ladbroke Grove. The result was a masterpiece of graphic art – and as much a visual manifesto as 'Re-make/Re-model' was a musical manifesto. The cover art to *Roxy Music* – both the outward cover of Kari-Ann, and the inside sleeve photographs of the group members, credits, and Simon Puxley's sleeve note – was a single statement about the process, brought together in Ferry's generational milieu of art students (the cast, in fact, of the present book), of turning oneself and one's lifestyle into a meticulously considered and poised work of art. It raised issues of gender, sexuality, personae, irony, Pop art, popular culture, revivalism, identity, fandom, humour, technical creativity and cultural status.

Juliet Mann: 'I was going around with Antony Price all the time at this point, and went to the photo shoot for the cover of the first album. Antony had made Kari-Ann's clothes; I'm sure that the concept of the girl was Bryan's and then they would have worked together on the look. And of course Antony had used Kari-Ann modelling his clothes before.'

Bryan Ferry: 'I liked designing the sleeves, for instance, from day one. However, once again, it was done with the help of other people. So I felt that I was like the sleeve director choosing the pictures and so on; but I needed people on that side of it as well – Antony Price was very important, and Nick de Ville, and Andy Mackay helped too.'

Nick de Ville: 'A range of people were involved, but Bryan was the arbiter, the conceptualiser. He had been very taken at Newcastle with that idea of assuming personae, and of being able to move across a range of ideas and styles – so there was this idea that you could be something, then something else, then something else. There was another idea connected to that, in the glamour shot of Kari-Ann on the cover of *Roxy Music*: the idea that the counterpoint to the band or the rock star was the fan. So there was this mythological notion going around that the more glamorous the fan, the more status you had as a star. The fan was thus an indicator. So Kari-Ann was supposed to be the rock star's "other" – which is the idealised fan.'

Within the masculine preserves of the rock music business, and its equally masculine press, *Roxy Music* brought with it a scent of artificiality – camp, even – all the way from the gay salons of Notting Hill. Antony Price's remark that 'fashion is nothing more, or less, than the seriousness of frivolity' seemed to come in a silent whisper from Kari-Ann's parted, pouting and pearlised lips.

Richard Williams: 'The image on the front cover of *Roxy Music* was a slap in the face for everything that was going on – it couldn't have been more explicitly so. It was frivolous in a way that nobody was supposed to be. "Rock" was supposed to be an expression of integrity in one form or another, and this was an expression of complete frivolity. There has never been an album cover that had a more strategic purpose than that, I would say.'

The strategy – whether intentional or not – certainly worked as regards Roxy Music being signed to Island. The final decision to sign the band was confirmed by Chris Blackwell when he happened to see the cover art.

Tim Clark: 'When we were going through an A&R meeting of potential new signings, I gave a pretty impassioned case for signing Roxy – but Chris Blackwell gave no sign at all of whether or not he liked this act.

'So the meeting broke up and I went away thinking, jeepers, what on earth am I going to tell David? Because it seems to me as though the A&R department don't like it, and if that's the case then we don't get Roxy signed.

'Anyway, about three days later, we were standing in the hallway of the office in Basing Street and it was unfeasibly early – around ten o'clock, and you never saw Chris at that time, because he'd have been in the studio until four. But Chris came in just as David and I were looking at the artwork for the first *Roxy Music* sleeve – which was quite, quite brilliant, as you know. And he looked at it and said, "Yes, that's great," and then he turned around to me and asked, "Have we got them signed yet?" At which point I realised that I was . . . off the hook.'

Having been signed at the beginning of May, *Roxy Music* would be released on 16 June 1972. As managed by Enthoven, the group were now following a busy schedule of concerts, press and radio sessions. They were beginning to be known – entering what might be termed their moment of becoming, chaperoned by Dr Simon Puxley.

Brian Eno: 'Simon Puxley was with us, but he wasn't a proactive publicist in the known sense. He wouldn't have dreamt of calling anybody up and asking if they would like to write about us – it wouldn't cross his mind.

'He spent years threatening to write a book about Swinburne. I don't know what became of the idea, or whether he ever did. It was one of those life projects. He was a very interesting person to have as a publicist; and funnily enough I think that it was a big part of Roxy's appeal to the press, because he was so bumbling and hopelessly inefficient as a publicist. He was really nice chap – always forgetting what he was saying, absent-minded, would never dream of pressurising anyone to anything. He was the opposite to all other publicists. In fact, he was almost reluctant to talk about the band. And people really liked him for this.

'This was a very fluid moment in cultural history, when there was a lot of swapping around in what people did – you never quite knew who you were going to bump into, and where. So somebody like Andy Mackay, who came from a humanities and classical music background, and Simon, who came from his interest in Pre-Raphaelitism, Bryan, from Pop art and soul – it was a very peculiar group of people to have come together.'

Puxley's sleeve note would capture in prose the exact essence of Roxy Music's modernity and appeal – and is unequalled, within the literary subgenre of sleeve-note writing, in its accuracy and poetry. Printed in a sans serif typeface, with no capitals but a bravura use of punctuation, it was the neo-Beat swerving of the prose that gave greatest evidence of the immense literary sophistication of its author. For example:

musicians lie rigid-&-fluid in a mannerist canvas of hard-edged black-leather glintings, red-satin slashes, smokey surrounding gloom . . .

. . . listening to the music re-sounding, cutting the air like it was glass, rock 'n 'roll juggernauted into demonic electronic supersonic mo-mo-momentum – by a panoptic machine-pile, hifi or scifi who can tell?

The relationship between Ferry and Puxley would be profound and absolute. As a publicist, Puxley was entirely eccentric; his true nature was entirely literary. In this he would become a crucial creative partner to Bryan Ferry; but in his struggle with addiction, and all of the chaos that addiction pulls down on the addict and their circle, he would never, tragically, be able to write his own work.

In a flash-forward to the later 1970s, his alter ego Rex Balfour would write *The Bryan Ferry Story*, which would be published by Michael Dempsey – who believed deeply in Puxley's writing, and who died ludicrously following a simple domestic fall. The death of Michael Dempsey would be crushing for Simon, whose own creativity – were it to flourish independently of the imperial monolith which Roxy Music had by then become – desperately required, like that of all writers, a reader in whom he could trust, and who would be eager to read his work. Simon would attempt to work on a novel, intermittently, but this, sadly, came to nothing.

Polly Eltes: 'Simon found writing very difficult and very painful and it took him a long, long time. He had many influences. When Pynchon's

Gravity's Rainbow was published [Picador, UK, 1975], he struck up a very close friendship with a publisher called Michael Dempsey, and under the influence of Pynchon he started writing a novel. Which I think was destroyed – which is really, really sad. Michael Dempsey, I think, was Simon's way out – his route, and his support through to his own career, and to expressing himself for himself.

'But tragically he died, Michael Dempsey. He made a strange switch from being a very successful publisher, to absolutely falling in love with Roxy Music and with the music business. And following Roxy Music around, and getting deeper and deeper into drugs and so on. He was a wonderful Irishman.

'I remember Simon being dismayed that no one seemed to take his reaction to Michael's death seriously. Nobody seemed to care or understand that this was an important person for him – and that was the end of the novel. And that caused Simon an immense – probably a complete – breakdown. Because Michael had represented support to Simon as an artist.'

Richard Williams: 'I first met Simon through Bryan, and it was amusing that he was totally unlike any other music PR. Charming, untogether, ungrasping, and didn't really mind if you wrote anything about the group or not. Simon's reputation was almost as big in the music papers as Bryan's for a while, because people began to take to this very eccentric English person, who was rather less together than the star he was representing. I thought his sleeve note for the first album was brilliant – scene setting, suggestive . . .'

Duncan Fallowell: 'My first encounter with Roxy Music must have been in either 1970 or 1971, at – of all places, although perhaps it was quite fitting – a garden party in Oriel College, Oxford – and Simon Puxley was there. I must have been the *Spectator*'s rock critic by then, which began in the summer of 1970. And so Simon came up to me – I don't know how he knew me, as I hadn't met him before – and said, "Are you Duncan Fallowell? I want to tell you about this new band we're putting together called Roxy Music . . ." Now Bryan had been friends with a man called Jeremy Catto, who taught history at Oriel, and this may have been how Simon came to be at the party . . .'

Bryan Ferry: 'He was crucial. It was like the best working relationship, based on friendship as much as anything.

'It's hard to describe Simon; he created a role for himself in my life, as general confidant and live-in producer, and spokesman. He was a very good critic for me, because he could be encouraging and yet at the same time say "absolutely not" about anything. Many's the time I would be writing lyrics, and he'd be in the same room, and I'd ask which line did he like better, this or that, and I'd generally trust his opinion pretty much all the time. We had some very good adventures together.

'Doomed by drugs, though. But he was always there, from the very, very beginning . . .'

On the evening of 25 June 1972, in one date on the busy schedule now prepared by EG, Roxy Music played at the Greyhound – a moderate-sized venue of around one thousand capacity in Croydon, on the southern suburban fringe of London. Towards the end of their set the applause became rapturous, roaring, sustained. The acknowledgement barely subsided, Ferry played the staccato, thrillingly anticipatory, opening piano chords of their final number of the night, 'Re-make/Re-model'.

To all intents and purposes, a constellation of ideas had now become Roxy Music.

Richard Hamilton: 'What I remember of Bryan is his extraordinary charisma. When I saw him performing I was absolutely knocked out. He became my idol – I thought he was really wonderful. How he would maintain this control over a big audience. And so I thought, "He's like Danny Kaye – he's got it!"'

The group's success would be almost immediate, creating a mass audience – particularly in the big, industrial cities of northern Britain – for whom joining the world proposed by the group's image, as a notion of constructed glamour, would become like membership of a vast but exclusive club. It was an image that was all the more potent for being so undefined – itself a montage, in which one might detect strands of Pop art or strands of revivalism, but never from a named source, only as a name itself, at once adjective and noun, 'Roxy'. It was in part, perhaps, a synthesis of Ladbroke Grove fashionability of the early 1970s, and in part a mutated form of that same fashionability;

it was an image which seemed fluid, ceaselessly re-making and re-modelling itself through a succession of copies.

Carol McNicoll: 'I remember one particular concert, and when they came on stage a group of girls near me all said, "He's wearing the feathers!" – meaning the costume that I'd made for Brian – and I felt like I'd really made it.

'Because one of the other things that was really important in the idea of the band was the notion that you could make things that were serious art, and they could also be popular – that was the ideal. Not to make something obscure that only a few people would ever see or listen to. The same was true for me: that I had made this costume, and hadn't compromised, but been as far out as I wanted to be, and it had become really popular. It was of the moment, that idea. One wanted to get away from being an artist in the art world sense – one wanted to move out of the art world. So you weren't making paintings or making a big splash at the ICA; you were actually out there in the 100 Club or wherever, in popular culture, and loads of people were loving what you did.

'At the same time, it was all about elitism – and that's what was so wonderful. It was at a time when people were marching for this, that or the other, but there never seemed to be any real contradiction between this incredibly elitist life that one was living, and being quite happy to go to some workers' collective meeting. Somehow managing to have them all as part of your life without worrying about the contradiction. But it was very, very elitist; and it was about the celebration of that.'

Polly Eltes: 'I think there is something very interesting about that; and this ties in with what I said about Simon resenting the fact that he never went up to Oxford. I think it's that idea of this "invented aristocracy" in parallel to the real aristocracy – which Bryan Ferry, and Simon, in fact, of course eventually bridged.

'And that was an exciting thing to see: Simon and Bryan inventing this new class of people: rather as though they were saying, "We don't belong to that – but we've got this, which is much better." And that was exciting – and very funny. It was always humorous.'

Within the subcultural imagination, Roxy Music's 'invented aristocracy' was an outline left for others to colour in. This was particularly the case amongst Roxy's earlier, more literary critics. In the underground newspaper *Frendz*, Nick Kent would commence his analysis of the group by a semi-fictional description of two young women called Zelda and Mimi, who live in a Kensington apartment, drinking Pernod or mint julep, enthusing over Cole Porter or Noël Coward, with a Salvador Dali on the wall and a jukebox playing Bo Diddley and the Beach Boys.

In a similar journalistic fantasy, titled 'The Bryan Ferry story – a Hollywood Production', published in the American *Creem* magazine in June 1974, Ferry was described by Simon Frith in the closing 'Act' of the feature being driven around the ring roads of Newcastle in a Rolls Royce, cocooned in a luxury car that intensifies his endless romantic reverie upon a vanished childhood landscape.

In both would be the suggestion that Roxy Music's identification with a particular notion of style and exclusivity is so alchemically potent that it would perform an act of transubstantiation on the group's creator – in effect turning Ferry the artist into both the subject of his art, and an artwork in his own right.

This notion would be clinched in 1974 by Eric Boman's photograph of Ferry wearing a white tuxedo, standing beside the swimming pool at the Bel Air Hotel, Los Angeles, during the violet coloured cocktail hour, while in the penumbral background various anonymously chic, exquisitely posed guests (one of whom was in fact Manolo Blahnik) appeared to fill the fragrant dusk with the low murmur of high society's feather-light talk.

In this pop-enabled process of self re-creation there was also a generous exchange with the fans, for whom Roxy Music proposed not just a style, but a template for developing one's own style. A film made by a group of five students at Manchester Polytechnic in 1975, for example, called *Roxette*, depicts a coterie of friends who have turned themselves into the glamorous stars of their own movie – that movie being their lives, which has been invented by their interpretation of Roxy Music, and which is dedicated to a form of lived creativity.

Gathering colossal momentum during the first half of the 1970s, the potency of Roxy Music's glamour within the culturally and commercially powerful mainstream of popular culture would also have a softly political resonance. Concluding his article for *New Society* in 1975, Andrew

Weiner pronounced on Roxy Music, and on Bryan Ferry in particular. The crescendo of his thesis proposed Ferry as a kind of postmodern Jay Gatsby, hosting a vast and ultimately aimless style party in the face of a modern void:

> A great deal of style, but little apparent meaning. Because for Bryan Ferry style was meaning – you couldn't separate the two ... Styles of disguise. Styles of survival for bewildering times ... It is the obvious intensity behind all those ornate visions that reaches out to Ferry's now enormous teen constituency, and seizes them. Ferry's audience must, at some level, understand and share his own urgent need – to live through his dreams and finally transcend them, to find some kind of safety or idealism at the end of it all, any home anywhere, anything at all beyond just dressing up with nowhere to go but another spectacular Roxy Music show ... Or the front stalls of the Roxy cinema.

Bryan Ferry had mentioned the previous month, to a reporter from the *New York Times* – who compared Roxy Music to the Weimar political cabaret of Kurt Weill, and 'what might be called post-glitter decadence in rock' – that: 'In England, the kids with the most style and the ones most into our music come from places like Liverpool, Birmingham and Newcastle. In England you see kids at our concerts not only in glitter and platforms, but full black tie.'

The image absorbed within the cultural imagination of Roxy Music would also emerge in an episode of *Rock Follies* – summoned up to pronounce the passing of an era by the maitre d' of the Bibaesque 'Idols' nightclub: 'Remember, we opened in 1974 – now that's a long time ago. It was the heyday of the elegance renaissance – Bryan Ferry in his white dinner jacket: a great era.'

What was the distance between achieving total cool – in the Mark Lancaster mode, for example – and becoming a work of art? Certainly, for some people, such a translation is possible; and in the case of Ferry, perhaps, the process took the form of a transaction between one's early self and an idea of accumulating overwhelming emotional urgency. And hence we leave Roxy Music, in this account, at its moment of becoming.

Bryan Ferry: 'The reality was, that after each show I was so tired – because it was a lot of singing, and I was punishing myself. It was hard work. It's always hardest work being the singer – which is why they get so crazy. I quite liked, in some ways, hiding behind the name of "Roxy Music", because Roxy Music is a glamorisation. And I didn't think my own name was terribly glamorous; and I suppose, all those years ago, I changed my name to Roxy Music.'

Roxy

Roxy are "goi
by storm"
JOHN PEEL C

mark my word
months they'll
RICHARD WI

....this is the f
this year and t
EVER remem

ROXY MUSIC
ILPS 9200
Produced by P

Music

world

atter of
ormous.
M

ve heard
I can
YLER NME

selected bibliography

Abrahams, Anna, *Warhol Films* (A Rongwrong Production by order of Wiederhall Editions, 1989)

Balfour, Rex (Dr Simon Puxley), *The Bryan Ferry Story* (Michael Dempsey, 1976)

Barnes, Richard, *Mods!* (Plexus, 1979)

Bean, Anne, *Autobituary Shadow Deeds* (Matt's Gallery, London, 2006)

Beaudelaire, Charles, *The Painter of Modern Life and Other Essays* (Da Capo Press, 1986)

Bockris, Victor, *Warhol: The Biography* (Da Capo Press, 2003)

Breward, Christopher, *Fashioning London: Clothing and the Modern Metropolis* (Berg, 2004)

Calloway, Stephen, *Aubrey Beardsley* (Harry N. Abrams, 1998)

Crisp, Quentin, *How to Have a Life-style* (Alyson Publications, 1998)

Donagh, Rita, *Paintings and Drawings* (Whitworth Art Gallery/Arts Council of Great Britain, 1977) .

Fitzgerald, F. Scott, *Tender Is the Night* (1934; Penguin Books, 1955)

Fitzgerald, F. Scott, *The Last Tycoon* (1941; Penguin Books, 1960)

Fogg, Marnie, *Boutique: A '60s Cultural Phenomenon* (Mitchell Beazley, 2003)

Goldberg, Rosehee and Harrod, Tanya, *Carol McNicoll* (The City Gallery, Leicester/ Lund Humphries, 2003)

Green, Jonathon, *All Dressed Up: The Sixties and the Counterculture* (Pimlico, 1999)

Grunenberg, Christoph (ed.), *Summer of Love: Art of the Psychedelic Era* (Tate Publishing, 2005)

Hamilton, Richard, *Collected Words 1953–1982* (Thames & Hudson, 1982)

Hamilton, Richard, *Retrospective: Paintings and Drawings, 1937–2002* (Walther König, 2003)

Harrison, Martin, *Transition: The Art Scene in London in the Fifties* (Merrell Publishers, 2002)

Hewitt, Paolo (ed.), *The Sharper Word: A Mod Anthology* (Helter Skelter Books, 1999)

Hill, John, *Sex, Class and Realism: British Cinema 1956–1963* (BFI Books, 1986)

Hillier, Bevis, *The Style of the Century 1900–1980* (New Amsterdam Books, 1990)

Hockney, David, *David Hockney by David Hockney: My Early Years* (Harry N. Abrams, 1988)

Howard, Delisia, *In BIBA* (Hazard Books, 2004)

Ironside, Virginia, *Janey and Me: Growing Up with My Mother* (Harper Perennial, 2004)

Kracauer, Siegfried, *The Mass Ornament: Weimar Essays* (1963; trans. Thomas Y. Levin, Harvard University Press, 1995)

Lichtenstein, Claude and Schregenberger, Thomas (eds.), *As Found: The Discovery of The Ordinary* (Lars Muller Publishers, 2001)

Livingstone, Marco, *British Pop* (Museo de Bellas Artes de Bilbao, 2005)

Livingstone, Marco, *Pop Art: A Continuing History* (Thames & Hudson, 1990 and 2000)

Livingstone, Marco and Heymer, Kay, *Hockney's Portraits and People* (Thames & Hudson, 2003)

Marinetti, Filippo, *Futurist Cookbook* (Chronicle Books, 1991)

McAleer, Dave, *Hit Parade Heroes: British Beat Before the Beatles* (Hamlyn, 1993)

McLuhan, Marshall, *The Mechanical Bride: Folklore of Industrial Man* (Gingko Press, 2002)

McShine, Kynaston (ed.), *Andy Warhol: A Retrospective* (Museum of Modern Art, 1989)

Mellor, David, *The Sixties Art Scene in London* (Phaidon, 1993)

Murphy, Robert, *Sixties British Cinema* (BFI Books, 1992)

Phillpot, Clive and Tarsia, Andrea, *Live in Your Head: Concept and Experiment in Britain, 1965–1975* (Whitechapel Art Gallery, 2000)

Rous, Lady Henrietta (ed.), *The Ossie Clark Diaries* (Bloomsbury, 1998)

Schlesinger, Peter, *A Chequered Past: My Visual Diary of the 60s and 70s* (UK edition, Thames & Hudson, 2004)

Seago, Alex, *Burning the Box of Beautiful Things: The Development of a Postmodern Sensibility* (Oxford University Press, 1995)

Stuart, Johnny, *Rockers!* (Plexus, 1987)

Turner, Alwyn W., *BIBA: The Biba Experience* (Antique Collectors Club, 2004)

Walker, John A., *Cultural Offensive: America's Impact on British Art Since 1945* (Pluto Press, 1998)

Walker, John A., *Learning to Paint: A British Art Student and Art School 1956–1961* (Institute of Artology, 2003)

Watkins, Jonathan, *Rita Donagh* (Ikon, 2005)

Watt, Judith, *Ossie Clark 1965–1974* (Victoria & Albert Museum, 2003)

York, Peter, *Modern Times* (Heinemann, 1984)

York, Peter, *Style Wars* (Sidgwick & Jackson, 1980)

selected filmography

Gala Day, dir. John Irvin, British Film Institute, 1963
Dreams That Money Can Buy, dir. Hans Richter, 1947
A Bigger Splash, dir. Jack Hazan, 1974
This Is Tomorrow, Without Walls/Channel 4 television documentary, 1992
Roxette, Manchester Polytechnic, 1975 (North West Film Archive)
Rock Follies, Series 1. Thames Television, 1976

index

Figures in italics indicate captions. 'BF' indicates Bryan Ferry.